THE MODERN SENATE OF CANADA 1925–1963

The role of the Senate has changed much in recent years and, judging by the amount of recent public discussion on its role, it might change even more in the future. It has, however, long been among the least known institutions of the country, and, although it is one of the Houses of Parliament, it has remained, to a large extent, a "terra incognita" in the literature of Canadian political science.

This new study sets out to remedy this situation by presenting a picture of the Senate at work as a part of the effective system of government in Canada in recent times. It contains a great deal of well-marshalled new material, from manuscript and ephemeral sources as well as from the printed Senate Debates, Journals, and Reports of Committees, while the theoretical discussion which it presents and the theoretical framework in which it is set make it more than merely descriptive. Dr. Kunz distinguishes such "technical" functions as the improvement of legislative draftsmanship, the first consideration of certain types of legislation, and the conduct of general debates, from such "substantive" functions as the checking of executive extravagance and the representation of the interests of the territorial and societal minorities in a federal state. He also discusses such organizational aspects as the appointing system, the question of partisanship, the composition of the Senate, and its committee system, and reviews various reform proposals. He recommends no drastic change in the Senate's composition, but believes, rather, that improvement lies in further exploiting the potentials of the Senate's present structure and organization. Political scientists, historians, sociologists, and Members of Parliament will learn much from this book, and it will appeal as well to the growing number of citizens interested in learning more about the way government operates.

F. A. KUNZ, a native of Hungary, has degrees from the University of Budapest, Sir George Williams University and McGill University. He studied for two years on a Ford Foundation post-doctoral travelling fellowship in California and East Africa, and has taught at Sir George Williams University and the University College in Southern Rhodesia. At present he is Assistant Professor in the Department of Economics and Political Science, McGill University.

CANADIAN GOVERNMENT SERIES

General Editors
R. MacG. DAWSON, 1946–58
J. A. CORRY, 1958–61
C. B. MACPHERSON, 1961–87

1. *Democratic Government and Politics.* By J. A. Corry and J. E. Hodgetts
2. *The Government of Canada.* By R. MacGregor Dawson; revised by Norman Ward
3. *Constitutional Amendment in Canada.* By Paul Gérin-Lajoie
4. *The Canadian House of Commons: Representation.* By Norman Ward
5. *The Government of Prince Edward Island.* By Frank MacKinnon
6. *Canadian Municipal Government.* By Kenneth Grant Crawford
7. *Pioneer Public Service: An Administrative History of the United Canadas, 1841–1867.* By J. E. Hodgetts
8. *The Government of Nova Scotia.* By J. Murray Beck
9. *The Office of Lieutenant-Governor.* By John T. Saywell
10. *Politics in New Brunswick.* By Hugh G. Thorburn
11. *The Public Purse.* By Norman Ward
12. *Procedure in the Canadian House of Commons.* By W. F. Dawson
13. *The Canadian General Election of 1957.* By John Meisel
14. *The Government of Manitoba.* By M. S. Donnelly
15. *The Modern Senate of Canada, 1925–63: A Re-appraisal.* By F. A. Kunz

The Modern Senate of Canada 1925-1963

A RE-APPRAISAL

F. A. Kunz

UNIVERSITY OF
TORONTO PRESS

Reprinted 1967, 2017

ISBN 978-1-4875-9247-9 (paper)

PREFACE

PERHAPS THE FIRST THING that strikes the student of the Canadian Senate is the almost universal ignorance which prevails in the public mind[1] and even in academic thinking with regard to the proper role and functioning of the Senate in the over-all context of the Canadian political system. Combined with this intellectual indifference there is a well discernible emotional hostility, fed partly by the underlying ignorance and partly by a vague lingering notion of century-old liberal-radical-socialist antagonism towards second chambers in general. Often, abusive description of the Senate is offered in place of intelligent opinion —a trend which may be taken as further evidence of the declining interest in, and respect for, legislative institutions in general.

As a result of, and perhaps one additional reason for, this situation has been a scarcity of literature on the Senate. Apart from Sir George Ross's pioneer work, *The Senate of Canada* (Toronto, 1914), the only important contribution has been Professor R. A. MacKay's book *The Unreformed Senate of Canada*, which was first published in 1926. Both of these books were written in a period of renewed interest in the question of second chambers, following the conflict of the House of Lords and the House of Commons and subsequent constitutional discussions in the United Kingdom.[2] There have been some half-dozen articles scattered in the learned journals, the rest of the available literature on the Senate being made up of occasional references in books of varied nature and of journalistic reports and comments in the press. In the field of academic theses I have found one discussion of the Senate during the period of 1950–54[3] and two others which took a somewhat

[1]See the revealing results of the Gallup Poll following the Senate's handling of the controversial Tariff bill and Bank of Canada bill in 1961. *Montreal Star*, Sept. 16, 1961.

[2]In particular, H. W. V. Temperley, *Senates and Upper Chambers* (London, 1910); J. A. R. Marriott, *Second Chambers* (Oxford, 1910; rev. ed., 1929); H. B. Lees-Smith, *Second Chambers in Theory and Practice* (London, 1923); Lord Bryce, *Conference on the Reform of the Second Chamber* (London, 1918, Cmd 9038).

[3]L. M. Wiles, "The Senate of Canada, 1950–54," Queen's University, 1955.

larger view.[4] In 1963, by which time the writing of this book had been completed, a new printing of Professor MacKay's book was issued, which incorporated new data from the years since 1924 but left the design of the previous edition basically unaltered.

The essential purpose of this study is to place the discussion of the structure and functioning of the modern Senate in a broad theoretical setting, which would take account of the changed role of second chambers in parliamentary regimes. To this end, it opens with a diachronic analysis of the functions of second chambers in changing historical circumstances. This functional approach is today widely used in political studies, as a result of the more intimate relationship of political science with sociology and anthropology, where functionalism has been a generally accepted tool of investigation since Durkheim. By function in our context is simply meant the contribution which second chambers as unit entities make to the total political life and the functioning of the total political system in parliamentary democracies. It is in this larger conceptual framework that the Senate's work as a part of the effective system of government in Canada in recent times is viewed.

There is, it should be noted, often a discrepancy between the ends intended and the ends actually served by institutions. Therefore, although I avoided covering old ground or discussing in detail historic aspects which have already been thoroughly treated elsewhere, I tried to maintain the historical perspective by linking each compartment of the book to the original ideas of the Fathers. By this means, it is hoped, the study will stand as a self-contained whole, despite its concentration on developments since 1925. Again, in order to keep the size as manageable as possible, I have made very little comparison with similar institutions in other countries, with the possible exception of the House of Lords in the United Kingdom. In this respect Peter Bromhead's book on the House of Lords, published in 1958, was of great value; I derived many useful ideas from this excellent survey.[5]

Admittedly, the functional approach, by the nature of its method, involves a subtle danger of operating with a concealed value judgment, of passing from the argument that everything observed in political systems as "functioning wholes" is meaningful to the argument that everything is indispensable. To forestall criticism that I read into the

[4]J. H. Turner, "The Senate of Canada," University of British Columbia, 1949; W. L. Hoyt, "The Composition of the Canadian Senate, 1935–51," Acadia University, 1962.

[5]*The House of Lords and Contemporary Politics, 1911–1957* (London, 1958).

record of the Senate some deductive assumptions unsubstantiated by empirical evidence, I should point out that I had begun my investigation with no preconceived idea as to the exact nature or significance of the Senate's contribution. But having set out on my research, I soon discovered that there was a pattern discernible in the Senate's activities and this in turn led me to formulate my hypothesis about the technical and substantive functions of second chambers.

Even if there be disagreement about the interpretation of these functions, the least that can be said for the functional approach is that it secures a unity of direction and provides a good practical framework, in which all the factual data and information intended to bring the Senate to life can be arranged in a well-ordered and logical manner. It is hoped also that the functional discussion will serve as a background against which any proposals for the reconstruction of the Senate's composition may be weighed.

In the preparation of this book I have received much help from many quarters. I drew much inspiration from Professor MacKay's exploratory work as well as from the encouragement he gave me. I find much satisfaction in the fact that many of the conclusions of the new edition of his book and mine seem to point in the same direction, despite the difference of the approaches used. I have special acknowledgement to make to Dr. K. Lamb, Archivist, and Messrs. Ormsby, Regehr, and Weilbrenner of the Public Archives, for the co-operation that was extended to me while consulting a number of private papers, a list of which appears in the Bibliographical Note. I have found equally generous help and assistance in the Senate itself. I am greatly indebted to Senators Hugessen, Kinley, Macdonald, Pouliot, Power, Robertson, and Roebuck, for the advice and encouragement they have given and particularly for their patience and readiness in answering questions and explaining points of difficulty. I also owe thanks to Mr. John F. MacNeill, Clerk of the Senate and Clerk of the Parliaments; Mr. E. Russell Hopkins, Law Clerk and Parliamentary Counsel to the Senate; Mr. Harvey Armstrong, Chief Clerk of Committees; Mr. A. Hinds, Assistant Clerk of Committees; and Mrs. Jean M. Sutherland, Secretary of the Clerk of the Senate, for their invaluable information on points of fact and procedure.

To Professor J. R. Mallory, Chairman of the Department of Economics and Political Science, McGill University, I must express my warmest gratitude for his suggestions in revising for publication the original doctoral dissertation which in 1963 had been accepted by

McGill University, and for giving me the immense benefit of his knowledge of Canadian government and politics. Of course, for all errors of fact and judgment I alone am responsible.

I should like also to thank my wife for her patient collaboration and for her assistance in preparing tables and statistics.

This work has been published with the help of grants from the Social Science Research Council of Canada, using funds provided by the Canada Council, and from the Publications Fund of the University of Toronto Press.

F. A. K.

CONTENTS

BIBLIOGRAPHICAL NOTE

MOST OF THE MATERIAL for this study has been derived from the *Debates* (cited as *SD*) and the *Journals* (cited as *SJ*) of the Senate and of the House of Commons, the *Minutes* of Proceedings and *Reports* of various standing and special committees, supplemented by data drawn from the *Canadian Parliamentary Guide* and the *Canadian Annual Review*.

A second stream of primary information comes from four unpublished private papers relating to this era, which have been deposited in the Public Archives at Ottawa. They are: the Meighen Papers from 1917 to 1941, grouped into five series and 202 volumes (equipped with a complete subject index) and covering the correspondence of Arthur Meighen as Secretary of State, Minister of Mines and Minister of Interior (1917–20), Prime Minister (1920–21), Opposition Leader in the House of Commons (1922–26), Prime Minister for the second time (1926) and Senator (1932–41), first as Government Leader (1932–35), then as Leader of the Opposition in the Senate (1935–41); the Murphy Papers, containing thirty-one volumes of the personal correspondence of the late Hon. Charles Murphy, former Secretary of State and Postmaster General, then member of the Senate between 1925 and 1935; the Manion Papers, especially useful during the period when R. J. Manion was Leader of the Opposition in the Commons and Arthur Meighen was Leader of the Opposition in the Senate; and finally the Dandurand Papers—a closed collection of the diary and memoirs of Sen. Raoul Dandurand; for its consultation I was granted special permission by M. de Gaspé Beaubien.

Books and articles containing reference to the Senate, or those which were used for the introductory chapter and for occasional comparisons throughout the survey, are noted in the text. Perhaps special mention might be made of the following contributions of members of the Senate: Sen. J. J. Connolly, "The Canadian Senate," *Canadian Liberal*, vol. VII, nos. 3–4 (1954); Sen. J. T. Haig, "The Watchdog of Our Constitution," *Financial Post*, July 5, 1952; Sen. N. Lambert, "Reform of the Senate,"

Winnipeg Free Press, April 1950; Sen. A. Meighen, "The Canadian Senate," *Queen's Quarterly*, vol. XLIV (1937); and Sen. A. Roebuck, "Tinkering with the Senate of Doubtful Value," *Saturday Night*, vol. LXIX, Feb. 27, 1954.

THE MODERN SENATE OF CANADA 1925-1963

A THEORY OF SECOND CHAMBERS

INTRODUCTION

SECOND CHAMBERS have traditionally been looked upon as the structural manifestation of conservative principles and their development as an integral part of the story of conservatism itself. It is only logical that this should be so, since the rationale for the performance of the two functions that have historically been assigned to these bodies—the technical and the substantive functions—has been deduced from an essentially conservative attitude, temperamental in the one case, ideological in the other. It is the general thesis of this chapter that whilst during the last fifty years or so the *technical* functions of second chambers have remained basically unaltered, their *substantive* role has changed, according to a general reorientation of conservatism itself, from being a primary institutional check upon democracy and progress as represented in the lower house (House of Commons) to becoming an auxiliary institutional check upon the lower house (House of Commons) dominated by the cabinet.

Consideration of the technical functions need not here detain us too long. The advantages that are to be gained from going slowly in matters of procedure, from thinking twice before a final decision is made, from having more than a single body of men deliberating, have been a recognized principle of deliberative assemblies all through the ages and derive from what Herman Finer calls a universal desire for "a multitude of counsellors."[1] In the ancient world, despite the difference in the political environment and the corresponding simplicity in group discussion, and despite the fact that the functions of what comes closest to our

[1]H. Finer, *Theory and Practice of Modern Government* (rev. ed., New York, 1951), p. 399.

concept of a second chamber were not so much to revise the decisions of the first assembly as to consider the topics that were to come before it,[2] the principle was nevertheless the same and was incorporated in the historically known councils of Greece,[3] the Senate of Rome, and the small councils of elders among the primitive Germans, as described by Tacitus, which held a preliminary debate on those graver questions which were to be raised in the more populous assembly. "The ancient governments of Germans," wrote Laurence Sterne, "had all of them a wise custom of debating everything of importance to their state, twice; that is, once drunk, and once sober; drunk—that their councils might not want vigour; and sober—that they might not want discretion."[4]

When the general debate over the relative merits and demerits of the bicameral and the unicameral system opened in the late eighteenth and early nineteenth century, the stage had not yet been reached in the development of the rules and procedures, as well as the expansion of the scope, of parliamentary business that would allow a clear perception of the type of technical usefulness that second chambers could well have offered. This may explain, in part, the unyielding antipathy of such legislative innovators as Bentham to second chambers even within this restricted domain of service.[5] Bentham refused to accept the notion that a second chamber might perhaps possess a special fitness, on the ground that "if the special fitness is for legislation, then the second chamber should be the first and no other is necessary."[6] He had no belief in the ultimate connection between age and wisdom. True, the second chamber is the place of the elder. But "wisdom without moral purpose is dangerous, and moral purpose has no relation to age."[7] He equally denied the notion, so eloquently advocated in No. 62 of *The Federalist*, that the members of second chambers would usually possess greater experience in conducting state affairs than the popularly elected members of the lower house. Nor could a bicameral legislature be justified in his eyes on the ground that a second chamber would check the haste and inevitable carelessness of the first, because if greater consideration were desirable, why should it not take place in the first, instead of the second chamber? In fact, he would oppose a second chamber regardless of its composition,

[2]Lord Bryce, *Modern Democracies* (London, 1921), vol. II, p. 398, n. 2.

[3]See discussion of the "boulé" in Aristotle's *Politics*, book VI.

[4]Quoted in S. D. Bailey, *The Future of the House of Lords* (London, 1954), p. 7.

[5]A good summary of Bentham's views on the topic can be found in an article by L. Rockow, "Bentham on the Theory of Second Chambers," *American Political Science Review*, vol. XXII (1928), no. 3.

[6]Quoted in *ibid.*, p. 587.

[7]*Ibid.*

powers, and relations with the other house. A second chamber was for him "needless, useless, worse than useless . . . a bar, or a drag,"[8] for it would involve useless delay in the process of legislation. Even John Stuart Mill, despite his otherwise friendly disposition to second chambers, was of the view that "it must be a very ill-constituted representative assembly, in which the established forms of business do not require many more than two deliberations."[9]

In the light of our contemporary experience these demands as formulated one hundred years ago for a more leisurely conduct of parliamentary business may seem to be somewhat naive. Indeed, to the extent that the duties of Parliament grew in number and in complexity and the lower house was obliged to act under special rules limiting debates, the conviction was gaining ground that if the legislative function of Parliament was to be discharged at a tolerably satisfactory level, the technical assistance of a second house was virtually a prerequisite. With his keen sense of constitutional realities Bagehot pointed out that "if we had an ideal House of Commons . . . it is certain we should not need a higher Chamber . . . but, besides the actual House, a revising and leisured legislature is extremely useful, if not quite necessary."[10] It became generally accepted that in straightening out "the tangles in the legislation of the popular Chamber," as Stead said, and in providing ministers an opportunity of putting into shape concessions promised there and in clarifying the drafting, a second chamber had an eminently useful field. Moreover, with the advance of the idea of government by experts, and in the same proportion as the House of Commons became less and less a "checking" and "choosing" body and more and more a debating and educating body, there appeared added reasons for maintaining, within the framework of Parliament, an assembly capable of devoting attention to the less exciting, yet by no means negligible, aspects of legislation that was dealt with mainly from a political and controversial angle in another place. The scope and nature of such technical contribution is varied; it ranges from the traditional reviewing function to such fairly recently acquired ones as the initiation and preliminary discussion, in a steadily increasing degree, of public legislation of an essentially technical character, a virtual monopoly over the introduction of private legislation, etc. Be it a service by a first look or by a second look—or indeed any other form of service—the common feature of this ever widening

[8]*Ibid.*, p. 582.

[9]J. S. Mill, *On Liberty and Considerations on representative Government*, R. B. McCallum, ed. (Oxford, 1946), p. 296.

[10]Quoted in Bailey, *The Future of the House of Lords*, p. 21.

area of technical functionalism is to alleviate the legislative burden of the elected chamber, and to save its time for a more adequate fulfilment of its primary role, which is to be the great forum of political discussion carried on in full publicity on the national level. As the performance of these technical functions requires no legal or political powers on the part of second chambers, even such traditionally ardent opponents of bicameralism as the British Labour party have "come around to the view that the House of Lords . . . does little harm and some good."[11] In fact, opinion everywhere is almost unanimous that some kind of second chamber is desirable, which seems to justify Sir Henry Maine's dictum that "almost any sort of second chamber is better than none."[12] Compared to the inflexible radicalism of Bentham, this is certainly a concession, albeit a minor one, to a kind of temperamental conservatism in matters technical and procedural. In essence, it is not different from the idea concerning the advantages of two-stage discussions manifested in earlier ages. Only its forms changed, in order to conform better to the new requirements of a modern political system.

It is easy to see, however, that this technical serviceability of second chambers in contributing to greater procedural efficacy has been merely a historical by-product and an almost incidental derivative of a more substantive role and a more deeply rooted conservatism, which has been the basis of their functioning in modern times. "All second chambers," says Finer, "have been instituted . . . not from disinterested love of mature deliberation, but because there is something their makers wished to defend against the rest of the community, especially inherited possessions and status."[13] Comparison with ancient institutions has little or no validity in this respect, for what we are confronted with here has been an upshot of the social and political changes of the periods of "take-off" and "maturity," preceding and following the Industrial Revolution. With due allowance for the difference in timing, this holds true of the House of Lords in England as well as of second chambers in other countries. However, a point of considerable practical importance is that whereas the House of Lords was the only second chamber of any

[11]W. I. Jennings, *The Approach to Self-Government* (Boston, 1963), p. 111. See also, amongst others, H. Morrison, *Government and Parliament* (London, 1959), p. 196; and his remarks on second reading of the Parliament Bill, *HD* (UK), 1947, vol. 444; Lord Campion *et al.*, *Parliament* (London, 1952), p. 210; Lord Chorley *et al.*, *Reform of the Lords* (London, 1954), pp. 16–17.

[12]As a result, only Denmark (since 1953), Finland, Greece (since 1864), Israel, the Lebanon, Luxembourg, Monaco, New Zealand (since 1951), Syria, and Turkey—to count states adhering to the cabinet system—have done without a second chamber. See Bailey, *The Future of the House of Lords*, p. 17.

[13]Finer, *Theory and Practice of Modern Government*, p. 400.

magnitude in Western democracies that had been the product of an almost uninterrupted historical evolution, similar institutions in other countries were devised and created by professional constitution-makers on the basis of a carefully reasoned set of principles at a certain point of time. Indeed, historically the idea of the bicameral legislature was rooted in the stratified society of the Middle Ages, in which the different classes of nobility, clergy, and townsmen made up politically independent estates. It was only through the seventeenth century's political struggles that the foundations of modern English constitutional government were laid, while in France, for example, the three estates were not summoned after 1614 for one-hundred-and-seventy-five years, to meet again in 1789, on the eve and as the harbinger of the Revolution. Thus, the modern bicameral system in Europe, says Shepard, "really dates from the late eighteenth century when French revolutionary ideas, reinforced by English example, ushered in the new epoch of constitutionalism."[14] It is fair to say that, whether copying it or refuting it, members of modern constituent assemblies were all influenced to a varying degree by the experience and practice of the British Upper House and its position within that much admired and no less often misinterpreted English Constitution. As Bentham wrote in his benign manner, in the case of England the existence of a second chamber was due to "authority-begotten and blind custom-begotten prejudice"; in the case of other countries, its "adoption was due to the mere imitation of the English model."[15]

The substantive role of second chambers, as it emerged during this period of constitutional development, can be summed up in brief as being an institutional check upon the popular principle in the constitution and an arresting influence upon change and the onward march of democracy. Clashes between the two houses in the United Kingdom had not been infrequent before, and, indeed, after the Restoration the Lords became an instrument in court intrigues which the King could successfully play off against the Commons.[16] It should be emphasized, however, that although the House of Lords had been based from its inception upon the triple principle of feudal land tenure, heredity, and primogeniture, conflicts between the two houses had traditionally been conflicts of interests owing to disagreements between alignments of personal and

[14] *Encyclopaedia of the Social Sciences*, vol. II, p. 534.

[15] Quoted in Rockow, "Bentham on the Theory of Second Chambers," p. 578.

[16] Cf. Charles II's fight over the issue of his brother's succession, William III's over the distribution of land in Ireland, or George III's conflict with Fox over the latter's East India bill.

party forces in them.[17] Nevertheless, since both houses represented substantially the same interests and the same strata of society, these clashes lacked that deeper economic/social content which could only come when the gap in the class-composition of the chambers grew wider and more evident, as a result of the changes in technology and the gradual extension of the franchise following the three Reform Acts. It was at this point that, on the one hand, the Lords became an institutional embodiment of conservative ambitions to check a self-willed democratic assembly, and that, on the other, "a powerful and self-conscious democracy began to ask the question quo warranto? of a House of Lords founded upon every sort of title except democratic functional utility."[18]

To be sure, around the middle of the nineteenth century democracy still denoted something to be dreaded and avoided. "The assumptions underlying the lamentations of the Tory prophets of woe," Tuberville says, "were that the fundamental and permanent functions alike of conservatism and of the House of Lords were *to resist organic change and the advent of democracy*."[19] Thus, the conflicts, when they occurred, were now conflicts, generally speaking, between two houses, one standing for progress and democracy, the other representing reactionary tendencies and a curious brand of benevolent authoritarianism.[20] As a result, the whole movement of parliamentary reform "was regarded as suspect by a number of lords who saw in the efforts of the reformers less a design for the reconstruction of the House of Commons than an attack upon their own House and the whole system of government with which they felt themselves to be identified. It was an attack upon two great principles which they looked upon as fundamental—the sacredness of property and the proper balance of the constitution."[21] And although the Great Reform Bill was truly one of the chief turning points in English constitutional history, the aristocracy, and thus the House of Lords, still remained exceedingly powerful, for the simple reason that there could be no real revolution in the distribution of political power without a revolution in the distribution of real property, as James Harrington had contended in his *Oceana*, some two hundred years before *Das Kapital*.

[17]W. I. Jennings, *Party Politics* (Cambridge, 1960–62), Part I, vol. II.

[18]Finer, *Theory and Practice of Modern Government*, p. 401.

[19]A. S. Tuberville, *The House of Lords in the Age of Reform, 1784–1837* (London, 1958), p. 419. Italics added.

[20]This coincides with the fourth stage of the historical development of opposition, as Duverger sees it, the first three being: tribunes-plebs; Church-feudal lords; King-Parliament; the fifth, last one being conflict between organized political parties. In M. Duverger, *Political Parties* (2nd ed., London, 1959), pp. 412 ff.

[21]Tuberville, *The House of Lords in the Age of Reform*, p. 252.

This may explain the Lords' determined, although ultimately unsuccessful, fight against the Corporation bill, the Corn Laws, or the admission of the Jews to Parliament. They had, in fact, become the very citadel of obstruction, an institutionalized stronghold of atavistic interests. For those who felt sympathetic with these interests the Upper House seemed to fulfil an important political role. Writing in 1895 Lecky said that "the existence of a strong Upper Chamber is a matter of first necessity. It is probable that the continuance, without a great catastrophe, of democratic government depends mainly upon the possibility of organizing such a chamber, representing the great social and industrial interests in the country, and sufficiently powerful to avert the evils that must, sooner or later, follow from the unbridled power of a purely democratic House Of Commons."[22] The effect of all this in terms of practical politics was that during the latter part of the nineteenth century, and indeed right up to the outbreak of the Great War, the role of the English upper chamber in the British political system could hardly be described except in terms of a permanent conflict between its Tory majority and the Liberals in the lower house. Much of the authoritative writing on the subject was framed on the assumption that the Lords would naturally act as a steady drag upon a House of Commons, normally of liberal, or radical, tendencies.[23] What happened is well known; "with the passage of time, as the number of peers increased, and as the Liberals' policies became more and more objectionable to the established interests represented by the conservative element in the Lords, the conflict became sharper until it came to a head in the crisis of 1909–11,"[24] resulting in the emasculation of the constitutional powers of the House of Lords in the first Parliament Act.

Significantly, the essential features of this conservatism, the fear and suspicion of "too much democracy," and the corresponding image of a second chamber as an effective bulwark against popular encroachment, found expression in the constitutions even of those countries where landed aristocracy and rights based upon inheritance formed no part of the social structure. Speaking of the problems confronting the composers of federal constitutions during this period, Finer aptly remarks that "there would have been some sort of second chamber, even if it were not required by the federal principle. There is not absent from the United States Senate and the German Reichsrat of Weimar the *intention*

[22]W. E. H. Lecky, *Democracy and Liberty* (London, 1899), vol. I. pp. 363–4.

[23]See Bagehot's introduction to the second edition of his work *The English Constitution* (London, 1872); H. Sidgwick, *Elements of Politics* (2nd ed., London, 1897), p. 468; S. Low, *The Governance of England*, p. 222 ff.

[24]P. Bromhead, *The House of Lords and Contemporary Politics, 1911–1957* (London, 1958), p. 12.

or spirit of a curb."[25] Indeed, both the *Records* of the Federal Convention and *The Federalist* indicate that the convention of 1787 was impelled towards the creation of a second chamber not only by federal considerations but by the practical and immediate fear of "tumultuous democracy." Therefore, a fence was required and this function was assigned to a body equipped, in Madison's language, with the "firmness seasonably to interpose against impetuous counsels."[26] Both he and Randolph, a delegate from Virginia, campaigned for a seven-year Senate on the professed basis that as this branch was to be "a check on the democracy—it cannot therefore be made too strong."[27] Hamilton, on the other hand, scorned those who were satisfied with a Senate of seven years in view of "the amazing violence and turbulence of the democratic spirit,"[28] and he went so far as to suggest that the Senate should be elected to serve during good behaviour. A later edition of the suggestion required that candidates should also have an estate in land.[29] In Nos. 62 and 63 of *The Federalist* the authors reiterated the necessity of a Senate "*as a defence to the people against their own temporary errors and delusions*. . . ." These phrases, coupled with George Washington's famous simile—which so much caught the imagination of Sir John A. Macdonald[30]—about the senatorial saucer to cool the legislation that was poured into it, were, of course, part of that superciliously magnificent system which has come to be known as "Madisonian democracy," and at the root of which there was a strong fear of popular majorities.[31]

It is not surprising to find that when the time arrived for the Canadian provinces to unite into a federal state, the Fathers of that delicate edifice shared the prevailing sentiments of the era. As in the United States, the absence of feudal-aristocratic elements from the social environment made no difference in the expectations as to the substantive function of a second chamber. Although this aspect of the question received no extensive treatment either at the Quebec Conference or in the Confederation Debates, and was overshadowed by the paramount task facing the participants to convince themselves that in the Senate they had found a panacea for their respective sectional fears, it is still possible to reconstruct from the few glimpses the stand taken by the men in this respect.

[25]Finer, *Theory and Practice of Modern Government*, p. 399. Italics added.

[26]Max Ferrand, *Records of the Federal Convention* (New Haven, 1911), I, p. 422.

[27]*Ibid.*, p. 222.

[28]*Ibid.*, p. 282.

[29]*Ibid.*, p. 291; and vol. III, App. F, p. 621.

[30]J. Pope, *Memoirs of the Rt. Hon. Sir John Alexander Macdonald* (Ottawa, 1894), vol. II, p. 233.

[31]See R. A. Dahl, *A Preface to Democratic Theory* (Chicago, 1956).

It was generally accepted that the Senate should be a check upon the House of Commons. "The weak point in democratic institutions," Cartier said, "is the leaving of all power in the hands of the popular element. . . . In order that institutions may be stable and work harmoniously there must be a power of resistance to oppose the democratic element."[32] Cauchon also warned, reminiscent of the language of *The Federalist*: "We ought to place in the constitution a counterpoise to prevent any party legislation, and to moderate the precipitancy of any government which might be disposed to move too fast and go too far—I mean a legislative body able *to protect the people against itself* and against the encroachment of power."[33] Similarly, the Father of the Fathers, John A. Macdonald, held "there would be no use of an Upper House if it did not exercise . . . the right of opposing or amending or postponing the legislation of the Lower House. . . . It must be an independent House . . ., for it is only valuable as being a regulating body, calmly considering the legislation initiated by the popular branch, and preventing any hasty or ill-considered legislation. . . ."[34] Significantly, he wholeheartedly supported the stand taken by the House of Lords in their rejection of the Paper Duties bill five years previously and said the Lords had acted not only according to the letter but also according to the spirit of the constitution. Although he took great pains in emphasizing that in Canada members of the second chamber would be basically the same type of people as those sitting in the Commons,[35] he reminded the delegates at the Quebec Conference that a "large qualification should be necessary for membership of the Upper House, in order to represent the principle of property. The rights of the minority must be protected," he added in a Machiavellian afterthought, "and the rich are always fewer in number than the poor."[36] Consequently, a high qualification was agreed upon, which was later reduced to suit Prince Edward Island and Newfoundland and was fixed at $4,000 in real property. Thus, if Hamilton's

[32]*Parliamentary Debates on Confederation of British North American Provinces* (Quebec, 1865; Ottawa, 1951), p. 571.

[33]*Ibid.*, p. 572. Italics added.

[34]*Ibid.*, p. 36.

[35]"The members of our Upper House will be like those of the Lower men of the people, and from the people. The man put into the Upper House is as much a man of the people the day after, as the day before his elevation. Springing from the people, and one of them, he takes his seat in the Council with all his sympathies and feelings of a man of the people, and when he returns home . . . he mingles with them on equal terms, and is influenced by the same feelings and associations, and events, as those which affect the mass around him." *Ibid.*

[36]Sir Joseph Pope, ed., *Confederation: Being a Series of Unpublished Documents Bearing on the British North America Act* (Toronto, 1895), p. 58.

suggestion was ignored at Philadelphia, it was carried into effect in London.[37]

What made the question of second chambers part of the theoretical debate of the time was the fact that arguments for or against them were invariably linked to some fundamental body of political principles. There were, in particular, two eighteenth century doctrines which had an important bearing upon the subject, one supporting the bicameral, the other the unicameral, principle. For those who felt in sympathy with the substantive role of second chambers, as interpreted at the time, Montesquieu's system of checks and balances came in handy. Influenced by the scientific point of view of the eighteenth century and by his fortunate (in its effects anyway) misreading of the unfolding trend of the British constitution, Montesquieu's theory of the state was the conception of equilibrium of forces. The bicameral system is merely an application of this doctrine of checks and balances. Montesquieu's influence upon the drafters of the American constitution, and, thus, on many a more recent constitution, is common knowledge. He himself argued for the desirability of a legislature of two chambers, on the ground that it would secure the necessary deliberation, avoid haste, and, most important, balance the judgment of the representatives of the masses of the people by that of the representatives of the wealthy and aristocratic elements in society. Although the idea of checks and balances itself is not necessarily to be associated with socially conservative values, its promulgation at this particular point of political development had important ideological connotations; so did, as we have seen, the consequent advocacy of second chambers.

By way of digression, it should be mentioned here that in federal states through a territorial expression of this system of checks and balances the substantive functions of second chambers have received additional stimuli. Whenever a federal state was established, it was invariably one of the greatest concerns of the founders to guarantee the observance of some rights, privileges, and interests of the composing units which had previously been independent. There was a constant fear, says Professor Wheare, that "the general executive and legislature depending primarily on numbers, may adopt policies in foreign and . . . in domestic affairs, which might be opposed but ineffectually opposed by the less populous states which are less strongly represented in the lower house."[38] Consequently, it has been one of the most enduring myths in the field of constitution writing that the maintenance of the desired equilibrium

[37] *Ibid.*, p. 120.
[38] K. C. Wheare, *Federal Government*, 3rd ed. (London, 1953), p. 189.

between units and the federation as a whole could effectively be secured through the arrangement of a second chamber in which the units are represented regardless of population, that is, represented as distinct political organizations, whether on the basis of equal (USA, Switzerland, Australia) or unequal (Germany, India) representation, or some combination of the two (Canada). The strength of this myth has been manifest in the constitution of old (such as USA, Switzerland, Canada) and new (such as Australia, Germany, India) federations alike and it may find an important role to play in shaping the constitutional structure of intensively plural excolonial areas where a second chamber may well be expected to produce a different communal balance from the first, by representing the various caste, linguistic, racial, and religious ingredients of the system.[39] The myth has never failed to find fertile ground whether it has been in accordance with the general tenor of the constitution of the country (as in the case of the USA) or not (as in the case of countries with a responsible cabinet government).

But to return to our main theme, there can be nothing surprising about the genuine hostility of eighteenth century French radical thinkers to a legislative institution whose chief function, by general admission, was to resist democratic aspirations. It must have been particularly appalling to believers in an indivisible national unity as expressed through the philosophical idea of the general will and its corresponding political notion of popular sovereignty. They could hardly be enamoured of the idea of checks and balances, which was aimed at checking precisely what they were trying to set free. Although Rousseau himself was mainly concerned with the question of direct democracy, his disciples were more ready to consider the principles of representation and they tried to secure for the representative assembly the attributes of sovereignty which Rousseau sought for the people themselves. Thus, their chief argument in favour of the unicameral system was that it secured unity instead of duality in the organization of the legislature. Two or three chambers, it was said, implied two or three sovereignties. But if there was a single general will it could only be expressed through a single organ, elected by the majority vote, not through several organs. "The law," said the Abbé Sieyès, "is the will of the people; the people cannot at the same time have two different wills on the same subject; therefore, the legislative body which represents the people ought to be essentially one. Where there are two chambers, discord and division will be inevitable and the will of the people will be paralyzed by inaction."[40] And

[39]Jennings, *Approach to Self-Government*, pp. 113–20.

[40]In J. W. Garner, *Introduction to Political Science* (New York, 1910), p. 43.

summing up the problem he put forward his famous, though somewhat superficial,[41] dilemma: "If the Upper House agrees with the lower it is superfluous; if it disagrees, it ought to be abolished." Basically the same view was expressed by Condorcet, Turgot, Robespierre, and other leaders in France at the time of the Revolution, and the principle was incorporated in the constitutions of 1791 and 1793. Distrust in a second house became a tradition in French political thinking and whenever radicalism was the ruling sentiment of the day, as in 1848, upon Lamartine's agitation, or in the first draft constitution in 1946—subsequently defeated—the idea of unicameralism was again reverted to.

The theme of the French radicals received further elaboration at the hand of Jeremy Bentham, whose views on the technical usefulness of second chambers we have already seen. His negative answer on that point was, of course, derived from a more general scheme of things in which there was no room left for second chambers of whatever type. Although he touched the question in his *Fragment*, he wrote a book especially on this subject, entitled *Jeremy Bentham to his Fellow-Citizens of France on Houses of Peers and Senates*, when he was asked as an honorary French citizen by the aged Lafayette to give advisory opinion on the question, "In France, shall we, or shall we not, have a Chamber of Peers?" As could be expected, Bentham's answer was an uncompromising "No." Since the end of government for him was "the greatest happiness of the greatest number," a legislative assembly, he thought, should be based on universal suffrage. Just as for the Rousseauists the kernel of the question was the most perfect representation of the general will, for Bentham if a second chamber represents the general interests it is useless; while if it represents a particular interest it is mischievous. This was the Abbé clothed in utilitarian surplice.

These opposing views, deriving from opposing systems of philosophy and political theory and reinforced by actual experience, help us define clearly the position and substantive role of second chambers during the late eighteenth and better part of the nineteenth century. They were intended to serve as a primary institutional check in the political system upon the newly enfranchised and politically activized part of the population as represented in the lower house of the legislature. There was no need in this period preceding the development of organized mass parties to try to utilize second chambers in parliamentary democracies as a control mechanism vis-à-vis the executive, for this era happily coincided with the golden age of Parliament, characterized by the independence of the private member and the concept of limited government and the

[41]For any easy refutal, see Finer, *Theory and Practice of Modern Government.*

negative state flowing from the underlying "Weltanschauung" of *laissez-faire* Whig liberalism. Laws were made, in the main, not only by but also in Parliament. In these circumstances the House of Commons was perfectly capable of looking after the executive itself. "No Government between 1834 and 1868," Ramsay Muir wrote nostalgically in 1933, "ever enjoyed a large majority, and members frequently and easily 'crossed the floor of the House', and still more frequently voted against their parties. . . . 'Cabinet dictatorship' did not yet exist; no Government could suppress the free judgment of the House of Commons or afford to disregard it. Party allegiance was not yet rigid, and the crack of the party whip had none of its modern terrors."[42] Bagehot could still believe that the fear of elections in the future was in itself an effective counterpoise of "the dangers arising from a party spirit in Parliament exceeding that of the nation and of a selfishness in Parliament contradicting the true interests of the nation,"[43] and Sidgwick, his contemporary, was satisfied that the Commons possessed enough power to control "the temptations which the consciousness of possessing supreme power carries with it."[44]

However, this political interdependence of Parliament and government, which was part of a greater harmony that Dicey called the Rule of Law, was slowly withering away under the impulse of a complexity of changes in the political and social order and in the philosophy that permeated both. In simplified terms, all that happened was an expansion of the notion of liberalism, so as to give bread to those who already had the franchise but could not enjoy it because they were starving. However, this gradual process of the economic enfranchisement of the people, as it turned out, could not be accomplished except through a gradual aggrandizement of the whole of the executive department of the state. If this process in parliamentary democracies of the cabinet type, where the executive and legislative branches are fused, established the primacy of the executive as such over Parliament as a whole, the accompanying development of party machinery, the increasing stringency of party discipline, and the replacement of the House of Commons by the electorate as the government-selecting agency put an end to the independence of the private member and to the political interdependence of the nineteenth century, and secured the domination of the House of Commons by the cabinet. This shift in the "constitutional centre of gravity," as Schwarz called it,[45] strengthened by the repeated occurrence of a state

[42]R. Muir, *How Britain is Governed* (3rd. ed., London, 1937), p. 8.
[43]Bagehot, *English Constitution*, p. 241.
[44]Sidgwick, *Elements of Politics*, p. 467.
[45]B. Schwarz, *An Introduction to American Administrative Law* (London, 1958), p. 128.

of national emergency in the first half of the century, has been, no doubt, the overriding constitutional phenomenon of our time and has been termed alternately "parliamentary bureaucracy,"[46] "cabinet government,"[47] and "cabinet bureaucracy."[48] In the course of this complex process conservatism received a new profile. As a result of the world-wide shift to the Left that has been evident in the last fifty years or so, yester-year's Whig liberals have become today's conservatives; the target of this new conservatism was no longer the arresting of the progress of the elementary aspirations of democracy, which had been accepted *in toto*, but the arresting of the new phenomenon of excessive concentration of power in the executive, whether it took the form of an accelerated rate of subordinate legislation, a formidable growth of departmental bureaucracy, or the advance of administrative law with a consequent reduction of the effectiveness of the courts to hold the executive at bay. It is perhaps no accident that those who felt most sensitive about this change in the constitutional balance and reacted promptly to it were members of the legal profession. The result was an upsurge in constitutional writings, pre-occupied with the dangers inherent in the new *status quo*. If it was still hoped in the 1920's and '30's that the new phenomenon was a passing one, these hopes were crudely shattered after the Second World War. The enhanced powers of the cabinet, and indeed, of the executive as a whole, survived into the post-war years, and the relationship between Parliament and the executive has become a major peace-time issue. From the briefest survey of relevant criticisms it is beyond doubt that most writers consider the unprecedented authority of cabinet and executive the true source of existing dissatisfaction.[49]

It was these changes in the general constitutional environment, and the corresponding reorientation of conservative objectives, that shaped the new substantive function of second chambers in countries adhering to the cabinet system. A tentative recognition of this emerging new role was not altogether absent from certain liberal writers in the latter part of the nineteenth century. Their views derived from the belief that wherever democracy was progressive and the people became more united and better educated, the idea of a chamber checking the people and their representatives was bound to disappear. In one of the rare books of political science that Hungary has produced, Baron J. Eotvos

[46]K. C. Wheare, "The Machinery of Government," *Public Administration*, vol. XXIV.

[47]W. I. Jennings, *Cabinet Government* (3rd ed., Cambridge, 1959).

[48]Sir Arthur Salter in Campion, *Parliament*, chap. v.

[49]*Parliamentary Reform, 1933–1960* (London, 1961), pp. 117–18.

warned that in so far as the upper chamber used its power to defend the interests of the wealthier strata of society against those of the nation as a whole, it would forfeit confidence and power.[50] Although not yet connected with our modern experience of cabinet supremacy, the consideration which told most to J. S. Mill in favour of second chambers was "the evil effect produced upon the mind of any holder of power. . . . A majority in a single chamber . . . when composed of the same persons habitually acting together . . . easily becomes despotic . . . if released from the necessity of considering whether its acts will be concurred in by another constitutional authority."[51] However, similarly to Eotvos, he emphasized that this end could not be achieved by means of a second chamber composed on an aristocratic basis. "An aristocratic House," he said, "is only powerful in an aristocratic state of society." Therefore, it was highly unlikely that "where democracy is the ruling power in society," such a second chamber "would have any real ability to resist even the aberration of the first."[52] In ideal circumstances, "if one House represents popular feeling, the other should represent personal merit, tested and guaranteed by actual public service, and fortified by practical experience. If one is the people's Chamber, the other should be the chamber of statesmen; a council composed of all living public men who have passed through important political offices or employment."[53] In fact, he advocated an appointed senate. Perhaps the clearest perception that was offered in this period of the new substantive function of second chambers is to be found in Professor W. S. McKechnie's *Reform of the House of Lords* in which it was definitely stated that "the House of Lords, which once stood guard over the actions of a too powerful House of Commons, now stands guard over a too powerful Cabinet. In these days . . . it is the Ministry of the day, and not the Lower Chamber of the Legislaturė, that threatens to become omnipotent. The House of Lords is the only barrier—a frail one, mayhap—that offers resistance to the power of the Cabinet, unrestrained and uncontrolled."[54]

As the process of the "passing of Parliament" became an everyday reality, such views have multiplied. Both Temperley and Lees-Smith, writers of the last two comprehensive works on upper chambers, advocated the idea of a second house protecting the rights of minorities in

[50]An untranslated work on the impact of the hereditary ideas of the nineteenth century upon the state. *Der Einfluss der Herrschenden Ideen des XIX Jahrhunderts auf den Staat* (Leipzig, 1854), vol. II, pp. 161 ff.

[51]Mill, *Representative Government*, p. 325.

[52]*Ibid.*, pp. 326–7.

[53]*Ibid.*, p. 328.

[54]Quoted in G. Ross, *The Senate of Canada* (Toronto, 1914), p. 84.

a constitutional democracy.[55] Their Canadian contemporary, Sir Clifford Sifton, a man who possessed a rare combination of creative and prophetic imagination, wrote in 1917, that is, at a relatively early stage of the development of cabinet preponderance in Canada: "No nation should be under unchecked, single-chamber government. . . . According to my experience, the will of the people is very often better expressed after a check, and after a period of searching and critical discussion which generally arises from such a check, than it is in the first instance." And he added: "It must also be remembered that, under our system, the power of the Cabinet tends to grow at the expense of the House of Commons . . . *The Senate is not so much a check on the House of Commons as it is upon the Cabinet,* and there can be no doubt that its influence in this respect is salutary."[56] The passage of years has not at all faded these arguments. On the contrary, we find L. S. Amery arguing some forty years later that in view of the danger of party caucus dictatorship, "some substantial easement could and should be afforded by once more making a reality of the House of Lords."[57] In a similar vein Craik Henderson called for the establishment of a strong second chamber "with general powers of rejection of measures which offend against subjects . . . such as freedom of speech and the press, Habeas Corpus, . . . etc."[58] And F. W. Lascelles, contributing to the same symposium, posed the question: "Do the principles of democratic government require that the second House should be merely a 'useful' chamber . . . or should it be a Chamber which could have enough power and authority, if circumstances ever made it necessary, to assert itself as a balancing factor in the Constitution?"[59]

Thus, as in the eighteenth and nineteenth century, second chambers again became involved in an ideological controversy. Since the opposing sides of the battle also normally represented distinct political groupings, arguments tended to be dramatized and the issue at stake to be obscured. It is hoped that through divesting these arguments of their emotional trappings we shall be able to formulate in realistic terms the substantive role to be played by second chambers in the modern constitutional milieu. Clearly, for those who maximized the political dangers and

[55]H. W. V. Temperley, *Senates and Upper Chambers* (London, 1910), p. 148; H. B. Lees-Smith, *Second Chambers in Theory and Practice* (London, 1923), pp. 139–40.

[56]Sir Clifford Sifton, "The Foundation of the New Era," in J. O. Miller, ed., *The New Era in Canada* (London, 1917), p. 50. Italics added.

[57]Quoted in Sen. J. J. Connolly, "The Canadian Senate," *Canadian Liberal,* vol. VII (1954), pp. 7–8.

[58]Campion, *Parliament,* p. 104.

[59]*Ibid.,* pp. 217–18.

minimized the social advantages flowing from the new constitutional relationship between executive and Parliament, the main function of second chambers was to delay and postpone until the next general election any legislation of a controversial character for which the government of the day received no specific mandate at the polls. This was certainly a considerable improvement over the substantive role that eighteenth and nineteenth century conservatism assigned to second chambers. Then, based upon a viciously militant type of ultra-conservatism, sceptical of the ability of the people to interpret their own interests, second chambers were designed to check the people and to thwart democratic progress; now, after the triumph of democracy, they were no longer expected to challenge the innate rights of the political sovereign, but rather the right of an omnipotent cabinet to interpret *ex cathedra* the demands of that sovereign without previous contact through election. If in their former role they were motivated by a pessimistic and anachronistic conservatism of the Bonald and DeMaistre type, their new complexion bore closer resemblance to Burke's image of a second chamber—"something to which, in the ordinary detail of government, the people could look up; something which might give a bias, and steadiness, and preserve something like consistency in the proceedings of state . . ."[60] Thus, instead of circumventing the people, second chambers were now conceived as a means by which the explicit views of the people could be put to a test whenever it was felt necessary. This notion had perhaps its most distinguished advocate in Mr. Churchill, first as a Liberal in 1910, then as a Conservative in 1947, on both occasions during second reading debate of the Parliament bill. His argument can be summed up as follows: parliaments will on the average last for about four years and in the first two years of a parliament the controversial questions upon which the election had been fought will normally have been disposed of. Then, in the second two years of the parliament there will be two classes of bills—bills upon which there is a broad measure of agreement between parties, and fresh controversial measures, which the Government might bring forward, but which, if rejected by the Upper House, will await what he called "the ratification of a new decision of the electorate."[61] Basically, the same idea was incorporated in the Bryce Report of 1918, which held that the main function of second chambers was "the interposition of so much delay (and no more) in the passing of a bill into law as may be needed to enable the opinion of the nation to be adequately expressed upon it."

[60]E. Burke, *Reflections on the French Revolution* (Everyman ed., London, 1955), p. 194.
[61]*HD* (UK), *1947*, vol. 444, col. 39.

If a second chamber with powers to force an election on *any* undecided controversial issue was a prime necessity for those who were terrified by the overflow of executive powers, for those who maximized the social advantages and minimized the political dangers of the new constitutional balance this was sheer obstructionism. Thus, Herbert Morrison, sponsor of the Parliament bill of 1947, found the Churchillian concept of a second chamber totally unacceptable for the Labour party. "Matters may well arise," he contended, "in the second half of a Government's terms of office, or before, which have to be dealt with promptly in the public interest. . . . Any other interpretation than this would, in effect, mean that [a non-elective Upper House], in spite of the expressed will of the Chamber elected by the people, would have the final voice in determining what was or what was not the will of the people."[62] Depositories of eighteenth and nineteenth century radicalism, socialists in general looked upon any resistance to the political implications of the phenomenon of a growing executive as being merely an ideological camouflage for a deeper hostility to the economic/social implications of the same phenomenon. They viewed any attempt to fight cabinet preponderance or excessive executive powers as *eo ipso* an attempt to fight the social achievements due to such powers under the banner of laissez-faire Whig liberalism. "The proposals for economic reconstruction," the authors of *Social Planning for Canada* said, ". . . will certainly . . . strengthen . . . the growth in power of the executive at the expense of the power of the legislature, and the extension of the practice of government by independent experts. Is there anything essentially undemocratic in this? Those who affirm that there is, are confusing the general principle of democracy with the particular machinery which was developed in the nineteenth century for giving effect to popular sovereignty."[63] Condemning Dicey for his preoccupation with the rule of law rather than with the economic and social problems of industrial Britain, Jennings could likewise postulate that any worrying about the growing discretionary powers of the executive was pure nostalgia for the individualistic theories of the nineteenth century Whigs.[64] And although he felt he had to admit that "in the political sphere there is much in the Whig philosophy with which any democracy will agree,"[65] there was nevertheless implicit in his whole argument an *a priori* and rigid equation of the economic with the political side of Whiggism. It is not surprising,

[62]*Ibid.*, cols. 42–3.

[63]*Social Planning for Canada* (Toronto, 1935), p. 494.

[64]W. I. Jennings, *The Law and the Constitution*, 5th ed. (London, 1959), pp. 310–11.

[65]*Ibid.*, pp. 314–15.

therefore, that, just as for radicals of the eighteenth and nineteenth century there was no need for an institution with the avowed purpose of checking what constituted the chief radical aspirations of that time, in the new scheme of twentieth century radicalism there was equally no room for any body which, through asserting the traditional concept of parliamentary supremacy, could easily become an obstacle to smooth executive action. According to this scheme, fear of executive preponderance implied fear of the positive state and a reassertion of the discarded economic-social principles of *laissez-faire* Whiggism.

We now know that neither of the extreme attitudes regarding the dangers inherent in the new constitutional relationship of Parliament and the executive, and, consequently, the role that a second chamber should play, was entirely correct. Only through a realistic reappraisal of these supposed dangers can we expect to define the substantive functions of second chambers in the middle of the twentieth century.

It is now clear that fears of a "new despotism," of a sinister plot of autocratic bureaucrats acting under the cloak of secrecy[66] and paving "the road to Moscow,"[67] were exaggerated, and historical analogies between Stuart times and today somewhat fanciful. Yet the off-hand dismissal of such anxieties by the other side has also turned out to be premature, in the light of the socialist experience that the diminution of capitalist power may be followed by an increase in the irresponsible power and oligopolistic privileges of a new managerial oligarchy. A reconsideration of the political factor in its relation to economic institutions—traditionally underestimated by socialists—was attempted by R. H. S. Crossman, a leading intellectual in the British Labour party, in a most remarkable piece of political introspection, in which he found that realization of the ultimate socialist goal—nationalization of the means of production—does not in itself solve the problem of responsible power. "Since our socialism," he said, "is based on the moral demand for greater equality and an enlargment of freedom, and postulates that irresponsible power corrupts, the socialist must be courageous enough to admit that the evils of oligopoly are not limited to the private sector of the economy. Public corporations and Departments of State can also exhibit managerialist tendencies, favour inequality and become a threat to freedom."[68] And he also stated: ". . . the growth of a vast, centralized state bureaucracy constitutes a grave potential threat to social democracy.

[66]Lord Hewart of Bury, *The New Despotism* (London, 1929), p. 8.

[67]G. W. Keeton, *The Passing of Parliament* (London, 1952).

[68]R. H. S. Crossman, "Socialism and the New Despotism," reprinted in W. Ebenstein, ed., *Modern Political Thought* (2nd. ed., New York, 1960), p. 623.

The idea that we are being disloyal to our socialist principles if we . . . defend the individual against its incipient despotism is a fallacy."[69]

The dangers posed by the emergence—inevitable and, in a sense, desirable though this process may be—of an over-powerful executive are now obvious. The threat is not that a sudden eruption into some form of absolutism is imminent, but rather that the constitutional structure may gradually be eroded and the consciousness of future generations of the meaning and importance of constitutionalism weakened to the point of disappearance. "At what stage," asks Professor Corry, "in the multiplying of official powers . . . [does] the Rule of Law disappear? When 1,000 discretionary powers had accumulated, or when 5,000 had been stockpiled? A little reflection would suggest that there is no arithmetical or statistical test for the presence of the Rule of Law. We cannot identify the additional straw of discretionary power which breaks the back of the constitutional state."[70] The problem is the preservation (one would say the discovery) of a fair, effective balance between Parliament and bureaucratic elements, the maintenance of what some call "constitutional ethics,"[71] or the "accepted moral code,"[72] or the "aims, spirit, and predicaments of the community,"[73] or, briefly, of the constitutional climate of the polity. To quote Crossman again, ". . . constitutional reform, designed to enlarge freedom and stimulate an active democracy, is at least as important as the extension of public ownership and redistribution of wealth—which are important only as another means to the same end. . . . *The modern State . . . is inherently totalitarian, and its natural tendency is towards despotism. These tendencies can only be held in check if we are determined to build the constitutional safeguards of freedom—and personal responsibility.*"[74]

This sets the stage for a tentative formulation of the substantive role of second chambers in parliamentary democracies of the cabinet type. They cannot, and ought not to, be expected to perform the over-ambitious and quixotic function of sitting in judgment over the executive and trying to prevent the emergence of a dictator. No senate could possibly stop a Hitler! Acceptance of such a function would only lead to obstruction and resentment. No second chamber should try to take the place of elections and of an operative party system—the ultimate safeguards of constitutional democracy. But, as we have seen, the danger

[69]*Ibid.*, p. 622.

[70]J. A. Corry, "The Prospects for the Rule of Law," *Canadian Journal of Economics and Political Science*, vol. XXI (1955), p. 405.

[71]Keeton, *Passing of Parliament*, p. 124.

[72]M. A. Sieghart, *Government by Decree* (London, 1950), p. 318.

[73]Corry, "Prospects for the Rule of Law," p. 414.

[74]Crossman, "Socialism and the New Despotism," pp. 627–8.

is much more subtle than that, and so must be the functions of second chambers. Accordingly, what second chambers may rightly be called upon to do is to help sustain, together with other institutional and non-institutional elements in the political and social system, the constitutional atmosphere in the body politic. To that end, second chambers may operate on two levels; first—and this is admittedly the more controversial one—in countries with no written constitution (such as the United Kingdom) they should keep a vigilant eye on and delay, if necessary, legislation which in countries with a written constitution would amount to a constitutional amendment, in order to make doubly sure that such legislation carries a mandate from the people and is not merely a product of partisan politicking; in countries which have a written constitution, and especially if they are also of a federal nature (such as Canada), this function takes the form of seeing to it that the method of formal constitutional amendment is not used lightly or to the express detriment of the component units of the federal state. Second, they should maintain a suspicious watch over any attempt on the part of the executive to act arbitrarily or to by-pass Parliament by sheer force of administrative habit or bureaucratic usage and thus unduly further increase its grip over the other branches of Government; for discharging this function second chambers may have various methods of control at their disposal, the effectiveness of which depends on the willingness and the skill to use them. They may consist of a special committee system to oversee all kinds of administrative law-making (as in the case of the United Kingdom and Australia, for example), or of developing a tradition in effecting modification in legislation for the purpose of countervailing executive power through restating—in various forms—the supremacy of Parliament and the rights of the individual (as in the case of Canada, for example). Through an effective discharge of their substantive functions, brought about by recent changes in the political and social system, second chambers may offer a modest yet important service. Instead of being a primary institutional check, as they used to be, upon the people's house, they are now an auxiliary institutional check upon an inflated executive dominating the people's house. As one of the elements of the ever-changing constitutional equilibrium they help to keep awake general interest in the interplay of constitutional forces, thus furthering, perchance, in their own way, the best possible compromise between liberty and authority—between Parliament and government, a compromise Lord Salisbury described as "the basis of ordered freedom." Once a stumbling block to democratic progress, second chambers, in their new role, may well become one of the institutional pillars of constitutional democracy.

Part I

THE STRUCTURE OF THE SENATE

THE APPOINTING SYSTEM

1

THE CANADIAN SENATE is the only legislative body in the Commonwealth, apart from modern Trinidad and Tobago, which is based upon the principle of pure nomination.[1] Its adoption was not a matter of light decision. In addition to the example of the United States, which they tried to avoid, and the example of the United Kingdom, which they tried to copy, the Fathers of Confederation were helped by the experience of all the provincial governments for nearly seventy-five years and fortified by the experience of Upper and Lower Canada under the Union Act, where the elective system for the Legislative Council had been used for a period of ten years. The final choice was in the nature of a compromise between lack of an appropriate social milieu for adopting a house of peers and lack of confidence in an elected senate. When the Quebec Conference opened on October 10, 1864, it was clear that although the Conference acted under no preconceived dominant notion,[2] there was a

[1]It was adopted in New Zealand in 1852 and retained, after the reduction of the life period to a term of seven years in 1891, until the Council was abolished in 1951. In some of the other Commonwealth countries nomination is combined with other methods of construction: in Ceylon for one-half of the Senate; in the Indian Council of States twelve members are nominated by the president on grounds similar to the principles governing life peerages in the United Kingdom; while in Nigeria four Senators are appointed by the president on the advice of the prime minister, the rest being selected by the regional legislatures from among persons nominated by the president. For Trinidad and Tobago, see below, p. 373, n. 11.

[2]Sir John A. Macdonald assured the Conference that he would keep his "own mind open on that point as if it were a new question to me altogether." However, it was equally clear that he was in favour of the appointing system: "While I do not admit that the elective principle has been a failure in Canada, I think we had better return to the original principle and . . . endeavour to make ours 'an image

general disinclination on the part of the Lower Provinces to adopt the elective principle; indeed, the delegates from New Brunswick, Nova Scotia and Newfoundland all supported the system of nomination,[3] with Prince Edward Island alone in its favour for election. However, a difference of opinion developed among the delegates respecting the mode of appointment. While some wanted the selection of members of the upper chamber made by the local legislatures, others, including Tupper, thought that this would be imposing an irritating subject on such legislatures, and suggested that the first legislative councillors (as the members of the Senate were to be called) should be chosen from the members of the existing Councils of the several colonies, care being taken to give to the Opposition adequate representation in the new federal Legislative Council. Further discussion ensued and, objection being raised to leave the appointment of the first members of the upper house to the local legislatures, the following resolution was unanimously agreed to:

> That the members of the first Legislative Council in the Federal Legislature shall be appointed by the Crown at the recommendation of the Federal Executive Government upon the nomination of the respective Local Governments. And that in such nomination due regard be had to the claims of the members of the Legislative Council of the Opposition in each Province, so as that all political parties be as nearly as possible fairly represented.[4]

While this resolution contained an express limitation on the mobility of the executive in making the first appointments, no restrictions were attached to any future appointments to be made by the federal government, and the resolution laid the constitutional principle on which the Canadian Senate was to be constructed. In idealistic terms it was expected that the method of appointment would enable men to be chosen for their acknowledged moral and intellectual qualities and produce a body which would lend dignity and distinction to the public life of the country. In more realistic terms, it must have been contemplated by those having a Hamiltonian frame of mind that the system of appointment by a central agency would eventually strengthen the position of the federal government and might help lead to a more unified form of political system.

---

and transcript of the British Constitution.' " J. Pope, ed., *Confederation: Being a Series of Unpublished Documents Bearing on the British North America Act* (Toronto, 1895), p. 57. Cited hereafter as *Confederation Documents.*

[3]*Parliamentary Debates on Confederation of British North American Provinces* (Quebec, 1865; Ottawa, 1951), p. 35. Cited hereafter as *Confederation Debates.*

[4]Pope, ed., *Confederation Documents,* p. 40. Quoted in J. F. MacNeill, Law Clerk and Parliamentary Counsel to the Senate, memo to Sen. Robertson, "Reasons Given for Senate by Confederation People" (1950).

1. *The Prime Minister's Prerogative*

The Crown's historic position in regard to making appointments to the upper chamber is expressed in the notion that Senators are not appointed but summoned, as are members of the British House of Lords. The section of the BNA Act governing summons of Senators says: "The Governor General shall from time to time, in the Queen's name, by instrument under the Great Seal of Canada, summon qualified persons to the Senate; and, subject to the provisions of this Act, every person so summoned shall become and be a member of the Senate and a Senator."[5] The duty of making appointments was, thus, placed upon the governor general, not upon the governor in council. Of course, in accordance with modern constitutional principles, the governor general acts upon the advice of his constitutional advisers—in this instance the prime minister of the day and of the Cabinet as a whole. The governor general's assent to the recommendation of the prime minister is practically automatic. However, as with other aspects of this prerogative that are ordinarily dormant, the governor general has, in theory, the right to refuse his consent or to defer a summons. In the last moments of the Liberal Government in June 1926 several appointments were made, including some to the Senate. It was reported at the time, however, that the Governor General consented to sign only such of the appointments submitted to him by the Prime Minister (King) as had been made on Friday (June 25) before the vote adverse to the Government. As a result, Senators W. L. McDougald (who later resigned following the Beauharnois incident) and D. Riley from Alberta were duly summoned to the Senate. It was alleged, however, that the Government had also determined to make appointments to the vacant senatorships in Nova Scotia; since these were not submitted to the Governor General until after Friday's vote, Lord Byng felt himself unable to assent to them.[6] This episode, however, was a rather extraordinary one, flowing from a rather extraordinary constitutional situation, and it would be misleading to attach too much importance to it.

For all practical purposes, therefore, it is virtually certain that the recommendation of the prime minister of the day will be carried into effect. The only constitutional restrictions on his choice are those sections

[5]Sec. 24 of the BNA Act.

[6]These reports were denied by King in the House of Commons: "Appointment to the vacant senatorships in Nova Scotia was never determined by the Government and no recommendation whatever was made to his Excellency." *HD, 1926,* p. 5098.

of the BNA Act regulating the federally fixed maximum of the number of Senators that can represent the senatorial sections of the country at any given point of time,[7] as well as the age, residence, and property qualifications of members of the Senate.[8] Otherwise, the prime minister's freedom of selection is subject to no limitations, except to the dictates of partisan-political expediency. However, in view of the limited number of seats available and the unlimited number of those seeking them, the task of recommending appointments to the Senate is one of the most difficult duties of a prime minister. As the ultimate decision rests with him he is subjected to constant and varied forms of pressure from all interested quarters. A considerable part of the personal correspondence of Arthur Meighen as prime minister of Canada in 1920–21 is made up of all kinds of literary communication between him and self-nominated senatorial candidates who were trying to catch the Prime Minister's eye. "I fear," he wrote, "the difficulties that a Government meets in connection with these appointments are not as a rule fully comprehended. . . . The task I am at is one I will never envy another when he undertakes it in future. It is . . . impossible for me to argue out the pros and cons of decisions I may come to. There are many considerations affecting and balancing each other."[9]

Although the prime minister is not unaided in making his choice, no hard and fast rules can be laid as to the exact nature of the advice he will seek and the extent to which he will accept it as binding upon him. Members of the cabinet will probably be listened to more attentively than members of Parliament or senators, although friendship and other personal ties cutting through party lines may enable those outside the immediate circle of political office-holders to have the prime minister's ear. In view of the federal-sectional character of senatorial representation, however, the overriding consideration seems to be attached to the advice flowing from representatives of the area from which the appointment is to be made. It is a well-established practice that the prime minister will consult as a "rule of courtesy" the minister from the province concerned and, if further information is needed, MP's and Senators from the same part of the country. "The number of aspirants,"

[7]For membership of the Senate, Canada is divided into four divisions representing the four naturally differentiated areas of the country. The Senate gives equal representation, 24 members each, to the main areas, thus making a total of 96. This number was increased to 102 when the entrance of Newfoundland added 6 more. This provision is only subject to the obsolescent swamping sec. 26, as amended in 1915, of the Act.

[8]Sec. 23 of the BNA Act.

[9]Meighen to J. G. Elliott and A. E. Fripp, MP, on July 29, 1920, and Sept. 14, 1921, respectively. Meighen Papers, series 2, no. 196.

wrote Meighen as Leader of the Senate to an aspirant from Quebec in 1932, "is very great and the Prime Minister will have considerable difficulty in deciding. I fancy he will be guided *only by the Quebec Ministers and Members*."[10]

It would seem logical that the leader of the Senate, who is the representative of the government in that chamber and has traditionally been, at least until recently, a member of the cabinet, should be consulted before decision is reached regarding new appointments. However, curious though it may seem, this is not the case. The office of leader of the Senate carries no privileged status with it beyond that possessed by other members of the Senate, unless, of course, the occupant of the post comes from the same province as the prospective candidate or has an easy and perhaps direct access to the prime minister. "The fact is," wrote Meighen in his capacity as leader of the Senate to someone from Manitoba, "that I am considered first of all a Senator, and a Senator has nothing, or less than nothing, to say about new appointments. Next, I am a Senator from Ontario and representatives of one province are not heard as regards another." As a result, he had "not the slightest idea of what the Prime Minister has in mind . . . and probably will know only when the appointment is made." The only thing he could promise was to try to keep the relevant "facts in mind if I can by any chance be present when the matter is reviewed, that is if indeed it is reviewed in Council at all."[11]

The real position of the leader of the Senate with regard to senatorial appointments is more often than not misunderstood. This may explain why between 1932 and 1935 Sen. Meighen received a total of eighty-nine pieces of correspondence[12] from petitioners and their sponsors, including a letter from Lieutenant-Governor Munroe of Saskatchewan, asking his prompt intercession on their behalf. Meighen parried each with such politeness as he could muster, explaining the limited opportunities he had as Senate leader in these matters. "I could not say definitely," he wrote to a wife advocating her husband's case, "that there is absolutely nothing I can do, but the Prime Minister considers and no doubt rightly considers this his own prerogative. . . ."[13] The influence the leader of the Senate may wield will ultimately depend on the character of his relations with the prime minister and, to a lesser

[10]Meighen to N. Garceau, on March 10, 1932. *Ibid.*, series 5, no. 223. Italic added.

[11]Meighen to J. W. on Jan. 10, 1935. *Ibid.*, no. 224.

[12]33 from Quebec, 18 from Manitoba, 15-15 from Saskatchewan and Ontario, 5 from New Brunswick, 3 from Nova Scotia.

[13]Meighen to Mrs. R. D. on Jan. 16, 1934. Meighen Papers, series 5, no. 224.

degree, on the frequency with which he will attend Council meetings where the question of appointments may be discussed. Thus Sen. Dandurand, who enjoyed the confidence of Mackenzie King, probably had more say in senatorial appointments than Meighen, whose relationship with Bennett had never warmed up to the point of friendship and who kept himself aloof from cabinet meetings whilst in Ottawa. "Personally I am here so little," he wrote in 1933, "that virtually no appointments are influenced by me in the least. Indeed, I do not remember being present when any appointments to the Senate have been made. . . . I am here only for purposes of Senate leadership."[14] As a result, after two years as leader of the Senate he could say that, "I have not yet been spoken to on the matter of any senatorship and am making this statement in no spirit of criticism whatever."[15]

If this holds true of the leader of the Senate, it is even more characteristic of the position of ordinary members of the House who "are supposed to keep away from politics and . . . act up to the expectation by refraining, among other things, from making any suggestions about" purely political matters such as appointments to the Senate.[16] Thus, even such a towering political figure of his day as Sir George E. Foster, Senator from Ontario, 1921–31, had to admit that he had "only an advisory influence in respect to appointments. . . . The appointment is really in the hands of the Prime Minister, subject to the special advice of the representative in the Cabinet for the province, and the general advice of his colleagues from other points."[17] In spite of their self-imposed political neutralism, senators belonging to a different political party from the prime minister's cannot help feeling handicapped in trying to promote the cause of a friend. The dilemma involved was well illustrated in the scruples of Sen. Murphy, who for all his friendly ties with Prime Minister Bennett did not feel at liberty to approach him in regard to senatorial appointments. Were he to do so, he thought, he would run a double risk: "either of being met with a rebuff, which of course, would seriously affect, if it did not destroy, our friendship; or I would be pointed to by Liberals as having turned Conservative, and of seeking to exercise an influence with the Conservative Party." Therefore, no matter how much he wished to see the Senate vacancy filled with an English-speaking Catholic, he felt he could not "make any repre-

[14]Meighen to C. J. Hamilton, Feb. 3, 1933. *Ibid.*, no. 223.
[15]Meighen to C. W. McMillan, Jan. 23, 1934. *Ibid.*, no. 224.
[16]Murphy to H. Timmins, Apr. 29, 1930. Murphy Papers, vol. 29, no. 12410.
[17]Foster to S. E. Elkin, MP, August 4, 1921. Meighen Papers, series 2, no. 194.

sentation to Mr. Bennett, or to any other Conservative, in the matter, because the appointment is purely a political one to be made by the Party of which I am not a member."[18]

In view of the intricacies of the decision to be made and in order to reduce as much as possible the number of frustrated parties, the prime minister will often decide to reach out for advice from any source of "associational" or "non-associational" interest formations, if he feels that such sources are better equipped to furnish him with the information he needs. This device has its best application in making senatorial appointments from various ethnic or religious minority groups which are not adequately represented in the cabinet. In such cases the prime minister will not hesitate to turn even to his political opponents for suggestions, lest by an unrepresentative, and, therefore, unpopular, appointment he antagonize a whole segment of the population. Thus, in 1935 Prime Minister Bennett sent the following letter to Sen. Veniot, a Liberal member of the Senate: "As a leader among the Acadians you are in a better position than I to judge which one of the gentlemen whose names I submit to you is best qualified to represent the Acadians of New Brunswick in the Senate as successor to the late Sen. Pascal Poirier. . . . *I shall abide by your recommendation and make the appointment as you suggest. . . .*"[19] In a similar manner he wrote to the editor of the *Catholic Record*, a politically non-partisan paper: "There is a Senate vacancy in Saskatchewan. I have told my supporters from that province, and my friends, that the minority is entitled to representation and that a Catholic should be appointed. . . . I may say to you very confidentially that I have asked some of our friends to give me the name of some outstanding Catholic in northern Saskatchewan who would be a credit to his Church and an honour to the position. Can you help me?"[20]

Normally, of course, prospective appointees would follow with a watchful eye the fluctuation of their chances on the senatorial stock-market, as, indeed, it is they themselves who will try to push their case with such firmness as would seem wise under the circumstances. Yet nothing illustrates better the absolute monopoly the prime minister has

[18]Murphy to J. J. Leddy, Jan. 12, 1931. Murphy Papers, vol. 16, nos. 6699–6700.

[19]Fifteen days later J. A. Léger was summoned to the Senate. "Here is a case," Sen. Veniot, Jr., later commented, "of a Conservative Prime Minister asking one of his bitterest political opponents . . . to practically make an appointment to the Senate for him." *SD, 1951*, p. 344. Italics added.

[20]Bennett to Rt. Rev. J. Foley, Feb. 24, 1931. Murphy Papers, vol. 10, no. 4281.

in regard to appointments to the Senate than the fact that at times, for reasons only known to him, he may decide to confer senatorships upon persons who never asked for them or even upon those who do not want them. Sen. Haig, former Conservative leader of the Senate, viewed his own appointment in 1935 as a good example of the sole prerogative of the prime minister:

"I speak with authority. I know how I was appointed. I was not appointed by any committee. A man telephoned me long distance and said, 'Will you accept a Senatorship?' I said 'What?' He said again, 'Will you accept a Senatorship?' I replied, 'Well, I thought you had to be a member of the House of Commons to become a Senator.' He said, 'Oh, no; anybody can be a Senator if he is appointed.' So I asked, 'Will the Prime Minister appoint me?' The reply came back, 'He says he will.' I said, 'But he does not like me.' The man answered, 'Oh, that doesn't make any difference—he wants you.' So I became a Senator." And he added: "An appointment to the Senate is a personal matter . . . 165 people wanted the place I occupy here. I have never asked for it. The others asked too hard, and the Prime Minister at the time did not listen to them. If I had asked, I think he would have turned me down."[21]

Sometimes an appointment to the Senate comes out of the blue. Thus, Sen. Donnelly recalled that he was in his seat in the House of Commons in 1913 when a pageboy came up to him with a message that the Prime Minister's messenger wished to see him at the entrance to the Commons Chamber. When he started out he did not know that this was the last time he would cross the threshold of the House as one of its members. At the entrance he was told that Prime Minister Borden wanted to see him in his office in the East Block. Following the instructions he went to the Prime Minister's private office, where he was simply told that he had been recommended for the Senate a short while ago. His resignation as a member of the House of Commons was already written out and he signed it upon the Prime Minister's advice, although it was not absolutely necessary. Sir Robert then told him that it would be better for him not to return to his seat in the Commons but rather to wait till the following day and take his seat in the Senate. Thus was J. J. Donnelly elevated, much to his surprise, from the Lower to the Upper House.[22]

If the ultimate decision respecting senatorial appointments rests with the prime minister of the day, the next question that must be considered is the principles governing the exercise of that prerogative.

[21]*SD, 1955*, pp. 454–5.
[22]*SD, 1938*, p. 398.

2. *The Principles Governing Appointments to the Senate*

Although the social symbols attached to membership in the Senate are not comparable to those surrounding the conferment of peerages in the United Kingdom,[23] appointments to the Senate have been considered a highly effective device for recognizing various claims arising out of the political life as well as of the territorial and societal diversity of the country. As they are in both instances manipulated by the prime minister, senatorial appointments are essentially an instrument of politics, for the purpose of either lubricating the machinery of the party or befriending (or trying to avoid insulting) various group-claimants.

The first principle, therefore, governing appointments to the Senate is in the more narrowly defined realm of party politics. Because of the complexity and comprehensiveness of the political life, claims based upon services rendered in that wide area have almost an infinite variety and can prove truly baffling for a prime minister trying to do justice among them. It is instructive to compare the more often recurring ones, in order to see the respective weight petitioners attach to them in their race for a Senate seat.

There are the odd ones, only loosely connected with party service. "My daughters," an ambitious mother wrote to Sen. Meighen, "are both married. May I dream of reaching to the Upper House, Ottawa?" To this a remarkably patient Meighen sent the following coolly correct answer: "A Senate seat is a legitimate aspiration of any Canadian."[24] Others have more relevance to politics, though still moving in general terms. "Please think of . . . myself," an old Conservative asked the Prime Minister, "when you come to appoint a new Senator in the place of Sen. Landry. I am still on my feet you know!"[25] Still others prefer bluntness, even at the risk of sounding aggressive: ". . . as one who has stood by the party from my infancy, long before you were able to know what politics meant," someone wrote to Meighen from Saskatchewan, "I feel that there is something due me. . . ."[26] In contrast, there are those who humbly recognize the shallowness of their request and leave their case

[23]P. Bromhead, *The House of Lords and Contemporary Politics, 1911–1957* (London, 1958), pp. 20 ff.

[24]Meighen to Mrs. E. T., May 31, 1935. Meighen Papers, series 5, no. 224.

[25]J. H. R. to Meighen, Dec. 20, 1919. Meighen's reply: "I do not know what the future has in store, but I for one will not forget you or any others who made the sacrifice for true Canadianism that you did." *Ibid.*, series 1, no. 60.

[26]C. J. H. to Meighen, Jan. 30, 1933. *Ibid.*

to the benevolence and wisdom of the Prime Minister. "I am too true a Conservative not to understand the Prime Minister's views on the matter," someone wrote to Meighen as leader of the Senate, "and . . . I would consent to resign honorably at his request at any time, my ambition being amply satisfied with, as an official recognition of my services, the honour of being allotted a seat in the Senate for no matter however a limited period."[27]

Claims supported by more concrete evidence may in their turn be divided into those based upon past services and those based upon future services to be rendered after appointment. Within the class of past services further subcategories may be established according to the placing of emphasis. Clearly, priority is expected for prolonged work done in connection with elections in general and party organization in particular on any of the three levels of government. This group includes those who did not distinguish themselves by running for office but by helping others, directly or indirectly, to fight the election. "I have supported the Conservative Party very actively since 1908," one claim reads, "in which year I campaigned for the Party's candidate. . . . It is true that in 1917 I withdrew shortly before the election, at the request of the leaders of the Party in the province, to make possible acclamation for Hon. F. Carvell, Minister of Public Works in the Borden Cabinet. . . . I can well appreciate the fact that those who have fought the Party's battles and have been successful deserve first consideration. But I feel that one who has worked wholeheartedly for the Party for many years, who has given of his time, his energy, his means, has a right to some consideration. I have stood up for the Party at the time . . . when few men would undertake the task. Thus I have contributed considerably to keeping the Party alive."[28] Others thought they could strengthen the case of their protégé by pointing out that "he was the Conservative Standard Bearer in the South B–constituency in the elections of 1925–26, and laid the foundation, in these elections, for the increased support that Dr. — received in the election of 1930. . . ."[29]

Party organizers have an equally well-founded claim to a seat in the Senate. "I think there is some credit due to me," a Manitoba organizer of the Conservative party wrote to A. Meighen, "for having kept this district and every poll organized when many of our own people had deserted us in both provincial and federal politics. You in your time

27J. N. D. to Meighen, May 20, 1932. *Ibid.*, series 5, no. 223.
28J. E. D. to Meighen, Nov. 24, 1933. *Ibid.*
29Major B. to Meighen, Jan. 23, 1933. *Ibid.*

. . . could always depend on this district for a majority."[30] In fact, the Senate has always included amongst its members persons who had formerly been active organizers of either of the two major parties. It is sufficient to note only the most famous examples. Sen. Haydon, who later became entangled in the unfortunate Beauharnois scandal, had been for years General Secretary of the National Liberal Organization Committee before he was summoned to the Senate in 1924. General McRae had the direction of the Conservative Convention held in Winnipeg in the late 1920's and took full charge of the election campaign which returned the Bennett Government afterwards. He was subsequently appointed to the Senate, on September 4, 1933.[31] After many years of loyal service to the Liberal cause, both on provincial and federal levels, J. A. Lesage won the confidence of the leaders of his party and became the chief organizer for the whole eastern section of the Province of Quebec. He took his seat in the Senate in 1944, together with J. Nicol, who had been chief organizer of the Liberal party in the province.[32] An even more sparkling career as party organizer was that of Sen. Fogo, who never ran for public office himself but maintained an unswerving loyalty to the Liberal party from his youth. Since his first political encounter in 1920 to support Col. Ralston's attempt to gain a Cumberland County seat in the Nova Scotia legislature, he continued to maintain an active interest in the Nova Scotia Liberal organization, of which he later became president. In 1945, he was drafted by the National Liberal Federation to organize the Liberal campaign in the federal election of that year. The campaign being successful, Fogo was elected president of the national organization. His greatest political task and the one that orbited him into the Senate was yet to come. It was the organizing of the National Liberal Convention in Ottawa in the summer of 1948, where Mr. St. Laurent was chosen as leader of the party. In the following year Fogo was summoned to the Senate.[33] Prime ministers do not usually forget such services as those of Sen. J. Davis who was one of the very few persons who went out to greet Mackenzie King in the town of St. Boniface, Man., when the latter first crossed Canada as leader of the Liberal party. Afterwards he took an important managerial part in the election and continued his organizational work until 1949 when he was elevated to the upper house. Among the more recent appointments one finds Sen. (Mrs.) Irvine, former

[30]R. J. W. to Meighen, Jan. 3, 1935. *Ibid.*, no. 224.

[31]*SD, 1946*, p. 407. Also J. R. Williams, *The Conservative Party of Canada, 1920–1949* (Durham, NC, 1956), pp. 124–5.

[32]*SD, 1950*, p. 58.

[33]*SD, 1953*, pp. 7–8.

president of the Women's Conservative Association of Manitoba; M. R. Drouin, chairman of the Quebec Conservative Organization and first vice president of the National Progressive Conservative party, who served as Speaker of the Senate from 1957 to 1962; Frank C. Welch, president of the Nova Scotia PC Association between 1953–62; and Allister Grosart, national director of the PC Association of Canada.

If claims built on organizational and election services can be made more convincing through reference to material and financial sacrifices encountered during the process, so much the better. There is, of course, a difference—often blurred in the critical comments—between being generous to the party in actual combat and offering money for the express purpose of purchasing a seat in the Senate. Much of the loose talk on this subject probably dates back to a post-election remark of Sir Wilfrid Laurier,[34] or, indeed, to a famous row between Herman Henry Cook and Sir Richard Cartwright, after the former alleged that he had been asked by someone, purporting to represent Sir Richard, to contribute $10,000 as the price of a seat in the Senate. Cook did not get any appointment, and, by reason of his peculiar notion of public morality, he was forever debarred from being even considered for an appointment.[35] This is why Sen. Murphy warned a determined claimant who did "not know much about how these appointments are made but would be quite willing to make good and proper contribution," by offering the following advice: "it would be all right for you to mention what you have done in the political campaigns to which you refer; but, on your life, do not make any reference" to "proper contributions." "In the first place it would be the worst kind of bad tactics to do so; and in the second place, there is absolutely no need for doing so, because nothing of the kind ever enters into any of the appointments. . . ."[36] Granted that this is true, dramatized accounts of financial losses suffered in the interest of the party are still numbered among the strongest claims in the contestants' armoury. There are those who sacrifice their business for the party. "I have been a staunch and loyal supporter of the Liberal Party all my life," one wrote, "and in 1921, at the solicitation of the Party here, resigned the Postmastership of B— to become a Standard Bearer of the

[34]"At present, just after an election, we have no great amount of campaign funds, but we expect to have a few Senate seats to dispose of before long, and that will help us through." Quoted by Bourassa in *HD, 1929*, p. 95. To which King replied: "I knew Sir Wilfrid Laurier very intimately and I feel certain that anything of the kind was the last thought in his mind. I do not believe Sir Wilfrid Laurier ever appointed anyone to the Senate because of a financial consideration." *Ibid.*, p. 96.

[35]Murphy to W. A. F., Oct. 12, 1927. Murphy Papers, vol. 11, nos. 4475–76.

[36]*Ibid.*

Party in the General Elections and redeemed this riding which was considered hopelessly Conservative."[37] Another, who was chairman of the Patronage Committee of the Conservative party in St. John, NB, called the Prime Minister's attention to the fact that "to the detriment of my own business, I worked night and day for the party and when Sir Douglas Hazen retired from the Cabinet, he wrote me a letter stating that he could never repay me for what I had done for him and the Party."[38] Even more convincing are claims supported by exact calculations: "This election was of very great importance from a party standpoint . . .," one letter reads, "it cost me personally over $20,000 over and above what assistance I received from outside sources."[39] Those who made financial contributions to the party's success tend to regard theirs as priority claims over all others. "It just struck me on checking over the list . . .," an indignant correspondent of the Hon. Charles Murphy wrote in 1927, "that although I have to work for a living, it might be considered that I had about as much claim to the appointment as any of the rest of these chaps, in view of the amount of money . . . I have spent on behalf of the Liberal Party during the last few years, including the West H— By-election of 1924, to say nothing of the beautiful fight in N— county that caused me personally . . . about $20,000, last Fall."[40] No wonder that failure to obtain a seat in the Senate after such muscular services may cause a feeling of resignation. ". . . I have been the acknowledged leader of the Conservative Party for the last 20 years," somebody argued from one of the Maritime provinces. "At times it has cost me so much money that I dare not tell my bankers. . . . If my services . . . are not recognized, there is not much inducement for any young man to start in and devote his time to the cause."[41]

Those who have very little accomplishment of their own to point to, prefer leaning back on the services of their ancestors as the magic key to open the door to the Senate. The appointment of Sen. Thibaudeau in 1896 as the first appointee of a grateful Sir Wilfrid Laurier was admittedly due to the fact that his father, the Hon. Isidore Thibaudeau, had given his seat in Quebec East to Laurier after his defeat in Drummond-Arthabaska, when he was seeking re-election as a member of the Mackenzie Administration.[42] "My own claims are," somebody wrote candidly to Prime Minister Meighen, "that both my Grandfathers, two of my

[37]W. G. R. to Murphy, Dec. 3, 1926. *Ibid.*, vol. 25, no. 10771.
[38]F. C. M. to Meighen, Aug. 26, 1921. Meighen Papers, series 2, no. 194.
[39]R. W. W. to Meighen, Sept. 19, 1921. *Ibid.*
[40]W. A. F. to Murphy. Murphy Papers, vol. 11, no. 4473.
[41]W. S. M. to Meighen, Sept. 8, 1921, Meighen Papers, series 2, no. 194.
[42]*SD, 1927*, p. 4.

uncles and my Father have represented this county as Conservatives . . ."[43] The fact that a person's father was a member of the Senate is sometimes used as an argument to stress the desirability of continuing the family tradition. "As you know," Sen. Meighen was reminded, "my father spent his life and resources in the service of the Party. He was very happy to receive a seat in the Senate . . . I have carried on the work ever since and I have always been at the service of the Party."[44] The inference is obvious. The ancestral claim has perhaps nowhere received a more elegantly convincing presentation than in the following Gallic systematization: "*a*) Mon arrière-grand-père . . . s'occupa toujours activement de la politique conservative. *b*) Mon grand-père maternel . . . fut député conservateur . . . *c*) Mon oncle . . . a été député provincial fédéral et conseiller législatif . . . *d*) Mon père a été un des principaux organisateurs durant plus de quarante ans. . . ."[45]

On the other hand, there are also grateful sons and daughters campaigning hard on behalf of elderly fathers. "I do not want to go into too many details regarding the merits of my father and reasons in claiming this honor," a son approached Sen. Meighen as Government leader in the Senate in 1934. "Suffice it to say that our strongest Conservative supporters . . . are unanimous in this case. He is and has been a life-long supporter of the Party; he also fought along with our candidates many an election campaign; he has devoted the time necessary and even spent his own money to bring these elections to successful issue; he is still active in politics."[46] A similarly suggestive picture is drawn in the fol-following account of "papa's" merits:

Honorable Monsieur Meighen, vous n'avez pas oublié papa, j'espère? Vous souvient-il qu'il a marché à vos côtés lorsque votre [?] dans notre province? Vous souvient-il qu'il est allé faire votre campagne dans l'Ouest canadien et qu'il a beaucoup travaillé pour gagner votre cause? Vous savez aussi que papa, directeur du Journal "La Minerve" a mis de son temps, de son argent pour le parti et cela sans jamais retirer un sou de salaire. [What else did papa do?] Président du club conservateur Cartier-McDonald [*sic*], papa a tout fait pour le ralliement et l'union des conservateurs dans notre province. A chaque election, mon père a été d'une ardeur inlassable pour que le parti soit à l'honneur. Et papa est cependent le seul que l'on est oublié; tous ceux qui étaient de ce temps ont reçu du Gouvernement une charge, entre autres, l'Honorable André Fauteux, M. Félix Desroches. Je puis vous dire que papa a peut-être fait plus que ceux-ci.[47]

---

[43]W. S. M. to Meighen. Meighen Papers, series 2, no. 194.
[44]J. B. to Meighen, July 15, 1932. Meighen Papers, series 5, no. 223.
[45]J. A. A. to Meighen, June 22, 1933. *Ibid.*
[46]A. L. R. to Meighen, Jan. 18. 1934. *Ibid.*
[47]Mlle L. to Meighen, April 22, 1934. *Ibid.*

Although claims based upon services to be rendered in the future are recognized as being less effective than those based upon services already done in the past,[48] they are used as supporting argument in building up a strong case for a Senate appointment. "There is a great need at the present time for organization and publicity work in connection with the business of the Party within this province," someone suggested from Saskatchewan, "and I have offered, should this appointment be made as suggested, to give my entire time to the business of the Party."[49] It is usually contended that the added prestige of a senatorship would considerably increase the effectiveness of a person's contribution to organizational and campaign activities.[50] "I would be most deeply grateful and highly appreciative of this appointment," one of the letters reads, "and believe from the standpoint of party good and usefulness that I could be of very material benefit and assistance to the Minister of New Brunswick and to the Government also."[51] And one of the supporters of his claim repeated that his "appointment would enable him to appropriately and efficiently cooperate in the organization and guidance of the Party's forces."[52] Another promised that if he "received that appointment, I would be in a position to look after the question of the French press for the province of New Brunswick."[53]

Those with service in the House of Commons can always expect especial consideration when decisions regarding appointments to the Senate are made. Nearly half (45 per cent) of the members of the Senate who were appointed between 1925 and 1963 have been persons from the House of Commons. These in their turn may be divided into a number of loosely defined groups. First come the ministers on whom senatorships are conferred as rewards for their services when they retire from office. Table I shows the number of ministers appointed by each administration during the last thirty-seven years, their proportion to the

[48]Said Meighen of such claims: "I like myself to recognize work done, rather than work promised, in the event of appointment. . . ." Meighen to E. K. S., Sept. 15, 1921. *Ibid.*, series 2, no. 195.

[49]J. A. H. to Meighen, Jan. 31, 1933. *Ibid.*, series 2, no. 223.

[50]"Friends as well as myself are very strongly in favour of my taking the Senatorship, as in doing so I could be of tremendous service to the party at this and future elections." R. W. W. to Meighen. Sept. 19, 1921. Meighen Papers, series 2, no. 194. And also: "During the last General Election I addressed a large number of meetings . . . on behalf of the Liberal candidates . . . I believe that in this way I could still be of great use to the Liberal Party; especially if I had the added prestige of being a Senator." W. G. R. to Murphy, Dec. 3, 1926. Murphy Papers, vol. 25, no. 10771.

[51]J. D. P. to Meighen, Aug. 3, 1921. Meighen Papers, series 2, no. 194.

[52]C. D. R. to Meighen, Aug. 13, 1921. *Ibid.*

[53]F. J. R. to Meighen, Aug. 22, 1921. *Ibid.*

total number of appointments, and the average age of them at the time of their appointment.

TABLE I

Percentage of Ministers Appointed to the Senate, 1925–63

Appointed by	Total appointments	No. of ministers	Percentage of ministers	Average age at appointment
King, '25–'30*	35	11	31%	60
Bennett, '30–'35	33	9	27%	64
King, '35–'49	59	4	7%	65
St. Laurent, '49–'57	55	3	5%	67
Diefenbaker, '57–'63	37	4	11%	55
Total	219	31	14.2%	62.2

*No appointments were made to the Senate during the brief period of the Meighen Government in 1926.

However, it would be a mistake to suggest that senatorships conferred upon ministers are always conferred at the end of glorious careers wound up by voluntary retirement. In fact, they may often indicate dismissal, as when a prime minister wants to rid himself of a minister, either because he is old, or because he has failed to live up to the expectations attached to his administrative abilities, or because a political or personal antagonism has developed between the two,[54] or simply because the prime minister wishes him out of the way in order that he may reorganize his cabinet. In these circumstances the Senate may provide a comfortable way for the prime minister of soothing and gratifying the individual concerned, or at any rate his relatives, while removing him from the Commons where his continuing presence might otherwise prove embarrassing to the government.

Senatorships are also due to members of the House of Commons who have held no ministerial office. Back-bench members who are appointed

[54]The appointment of the Hon. Charles Murphy to the Senate was clearly the result of such an irreconcilable difference of opinion between King and himself, dating back to the Liberal Convention in 1919 and reaching its climax by the mid-twenties. Murphy's feelings towards the Prime Minister are well illustrated by the following excerpt from a letter to Viscount Willingdon, dated July 30, 1931: ". . . I want to say that my reason for depriving myself of the pleasure of accepting invitations from Rideau Hall during your term of office was that I would not associate myself publicly or privately with Mackenzie King . . . Just as Lloyd George has ruined the Liberal Party in England, by his treachery, so Mackenzie King has ruined the Liberal Party in Canada. Even as I write King is probably throwing his friends of yesterday to the wolves in the House of Commons. That, of course, will not surprise those of us who have known him for years and who have never trusted him." Murphy Papers, vol. 30, no. 12986. For such views, of course, there can be no room in the cabinet; they must be elevated into another place.

to the Senate have usually many years of faithful party service to their credit; as Table II indicates, nearly one-third of the total appointments made under five administrations during a period of thirty-seven years went to former back-benchers, 38 per cent of whom had been successful candidates of their parties in at least four general elections. This may be one of the reasons for the relatively high average age (60.8) of this group. The table also reveals that the principle of recognizing party service in the form of electoral victories is not the exclusive property of

TABLE II

Percentage of Back-Benchers Appointed to the Senate, 1925–63

Appointed by	Total appoint-ments	No. of back-benchers	Percentage	Re-elected four times or more: No.	Re-elected four times or more: %	Average age
King, '25–'30	35	11	34	5	49	61
Bennett, '30–'35	33	11	33	2	2	64
King, '35–'49	59	23	38	11	48	67
St. Laurent, '49–'57	55	19	35	8	42	62
Diefenbaker, '57–'63	37	4	11	1	25	50
Total	219	68	31.2	27	38.0	60.8

any one party, but it is liberally applied by both, practically to the same extent.[55] In addition to defeated candidates who were successful in the past, claims are also formulated by those members of this group who no longer feel able or willing to fight further elections. ". . . my health forbids me to enter into another fight and to undertake the duties of a new mandate," a Quebec member wrote to M. Dupré, representative of the province in the cabinet, in 1934. "I appeal, my minister, to your loyalty as leader and to your sentiment of justice. Give his reward to an old fighter who never spared you his support nor his efforts. . . . My humble contributions as well as the very heavy sacrifices I made for my party, my age and my health, are all reasons which incline me to believe that you will give me your heartful help."[56] Even more to the point was the following appeal made on behalf of a Conservative back-bencher from Ontario: "It is my firm conviction," ran the letter, "that Col. Robinson can not be re-elected in his riding. It is not because he is not

[55]The reason for the comparatively low percentage under the Conservative Government 1957–63 was that the party started, as it were, from new foundations and had not been able to develop adequate human resources for purposes of Senate membership out of its back-bench members.

[56]Meighen Papers, series 5, no. 224.

popular and well liked but because he is getting old and besides he has never been a strong member. He has gone through three campaigns and I believe has spent some 60 or 70,000 dollars of his money in these three campaigns. . . . He has in the past with the talents and finances at his disposal, done his very best for the Conservative Party. Now he is in more need of help than the Party. Don't you think it would be a fitting reward for one who has been so faithful and so generous to promote him to the Senate, and *thereby give him an income that will keep him to the end of his days*?"[57]

Claims like these cannot, of course, be easily ignored by a prime minister. They may only become endangered when they are overshadowed by more robust political considerations. Clearly, the urging of a sitting member that he "can be of far more service to the Party in British Columbia as a Senator than as a Private Member," and that "to appoint someone else in my stead would be fatal with my friends and party," would probably have been effective in ordinary circumstances. However, this was in 1920 when the need of cementing Liberal Unionist support for the Conservative party loomed larger than the need of recognizing the services of the already faithful. At first, a hesitant Prime Minister[58] attempted delay but the wire from the party organizer in the province decided the issue: "Strong organizations working in 3 Vancouver constituencies with generous Liberal support stop. Feeling however apparently developing that delay in making Senate appointment means shelving of Crowe [a Liberal-Unionist aspirant for a Senate seat] stop. If this feeling allowed develop further it means serious harm to our organization work here stop. Believe immediate appointment of Crowe would inspire enthusiasm and firmly and permanently establish confidence. . . ." That is how S. J. Crowe became a Senator.[59]

On occasion an MP may find himself prematurely elevated to the Senate as a result of what Sir Stephen King-Hall has called, in relation to the British practice, "the co-incidental operation of the honours list." If a prominent member of the Government party has been defeated at the polls or if the services of a person are badly needed in the cabinet, the prime minister may wish to find a seat in the House of Commons for him quickly. A convenient way of doing this is by conferring a senatorship upon a back-bencher who occupies a safe Government seat. As Peter Bromhead remarks, drawing on British precedents, the offer

[57]H. J. M. to Meighen, June 12, 1935. *Ibid.* Italics added.

[58]"I sincerely wish the present responsibility as to these Senate appointments was not mine." Meighen to H. S. C., Sept. 10, 1921. *Ibid.*, series 2, no. 193.

[59]M. S. to Meighen, Oct. 26, 1921. *Ibid.*

of a seat in the Upper Chamber can, as a rule, "be relied on to induce a suitable person to sacrifice his seat for the sake of the party's interests."[60] Thus, J. A. Macdonald (Nova Scotia) was appointed to the Senate in 1932 after he resigned his seat in the House of Commons to make way for the entry into the cabinet of the late E. N. Rhodes, the premier of Nova Scotia, whom R. B. Bennett had invited to join his government.[61] Similarly, when in 1942 Mackenzie King wished to fill the vacancies in the cabinet's representation from Quebec caused by Casgrain's appointment to the Bench, Cardin's resignation, and Senator Dandurand's death, he decided to appoint T. Vien to the Senate and run Major-General L. R. LaFlèche in his constituency—Outremont.[62] Sometimes, reward for resignation from a Commons seat comes somewhat belatedly. Although C. McDonald (British Columbia) resigned his seat in favour of Mackenzie King in 1925, he received his summons to the Senate only in 1935, ten years later. Indeed, the value of the Senate as an indirect way of enabling outsiders to enter the cabinet is so important that it actually overrides otherwise formidable claims. The appointment of P. L. Hatfield to the vacant Nova Scotia senatorship in 1926 is a case in point. The seat was promised in 1925 to George W. Kyte, the Chief Liberal Whip, both verbally and in writing by King, and the choice was a perfectly sound one in view of the fact that whips are usually promoted when the party is in office.[63] Indeed, he was brought from Nova Scotia to Ottawa upon the understanding that he was to receive an appointment immediately. "After hanging around Ottawa for about six weeks," Sen. Murphy recorded, "he became aware that promises made by the Prime Minister had little or no value . . . and he returned home a disgusted man. . . .[64] The sudden change in the Prime Minister's plans was, of course, caused by his decision to bring Colonel Ralston into the Government and in order to accomplish it he traded Hatfield's seat of Yarmouth-Shelburne in the Commons for the vacant Nova Scotia senatorship![65]

If, in recognizing partisan claims based upon past or future services, the Senate's chief value seems to be in the pecuniary compensation

[60]Bromhead, *The House of Lords*, p. 24.

[61]*SD, 1945*, p. 7.

[62]J. W. Pickersgill, *The Mackenzie King Record* (Toronto, 1960), vol. I, p. 442.

[63]For instance, on the Liberal side Sutherland and Robb were appointed to the cabinet, Calvert to the Railway Commission, and Gibson, Pardee, Taylor, Tremblay, Boucher and Fraser to the Senate.

[64]Murphy to D. A. McIntyre, Oct. 9, 1926. Murphy Papers, vol. 19, no. 8009–10.

[65]G. W. K. to Murphy, Sept. 28, 1926. *Ibid.*, vol. 15, no. 6128. (The real reason for the wrath of Murphy, a devout Catholic, was that Hatfield was a Methodist, while Kyte was a Catholic!)

afforded by the office, in granting senatorships to various minorities it is rather the social symbol aspect of the appointments that receives emphasis. The written part of the constitution contains no provision, apart from those regulating representation in the Senate of the four basic sections of the country as well as the twenty-four electoral divisions in the Province of Quebec,[66] as to how vacancies in the Senate should be filled. But it has been a conventional practice of prime ministers to go beyond these fundamental aspects of senatorial representation and satisfy certain minority group claims, whether on territorial, religious, racial/ethnic, linguistic, or any other grounds, by appointing some of their members to the Senate. Before going any further, two factors should be emphasized regarding these appointments. First, the apparently non-partisan character of the claims does not necessarily imply that appointments made on such basis are altogether free from political considerations. Apart from their general political purpose, viz., to please and cajole, they are usually given to those members of the group who are acknowledged supporters of the party that makes the appointments. Having said this, however, it should be admitted that the purely partisan character of senatorial appointments is considerably less marked in this second category of claims than in the case of those motivated by sheer patronage. Second, as Mr. Zaplitny (CCF, Dauphin) very aptly remarked —forgetting for the moment the official stand of his party on the Senate—the right objective of these appointments "is not so much a matter of protecting minority rights as it is a matter of doing the democratic thing, and that is to see that all so-called minorities are represented to the greatest extent possible in the Senate Chamber."[67] Even the minorities themselves do not look upon Senate seats as a truly effective guarantee of safeguarding their interests; they regard a senatorship as a token of recognition of their relative importance in the social and political system of the country.

Special territorial units may formulate claims within the general quota allotted to that larger area of which they are parts. It has become a practice, for instance, to have one Senator from Vancouver Island out of the six from the province of British Columbia. When the vacancy created by the death of the incumbent member was not filled for a few years, complaints were made during the Throne Speech debate in the House of Commons in 1951 to the effect that "the fact that Vancouver Island, with its importance industrially, is not represented in the Senate, is one of those situations which should be corrected as soon as pos-

[66]Sec. 22 of the BNA Act.
[67]*HD, 1955*, p. 5352.

sible."[68] For similar reasons, a private member's bill was introduced by Mr. Nielsen (PC, Yukon) in the House of Commons in 1959 to amend the British North America Act to provide for representation in the Senate by one representative for Yukon and one for the Northwest Territories. Although the bill died on the order paper in 1959 and did not get beyond first reading in 1960 and 1962, the attempt well illustrated the type of considerations that are associated with the conferment of senatorships.

The main groups, however, whose traditional claims to senatorial representation form part of the principles governing appointments are the Acadians in the Maritime provinces, the French in the West and in Ontario, English-speaking Catholics in the English-speaking provinces, and English-speaking Protestants in the Province of Quebec. As Table III indicates, each of the groups continued to receive basically the same degree of attention from five different administrations. Where the percentage drops below the average (as in some of the appointments under the King Government, 1925–30, and the Diefenbaker Administration, 1957–63) it is simply because representatives of the minorities appointed under previous administrations are still active members of the Senate at the end of the period.

Perhaps the oldest claim to senatorial representation amongst the various groups is that of the Acadians in New Brunswick and Nova Scotia.[69] The appointment of the first Acadian to the Senate in 1881 was regarded as a highly considerate act both politically and socially on the part of Sir John A. Macdonald, who probably recognized, with John Costigan, Sir Leonard Tilley, Sir Charles Tupper, Sir Hector Langevin, and others, that it was desirable, even necessary, to give representation in the Upper Chamber to the people who first implanted European civilization in Canada, Port Royal having been founded two years before Quebec. The choice, as is known, fell upon Pascal Poirier, who had already acquired, by the age of thirty-three, an enviable

[68]Mr. Gibson (Ind., Comox Alberni). *HD, 1951* (2nd session), p. 367.

[69]Similar claims of the French element in Prince Edward Island have not been so effective. When the Hon. Joseph Octave Arsenault, who was appointed by Sir J. A. Macdonald in 1893, died in 1898, the Liberal party appointed the Hon. John Yeo to his place. "From that date," Mr. Doucet said during the Budget Debate in 1925, "the French-Acadians of P.E.I. . . . have no representative in the Senate," and he urged the Government "to do honour to the French-Acadians by appointing one of our race to represent in the Senate the French-Acadian people of P.E.I." *HD, 1925*, p. 1830.

TABLE III

Minorities in Senate Appointments, 1925–63

	Appointments in N.B. and N.S.			Appointments in the West			Appointments in Ontario			Appointments in Eng.-sp. provinces			Appointments in Quebec		
		Acadians			French			French			Eng.-sp. Catholics			Eng.-sp. Protestants	
Appointed by	Total	No.	%	Total	No.	%	Total	No.	%	Total	No.	%	Total	No.	%
King, '25–'30	4	0	0	5	1	20	13	2	15	25	4	14	10	0*	0
Bennett, '30–'35	9	2	20	6	1	17	8	1	13	25	4	14	8	1	13
King, '35–'49	9	1	11	7	2	30	16	1	6	40	6	13	19	3	16
St. Laurent, '49–'57	12	3	25	8	1	13	10	2	20	45	8	18	10	1†	10
Diefenbaker, '57–'63	7	1	14	6	0	0	11	2	17	30	4	13	7	0	0

*Senators McDougald and L. A. Wilson were English-speaking but both were Catholics.
†The same was true of Senators Hackett and Power.

reputation when as a young official of the House of Commons he was picked by Sir John to be the first, and for many years the sole, representative of Acadians in the Senate. He represented his group in that Chamber for forty-eight years and in his book, *La Langue acadienne*, he composed what was later to become the national anthem of the Acadians and for which he was recognized by the French Academy. He was subsequently joined by others, with the result that Acadians in modern times have had, in all, eleven representatives in the persons of Senators Girroir (1912–32), Bourque (1917–52), O. Turgeon (1923–44), A. J. Léger (1935–50), Robicheau (1935–48), Veniot (1945–), Comeau (1948–), A. D. Léger (1953–62), Savoie (1955–), and Fournier (1962–). However, despite the decline of English-speaking Protestant dominance and a marked improvement in Catholic and French-speaking representation,[70] Acadians are, generally speaking, dissatisfied with the number of seats they are allotted in the Senate. "If the total population of the province be now estimated at 375,000 . . ." an indignant Acadian wrote to A. Meighen in 1921, "the Acadians would be entitled to three of the ten Senators appointed for that province. . . . We have no representation whatever on either the county court or the Superior Court bench—a situation for which there is no justification whatever."[71] Similar complaints are numerous.[72] Knowing the weak points of all party leaders, Acadians often resort to virtually blackmailing prime ministers into embarking upon a more generous policy of senatorial appointments for their groups. "There is . . .," a party organizer from New Brunswick reminded the Prime Minister, "a very active demand presently that the Northern part of New Brunswick be given representation in the Senate . . . but to appoint an English senator in any of the counties . . . would not be giving proper representation to the people forming the population of these counties which are three-fourths French . . . we don't want an English-speaking senator appointed from any of these French counties as," the whip cracks, "it would hurt

[70]See Hugh G. Thorburn, *Politics in New Brunswick* (Toronto, 1961), pp. 166 ff.

[71]F. J. Robidoux to Meighen, Aug. 22, 1921. Meighen Papers, series 2, no. 194.

[72]H. G. Thorburn quotes the following editorial of *L'Evangéline*, Dec. 10, 1953: "S'il veut réellement faire tout en son pouvoir pour raffermir le prestige du sénat, il est évident que le premier ministre devra donner au sénat son caractère représentatif. Il fut un temps où deux sénateurs, trois sénateurs, représentaient adéquatement la population française du Nouveau-Brunswick à la Chambre haute. Ce temps-là est révolu. La population française forme 40 pour-cent de la population et–le calcul est facile—cela nous donne droit à quatre sénateurs sur 10." *Politics in New Brunswick*, p. 166.

us politically in an election."[73] The same technique of persuasion was used in the following letter of the proprietor of the *Tribune*: "There is not the slightest doubt in my mind," he wrote to the Prime Minister, "that the ignoring of this section of the Province . . . will be keenly resented and this feeling will have a very marked effect upon the coming elections . . . there is a good prospect of carrying N– [county] for the Government, but if the North Shore is ignored in connection with this appointment . . . the fight there might as well be abandoned."[74] It follows from the psychosis of being a minority that Acadians attach so much importance to proper representation in the Senate. Similarly to other minorities they like to believe that the number of seats they hold in the Senate is a true reflection of their significance. They appreciate every little gesture in this connection and wise prime ministers can make good use of this attitude. It was noted, for example, how much Acadians were impressed by the fact that one of their members was summoned to the Senate on the occasion of the solemn festivities which marked the second centenary of the deportation of Acadians.[75]

Another group that has a well-articulated claim to representation in the Senate on the ground of their distinct identity is the English-speaking Catholics in the English-speaking provinces, particularly in Ontario. They try to secure a balance in Senate membership between English and French, Protestant and Catholic. The difficulty of course is that Protestants look upon a French-Canadian appointee as a Catholic appointment, whilst French Canadians look upon the appointment of an English-speaking Catholic as an English appointment. So between the French-Canadian Catholics on the one hand and the Protestants on the other, English-speaking Catholics are ground between the upper and nether mill-stones. No cyclical regularity can be established in alternating Senate seats between English-speaking and French-speaking appointments, although on occasion when a Frenchman held a seat that, prior to his appointment, was occupied by an Englishman, the seat was returned to an English-speaking person in case of a new vacancy, so as to restore the balance which was disturbed by the appointment of the Frenchman in the first place.[76] Some have gone farther than simply

[73]J. B. H. to Meighen, Aug. 16, 1921. Meighen Papers, series 2, no. 194.

[74]O. S. Crocket to Meighen, Sept. 17, 1921. *Ibid.*

[75]*SD, 1956*, p. 181.

[76]Thus, when Sen. McDougald, a Catholic, who was appointed to the seat formerly held by Sen. Mitchell, was forced out and the seat again became vacant, it was given to another English-speaking Protestant, thus again restoring the balance that was disturbed by McDougald's appointment.

demanding representation for English-speaking Catholics. Sen. Murphy, for example, an ardent advocate of the cause of the English-speaking Catholics, demanded that the English Catholic press as such should be given representation in the Senate from a nation-wide constituency.[77] Others tried to impress Prime Minister Bennett that since there already was a Protestant woman Senator (Sen. C. R. Wilson, appointed in 1930), there should also be a Catholic woman in the Senate. This put the Premier on his mettle and turning his attention to the question of representation in the Senate he discovered that, according to the quota which allots one-quarter of the Senators in Ontario to Catholics, they already had one more than they were entitled to and on that ground he declined to make the requested appointment.[78] This raises, of course, the question as to how, when, and by whom this Catholic quota from Ontario was fixed. The Fathers of Confederation knew nothing about it. As late as the year 1906 Sir Richard Cartwright raised the problem in a famous speech in the Senate,[79] wherein he pointed out that, to overcome the inadequate representation of Catholics from Ontario in the House of Commons, both parties had tried to compensate them by giving Catholics a number of seats in the Senate. However, he did not pretend that the number of Ontario Catholics in the Senate was limited to six. ". . . I never heard of any arguments of that kind," Sen. Murphy wrote in 1935, "until recent years, when, just because there happened to be only six Catholics in the Senate, wise-acres . . . began to talk as if the number six were as fixed as the Laws of the Medes and Persians."[80]

The French Canadians of Ontario and Western Canada seem to attach the same kind of political-social-psychological significance to representation in the Senate. When J. H. G. Lacasse from Ontario was summoned to the Upper House in 1928, Casgrain made a special point during the Address debate in the House of Commons: "I am pleased to observe," he said, "that the Government has fulfilled a duty: they have acknowledged the rights of the French Canadian minority in Ontario, by calling to the Upper House one of its distinguished citizens . . . and I think all the French Canadian people of the Province of Quebec, as well as those of other parts of Canada, will give credit to the Government . . . for such a fair and just act."[81] The corresponding worries and aspirations

[77]Murphy to R. M. Burns, Feb. 28, 1932. Murphy Papers, vol. 4, no. 1549.

[78]*Ibid.*, nos. 1550–52. Actually, the only woman he appointed to the Senate, Mrs. I. C. Fallis, belonged to the United Church of Canada.

[79]*SD, 1906*, p. 467.

[80]Murphy Papers, vol. 4, nos. 1550–52.

[81]*HD, 1928*, p. 136.

of the French Canadians in the Western provinces are well expressed in the following letter written by Sen. Blondin, Postmaster General, to Prime Minister Meighen in 1921.

> The appointment of a Senator in Saskatchewan to succeed the late Sen. Prince is a matter of great concern to the public of the Province of Quebec. Fear is expressed . . . that an English Protestant may have the position and, what should still be worse, that an Irish Catholic should be appointed. . . . Honourable Mr. Calder, I suppose, has given you full information regarding that appointment, and from all I hear, the man recommended by his Grace Archbishop Mathieu is the best candidate. His name and address are as follows: Mr. Arthur Marcotte, Barrister, Ponteix, Sask.
>
> If this appointment could be made with the least possible delay, . . . it would most favourably impress public opinion, both in Quebec and amongst the French Canadian population of the other provinces. . . .[82]

Claims of this nature are of course not restricted to the major minority groups. Indeed, there are nearly as many claims to representation in the Senate as there are minorities of whatever complexion. Thus, for example, the Hebrew Conservative Political Association, Montreal, said in its resolution, June 28, 1926, that, "Whereas from a National and Political point of view the time has arrived when it would be highly desirable that the Conservative Party should give due prominence and recognition to a Member of the Jewish race by an appointment to the Senate of Canada . . . be it resolved that we . . . hereby unanimously recommend the appointment of Isaac Lande to the Senate of Canada."[83] Again, when Mr. J. Hnatyshyn was summoned to the Senate in 1959, the Saskatoon *Star Phoenix* commented: "The appointment of Mr. John Hnatyshyn, Q.C., as a Senator of Canada is a meritorious one and is so acclaimed in Saskatoon and beyond, and regardless of party affiliations and party considerations . . . the underlying importance of this appointment to the Red Chamber is in the fact that Mr. Hnatyshyn is a native of the Ukraine, and his choice . . . as the first of his race in Saskatchewan to go to the Senate is a recognition of the great role Canadian Ukrainians have played, and are continuing to play in this growing country."[84] If it was felt that a group of relative newcomers should be distinctly recognized by giving them representation in the Senate, the same consideration could be applied with added force to the people who first populated the territory of the country. Indeed, as far back as 1955, Mr.

[82]*Meighen Papers*, series 2, no. 15. The advice was taken—but only ten years later, when in 1931 Marcotte was summoned to the Senate.

[83]*Ibid.*, series 4, no. 154. The first, and so far only, Jewish Senator, Sen. D. A. Croll, was appointed in 1955.

[84]Quoted in *SD*, *1959*, p. 39. The first member of Ukrainian descent, Sen. Wall of Manitoba, was appointed in 1955.

Diefenbaker urged that "there are 160,000 of these first citizens of Canada, and . . . one of the finest gestures this Government could make would be to appoint a full-blooded Indian to the Senate of Canada in order that the views of the Indians might be expressed and Indians in general would have an opportunity of having a spokesman in the parliament of this country."[85] In accordance with this statement, which he repeated in the following session of Parliament,[86] he promised during the 1957 election campaign[87] that if he was elected as head of the Government he would immediately name an Indian to the Senate. This pledge was subsequently implemented by the appointment in 1958 of James Gladstone, a Treaty Indian, to the Senate.[88]

With the ominous spread of the notion that women should have equal political rights with men, the days of the Senate as an exclusively male institution were numbered. The movement for having women in the Senate was given an impetus by Miss Agnes Macphail's election to the House of Commons as the first woman MP in Canadian history. In addition, although always in a majority, women professed to be just one of the many minorities of the country seeking representation in the Senate.[89] The only legal barrier appeared to lie in the ambiguous wording of the constitution. In section 21 of the BNA act, which provides that the Senate shall consist of seventy-two members, there is nothing to indicate that females might not be members of the Senate; in section 23 of the Act, however, which provides for the qualifications of a Senator, the masculine pronoun is used with the possible interpretation that men were only to be qualified. On the other hand, in Chapter I of the Revised Statutes of Canada, the Interpretation Act, by section 21, subsection (1), states "that in every Act of the Parliament of Canada, unless a contrary intention appears, words importing masculine shall include females." Both the National Council of Women and many women's clubs and societies strenuously campaigned for the candidature of Judge Emily Murphy of Edmonton. "If the matter were questionable on the ground

[85] *HD, 1955*, p. 2393.

[86] *Ibid., 1956*, p. 5567.

[87] Cf. speeches made in Prince Albert and Calgary.

[88] It should be mentioned, however, that the Prime Minister evaded answering a suggestion of Mr. Howard (CCF, Skeena), on Oct. 29, 1957, that the BNA Act should be amended to remove some of the real-estate qualifications for membership in the Senate, "inasmuch as many native Indians will not be able to qualify." *Ibid., 1957–58*, pp. 506–7.

[89] Indeed, in 1955 Mr. Dinsdale (PC, Brandon-Souris) made a strong plea on behalf of women as one of those minority groups the protection of which is the *raison d'être* of the Senate and he supported the idea, propagated by various women's organizations, that there should be at least one woman representative from every province in the Senate. *Ibid., 1955*, p. 5925.

that the Act was ambiguous, and the Government wished to surmount such a difficulty," Judge Murphy's brother, Judge Ferguson of Toronto, wrote to her, "it seems to me that the practical politics would be to appoint you and allow either the Senate to question your right to sit by reference to the Privileges Committee, or you to determine your right, and if they refuse to admit you to leave you to resort to the Courts."[90] However, after considering Judge Ferguson's opinion, the Justice Department concluded that there was nothing in it which would lead the Department to vary its conclusion that "in the absence of any precise authority to the contrary, women are not qualified."[91] The issue was not dropped, however, and on the occasion of Mackenzie King's visit to Calgary in 1924, the Women's Canadian Club was assured that "this was a matter which the Liberal Government would take up at once, and see a change."[92] Indeed, four years later, after the settlement of more acute constitutional crises, the Government of the day submitted to the Supreme Court of Canada the question whether under section 24 of the BNA Act women were qualified persons for admission to the Senate. The Court's decision was 4 to 1 in the negative, only Justice (later Chief Justice) Duff dissenting. In a powerful judgment Chief Justice Anglin said that by no conceivable stretch of the imagination could the Fathers of Confederation have been supposed to include women in the category of qualified persons in section 24 of the BNA Act, since in 1867 women were debarred by the Common Law of England from holding any public office, even down to that of Church warden. The judgment apparently left the Government dissatisfied.[93] Yet, it was primarily due to the persistence of a group of five women[94] that the question was finally referred by the Government to His Majesty's Privy Council. The appeal to London took place with the full support of Lapointe who seemed to have a high regard for women's capabilities.[95] Both the Attorney General of Canada and the Canadian women were represented before the Judicial Committee, which, reversing the judgment of the Supreme Court of

[90]Quoted in Meighen Papers, series 2, no. 192.

[91]Justice Department Memorandum, June 6, 1921. *Ibid.*

[92]Quoted in *ibid.*, series 4, no. 175.

[93]See Lapointe's remarks, *HD, 1928*, p. 2311.

[94]Judge Emily Murphy; the Hon. Irene Parlby, cabinet minister in the Alberta legislature; Mrs. Nellie McClung; Mrs. Louise McKinney, a national president of the WCTU; Mrs. Henrietta Muir Edwards, who, as convener of laws in the National Council of Women, became thoroughly versed in the legal position of women. See *SD, 1954*.

[95]He pledged in 1929 that "if the judgement of the Court is antagonistic to those views that is, those of the women I am willing to do my part to change the Constitution." *HD, 1929*, p. 3411.

Canada, ruled that "persons" in section 24 of the BNA Act included members of either sex.[96] Although as a matter of law, and considered solely as a matter of strict interpretation of the BNA Act, the Supreme Court decision was probably right, the decision of the Privy Council was essentially a political decision based on the belief—correctly as it turned out—that public opinion in Canada would welcome the admission of women to the Senate. As a result, Mrs. Cairine Mackay Wilson, daughter of the late Sen. Mackay from Ontario, was summoned to the Upper Chamber on Valentine's Day, 1930. Her reception in Parliament was a mixed one. In the Speech from the Throne the Government took pride to announce that "the eligibility of women for appointment to the Senate of Canada has been declared by the Judicial Committee of the Privy Council. . . . For the first time in Canadian history, women have been accorded an equal right with men to representation in both houses of parliament."[97] However, Bennett questioned the right of the Government to claim any part in the matter and when the Prime Minister suggested that Mrs. Wilson's appointment "is a very considerable measure of Senate reform,"[98] he was advised by Manion that "the next time he goes to the country he go on sex reform, not Senate reform."[99] In the Senate, if the question did not stir as much controversy as did the same event in the House of Lords twenty-eight years later,[100] there was no particularly jubilant spirit discernible on the historic occasion of Mrs. Wilson's introduction. Indeed, Sen. Willoughby, Leader of the Opposition, frankly told the House that although the judges of the Supreme Court failed to convince the Privy Council, they did convince him.[101] And Sen. Laird hastened to awaken his lady colleague from the pleasant dream that she represented Canadian womanhood in the Upper Chamber. Rather, he said, "she is a Senator from the Province of Ontario, and is one of the representatives in this Chamber of all the people of Ontario, men, women and children. She stands in a position no different from that of any other member of this House: no one of us represents any particular class, creed, or sex, but each member is here to speak for all the people."[102] Perhaps because of this welcome, Sen. Wilson did not utter

[96]Lord Sankey in Persons Case: *Edwards* v. *Att. Gen. of Canada* (1930) AC 124.

[97]*HD, 1930*, p. 3.

[98]*Ibid.*, p. 47.

[99]*Ibid.*, p. 880.

[100]Perhaps because the Senate did not suffer from the same shortage as the Lords, where Lord Redesdale warned how inconvenient females could be in a House with only one washroom.

[101]*SD, 1930*, p. 12.

[102]*Ibid.*, p. 47.

a single word during the whole session. It is a curious fact that having recommended one woman for appointment to the Senate, King never again recommended another. It is doubtful whether this was because of any failing on the part of Mrs. Wilson or whether, as he said, it was his first and only experience of proposing and he did not wish to repeat it.[103]

As could have been expected, Canadian women were not satisfied with having only one representative in the Senate. Upon the agitation of the Women's Conservative Association, Prime Minister Bennett appointed Mrs. I. C. Fallis from Ontario in 1935. Further additions were made by the appointment in 1954 of M. Beauchamp Jodoin (Quebec), M. McQueen Fergusson and Nancy Hodges (BC),[104] who were joined in 1956 by Mrs. F. E. Inman (PEI), the sixth woman appointee. In 1960 the seventh and eighth women entered the Senate with the appointment of Mrs. O. L. Irvine from Manitoba and Mrs. J. D. Quart from Quebec. By that time women could point out that they were more favourably represented in the Senate than in the House of Commons (where at the dissolution of Parliament in 1962 there were only five women MP's).

Is it any wonder that, surrounded by such a multitude of claims from an almost numberless variety of minority groups and loyal party men, prime ministers will often decide to defer decisions on appointments to the Senate? The result is an accumulation of vacancies over a certain period of time. It has been customary to describe this phenomenon purely in terms of party tactics—as a disciplinary device employed by an astute Prime Minister, "to keep his supporters eager, active, and toiling unceasingly for the party until the election is near at hand, and then, having wrung them dry, to reward the most faithful by translation to a higher and more restful sphere of usefulness."[105] What this interpretation ignores is the fact that it is usually the prime minister, rather than his supporters, who gets wrung dry by an unceasing flow of claims upon a limited number of seats. And although it is true that the bulk of appointments under each administration weighs heavily towards the closing months before dissolution of Parliament and a general election, the same evidence, I submit, could equally well support the argument that the accumulation of vacancies in the Senate reflects hesitancy as much as it reflects shrewdness on the part of a prime minister. This was

[103]*Ibid., 1955*, pp. 254–6.

[104]As ex-Speaker of the British Columbia Legislature in 1949, she was the first woman Speaker in the Commonwealth.

[105]R. M. Dawson, *The Government of Canada*, 4th ed. (Toronto, 1963), p. 309. Also see Mr. Green's remarks, *HD, 1955*, pp. 5340–1.

particularly the case during the second half of the St. Laurent Administration, when the Prime Minister was faced with the disturbing phenomenon of a growing political disequilibrium in the Senate's membership.

The maintenance, to be sure, of the specified number of members in the Senate was very carefully provided for by the wording of two sections of the BNA Act. In addition to section 24, which provides for the appointment of Senators, section 32 says: "When a vacancy happens in the Senate, by resignation, death, or otherwise, the Governor General shall by summons to a fit and qualified person fill the vacancy." The reason that the Senate does not have a provision similar to the one in force in the House of Commons regarding a time limit within which vacancies must be filled is that the constitution itself is so clear and plain upon that subject. It distinctly says that appointments shall (not "may") be made when vacancies occur. This certainly does not mean the moment they occur because that would be impracticable. The principle in interpreting directives of this kind is that action must be taken within a reasonable time.[106]

However, this rule seems to have had no effect upon the actions of Prime Ministers. Prior to the election of 1930 all the Senate vacancies were filled. In the eighteenth Parliament, 1930–35, under the Bennett Administration, there was an accumulation of nineteen vacancies in the Senate. They were filled before the general election. In the next Parliament, under the King Government, there was an accumulation of fourteen vacancies. Again, all but one—that one in Quebec—were filled before the general election of 1940. The Parliament of 1940–45 saw the accumulation of eighteen vacancies. All but one, in Nova Scotia, were filled before the election in that year. All these vacancies occurred under the King Administration, except the one in Nova Scotia. In the next Parliament of 1945–49, there was an accumulation of eleven vacancies. Only three were filled before the election and eight remained unfilled. By 1953 the number of vacancies increased to twenty-three, approaching one-quarter of the normal membership of the Senate; ten were filled before the election of 1953 and thirteen were left vacant. In 1955 the number of vacancies reached twenty-one with the gloomy prospect of climbing higher towards the end of that Parliament. They applied to all of Canada, with the exception of British Columbia and Saskatchewan; there were one in Alberta, two in Manitoba, three in Ontario, four in New Brunswick, three in Nova Scotia, one in Prince Edward Island,

[106]See Mr. MacLean's (PC, Queens) argument. *Ibid.*, p. 5482.

and one in Newfoundland. One of them existed for less than a year, while six for a year, five for two years, three for four years, five for five years, and one was in its seventh year.

The number of vacancies in 1955, with no immediate sign of relief, was so alarming that it was declared "contrary to the public interest and a challenge to the usefulness of the Senate, threatening the integrity of this Branch of Parliament."[107] To remedy the situation Sen. Euler introduced a private member's bill on May 11 to amend section 32 of the BNA Act by making it mandatory—upon the pattern of the House of Commons Act of 1919—to fill every vacancy within a period of six months from the date on which it occurred. Although from a strictly legal point of view[108] his measure would have had little, if any, effect at all, what the bill might have achieved was the moral effect of crystallizing something which was already in the Act, by defining the words "a reasonable time" within which Senate vacancies were to be filled as being a period not exceeding six months. However, in spite of the support it received from a number of influential members of the Senate, the bill was finally negatived on second reading by a vote of 37 to 12, mainly on the ground that its passage by the Senate might have proved embarrassing for the Government.[109]

The cause of so many vacancies under the Liberal Administration of 1949–57, and of the underlying vacillation of the Prime Minister to fill them, was the fact that by 1955, when there were twenty unfilled seats in the Senate, seven Conservatives faced seventy-five Liberals. The disproportion between the two groups grew steadily worse after 1949, with the Prime Minister facing the dilemma of how to fill the increasing number of vacancies without either violating the established precedents or further aggravating the state of disequilibrium. At the root of the dilemma lay the character of the Prime Minister; Mr. St. Laurent was a man of justice and of common sense enough to see the inherent unfairness of the continuation of the practice of appointments; but he was a politician enough not to be able to break with it. Unable to cut the Gordian knot, he, therefore, decided not to act. Nevertheless, under the pressure of continuing criticism he finally made up his mind and at the end of 1955 appointed eleven new Senators, including a Conservative and a few Independents.[110] However, the number of vacancies was still considerable. On April 11, 1957, Mr. Diefenbaker inquired whether it

[107]*SD, 1955*, p. 447.

[108]See P. B. Maxwell, *On the Interpretation of Statutes* (8th ed., London, 1937), pp. 189–90, 326–27, etc.

[109]*SD, 1955*, p. 540.

[110]See below, chap. 3.

was "the intention of the Prime Minister . . . to make any appointments to the Senate before the election writs are issued or after the writs are issued but before election day." Mr. St. Laurent told the House that since the writs were to be issued the following day there was no question of summoning anyone before that time. "As to whether or not there will be appointments made between the issue of the writs and the date of election," he said, "I would not like to make any commitment one way or the other." It "will depend upon whether I should find it in the public interest that I should take the responsibility . . . of recommending the appointments. . . ."[111] This was the last recorded statement of Mr. St. Laurent with regard to filling the fourteen vacancies which existed in 1957 and which were inherited by the appreciative Conservative Government that took office the same year.

[111] *HD, 1957*, p. 3402.

THE COMPOSITION OF THE SENATE 2

IN A FEDERAL COUNTRY of parallel and overlapping diversities the problem of finding universally accepted national personages is always more difficult than in a unitary state with a high level of homogeneity. Thus, the Senate will ill compare to a House of Lords, which, as a result of the operation of the Life Peerages Act, now includes amongst its members more and more of the most eminent representatives of the various walks of life in that land. But "how many men and women are nationally known" in Canada?—Sen. Davies posed the question in 1957. "The names of cabinet-ministers and a few other prominent men and women are known through the press, because their names are constantly in the newspapers, but few are personally known across Canada." In these circumstances it seemed of little consequence to him whether Senate appointees are known all across the country; what is important is that they should be known and respected in their own senatorial districts.[1]

Perhaps politics is the only field which transcends the effect of localism, and the Senate has, indeed, invariably included amongst its members some of the most shining political names of the era. In the more distant past the Senate had amongst its members such men as Sir Alexander Campbell, Fergusson Blair, Joseph Cauchon, P. J. Chauveau, George Brown, Sir C. B. de Boucherville, Louis Rodrigue Masson, Sir Alexandre Lacoste, Sir John Abbott, Sir George Drummond, Sir Mackenzie Bowell, Sir Auguste Réal Angers, Sir William Hingston, Sir Oliver Mowat, Sir Richard Cartwright, Sir George Ross, and others. During the period under study the Senate was enriched by the presence of such men as Sir Allen Aylesworth, Charles Ballantyne, J. A. Calder, Raoul Dan-

[1]*SD, 1957*, pp. 66–8.

durand, W. Euler, Sir George Foster, J. Haig, J. A. Godbout, Sir A. E. Kemp, Sir J. A. Lougheed, Ian Mackenzie, J. A. MacKinnon, Charles Murphy, Arthur Meighen, E. N. Rhodes—to mention only a few who have died. Some of them attained fame beyond the boundaries of Canada. Mention has already been made of Sen. Poirier, who was recognized by the Académie Française for his literary work. Sen. Aylesworth was knighted for his services in representing Canada and Britain, as agent, before the Hague Tribunal in the Fisheries Arbitration in 1910, following his participation in the Commission for settlement of the Alaska Boundary in 1903, when he refused, with Sir Louis Jetté, to sign the Boundary Award. His famous contemporary, Sir George Foster, who as a scholar and orator occupied a unique position in the parliamentary annals of Canada, greatly enhanced Canada's prestige throughout the world by the reputation he made at the meetings of the League of Nations in 1920, 1926, and 1929.[2] Of course, Dandurand himself represented Canada on several occasions before the League of Nations, was even chosen president of the Assembly and, as his diary testifies, established close personal relations with the leading statesmen of the day.[3] Functioning in a somewhat similar capacity, Sen. C. P. Beaubien was for many years chairman of the Canadian group of the Inter-Parliamentary Union; he represented Canada at Geneva in 1919, at Vienna in 1922, at Washington in 1925, at Paris in 1927, and at Berlin in 1928. In 1921 the Canadian government selected him to negotiate a reciprocal trade agreement with France, and he succeeded in bringing this very difficult undertaking to fruition. He was also entrusted with special missions to France in 1919, 1920, and 1922. He was also delegate to the League of Nations in 1931.[4]

These few examples, of course, symbolize the exception rather than the rule. But the presence of people of renown, even if their number is small, is an important factor not only in enhancing the status of the House vis-à-vis the outside world, but also in stimulating activity within the Senate itself.

1. *Membership Analysis*

From 1925 to the end of the 1962–63 session of Parliament, there were a total of 308 members of the Senate. Of these, 89 were sitting in the

[2]*Ibid., 1932*, p. 45.

[3]His memoirs are among the closed manuscripts in the Public Archives at Ottawa. I was granted special permission to read them by M. de Gaspé Beaubien.

[4]*SD, 1949*, p. 9

Senate at the beginning of 1925 as the appointees of previous regimes, while 219 received their summonses under five administrations[5] between 1925 and 1963, in the following ratio: 35 were appointed under the King Government, 1925–30; 33 under the Bennett Administration, 1930–35; 59, under the King Administration, 1936–1949; 55, under the St. Laurent Administration, 1949–57; and 37 under the Diefenbaker Administration, from 1957 to February 1963. What follows below is a five-fold classification of membership both from the total (308) and against a comparative background of five administrations.

LEGISLATIVE EXPERIENCE

Since the Senate is a parliamentary institution, whose main field of activity is in law-making, the most important question respecting its composition is the amount of legislative experience its members possess at the time of their appointment. As Table IV indicates, only 31 per cent

TABLE IV

Legislative Experience of Total Membership

Experience		No. out of total of 308	Percentage
House of Commons		137	45
Provincial legislatures		53	17.2
House of Commons *and* provincial legislatures		23	7.5
Ex-dominion minister	1 portfolio	41 < 20	13.3 < 6.5
	more than 1 portfolio	21	6.8
Ex-provincial minister		33	10.7
House of Commons Speaker		5	1.6
House of Commons Deputy Speaker		7	2.3
Whip		7	2.3
Provincial speaker		9	3
Local Government	Mayor	38	12.3
	Alderman	14	4.5
No experience except provincial legislature		33	10.8
No experience except local government		8	2.6
Other experience		2	0.4
No experience at all		94	31

of the total membership of the Senate (308) during the last thirty-seven years lacked legislative experience at the time of their appointment, while two-thirds had some kind of experience in their previous career. Significantly, nearly half (45 per cent) went through the apprenticeship of the House of Commons, and as the following brief statistics shows (Table V) nearly 40 per cent of those were re-elected to the Commons at least four times, while 12 per cent of them bore away the palm in

[5]No appointment was made by Meighen in 1926.

more than five federal elections. This last figure shows an interesting correlation with the percentage of former dominion ministers in the Senate (13.3 per cent), who in turn can be divided into those who had

TABLE V
Terms of Service in the House of Commons

Those with House of Commons experience (137) elected: (percentages)					
Once	Twice	Three times	Four times	Five times	More
31	24	29	27	9	17
22.6	17.5	21.2	19.8	6.6	12.4
			38%		

only had one portfolio (6 per cent) and into a somewhat larger class of those who had more (7 per cent). Apart from those who had no experience whatever, the proportion of those whose legislative experience was limited to the provincial sphere (11 per cent), to the field of municipal government (2.6 per cent), or to other public offices (0.64 per cent) has been, indeed, insignificant. However, when such experience is added to that gained in the House of Commons, the legislative competence and political horizon of the person widens considerably. The same holds true of such offices as dominion and provincial Speakers or Whips.

The next table (Table VI) is a comparative analysis of the pattern of legislative experience as presented in the original membership in 1925 and the subsequent appointments of five administrations. The most interesting phenomenon, no doubt, is the downward trend which has been manifest in the last two administrations with respect to the general level of legislative experience before entrance into the Senate. While the fluctuation in the relevant percentage figures of the pre-1925 appointments and those under the administrations of King and Bennett (75, 71, 79, and 75 per cent) was insignificant and the proportion of those who possessed some experience before appointment stood high, under Mr. St. Laurent this percentage fell to 61 per cent, only further to be brought down to an all-time low (46 per cent) during the years 1957–63. The effect of this trend has been most marked, of course, upon the relative proportion of persons graduating from the House of Commons. It was an impressive 43 per cent (pre-1925), 59 per cent (King), 59 per cent (Bennett), 47 per cent (King) up to 1949; then it dropped to 40 per cent (St. Laurent) from which it further fell to 22

TABLE VI

Comparative Analysis of Legislative Experience, 1925–63

	Pre-1925		King		Bennett		King		St. Laurent		Diefenbaker	
Total:	89		35		33		59		55		37	
Experience	No.	%	No.	%	No.	%	No.	%	No.	%	No.	%
House of Commons	39	43	21	59	9	59	28	47	22	40	8	22
Provincial Legislature	15	17	7	20	8	24	14	24	2	4	7	19
House of Commons *and* provincial legislature	4	5	2	12	4	12	9	15	2	4	—	—
Ex-dominion ministers:												
1 Portfolio	4	5	5	15	6	18	—	—	1	2	4	11
>1 Portfolio	6	7	6	17	3	9	4	7	2	4	—	—
Ex-provincial minister	6	7	3	9	3	9	8	12	13	24	—	—
House of Commons Speaker	2	2	1	3	1	3	—	—	1	2	—	—
House of Commons Deputy Speaker	1	1	—	—	—	—	3	5	1	2	2	5
Whip	3	3	—	—	—	—	1	2	3	5	—	—
Provincial Speaker	5	6	—	—	—	—	2	4	1	2	1	2.7
Local government												
Mayor	22	25	3	9	2	6	8	12	2	4	1	2.7
Alderman	7	8	1	3	1	3	4	7	1	2	—	—
No experience except provincial legislature	11	13	3	9	4	12	8	12	11	20	6	16
No experience except local government	4	5	1	3	—	—	2	4	—	—	1	2.7
Other	1	1	—	—	1	3	—	—	—	—	—	—
Nil	21	25	10	29	7	21	15	25	21	39	20	54
Some experience	68	75	25	71	26	79	44	75	34	61	17	46

per cent (Diefenbaker). A corresponding phenomenon has been a gradual elimination of local government experience from the legislative background of new appointees to the Senate. While it was as high as 33 per cent in the pre-1925 crop, it fluctuated between 12 to 9 to 19 per cent under the three successive administrations; under Mr. St. Laurent it was drastically reduced to 6 per cent while during the years 1957–63 it almost completely vanished. The reasons for the decline in legislative experience during the last two administrations are not hard to find. With Mr. St. Laurent's hesitant resolution to retard the process of deteriorating partisan equilibrium in the Senate the bulk of the appointments under his Administration was made from outside the House of Commons. On the other hand, the new Conservative Government after 1957 had not been in power long enough to be able to use effectively its human resources in the Commons for Senate appointments. However, since the most obvious source of legislative experience is the House of Commons, any embargo on MP's would automatically reduce the experience-quotient. So far, the effect of the recent trend has not been too disturbing. But it requires little prophecy to say that its continuance may perceptibly affect the legislative competence of the Senate.

PROFESSIONAL AND EDUCATIONAL BACKGROUND

The occupational breakdown of the membership of the Senate is illustrated in Table VII. It cannot be claimed that this table is entirely accurate, because there are so many individuals who could be classified under a number of categories. The compiler of a table of this sort cannot escape from the need to make rather arbitrary decisions from time to time in individual cases. The chief source of possible misleading impressions is probably with relation to members of the legal profession, who in addition to their actual practices may also be on the boards of directors of various financial and banking institutions or some other business concerns. Their final classification was decided on the basis of what appeared to be their major interest. On the whole, however, it can be claimed the general picture probably corresponds fairly well with the reality.

This picture of the professional background of Senators must be supplemented by a statement (Table VIII) regarding the proportion of those who had college or university training. The top position of law as the largest single area of activity (with more than half of the lawyers being QC's) in the aggregate picture of professions in the Senate is hardly surprising in the light of the universal experience of the percentage of lawyers participating in legislation everywhere. Indeed, there is no serious deviation from the average in five of our six periods (it never fell below 20 per cent and it never rose above 35 per cent); however, the appointments of Mr. Diefenbaker show a sudden increase in the proportion of lawyers—sixteen of his thirty-seven appointees were members of the legal profession and fourteen out of the sixteen were QC's. On the other hand, there was a drop, almost by 50 per cent, in the number of manufacturers, the second largest single group in the total, and an even sharper decrease in the proportion of merchants, the third largest group, who were not allotted one representative in the appointments of the Government 1957–63. It is interesting to point out that the relevant figures of the previous Conservative Administration of Bennett regarding these two groups correspond to our findings under the Conservative Government of Mr. Diefenbaker. Then, too, there was a drop in the proportion of manufacturers and merchants, and also of agriculture which fell by one-third. What makes the picture even more instructive is the fact that in both instances the decrease in these two occupational

TABLE VII

Occupational Breakdown of Senate Membership, 1925–63

Occupation	From total		Pre-1925		King		Bennett		King		St.-Laurent		Diefenbaker	
	No.	%	No.	%	No.	%	No.	%	No.	%	No.	%	No.	%
Law	82	26	19	21	7	20	10	33	18	33	12	22	16	48
KC/QC	46	55	9	50	2	28	1	10	13	74	7	59	4	85
Manufacturing	53	16.9	22	25	4	12	3	9	9	15	11	20	4	11
Merchants	33	10.7	14	16	6	17	3	9	4	6	6	11	—	—
Agriculture	28	9	9	10	3	8	1	3	9	15	3	5	3	8
Finance and banking	27	8.8	6	7	3	8	5	15	5	8	4	7	4	11
Medicine	23	7.4	4	5	6	17	3	9	5	8	3	5	2	5
Press and journalism	18	5.9	5	6	3	8	2	6	5	8	2	4	1	2.7
Education	10	3.2	3	3.3	—	—	—	—	1	2	6	11	—	—
Housewives	5	1.6	1	1.1	1	3.3	1	3	—	—	1	2	2	5
Engineering	4	1.3	—	—	—	—	—	—	—	—	2	4	1	2.7
Military	4	1.3	1	1.1	—	—	3	9	—	—	—	—	—	—
Labour	2	0.6	—	—	1	3.3	—	—	—	—	—	—	1	2.7
Undisclosed	6	1.9	2	2.2	—	—	—	—	1	2	2	4	2	5
Unclassified	13	3.2	3	3.3	1	3.3	2	6	2	3	3	5	2	5
Total	308	100	89	100	35	100	33	100	59	100	55	100	37	100

TABLE VIII
Educational Background of Senators, 1925–63

	From total		Pre-1925		King		Bennett		King		St. Laurent		Diefenbaker	
Total	308		89		35		33		59		55		37	
	No.	%	No.	%	No.	%	No.	%	No.	%	No.	%	No.	%
Those with a college or university degree	196	64	46	52	24	70	22	67	41	71	35	63	28	80

groups was balanced by an increase in the percentage of the "Finance and banking" class, which was elevated to the second place under both Bennett and Diefenbaker, although in the total average it ranks fifth. Contrariwise, in the appointments made before 1925 the percentage of financiers stood slightly below the average, while that of manufacturers and merchants was higher. Indeed, the pre-1925 columns show that the largest single element of the Senate, as it stood in 1925, was made up of manufacturers, who comprised 25 per cent of the Senate's membership, rather than of lawyers, whose percentage was only 21. The proportion of manufacturers in the 1925 membership, most of whom had made their fortunes as self-made men in the pioneer era of Canada, may partially explain the Whiggish suspicion of the Senate in the late '20's and perhaps '30's towards any legislation which tried to pave the way to the positive state.

Be that as it may, of the total of 308 Senators who have filled the Chamber during the last thirty-seven years, 223 (or 71 per cent) were recruited from the realm of law, business, and agriculture. This leaves the professional fields of medicine, engineering, education, and journalism, as well as labour, grossly under-represented in the membership of the Senate. The argument that they are not much better off in the House of Commons is not convincing. It is in this respect that the difference in the membership of the Senate and that of the modern House of Lords becomes most pronounced. Perhaps the percentage of educationalists in Mr. St. Laurent's appointments (11 per cent, or almost 75 per cent more than the average) and the proportion of engineers to the total number of appointments under the last two administrations may entail some hopes for the future. It is a sad fact, however, that in a basically "shopkeeper country" the percentage of the military in the membership of one of the houses of Parliament should be twice as high as the percentage of wage-earners.

The picture of the educational background of members of the Senate is perhaps somewhat more encouraging. A total of 188 of the 308 Senators in 1925–63 held a college or university degree, which falls only slightly short of the two-thirds mark. The level of education shows an interesting, though not surprising, connection with the correlation between the relevant percentage of law, on the one hand, and that of business, on the other. Where the proportion of manufacturers was higher than the lawyers' (as in the case of the pre-1925 appointments), or came within a striking distance (as in the St. Laurent appointments), the education quotient fell below the average, in the first instance to 52 per cent, in the second, to 63 per cent. On the other hand, where the proportion was undoubtedly in favour of members of the legal profession, as in the appointments of Mr. Diefenbaker, the quotient showed a steep increase to a record high of 80 per cent, twenty-eight of the thirty-seven new appointees holding a university degree. The percentage was also higher than the average in the appointments of King, both in 1925–30 and in 1936–49, and under Bennett, although it was never set as high as during the last three years.

RELIGION

Information regarding the composition of the Senate would not be complete without reference to the representation of religious denominations in its membership. Table IX, setting forth the division of Senators according to religion, needs little clarification. It shows that the various churches and sects have been fairly well represented in the Senate during the thirty-seven years under study, although nearly three-fourths of the membership have belonged to the four largest denominations. It is noteworthy that the amount of undisclosed information is here the greatest, the relevant figure of 9 per cent (which ranks as the fourth largest group) leaving the observer guessing whether it merely means unwillingness to shed light on such highly personal affair as one's religion, or it is an indication of the extent of agnosticism in the Senate.

AGE

A young Senate would be a contradiction in terms. Although, as we have seen in the case of Bentham,[6] wisdom or moral greatness is not always linked automatically with advanced age, it has been, generally speaking, part of the historical image of second chambers that for their basically dispassionate and meticulous work a human environment of elderly people would be a more appropriate framework than one in

[6]See above, p. 4.

TABLE IX

Religion of Senators, 1925–63

	From total		Pre-1925		King		Bennett		King		St. Laurent		Diefen-baker	
Denomination	No.	%	No.	%	No.	%	No.	%	No.	%	No.	%	No.	%
Roman Catholic	127	41.1	31	34	17	50	15	45	27	45	23	42	14	38
United Church of Canada	46	15.0	9*	10	9	25	6	18	8	12	14	26	9	25
Presbyterian	39	12.0	14	16	4	12	8	24	9	15	4	7	—	—
Church of England	35	11.4	17	19.1	3	9	1	3	4	7	5	9	5	13
Baptist	18	6.0	3	3.3	1	3	2	6	5	8	4	7	3	8
Lutherans	1	0.3	—	—	—	—	—	—	1	2	—	—	—	—
Hebrew	1	0.3	—	—	—	—	—	—	—	—	1	2	—	—
Ukrainian Catholic	1	0.3	—	—	—	—	—	—	—	—	1	2	—	—
Orthodox Catholic	1	0.3	—	—	—	—	—	—	—	—	—	—	1	2.7
Congregation-alist	1	0.3	1	1.1	—	—	—	—	—	—	—	—	—	—
Christian Scientist	1	0.3	1	1.1	—	—	—	—	—	—	—	—	—	—
Undisclosed	28	9.0	13	15	1	3	1	3	5	8	3	5	5	13
Total	308		89		35		33		59		55		37	

*These were Methodists.

which the median age is low. Nevertheless, apart from the partisan aspects of the appointing system, it has been for the allegedly high average age of its members that the Senate has received most of the scorn throughout the years. In characterizing Senators contemptuously as "old party hacks," the word "old" has been as important an element of contempt as the rest of the phrase. However, it is important to see the relevant figures before one can make any critical comments.

If we compare the data of 308 Senators in the last thirty-seven years from the point of view of how old they were when they entered the Senate, we shall find that the average age of Senators at the time of their appointment has been slightly higher than 58. This is borne out by the fact that, as we have seen before, 45 per cent of the total membership have been elevated from the House of Commons, of whom about 80 per cent served at least eight years in Parliament, but usually more than that. If we add to this that the median age of people entering the House of Commons for the first time is 51.1,[7] the average age of newly appointed Senators as fixed between 58 and 61 becomes well understandable. This correlation between the number of years served in the House of Com-

[7]See N. Ward, *The Canadian House of Commons: Representation* (Toronto, 1950), p. 129, Table VIII.

mons prior to appointment to the Senate and the average age at the time of the appointment, while not conclusive, is a contributory explanation of the fluctuation of the median appointment age in our six periods. If we relate this picture to the pattern of service in the House of Commons immediately preceding appointment to the Senate the fluctuation of the curve becomes easily explicable.

TABLE X

Correlation between Length of Service in the House of Commons and Median Appointment Age in the Senate, 1925–62

Appointment	Service in the House of Commons: One or two terms	Service in the House of Commons: Three or more terms	Median Appointment Age
Pre–1925	58%	42%	56
King	20%	80%	57
Bennett	49%	52%	58
King	36%	67%	58
St. Laurent	22%	78%	61
Diefenbaker	65%	35%	58

It usually escapes the attention of the Senate's critics, who are preoccupied with the high average age of the Senators, that the mortality rate in the House, and consequently, the frequency with which the membership changes is comparatively high. Between 1925 and 1963 the mortality rate in the Senate has been 4.9, that is, approximately five Senators died each year and their places were filled with new appointments, except when the vacancies were held over for political or other reasons. This means that a "Senate generation" does not last longer than approximately sixteen to eighteen years, or in other words, that it takes about eight or nine years to have a complete change in half of the Senate forces—the same period for which Senators are elected in the French Republic. As a result, there have been almost two full revolutions in the composition of the Senate since 1925, the first ending during the war, the second being accomplished in our own day. If the average appointment age and thus the mortality rate were lower, if the life expectancy of Senate generations were higher and opportunity for injecting new blood into the Senate scantier, charges about a growing gulf between the Senate and public opinion would be much sounder than they actually are. Of course, in spite of the mortality rate there is bound to be a difference between the average age at the time of appointment and the average age in any given year. Taking four typical two-year periods (1925–26, 1934–35, 1952–53, 1960–61) we find that the yearly average age over the last thirty-five years has been 69. However, it should be pointed out that while this figure represents a clear eleven-years-plus over the average appointment age, it is still six years below the constitutional and statutory retiring age on the Bench, which recently has been seriously considered for adoption in the Senate itself. Indeed, if, in addition to the average appointment age (58), we also take into account the fact that between 1925 and 1963 "life-tenure" in fact meant an average of sixteen years in the Senate, then it will be clear that Senators, on the average, die at the age of 74, that is, with a year to go before the theoretical limit of 75. Therefore, although there is always a varying number of people in the Senate who are over 75, the introduction of a compulsory retiring age at 75 would by no means seriously affect the existing situation in the Senate; it would rather formalize a practice already present.

2. *The Active Element in the Senate*

Although the Senate has no "backwoodsmen" amongst its members, who emerge from obscurity on occasion in order to swamp the House with their votes, it is nevertheless possible to speak of a regular nucleus of the active House as it performs its business from day to day. For the attempt to present a fairly reliable picture of the active element in the Senate in recent times, four two-year periods have been studied—the parliamentary sessions of 1925–26, 1934–35, 1952–53, and 1960–61—from the double viewpoint of attendance and of participation in debates.[8] In each instance three groups have been established and each Senator has been classified as "active," "moderately active," or "passive" according to certain criteria to be explained below. Then the classes assigned to the Senators have been checked against a four-fold classification of their legislative background, occupation, age, and education. The purpose of this detailed study is not so much to compare the four periods with one another as to try to define the type of persons who carry the bulk of the Senate's work load through analysing the combined figures of four periods covering a total of eight years and chosen in such a way as to be fairly representative of the thirty-seven years under review. However, a word of warning is necessary. This analysis is restricted to locating the active element as it

[8]This method combines the analysis used by Lord Chorley, Bernard Crick, and Donald Chapman in *Reform of the Lords* (London, 1954) on the one hand, and Peter Bromhead's method on the other. Bromhead, *The House of Lords and Contemporary Politics, 1911–57* (London, 1958), chap. III.

appears in the Senate Chamber and, thus, takes no cognizance of those who, for one reason or other, choose to keep the full scope of their activities for work in the Senate's committees where a considerable portion of the Senate's legislative business is done. However, apart from the inadequacy of printed records of committee proceedings, the overlapping membership of the committees and the arrangement under which they frequently meet simultaneously makes meaningful statistical analysis of the active element in committee practically impossible. But it is urged that apart from a few exceptional cases those who make up the core of the active nucleus in the Senate are the same who will be found taking the lion's share of work on the committee level. Similarly, this analysis, based upon purely quantitative measurement, cannot take into account the special and varied qualities of individual Senators. The Senate includes among its membership many elder statesmen of the day. Some of them speak often and others speak rarely, but the total effect of their experience and wisdom is something which defies statistical tabulation. It has been said, for example, that when he realized his powers were declining, Sir Allen Aylesworth rarely participated in debate. Strictly on the basis of his interventions, therefore, he would have to be classified among the "passive." But his ability was regarded so highly by his political opponent, Arthur Meighen, then leader of the Senate, that he was often requested by the latter to prepare and present to the House briefs on complicated constitutional problems which required the application of a keen legal mind. Sir Allen always complied with such requests and provided information, on the basis of which others could build up their speeches.[9] Such services, of course, will not appear in the following analysis. Again, a powerful address upon an important topic may often be more effective than a dozen smaller contributions, and yet in the statistics it will be counted as one. However, these loopholes are the inevitable results of any attempt to measure in quantitative terms basically intellectual endeavours.

ATTENDANCE

In Table XI, Senators have been classified into three groups according to the number of occasions their names appeared on the attendance sheet recorded daily in the Senate *Journals*. The qualification for inclusion in the "active" group (Group I) is to have been present at least at 80 per cent of the sittings in the two-year period. The second group, that of the "moderately active," consists of Senators who attended less than 80 per cent, but more than 50 per cent, of the sittings, while the third,

[9] *SD, 1952*, p. 17.

Table XI

Activity of Senators According to Attendance

		Class I					Class II					Class III				
		1925–6	1934–5	1952–3	1960–1	Total	1925–6	1934–5	1952–3	1960–1	Total	1925–6	1934–5	1952–3	1960–1	Total
Aggregate	No.	58	30	21	23	132	29	45	40	50	164	10	8	22	28	68
	%	60	36	25	23	33	28	54	50	50	45	10	8	25	28	19
Age		66	66	70	69	68	64	66	70	70	67	74	69	68	73	71
Education	No.	32	21	12	18	83	18	27	27	33	105	3	4	15	21	43
	%	55	71	57	78	66	62	50	68	61	64	33	50	66	75	63
Occupation																
Law	No.	15	10	3	10	38	5	8	10	12	35	1	—	5	4	10
	%	25	33	14	43	29	17	18	25	24	21	10	—	23	14	15
Business	No.	28	10	5	1	44	10	20	13	24	67	6	4	14	11	35
	%	50	33	24	4	33	34	44	33	48	41	60	50	66	39	52
Agriculture	No.	3	2	4	3	12	4	3	5	6	18	1	—	—	2	3
	%	5	7	19	13	9	14	7	13	12	11	10	—	—	7	4
Other professionals	No.	8	5	5	6	24	7	10	9	4	30	2	3	3	9	17
	%	14	17	24	26	18	24	22	23	28	18	20	38	14	32	25
Others	No.	4	3	4	3	14	3	4	3	4	14	—	1	—	2	3
	%	7	10	19	13	11	10	9	8	18	9	—	13	—	7	4
Legislative experience																
House of Commons	No.	27	16	9	7	59	19	21	19	19	78	3	3	6	8	20
	%	48	53	43	30	45	65	47	48	38	48	30	38	24	28	29
Provincial legis.	No.	11	6	4	2	23	6	5	7	9	27	1	—	5	6	12
	%	19	20	19	9	17	21	11	18	18	16	10	—	23	22	18
Local government	No.	5	2	1	1	9	—	1	1	2	4	2	—	1	—	3
	%	8	7	5	4	7	—	2	3	4	2	20	—	5	—	4
No experience	No.	15	6	7	13	41	4	18	13	20	55	4	5	10	14	33
	%	25	20	33	56	31	14	40	33	40	34	40	63	45	50	49

NOTE: Number of Sittings: 1925–6: 92; 1934–5: 116; 1952–3: 119; 1960–1: 178; Total: 505.
Number of Senators: 1925–6: 97; 1934–5: 83; 1952–3: 83; 1960–1: 101; Total: 364.

the "casuals," those who were present less than half the time. If the four two-year periods are considered a fairly representative sample of the three-and-a-half decades since 1925, it will follow that one-third of the Senate's membership falls into the category of regular attenders, 45 per cent are those who attend 50–80 per cent of the sittings, and a relatively minor group is made up of the casual attenders, those who are not present more than half the time. This means, *inter alia*, that approximately 78 per cent of the members of the Senate are present more than half the sittings per session. Indeed, the total attendance figures of the 505 sittings during the four two-year periods studied indicates that the *average* daily attendance in the Senate is 62.37, which compares favourably with the attendance statistics of the House of Commons.[10]

A closer scrutiny of the three classes, but particularly of the two extreme groups, would reveal that there is a discernible, even if limited, effect of age upon the frequency of attendance; the average age of those in the "active" group is practically the same as the median age in the Senate, while the average age of those who make up the third, "passive," group is three years higher. Similarly, two-thirds of the members of Class I are college or university graduates. From the point of view of occupation, it is the businessmen who make up the bulk of frequent attenders (33.4 per cent), while lawyers and professional people form only 29 per cent and 18 per cent of Group I respectively. However, the activity of businessmen as a group is somewhat counterbalanced by the fact that they are also in a majority in Class III, the "casuals," while lawyers make up a small portion (14.7 per cent) of this group. In this sense other professionals fare worse than lawyers, because they compose one-quarter of the "passive" third group. On the contrary, those whose major interest lies in agriculture maintain a steady 10 per cent in the first two classes and provide only an insignificant segment (4.4 per cent) of the "casuals." The most interesting difference, however, appears in connection with the relationship between legislative experience and the regularity of attendance. Those who had no legislative experience whatever before they were summoned to the Senate make up only 31 per cent of Class I and 34 per cent of Class II, while they form nearly an absolute majority (49 per cent) among those whose attendance rate is lower than 50 per cent. Furthermore, it is also evident that former MP's top the list of both the frequent and moderately regular attenders (45 and 48 per cent respectively), followed by those whose previous legislative experience was limited to provincial legislatures, and finally by those

[10]Cf. Norman Ward's comments in *Saturday Night*, June 5, 1954, pp. 7–8.

who had no other experience than that gained on the local government level. What emerges, then, from the classification according to our first criterion, i.e., the frequency of attendance, is that one-third of the membership of the Senate can be classed as regular attenders; that the average age of this vanguard group is lower than the median age in the Senate; that two-thirds of them had university training; that the largest single occupational element in it is made up of businessmen; and that their overwhelming majority had some form of legislative experience before starting to serve their life term in the Upper Chamber.

However, the relatively high attendance of Senators at the daily sittings is no indication in itself of what goes on in the Senate, and, therefore, to base our assessment of the active element in the House on the attendance figures might be misleading. After all, the majority of Senators come from places outside Ottawa and, in view of the cultural amenities offered by the capital they could not, even if they wished to, find better entertainment than that provided on Parliament Hill. Accordingly, it has been felt necessary to proceed a little beyond the results produced by the above survey and to attempt to supplement them by some further statistics of the same sort, based on different criteria.

CONTRIBUTION TO DEBATE

The method used for this purpose is a classification of Senators into the same number of groups as in the case of attendance, according to the frequency of their interventions in the four two-year periods analysed above. As indicated in Table XII, each Senator has been credited with the number of interventions shown against his name in the Senate Debates index and then classified as "active" (Class I), "occasional contributor" (Class II), and "passive" (Class III), according to the number of his interventions. The qualification for inclusion in the first group is to have spoken on twenty or more occasions in 1925–26 and in 1934–35 and on thirty or more occasions in 1952–53 and in 1960–61. The second group consists of Senators who spoke at least once each but less than twenty times in 1925–26 and in 1934–35 and thirty times in 1952–53 and in 1960–61, and the third, the "passive" class, those who did not speak at all.[11]

[11]The classification is inevitably subject to error, especially in borderline cases between groups. It has been difficult, for example, to decide how best to deal with speeches in Committee of the Whole or, indeed, during second reading and third reading debates, under the laxity of the Rules. In order that distortions in this respect may be minimized, all speeches made by a Senator on a particular bill on any one day at short intervals have been counted as one intervention. Despite such arbitrary decisions, however, it seems fair to claim an adequate degree of accuracy for the classification as a whole.

TABLE XII

Activity of Senators According to Interventions

		Class I					Class II					Class III				
		1925 –6	1934 –5	1952 –3	1960 –1	Total	1925 –6	1934 –5	1952 –3	1960 –1	Total	1925 –6	1934 –5	1952 –3	1960 –1	Total
Aggregate	No.	16	12	11	25	64	57	52	55	54	218	24	19	17	22	82
	%	17	7	13	25	18	58	70	66	54	60	25	23	20	22	23
Age		66	67	68	71	68	63	66	67	69	66	69	67	71	74	70
	No.	12	9	8	19	48	31	33	33	38	135	10	10	13	15	48
Education	%	77	75	73	76	75	55	62	60	71	62	41	50	77	69	59
Occupation																
Law	No.	9	3	4	11	27	9	11	11	14	45	3	4	3	1	11
	%	64	25	36	44	44	17	21	20	26	21	12	21	18	5	13
Business	No.	4	4	5	8	21	28	22	21	14	85	12	8	6	11	37
	%	24	33	45	32	33	54	42	38	26	39	50	42	35	50	45
Agriculture	No.	1	1	1	3	6	6	4	7	6	23	1	—	1	2	4
	%	6	8	9	12	9	11	8	11	11	11	4	—	6	9	5
Other professionals	No.	1	3	1	2	7	10	10	11	14	45	6	5	5	6	22
	%	6	25	9	8	11	18	19	20	26	21	25	26	30	27	27
Others	No.	1	1	—	1	3	4	5	5	6	20	2	2	2	2	8
	%	6	8	—	4	5	8	7	9	11	9	11	11	12	9	10
Legislative experience																
House of Commons	No.	8	9	3	9	29	29	25	23	15	92	12	6	6	10	34
	%	48	75	28	36	45	50	47	42	28	42	50	31	35	45	42
Provincial legis.	No.	3	1	2	5	11	11	8	11	9	39	4	2	4	3	13
	%	21	8	18	20	17	20	16	20	17	18	17	11	23	14	16
Local government	No.	1	—	2	2	5	3	—	—	1	4	3	3	1	—	7
	%	6	—	18	8	8	5	—	—	2	2	12	16	6	—	9
No experience	No.	4	2	4	9	19	14	19	21	29	83	5	8	6	9	28
	%	24	16	36	36	30	25	37	38	54	38	21	42	35	41	34

NOTE: Number of Sittings—1925–6: 92; 1934–5: 116; 1952–3: 119; 1960–1: 178; Total: 505.
Number of Senators—1925–6: 97; 1934–5: 83; 1952–3: 83; 1960–1: 101; Total: 364.

The most interesting aspect of the whole survey is to compare the results of the second classification with the figures produced by the first grouping based upon the frequency of attendance. Perhaps the most striking feature of the over-all picture is the difference in the size of Class I under the two classifications. While on the basis of attendance one-third of the Senators would be classed as "active," only half this number (17.7 per cent) qualified for the first class according to the criterion of active participation. In other words, there is a small group of Senators who attend at least 80 per cent of the sittings of the Senate but do not contribute to debate on a sufficient number of occasions to be regarded as "active." The effect of this shift in the size of Class I is most evident on the proportion of the second group, the "occasional contributors," which consists of as much as 60 per cent of the membership of the House in the second classification, while it was not higher than 45 per cent according to the criterion of attendance. As a result of the figures of the first two classes, it is not surprising to find that the percentage of those who never speak (22.8) is higher than that of Class I (17.7 per cent), although it was the reverse in the case of attendance (19 per cent "passive" as compared to 33 per cent "active"). One more general observation must be made. While it is true that the *total* percentage of Class I according to attendance is considerably higher than the total percentage of the same class according to interventions, a reverse *tendency* can be seen in the two classifications over the past thirty-five years. In the case of attendance, the proportion of Senators who can be classed as "active" has been dwindling; it was 60 per cent in 1925–26, 36 in 1934–35, 25 in 1952–53, and 23 in 1960–61. In the case of active participation in debate the proportion of first classers has produced a different curve; it was 17 per cent in 1925–26, fell to 7 per cent in 1934–35, for reasons to be explained in the next chapter, rose to 13 per cent in 1952–53, and reached its peak in 1960–61, when 25 per cent of the Senators spoke enough to be classified in the "active" group. What this double trend signifies is a shrinking of the group of first class ("active") attenders and an expansion of the group of first class ("active") contributors.

The main reason for this discrepancy seems to be closely connected with the occupational structure of the "active" group in both systems of classification. In the first classification, based upon the frequency of attendance, businessmen formed the bulk (33.4 per cent) of Class I, followed by lawyers and professionals. However, in the second classification, according to the frequency of interventions, it is lawyers who constitute 44 per cent of the "active" group, followed by businessmen

(33 per cent) and professionals (11 per cent). Indeed, if we compare the composition of the "active" class with those who never spoke at all, we shall find that the majority of the "passive" group is made up of businessmen (45 per cent) and professionals (27 per cent) and lawyers constitute a mere segment (13 per cent) of it. This means that, while members of the legal profession may not be among the most frequent attenders, when they do attend the frequency rate of their contribution is higher than that of any other occupational element in the House. If we combine this finding with the fact that, as we have seen, in the pre-1925 appointments the percentage of manufacturers was higher than the lawyers, but under successive administrations their proportion was drastically reversed, the phenomenon of the diverse trend in Class I under the two systems of classification will seem to be natural. The most disturbing factor in the relative contribution of the various occupational groups is the poor showing of professional people—doctors, engineers, teachers, journalists, etc. In both systems of classification they constituted one-fourth of the "passive" class: 25 per cent of those who did not attend more than half the sittings of the Senate and 27 per cent of those who made no contribution at all to debates. This fact must be taken into account when considering the numerous reform proposals to re-constitute the Senate on the basis of a more liberal representation of the various professions. It seems likely that a Senate composed entirely of such men would seriously lack continuity.

In the remaining aspects of classification the figures derived from the number of interventions reinforce our findings based upon the frequency of attendance. Accordingly, the average age of those in the "active" class was lower than the average age of those who never spoke; it was also lower than the median age in the Senate and the average age of Class I in the attendance statistics. Similarly, 75 per cent of those who have been classified as "active" contributors had higher education, while university graduates have constituted only 62 and 59 per cent of Classes II and III respectively. There seems to be, as might be expected, a direct relationship between the intensity of contribution, on the one hand, and the high level of education as well as the low level of the median age, on the other. Although the same relationship existed in the classification according to attendance, it was less pronounced there than in the case of interventions.

The most interesting figures, however, relate to the impact of previous legislative experience on the level of contribution. Again, the findings of the two classifications point in the same direction. But if in the case of mere attendance those who had no previous legislative experience could still make up 31 per cent of Class I, in the case of interventions 75 per cent of those who have been classified as "active" had some kind of legislative experience before they entered the Senate. Otherwise, the figures indicating the breakdown of Class I into House of Commons, provincial legislature, and local government experience are practically the same in both classifications. However, there is one important contrast: in the case of attendance, former members of the House of Commons constituted the bulk of both Class I and Class II, but they made up a much smaller proportion of the membership of Class III (29 per cent); in the case of contribution to debate they formed the bulk not only of the "active" (45.3 per cent) and "moderately active" (42.2 per cent) but also of the "passive" group (41.5 per cent), that is, those who have never spoken at all. It appears, then, that, on the whole, party politicians, elevated from the House of Commons tend either to be very active in debate in the Senate or to take hardly any part at all.

On the basis of this comparative analysis of activity-rate according to the double criteria of attendance and contribution to debate in four chosen two-year periods from 1925 to 1963, the following tentative conclusion may be hazarded; the main burden of the legislative work of the Senate is shouldered by a group of approximately fifteen to twenty Senators who attend more than 80 per cent of the sittings of the House and participate actively in the debates. Their average age is not higher than the median age in the Senate; their overwhelming majority have received university education, the dominant occupation among them is law, and almost all of them had some legislative experience before entering the Senate, a considerable portion of them having served in the House of Commons itself.

THE SENATE AND PARTISANSHIP: PARTY ORGANIZATION

3

THE PROBLEM OF HOW TO LIVE with the appointing system without falling victim to it has been, no doubt, one of the most taxing problems for the Senate throughout its history and one on which it has received most of its criticism. The Fathers, to be sure, although somewhat lofty in their general ideas concerning the Senate, had no illusions about the nature of the appointments.[1] It was never seriously contemplated that appointments by successive governments would be other than to the supporters of such governments. What was expected rather was that, on the one hand, the peripheral position of the Senate in the direct political battle would tend to tone down the partisan effects of the appointing system and emphasize, instead, the quasi-judicial attitude of the members of the Senate, and that, on the other, the regular alternation of government between the two major parties would never allow a wide gap to develop in the numerical balance of the appointees of those parties in the Senate.

As to the realization of the main expectations of an operative non-partisan spirit in despite of partisan appointments during the last thirty-seven years, this will be discussed in the next chapter. With regard to the exclusively partisan character of the appointments and the changing pattern of party stands in the Senate, a brief historical survey seems to be in order. The arrangement under which the first Senate was composed fairly equally of Conservatives and Liberals, as a result of a

[1]See in particular the remarks of Reesor and Taché, J. Pope, ed., *Confederation Documents* (Toronto, 1895), pp. 238 ff. and 331, and *Confederation Debates* (Ottawa, 1951), pp. 166 and 570.

gentleman's agreement incorporated in Resolution 14 of the Quebec Conference, was clearly not accepted as a meaningful precedent. During his nineteen years of office, Sir John A. Macdonald caused the appointment of 117 Senators, only one of them Liberal and one other Independent; both were his personal friends. As a result, in 1896 there were sixty-three Conservatives, ten Liberals, and three Independents in the Senate. Sir Wilfrid Laurier appointed eighty-one members of the Senate, of whom all were his own supporters. This reversed the balance, so that by 1912 the composition of the Chamber was fifty-seven Liberals, twelve Conservatives, and nine others. The tradition of pure partisan appointments was broken only once under the Borden Administration, by the appointment in 1918 of Sen. Harmer, a Liberal-Unionist from Alberta, who sided with the Liberals in twenty-two divisions between 1925 and 1947, the year of his death. As a result of the appointments of Sir Robert Borden and Arthur Meighen the stand of the parties in the Senate at the beginning of the period under review was fifty-nine Conservatives and thirty Liberals. Through filling the emerging vacancies consistently with his supporters during the period of 1925–30, King could achieve a transient Liberal majority of 48 : 47 in the Senate by the end of his Administration. The proportion was quickly reversed, however, during the following five years, and when the Liberals came back to power after the 1935 election, there were sixty-five Conservatives in the Senate as against thirty-one Liberals. Although Bennett openly admitted that in making his appointments to the Senate "it was assumed that they are supporters of the Conservative Party,"[2] it has been said that at least one of his appointees, Patrick Burns of Alberta (1931–37), was a life-long Liberal.[3] His example was not repeated by King, who needed six years to restore the dominance of his party in the Senate. By 1938 the Conservative majority had dropped to 56 : 34; between January and May 1940 Mackenzie King appointed fifteen Liberals to the Senate, which further reduced the gap. Although there were still forty-nine Conservatives to forty-six Liberals, the Liberal majority was practically established, for one Conservative was absent on military service and four others were wholly incapable of attending because of illness.[4] In the following session the numerical strength of the two parties, at least on paper, was in a complete balance, each having 41 supporters in the Senate. The tide finally turned in 1942 when, for the first time in twelve

[2]*HD, 1938*, p. 3703.
[3]Sen. Horner's remarks. *SD, 1951*, p. 260. Also *SD, 1937*, p. 94.
[4]*SD, 1940*, p. 443

years, the Liberals secured a majority of three (44 : 41). From then on the size of the Conservative group in the Senate gradually and continuously dwindled and with every new Liberal victory their hopes for an early recuperation further faded, with good chances of ultimate extinction. Indeed, by 1946 the ratio was 65 : 30 in favour of the Liberals; after the 1949 election it changed to 76 : 15, then to 80 : 8 in 1954. When the long Liberal reign ended in 1957, the Conservative party was represented in the Senate by a tiny contingent of five stubborn survivors of the Bennett era—a tenaciously optimistic island surrounded by a Liberal ocean.

As the process of the rapid weakening of the Conservative forces in the Senate became evident, pressure for some modifications in the appointing system gathered momentum. In 1947 there appeared an article in the *Dalhousie Review*, urging that "the system of filling the Senate by life appointments on the nomination of the Government of the day . . . offends against the principle of democracy, and it would become indefensible if the Senate's personnel came to be composed solely of Liberals."[5] Even members of the growing Liberal majority in the Senate felt that, even though the Senate was not to be conceived as a body composed of supporters of two great rival party machines, there was nevertheless something inherently wrong and silly about the distorted balance. In 1950 Sen. Reid, a relative newcomer in the Senate, observed that "the appointment of Senators at large would not bring about the changes which the public of this country are looking for. . . . The problems that we hear so much about today are being emphasized because in this House there are only a few Opposition members facing an overwhelming majority appointed by the present administration."[6] There could be no doubt that the growing pressure would effect some change in the system of future appointments. We have seen[7] the problems that faced Mr. St. Laurent in this regard during the second half of his Administration and his inability or unwillingness to come to grips with them. He preferred the Fabian tactics of delaying and postponing decision in filling the vacancies in the Senate. But in 1956 he finally decided to make a small gesture in the right direction, if not as the first move of a general reorientation of the appointing principles, at least as a token of his awareness that such reorientation was perhaps necessary. The upshot was the summoning in that year of one Conservative and three "Independents" to the Senate. The Conservative was J. T. Hackett, an

[5]"Topics of the Day," *Dalhousie Review*, vol. 26 (1946–47), p. 100.
[6]*SD, 1950*, p. 250.
[7]Above, pp. 57 ff.

English-speaking Catholic from Quebec, who had served twelve years as Conservative member in the House of Commons and who was seventy-one years of age at the time of his appointment. Although his appointment was regarded as an important precedent, it was generally understood that in addition to the lopsidedness of the Senate the friendship between Hackett and the Prime Minister was a no less important factor in his appointment.[8] Unfortunately, he could not become a lasting asset for his Conservative colleagues in the Senate because he died one year after his appointment. Apart from him there were three others among the 1956 appointees who bore partisan designation other than "Liberal." Donald Cameron of Alberta called himself an "Independent Liberal," while Senator Molson of Quebec and Senator Savoie of New Brunswick were pure "Independents." However, their independence of the Administration has been less manifestly obvious than that of Sen. Hackett. This was borne out even by two procedural aspects of their introduction; unlike Sen. Hackett they were all seated to the right of the Speaker and were all introduced by two Liberal members of the House, whereas in the case of Sen. Hackett the two Senators who performed the ceremony were Sen. Macdonald, Government Leader in the Senate, and Sen. Haig, the Leader of the Opposition. As to their stand in concrete cases, such as the total of five divisions in the Chamber over the Customs Tariff Bill and the Bank of Canada bill in 1961, the two most controversial measures since 1958 on which there was no cross-voting, their voting record reveals very little; Sen. Molson was absent on each of the five occasions; Sen. Cameron was not in the Senate four out of five times and abstained the one he was there; only Sen. Savoie's record is a little more revealing; he was absent on two occasions, on two other occasions he chose to abstain from voting, but on the one occasion when he did vote he voted against the Government.

Those four exceptions aside, the rest of Mr. St. Laurent's fifty-five appointments consisted entirely of his Liberal supporters. There was a last-minute appeal in 1957 from Sen. Haig, Opposition Leader in the Senate, asking that when the great number of "vacant seats were filled,

[8]Sen. Hackett gave the following explanation of his appointment: "it may be that the diminishing size of the Opposition is one reason why I am here. . . ." But, he added: "there is another possibility connected with my appointment . . . It is conceivable that I had a friend somewhere. There is a man, prominent in government circles, with whom I have been on intimate terms since boyhood and early manhood. I have not always had the grace to share his political views nor his political enthusiasms, but through all the years—60 odd—we have remained friends. It is not often that the sweet rose of sentiment buds and blooms in the weedy patch of politics . . . If I find myself here I think it is because of that friendship which has remained green throughout the years." *SD, 1956*, p. 176.

enough Conservatives shall be appointed to give some semblance of strength to the Opposition."[9] No action was taken, however, and the vacancies were passed on to the new Government as part of the dowry from the outgoing Administration. Mr. Diefenbaker's first action on the Senate was the appointment of six Conservatives to fill Ontario, Quebec, and Saskatchewan vacancies. Up to February 1963, he made a total of thirty-seven appointments to the Senate. They were all conferred upon his party supporters, with the possible exception of Sen. Gladstone, the first Treaty Indian to be summoned to the Senate, who had no party label for the simple reason that Treaty Indians did not have the franchise.[10] As a result of these appointments, the stand of the two parties in the Senate in February 1963 was fifty-nine Liberals as against thirty-six Conservatives.

Thus, apart from approximately half a dozen men, all the 308 persons who have had a seat in the Senate between 1925 and 1963 were supporters of the party and the prime minister who appointed them, whether for partisan services or on some other grounds. The question that must be considered in the light of the experience of the past thirty-seven years is whether, and to what extent, this motivation for conferring senatorships on persons influenced the functioning of the Senate as an institution. However, before actually reviewing the Senate's attitude in that respect, it is necessary to describe the pattern of party organization in the Chamber.

1. *Party Organization in the Senate*

Distance from the political centre of gravity inevitably fosters laxity both in the rules of procedure and in the organization of party forces.[11] Although the relative absence of the usual tightness of party organization does not necessarily imply lack of partisan spirit—indeed, one might argue that party organization in the Senate may afford laxity because Senators are so deeply partisan that they no longer need be reminded of their loyalties—its freedom from the domination of the two great rival party machines is often cited as one of the virtues of the Senate.

Nevertheless, while the stringency may be lacking, all the essential *forms* of party organization that are ordinarily associated with the mechanism of a legislative assembly are present on both sides of the

[9]*Ibid., 1957*, p. 363

[10]Since then he has become an "Independent Conservative."

[11]For procedure see chap. v.

Senate. Indeed, there is no difference in practice between the two parties, except that the party which happens to be in office may find it desirable to increase the efficiency of its organization for the sake of the smooth discharge of the legislative functions of the House. Otherwise, the following description may apply with equal force to both party organizations in the Senate.

Each party selects its leader at a caucus attended by the members of the party in the Senate. In their choice they are practically free from the dictates or even the wishes of the national leadership of the party. On the other hand, the Government appoints as its representative in the Senate any Senator it chooses. It is merely through custom that the offices of Leader of the Senate and Government leader are held by the same person. The Government could, if it chose, appoint someone else and that someone else would then introduce Government bills and pilot them in the Upper House. However, in practice it has always appointed the acknowledged leader of the party supporting the Government in the Senate. (For a list of Government leaders and Opposition leaders in the Senate, 1925–63, see Table XIII.) Thus, on June 28, 1926, Sen. Ross, Leader of the Conservative party in the Senate, automatically became Government Leader and held that post until the downfall of the Meighen Government in the House of Commons four days later. The change brought back Sen. Dandurand, who remained Leader of the Government till the Conservative victory in 1930, to be followed by Sen. Willoughby, who had been Leader of the Conservative group during the preceding years. Between 1930 and 1935 Dandurand acted as Leader of the Liberal Opposition in the Senate, so that the choice of Government leadership again naturally fell upon him with the return to power of the Liberals in 1936. It was for similar reasons that Sen. Haig, although 80 years old, was named Government Leader in 1957, and that Sen. Macdonald was reappointed Leader for the second time when his party assumed office in 1963.

Once elected the leader is not subjected to annual re-election and is unaffected by any change in national leadership. He remains leader in the Senate until he dies or resigns or otherwise vacates his office. If this happens while the party is in opposition the post will be filled through a new ballot at a meeting of the members of the party in the Senate. If the leader had an acknowledged lieutenant or someone otherwise designated for succession the vote is merely a matter of routine. Thus, shortly after W. B. Ross joined the Senate in 1912, Sir James Lougheed recognized and appreciated his particular ability as an interpreter of constitutional questions. So when Sir James laid down his work in 1925, it

TABLE XIII

Government Leaders and Opposition Leaders of the Senate, 1925–63

Year	Government leader	Opposition leader	Government
1925	Dandurand	Lougheed (died)	King
1926	"	Ross	"
1926	Ross	Dandurand	Meighen
1927	Dandurand	Ross	King
1928	"	" (died)	"
1929	"	Willoughby	"
1930	"	"	"
1931	Willoughby (resigned)	Dandurand	Bennett
1932	Meighen	"	"
1933	"	"	"
1934	"	"	"
1935	"	"	"
1936	Dandurand	Meighen	King
1937	"	"	"
1938	"	"	"
1939	"	"	"
1940	"	"	"
1941	" (died)	" (resigned from Senate)	"
1942	King	Ballantyne	"
1943	"	"	"
1944	" (appointed Speaker)	" (resigned)	"
1945	Robertson	Haig	"
1946	"	"	"
1947	"	"	"
1948	"	"	"
1949	"	"	St. Laurent
1950	"	"	"
1951	"	"	"
1952	"	"	"
1953	" (appointed Speaker)	"	"
1954	Macdonald	"	"
1955	"	"	"
1956	"	"	"
1957	"	"	"
1957–58	Haig (resigned)	Macdonald	Diefenbaker
1958	Aseltine	"	"
1959	"	"	"
1960	"	"	"
1961	"	"	"
1962	" (retired)	"	"
1962–63	Brooks	"	"

was fitting and natural that Ross should take it up.[12] Conversely, upon Ross's death in 1929 following a short illness, the unanimous choice of the Conservative group in the Senate fell upon Sen. Willoughby. In 1942 the Conservatives were again left without a leader through the resignation from the Senate of the Right Hon. Arthur Meighen, who decided to make a final effort to return to the summit of politics. For months Sen.

[12] *SD, 1929*, p. 9

Ballantyne, the former Leader's deskmate and right-hand man, was Acting Leader, until finally he was chosen Conservative Leader on May 6. It was in this capacity that he greeted Sen. Robertson, the newly appointed Government Leader of the Senate, at the commencement of the 1945 session, but shortly afterwards he announced his decision to resign as Leader of his party in the Chamber. The move came after weeks of strenuous efforts on the part of Conservative Senators to persuade their Leader to stay on. He, however, felt "it my duty to resign, because I believe the interests of our party can be better served by a younger man . . ."[13] With great reluctance his colleagues accepted his resignation and elected Sen. Haig of Manitoba as his successor, who was sixty-eight at this time and had ten years' experience as a Senator.

If a leader who is also Government leader in the Senate dies or resigns while his party is in power, his replacement will be a matter to be decided on by the Government. The procedure is thus reversed, in that it is now for the members of the party in the Senate to endorse the appointment of the representative of the Government by automatically electing him as their new leader. As in the case of appointments to the Senate in general, individual members of the Senate have practically no influence on the choice of the Government leader. The decision rests with the prime minister, and with him alone. When Bennett offered Meighen a senatorship in 1932 he did so on the expressed assumption that Meighen would be immediately elected leader.[14] Indeed, on the day of his appointment, February 3, 1932, Sen. Willoughby tendered his resignation as Leader of the Government in the Senate at a caucus of Conservative members of the Senate. Arthur Meighen was then nominated and unanimously chosen as his successor.[15] When Dandurand died in 1942, it was a matter of some urgency to find a successor to him quickly as the representative of the Government in the Senate. On the way to Dandurand's funeral, Sen. King suggested to Mackenzie King that he should name someone to carry on as leader in the Senate. Typically, the Prime Minister answered: "Well, we shall take time to think it over, but you carry on next week." Shortly afterwards, King was asked to take the oath of office as a member of the Government and given the honour of continuing as representative of the Government and Leader of the Senate. On their next trip together to the San Francisco Conference in 1945, Sen. King again brought up the question of Senate leadership and suggested to the Prime Minister that if his Government were returned after

[13]*Ibid., 1945*, p. 14.
[14]Meighen to Lederle, May 14, 1941. *Meighen Papers*, series 5, 121981–4.
[15]*Canadian Parliamentary Guide, 1932*, Supplement.

the impending election it would be wiser for him to nominate as Government leader in the Senate someone who during the parliamentary recess lived close to Ottawa and possibly a younger man than Sen. King.[16] Consequently, upon the elevation of Sen. King to the Speakership, Sen. Robertson of Nova Scotia was appointed by the Prime Minister as Government leader in the Senate, at the age of 54 and with only two years of experience in the Senate. Robertson openly condemned the system of appointment of Government leaders in which members of the Senate had no formalized influence whatever.[17] He proposed that some new machinery should be substituted for the position of leader of the Government in the Senate to enable Senators to be better informed on all aspects of Government policy and to provide them with leadership of their own choosing. He advocated a system of electing the Senate leader at regular intervals, having him subject to recall and generally deriving his power from the House.[18] However, his suggestion was not seriously considered and when he replaced Elie Beauregard as Speaker of the Senate in 1953, the new Government Leader, Sen. Macdonald, was appointed in the traditional way. The method was not altered under the Conservative Government after 1958 and the appointment of both Sen. Aseltine and Sen. Brooks followed the usual pattern. It would be too early to say whether the appointment of Sen. King and Sen. Robertson as Speakers immediately following their resignation as Senate leaders had established a precedent. However, if it had, the fact that neither Sen. Haig nor Sen. Aseltine was made Speaker when they stepped down as the Government's spokesmen in the Senate can hardly be regarded as a violation of the practice; the first was 81, the second 76, at the time of their replacement as Senate leaders.

If the Government leader is absent from the Senate for an extended period of time, business will be organized by the deputy leader, or acting leader of the Government, as he is sometimes called. Being primarily the representative of the leader, the deputy leader is personally chosen by him; neither the Government nor his fellow party-members in the Senate have anything to do with his selection.[19] As a result, there is no

[16]*SD, 1951*, p. 168.

[17]"I do not know what goes on behind the scenes, but the peculiar fact is that the members of the Senate have nothing whatever to do with the choice of their leader, except to the extent that some of them may be able to influence the Government of the day." *SD, 1951*, p. 54.

[18]*Ibid.*, p. 59.

[19]"I feel quite badly that certain of our Senator friends interviewed you recently suggesting that in your absence I act for you . . . I fully appreciate their goodwill, but am firmly convinced that you, as Leader of the Senate, must be free at all times to select whom you please to act in your absence." Sen. Ballantyne to Meighen, Feb. 27, 1934. Meighen Papers, series 5, no. 221.

formality regarding his appointment and no official announcement is made to define his position.[20] During a good part of the 1930 session, for example, Sen. Belcourt acted on behalf of Sen. Dandurand, by virtue of a simple mandate from the Leader. Again, whenever Sen. Robertson happened to be absent from the Chamber during the first four parliamentary sessions after the war, he was usually represented by Sen. Copp. Upon his death in 1949, Sen. Copp was succeeded as Deputy Leader by Sen. Hugessen, who acted in this capacity until 1953,[21] to be followed, for the rest of the session, by Sen. Lambert. With the change in the Senate leadership in 1954, the new Leader, Sen. Macdonald, chose as his Deputy Sen. Godbout, the former premier of Quebec, and this arrangement was not changed until 1957, when Sen. Godbout died and was replaced by Sen. Vaillancourt. Under the Conservative Government of 1957–63 the original set-up was disturbed twice; firstly, when Sen. Aseltine, who was Acting Leader under Sen. Haig in 1957, himself became Leader in 1958 and selected Sen. Brunt of Ontario as his Deputy; and the second time, when Sen. Brooks was appointed Leader in 1962 and he chose to rely on the assistance of Sen. Lionel Choquette.

Of course, the fact that the acting Government leader is a personal choice of the leader and his appointment is not a matter of Government policy imposes serious limitations upon his authority and competence. Since he is not a member of the Government, his knowledge of the background of certain pieces of legislation is even more inadequate than the leader's. Thus, when Sen. Belcourt stepped in to represent Sen. Dandurand, who was on an official mission to the League of Nations at Geneva in 1930, Sen. Taylor observed that the situation was "that of the blind leading the blind. He [Belcourt] is a Privy Councillor, in recognition of distinguished service as Speaker of the House of Commons . . . but he cannot know by intuition what are the policies and intentions of the ministers with whom he is not privileged to sit in Council."[22] Again, when Copp, temporarily replacing Robertson during the latter's absence in 1947, was pressed for an explanation of certain features of the Government's policy regarding the controversial Canadian Wheat Board Bill, he could only say: "As you are all aware, I am not very closely allied with the Government and I do not know anything about the inside

[20]Thus, during the closing days of the 1946 session, when circumstances beyond his control made it imperative for Sen. Robertson to be away from Ottawa, the post of acting leader of the Senate was held by Hugessen. "I have asked him," Robertson simply told the House, "to lead the House in my absence." *SD, 1946*, p. 776.

[21]In that year he became the senior partner of his law firm and was unable to look after properly the duties of deputy Government leader.

[22]*SD, 1930*, p. 270.

workings of the Cabinet." Therefore he urged that the bill be referred to a standing committee where all of them would be able to obtain some first-hand information from departmental officials.[23]

In the same way as they choose their leaders, Senators on both sides of the House appoint a whip and, possibly, an assistant whip, from their numbers. Although they could pick anyone, they would usually act upon the recommendation of their leader.[24] The whips, like other office-holders in the Senate, are not subject to annual re-election; they lay down their work only when they die or resign. As a result the number of persons who have acted as Whips in the past twelve years has been small. On the Liberal side, Sen. A. L. Beaubien of Manitoba was elected Chief Government Whip in May 1950 and he remained Liberal Whip after 1958. In 1951 Sen. W. H. Taylor of Ontario was appointed Assistant Government Whip. On the other side, Sen. Quinn of Nova Scotia acted as Conservative Whip from 1954 to 1958, when Sen. White, a newly appointed member of the House, took over the post of Chief Government Whip in the Senate. After his elevation to the Speakership in September 1962, the post went to J. M. Macdonald of Nova Scotia. Although the position is not just honorary, the whips' function in the Senate is not to secure party discipline. The nature of their work is purely organizational; to see to the attendance of party members, to maintain the quorum, to send out party notices (or "whips") about forthcoming business, meetings, etc.,[25] and perhaps to ensure a reasonable turnout of members of their party when important divisions take place, but they can in no way bring party pressure to bear upon their vote; their only weapon is persuasion.[26]

Similarly to the role of the whips in maintaining party discipline, the effectiveness and frequency of party caucuses in the Senate are not comparable to those in the House of Commons. When he assumed leadership in the Senate in 1942, Sen. King said that during the twelve years he had been in the House he had never attended a party caucus.[27] Looking

[23]*Ibid., 1947*, p. 265.

[24]"When I took the leadership I made no change in the Whips. If I desired to make a change in the Whips, I would call a caucus and ask that the change be made. Doubtless such caucus would follow my advice, but if it did not, it is probable I would not continue as Leader." Meighen to Lederle, May 14, 1941. Meighen Papers, series 5.

[25]Here is a sample of such "whips": "Dear Sir: You are requested to attend a meeting of the Conservative members of the Senate, in Committee Room No. 262, at 12 o'clock noon, tomorrow, Wednesday, the 25th instant."

[26]Meighen to Lederle, May 14, 1941. Meighen Papers, series 5. J. W. Lederle, "Party Forms in the Senate," *Queen's Quarterly*, vol. LVII (1950).

[27]*SD, 1942*, p. 148.

back on a greater span of time, Sen. Hardy told the Senate that during the whole of his twenty years' membership in the Chamber he had attended only one caucus and that was the only one held between 1922 and 1942.[28] Speaking for the Conservative party in the Senate, Sen. Calder said that although they had held caucuses more often than the Liberals, the purpose of such meetings was merely "to analyze some of the measures that come before us and to ascertain what our various viewpoints are. It is not for the purpose of having a united party stand one way or the other."[29] Such general purpose meetings are usually held early in the session or on exceptional occasions when some unforeseen event calls for quick action. A good example of this type of caucus was the one held by Liberal Senators on May 6, 1942, following the death of Sen. Dandurand, for the purpose of considering their position and trying "to arrange their affairs so that they might be better advised as to the activities of and the legislation coming from the other House, to the end that our activities should be of greater interest and usefulness."[30]

In addition to caucuses held in the Senate, Senators are cordially invited to joint caucuses with their opposite numbers in the Commons, called by the party leader and held in one of the committee rooms in the Commons. There they sit along with the Commons' members of the party and have a right to speak and to vote if ever a vote is taken. Although on occasion their presence may prove scandalous,[31] the main purpose of their attendance is to get an up-to-date picture of political development within the party and in the country at large. As the late Sen. W. B. Ross used to say, "it is a part of the liberal education to attend a caucus of one's Party, and hear what is said. How can one know the minds of people without that? . . . sometimes we hear folly, and sometimes we hear wisdom, but we have to make the best of it."[32] It appears from the evidence that when Senators do attend joint caucuses it is never for the purpose of receiving instructions with regard to the stand they should take on certain pieces of legislation.[33] Despite the relatively small number of Senators who regularly avail themselves of

[28]*Ibid.*, p. 151. [29]*Ibid.*, p. 148. [30]*Ibid.*, p. 149.

[31]As in one caucus during Bennett's premiership when the Prime Minister became so incensed at the criticism and general rebelliousness of Conservative Senators that he ordered them to get out and stay out. Not until Manion became party leader in 1938 did they return. Quoted in John R. Williams, *The Conservative Party of Canada, 1920–1948* (Durham, NC, 1956), p. 195, n. 9.

[32]*SD, 1926*, p. 414.

[33]Thus, for instance, Liberal Senators maintained that their position regarding the very controversial Bank of Canada bill in 1961 was not decided in concert with Liberal members of the Commons. Interview with Sen. A. K. Hugessen, Dec. 30, 1961.

the opportunity,[34] it seems that the general value attached to attending joint caucuses has increased in recent years. Thus, in 1961, Sen. Croll protested against holding committee meetings on Wednesday mornings, lest they clash with Liberal joint caucuses which are traditionally held on every second Wednesday. "When committee meetings are held," he said, ". . . we are unable to participate in discussion with members of the House of Commons. When that occurs we lose contact with them and misunderstandings result. . . . It is necessary for us to know what goes on. . . . Our highest priority for Wednesday is attendance at the caucus . . ."[35]

Typically, also, pairing as a generally useful device of maintaining party discipline in case of voting is looked upon as something alien to the spirit of the Senate. When following the division on a bill concerning divorce jurisdiction in 1929 Sen. Copp, who had recently been appointed to the Senate, declared that he was paired with Sen. Black but did not know how he would vote on such occasion, he was severely reprimanded by Sen. Daniel for being paired at all in the Senate.[36] Even when pairing is resorted to, it may be arranged, not between two senators belonging to two different parties, but between two members of the same party who know that they each have divergent views on a particular subject. How little importance is attached to pairing in general was well illustrated by the painful experience of Sen. Euler who completely forgot his agreement with Sen. Vaillancourt, a fellow-Liberal, as regards voting on the controversial Exchequer Court bill, May 30, 1956. Vaillancourt, who was touring Europe at the time the division took place in the Senate, learnt the breach of their agreement from reading Hansard. Although his pair subsequently made public apologies, the fact remained that pairing-deals in the Senate are simply not considered important enough to be remembered when the moment in question arrives.

The casualness of formal party organization in the Senate and the evident disregard for disciplinary devices of any kind are, no doubt, among the most characteristic features of the contemporary Senate and their adoption has been largely due to the effectiveness of what might be called the appeal of the Dandurand conception of the Senate. In brief, in his view the Senate was a sort of appendage to the Supreme Court of Canada, manned by politically dispassionate persons acting in

[34]There were approximately twenty Liberal Senators (or 29 per cent of the Liberal strength in the Senate) who can be said to have regularly attended joint caucuses during the 1961 session of Parliament. I owe this information to Mr. A. Fraser, Executive Assistant to the Leader of the Opposition in the Senate.

[35]*SD, 1961*, p. 123.

[36]*Ibid., 1929*, pp. 376–7.

a quasi-judicial capacity. Although an out-and-out politician and a lifelong Liberal, one of Laurier's chief lieutenants, and one of Mackenzie King's most confidential advisers,[37] Dandurand had never been a member of the House of Commons, and, therefore, he was not imbued with the mentality of an almost mechanical self-subordination to a parliamentary party machine as were former members of the Commons who had been elevated to the Senate after long years of service in the Lower House. He was 37 years old when he was summoned to the Senate in 1898 and he was 81 years of age when he died in 1942 as probably the most distinguished member in the whole history of his beloved Chamber. Between 1922, when he became Government leader, and the time of his death he completely dominated the House, and his personality, his views, and the manner of his leadership have become identified with the best features of the Senate. In his image of the Upper House as a body of independent-minded elder statesmen coolly exercising judicial impartiality there was no room for any formal party machinery, which would only accentuate a spirit that ought to be extirpated by all means. In a letter to Sen. Lambert shortly before his death, he confessed that in order to bring the Senate to his point of view he had thought "that an ideal Canadian Upper House should have no official Government Leader and that each minister at the head of a department should confide his bills when they reach the Senate to a member of his choice, to pilot them through. The Senators would no more sit in two separate groups, one to the right and the other to the left of the Speaker, so as not to be divided on party lines."[38] He laid down his policies when he was appointed Senate Leader in the early twenties by assuring his colleagues that he refused to lead a ministerial party in the House, that he claimed no followers, and that he shunned party discipline and the party whip. To provide a good example, he had attended only one joint caucus after his appointment as Senate leader and had asked the Whips in the House of Commons not to send notices to Senators to attend caucuses, because he preferred that members of the Upper House should remain away from the political atmosphere of the Commons.[39] In his crusade against all semblance of partisanship in the Senate he cut short any reference to such traditional terms as Government leader, Opposition leader, backbencher, etc.[40] He greeted newcomers in the Senate not as party-men

[37]For the relationship between the two and Mackenzie King's affection for Dandurand, see J. W. Pickersgill, *The Mackenzie King Record.* I, *1939–44* (Toronto, 1960), pp. 8; 92; 290–1; 361. Also *SD*, *1942*, pp. 47 and 102.

[38]*SD*, *1955*, p. 507. Similar views are expressed in his memoirs, a closed paper deposited in the Public Archives, Ottawa.

[39]*Ibid.*, *1926*, p. 412.

[40]*Ibid.*, *1926*, p. 366, 372.

but as "co-workers" and only recognized the existence of two trends of thought, "a Conservative trend and a Liberal trend, which must necessarily appear in our discussions; but here there is not, as there is in the House of Commons, what is referred to as His Majesty's loyal opposition."[41] Indeed, he refrained during the years when he was Senate Leader from calling his opposite number "the Leader of the Opposition," and went so far in this respect that after the Liberal victory at the polls in 1921 he suggested to Sir James Lougheed that he should remain on the right of the Speaker where he sat before, for he could not see "that we of the Senate ought to take notice of the change occurring" in the other House.[42]

There was so much élan and genuine sincerity in his efforts to purify the Senate of all aspects of party organization that no one could quite remove oneself from the impact of the Dandurand image. Thus, Sir Allen Aylesworth, one-time Minister of Justice, favoured the statutory disfranchisement of Senators,[43] and, even if for different reasons, Meighen himself became a convert to Dandurand's views soon after he was appointed Government Leader in 1932. Dandurand liked to relate of their first meeting in the Senate, when Meighen greeted him jubilantly, and said: "Here is my opponent. I hope I am worthy of his steel." To which Dandurand replied: "My friend, you are wrong on two counts. I am not your opponent, and I am not worthy of your steel."[44] As a matter of fact, Dandurand had been expecting for years the appointment of Sir Robert Borden. Faced now with a much more vigorous and more aggressive former prime minister, he warned Meighen that

> impulsiveness does not avail us to any extent in this Chamber, because as my right hon. friend will quickly observe, there is really no opposition here; there is no standing opposition to government measures. In other words, we are collaborators in the work of the Senate, and we are that by reason of the fact that we are appointed for life, are independent of electors, and have not to consider any constituency as a special unit from which we hold a mandate . . .[45]

In turn, Meighen promised he would "make an honest effort to escape from that atmosphere of the House of Commons and to acquire, even more than in the past, the habit of addressing myself to the question instead of to the public at large."[46] Indeed, he turned down invitations

[41] *Ibid., 1930* (2nd session), p. 61. [42] *Ibid.* [43] *Ibid., 1950*, p. 503.
[44] Sen. Lambert's recollections. *Ibid., 1951*, p. 149.
[45] *Ibid., 1932*, p. 6.
[46] *Ibid.*, p. 10. He also wrote to Lederle that "I have sought, since entering the Senate . . . to remove party ties to the utmost."

to caucuses in the House of Commons[47] and although he was member of the cabinet from 1932 to 1935 he made no pretence of attending Council meetings regularly, and made it plain in the Senate that he did not take the constitutional responsibility of cabinet membership with the same seriousness as if he had been a minister in the Commons.[48] Following in Dandurand's footsteps he developed the practice of utilizing caucuses in the Senate as little as possible.[49] When he summed up his ideas about the Senate in an article in the *Queen's Quarterly* in 1937, it sounded exactly like Dandurand:

> The Senate is worthless if it becomes merely another Commons divided upon party lines and indulging in party debates. . . . Members of the Second Chambers must get away, lift their minds far from those hard-drawn lines of party, or they cannot serve their country. They have to make up their minds to give every government fair play and not to stand in the way of legislation unless they are convinced it must be defeated on its merits, and that the consequences of failure to defeat it would be serious; nor to stand stubbornly in the path of any government unless it is brought there in their judgment to serve the ends of party by largess in this or some other part of the dominion rather than the true interests of the nation.[50]

The views of Meighen and Dandurand regarding partisanship and party organization in the Senate provided a useful rationalization for a practice that had always been, to varying degrees, part of the operative principles of the Senate. Conversely, they have played an important role in shaping the attitude of incoming generations, by helping them be adjusted to the established norms of the House and trimming, when necessary, the more glaring excrescences of their partisan past.

All other elements of a formal party machinery reduced to virtual

[47]"I receive regularly invitations to Caucus, but, as you know, have always made it a practice, since assuming Senate Leadership, not to attend Caucus." Letter to A. C. Casselman, MP, June 4, 1940. Meighen Papers, series 5, no. 47.

[48]To J. Lederle, May 14, 1941. *Ibid.*, series 5. See also Roger Graham, *Arthur Meighen*, vol. 3 (Toronto-Vancouver, 1965), pp. 30, 76.

[49]"These I call very rarely and mainly for the purpose of explaining the stand I contemplate taking and having it discussed. At each of these caucuses I make it plain that support of my stand should be based on its merits only and not on mere party affiliation." *Ibid.* When it was charged in 1938 that the fate of the Penitentiary bill, which was negatived on third reading, had been decided in a Conservative caucus, Meighen said that they "do not bother much about caucuses. . . . The rule is about this, that a caucus is called only when it becomes apparent that hon. gentlemen around me are not able to understand what I am doing." In respect of the bill in question he said that "we met only once this session, and the only subject discussed was the Transport bill of the Government, which has been passed." *SD, 1938*, p. 602. Referring to the practice under Meighen, Haig said: "True there are caucuses and I have had the pleasure of attending some of them, but I have never been asked to follow the caucus either for or against a measure." *SD, 1940*, p. 443 .

[50]"The Canadian Senate," *Queen's Quarterly* (1937), pp. 159–60.

nonexistence, the brunt of organization is borne by the two leaders of the Senate, of whom the representative of the Government is clearly the more important. In order that he may be able to perform his duties efficiently, the Government leader has to be familiar with the Government's policy and progress in all particulars. Therefore, he may have to attend cabinet meetings not only during the session but during parliamentary recess as well. In addition to the general aspects of Government policy, he has to be familiar with the background and the objectives of each particular bill that emanates from the various departments and comes before the Senate. In modern times, it is expected that the Government leader should develop a special interest in international problems and be a spokesman for the Government in the Senate with regard to the foreign policy of the country. He has to confer with the chairmen of the various committees and the Chief Clerk of Committees in arranging for committee meetings and deciding on the number and type of witnesses to be invited to such meetings. He has to consult with the leader of the other side in regard to the conduct of business from day to day. And on top of all this, being the sole official liaison between the Senate and government departments, it is his responsibility to obtain from the appropriate departments the answers to inquiries made in the Chamber. And on top of all this, being an important official liaison between the Senate and government departments, it is his responsibility to obtain from the appropriate departments the answers to inquiries made in the Chamber.

Despite their multifarious activities, it was not until 1946 that the Government leader and the leader of the Opposition were provided secretarial help.[51] Also, under mounting pressure from a number of influential members of the Senate,[52] the Government finally decided in 1947 to introduce a bill to amend the Senate and House of Commons Act to provide, for the first time, statutory recognition of the positions of Government leader and Opposition leader in the Senate. The resolution, introduced by King, read: "that it is expedient . . . to provide an additional annual allowance to the member of the Senate occupying the recognized position of leader of the Government in the Senate [$7,000] and the member occupying the recognized position of Leader of the Opposition in the Senate [$4,000]."[53]

[51]Thus, Meighen wrote to H. A. Stewart, Minister of Public Works in 1932: "On taking over the Leader's office in the Senate I find there is no accommodation for a secretary . . . At the present time, between answering the door, the telephone, and people walking in on me, I can't get my work done." Meighen Papers, series 5, no. 221.

[52]See in particular, the speeches of Senators Bench and Euler. *SD, 1945*, pp. 42, 291.

[53]*HD, 1947*, p. 5266.

Important though these provisions were, they offered no panacea for the inability of the Government leader to lay before the Senate an adequate volume of information respecting public legislation. It is highly unlikely that any single individual can amass all the details of the few dozen bills that come annually before the Senate. Even Dandurand and Meighen, despite their extraordinary skill, experience, and brilliance, suffered from the same handicap. Commenting upon the Government leader's anomalous position, Sen. Lemieux, former Speaker of the House of Commons, said: "Of course the hon. gentleman has great moral authority, but it has happened . . . that with all his imagination and all his ability he could not answer some questions that were put to him, because he had not been informed of the views of the Government in regard to certain legislation."[54] All that a Government leader can do in such a case is to promise to make enquiries and to bring their results to the Senate. But that throws, as Sir George Foster used to say, a "wet blanket over the whole discussion." Were an answer to the question available at the time, it would be a great advantage. As the information is usually not forthcoming for several days, when it is obtained it is frequently found inadequate, and in the meantime most of the interest in the discussion has been lost. Another inevitable result of the absurdity of the Government leader's position is an increasingly heavy reliance upon sketchy briefs submitted to him by the departments. To parry criticisms for basing his entire explanation of the important National Harbours bill of 1936 on a single memorandum from the department, Dandurand confessed "that it is difficult, and that at times I have had to work 18 hours a day in order to digest the data placed before me, I must apologize if occasionally I have had to make use of memoranda in the form in which they reached me from these departments."[55] Meighen himself was in no better position during the four years when he was Government leader from 1932 to 1935. Despite his great intellectual power he was often unable to provide satisfactory explanation for technically involved legislation. When, for example, the Fisheries bill of 1932, a consolidating measure along the lines laid down by the Privy Council in a judgment given the previous year, was considered in committee, proceedings had to be suspended because the Government leader simply could not answer certain vital questions and there was no one available from the department to clarify the disputed clauses.[56] Meighen found himself in a particularly hopeless situation when he was expected to explain a number of bills that reached him about the same time. Thus, he could not satisfy certain queries in 1932 concerning the estimated

[54]*SD, 1931*, p. 144. [55]*Ibid., 1936*, p. 376. [56]*Ibid., 1932*, p. 455.

cost of remissions in the highly complex Soldier Settlement bill, for the simple reason that a most exhaustive analysis of the bill had reached him five minutes before he entered the Senate Chamber. "The data furnished me," he apologized, "err on the side of being too voluminous. They would have been very appropriate earlier in the session, when it was not necessary to absorb a dozen Bills in a single day."[57] He had no illusions of the absolutely impractical task of the Government leader in the Senate and he was perfectly aware of the paralysing effects of his position upon the performance of the Senate as a whole. He knew that the long and arduous journey of a bill "necessitates on the part of the person guiding it a thorough command not only of the history of legislation on the subject treated, but of the details of the particular measure under consideration. . . ." He suggested that "while the burden of guiding Government legislation continues to rest upon the single member of the Government in this Chamber, it is not possible to increase very greatly . . . the volume of Government measures introduced here."[58]

In order to remedy this situation, various devices had been suggested and tried from time to time, the most important being the arrangement under which departmental officials had been invited to the Senate floor at the committee stage to explain the technical clauses of legislation. This device was particularly popular in the 1920's and '30's when bills were still fairly regularly discussed in Committee of the Whole. Both Dandurand and Willoughby had frequently availed themselves of this opportunity and gave practically a free hand to departmental experts in furnishing the necessary information.[59] On occasion direct interviews have been arranged between members of the Senate and departmental officials to argue out certain complicated aspects of a bill which the Government Leader was unable to explain.[60] However, all through this period, extending from 1925 to 1942, Senators on the whole were preoccupied with the question of cabinet representation in the Senate. Instead of

[57]*Ibid., 1933*, p. 486. [58]*Ibid., 1934*, p. 254.

[59]See, e.g., Varcoe of the Dept. of Justice on the Bankruptcy bill, 1925; Taylor of the Dept. of National Revenue on the Export bill, 1930; Deputy Minister Scammell on the Pension bill, 1931, etc. In the last mentioned case, Willoughby said: "if hon. gentlemen want any detailed information that is not in my possession, I shall ask the Deputy to take a seat on the floor." *Ibid., 1931*, p. 458.

[60]In 1931, for example, Sen. Graham, former Minister of Railways, raised certain doubts with regard to the bill to amend the Customs Act. The section he opposed was left standing, as Willoughby could not answer the questions, nor was there anybody on hand to satisfy Graham. On the following morning, however, an interview was arranged between him and Blair, an official of the sponsoring department. "He was so honest in his contention about this bill," Graham later said, "and gave such an explanation of it . . . that I will not oppose it further." *Ibid.*, p. 471.

utilizing to the greatest extent possible within the Senate the latent talents of its membership, it was expected that the right answer to the problem lay in an increased number of ministers in the Senate. Since this was not in harmony with the general trend of constitutional development, arguments tended to be academic and proposals to be impractical. The idea that the duties of government leadership in the Senate should be decentralized received only tentative recognition during these days. In 1934, Sen. McLennan suggested that the responsibility of the Government leader to familiarize himself with every piece of legislation should be evenly distributed amongst the chairmen of the various standing committees and even perhaps some other selected members. "In that way," he thought, "the Leader of the House would be spared a great deal of work . . . if such assignments were made to lieutenants . . . the result would be notable improvement over the handling of all Government measures exclusively by the Leader, however able he may be."[61] Yet, typically, his suggestion was not considered practical enough. And herein lay perhaps the most serious defect of the combined leadership of Dandurand and Meighen. If on rare occasions a few members of the Senate were assigned the task of introducing and piloting Government legislation in the Senate, it was the exception rather than the rule.[62] Although both knew that the job was superhuman in its proportions, they nevertheless persisted in performing it alone. The Senate has never had two more distinguished men for the positions of Government leader and Opposition leader at one and the same time in its history. However, their very ambition and energy detracted from the effectiveness of the Senate as a body of legislators. Dandurand made it a sport of explaining a bill about the subject-matter of which he knew virtually nothing, yet proving to everybody that it was all right. Meighen, who, as a matter of fact, was a very close friend of his, enjoyed baiting him only to watch how he would respond. Senators sitting opposite Meighen could see "the smile that came over his face as Sen. Dandurand dealt so adroitly with every question that arose" from the higher intricacies of insurance to the economy of internal combustion engines.[63] But Meighen himself was no better. Indeed, if he was a failure as national party leader, he was a double failure as Leader of the Senate. It was precisely for the reputed

[61]*Ibid., 1934*, p. 161.

[62]In 1929 Bureau, former Minister of Customs, took care of the Precious Metals bill; similarly Dandurand let Graham handle some of the railway legislation and in 1939, when he was 78 years old, he allowed Marshall to explain such agricultural bills as the Grain bill, the Grain Futures bill, the Prairie Farm Assistance bill, the Wheat Board bill, or the Wheat Co-operative Marketing bill.

[63]*SD, 1957–58*, p. 209.

qualities of his genius that he was totally unsuited to that post. The sharpness of his mind as well as his tongue, his feared wit, his occasional impatience and aggressiveness, his accentuated vigour, and deadly punctuality separated him from the rest of the House. In sum, he was too intelligent for the Senate, as, indeed, perhaps, for politics in general. He was warned as a relative newcomer to the Senate that he was possibly not acquainted with its tone and temper and he was emphatically urged "to disabuse his mind of the idea that he is a sort of censor and schoolmaster of this assembly, entitled to dictate to us as to the course we are to follow or the sort of speeches we are to make."[64] Due to his failure to realize that although all the members of the Senate were probably not equal in ability they were all equal in status, Meighen was highly respected and deeply disliked by his colleagues.

The refusal of the two leaders to delegate some of their authority resulted in reducing their followers to a group of silent spectators of a drama of which the two main characters were the Leader of the Government and the Leader of the Opposition. Discussion in the Senate was practically limited to dialogues between the two, with the rest of the Senate sitting "around cooling our heels, for very seldom did we get a chance to participate in debate."[65] The result was not only a low level of general activity, as we have seen in the previous chapter,[66] but a lack of genuine comradeship and effective co-operation. Therefore, it was befitting, in a sense, that Dandurand's death and Meighen's resignation should occur in the same year. Their departure in 1942 marked the end of a whole era in the modern history of the Senate—the period of centralized one-man leadership. Their successors, King, Robertson, and Macdonald on the one hand, and Ballantyne, Haig, Aseltine, and Brooks on the other, could hardly be compared to them either in terms of parliamentary experience and general stature or in intellectual brilliance. But perhaps because of this, they have been more efficient and under their leadership the Senate has accomplished more through joint effort than when it was ruled by statesmen.

In view of the limited scope of parliamentary activity during the war, Sen. King had little opportunity for making substantial innovations in

[64] *Ibid., 1933*, p. 249.

[65] Sen. Farris recalled that on one occasion, at least, he could no longer resist the temptation and rose to deliver a severe criticism of Meighen. "I was sitting," he later recalled, "right behind my leader, Sen. Dandurand, and was very conscious of the way in which he looked around and glared at me. It was not a popular thing for me to do; however, I got away with it." *SD, 1957–58*, p. 209. See also Sen. Hardy's remarks in *ibid., 1945*, p. 297.

[66] P. 77.

the conduct of legislation in the Senate. Nevertheless, by originating the practice of referring the Estimates to standing committees *before* they actually reached the House, he made a small yet important step in taking off part of the Government leader's responsibilities of preparing explanations about highly involved pieces of legislation.

The first major attempt to diffuse leadership in the Senate came with the appointment of Sen. Robertson as Government leader in 1945. Young (fifty-four) and lacking in experience (he had only two years' experience in the Senate when he became Leader), he was all too conscious of the vulnerability of his position in a group of men most of whom were his seniors in years as well as in parliamentary experience.[67] Therefore, he felt impelled to decentralize his legislative functions, by delegating the task of introducing, explaining, and piloting bills in the Senate to practically anybody who indicated that he wished to do so. As a result, in the first year out of a total of thirty-nine public bills that came before the Senate he assigned the handling of twenty to thirteen Liberal Senators. This tactic enabled him to achieve two objectives; first, it relieved him of the monstrous task of preparation in regard to every piece of legislation before the Senate, thus giving him more time for general organization and committee work; second, and even more important, it enlarged the circle of Senators who became involved and actively interested in legislation, which, conversely, greatly improved the general state of vitality and competence of the body as a whole. All the thirteen Senators who formed the first group to father half the legislative crop of the 1945 session[68] took their job seriously and felt honoured for being selected to explain and defend legislation before the House. In his survey for the most suitable persons, Robertson was only guided by one consideration, that is, to find those who through their legislative interest, training, and general willingness to work seemed most deserving of a share in the leadership of the Senate. Thus, the choice fell upon MacLennan to explain the Fishery Inspection bill because "he is keenly interested in matters of this kind,"[69] whereas Buchanan was picked for the Dominion-Alberta Supplementary Taxation Agreement bill because he was one of the Alberta Senators and it was felt only fair to let the representative sponsor a bill affecting his section.

[67]"I realize that I am surrounded by men of great and long experience. They have been most forbearing with regard to the sins of omission and commission which, due to inexperience, I have undoubtedly committed." *SD, 1946*, p. 776.

[68]Farris introduced four; Campbell, three; Buchanan and Mrs. Wilson, two each; and Hayden, Bench, Roebuck, Paterson, MacLennan, Vaillancourt, Kinley, Bishop, and McGeer, one each.

[69]*SD, 1945*, p. 354.

Robertson's method of decentralized leadership proved a success. In the following year the percentage of bills distributed for introduction grew from 50 to 59 per cent, whilst the size of the group activized through the process, from 27 to 36 per cent. By 1950 the practice had become so well established that only one Senator in a group of twelve considered it a privilege being asked to introduce legislation.[70] As Table XIV

TABLE XIV

Distribution of Government Legislation for Introduction in the Senate, 1945–1963

Government leader	Session	Total no. of bills	Assigned for introduction		Rate of activization	
			No.	%	No.	%
Robertson	1945	39	20	50	13	27
"	1946	77	46	59	23	36
"*	1947	78	55	71	22	32
"	1948	78	34	43	15	23
"	1949[1]	27	15	56	13	20
"	1949[2]	43	31	71	16	22
"	1950	55	30	55	12	16
"	1951	65	58	91	22	29
"	1952	56	35	63	15	19
"	1953	56	41	73	20	26
Macdonald	1954	67	41	67	23	29
"	1955	60	42	66	29	38
"	1956	50	32	64	18	23
"	1957	42	25	60	17	21
Haig	1957–58	32	16	50	7	43
Aseltine	1958	44	30	68	13	83
"	1959	56	37	66	11	63
"	1960	48	38	79	15	71
"	1961	66	53	80	17	71
"	1962	27	21	77	14	59
Brooks	1962–63	18	13	71	9	25

*Thirteen bills were introduced by Sen. Copp, Acting Government Leader, during Robertson's illness.

indicates, the practice was continued under successive leaders, whether Liberal or Conservative, with the result that approximately two-thirds of the total amount of legislation between 1945 and 1963 was handled by individual members of the Senate. Although there is little use of making comparisons because of the divergent size of the Liberal and Conservative groups in the Senate, it may be noted that while during the nine years of Robertson's leadership the average rate of activization was 25 per cent, it was 28 per cent under Sen. Macdonald, 43 per cent

[70]Before the opening his explanatory remarks on the Prairie Farm Assistance bill, Sen. Gershaw wished "to thank the hon. leader for asking me to move the second reading of this bill and explain the . . . amendments it contains." *Ibid., 1950*, p. 480.

under Sen. Haig, 69 per cent when Sen. Aseltine was Government leader in the Senate, and 25 per cent during the short period of leadership of Sen. Brooks. The figures since 1958 suggest that during the years 1958–63 the great majority of Conservative Senators took an active part in carrying the burden of legislative leadership.

The new system has also enabled many Senators to develop a continued pattern of interest and become specialized in certain subjects of legislation. Under the Liberal regime till 1958 Sen. Hayden and later Sen. Connolly enjoyed a virtual monopoly over annual income tax legislation as well as bills affecting customs, customs tariff, and excise. Hayden achieved such a mastery of explaining complicated and dull income tax measures in a lucid and fascinating manner that he was warmly applauded on several occasions.[71] In a similar way, Sen. Crerar specialized in legislation dealing with natural resources and agriculture in general, Senators Lambert and Pratt in treaties and legislation implementing international trade and tax conventions; Sen. Burchill displayed a special interest in the broad field of railway and transportation as well as pensions and veteran affairs, Sen. Roebuck in legislation concerning citizenship, Senators Hugessen and Farris in bills relating to the Criminal Code, the Supreme Court of Canada, and the judiciary in general, Sen. Kinley in measures doing with the merchant marine, Sen. Reid in fisheries legislation, Sen. Bradette in mining, while doctors like Gershaw and Veniot in bills respecting disabled persons, narcotic drugs, and similar matters. Although the period 1958–63 had been too short to enable us to establish any clearly definable patterns amongst Conservative Senators, it was possible to see developing lines of interest. Accordingly, the important field of taxation and tariff legislation, once dominated by Hayden and Connolly, came under the able command of Senators Thorvaldson and Choquette; Sen. Pearson consistently sponsored agricultural measures; Senators Brooks and Gladstone have looked after legislation affecting veterans and Indians, respectively, while the early doctor appointee of the Diefenbaker regime, Sen. Sullivan, has inherited from his Liberal colleagues the field of disabled persons and old age assistance legislation.

Thus, what used to be the exception under the glittering management of Dandurand and Meighen, has become the rule under the "administrator leaders" since 1945. Co-operation and collective leadership have replaced a system based upon the spectacular one-man show. In the changed circumstances artificial solutions, such as the assignment of

[71]Sen. Robertson pointed out that he had always entrusted "the mysteries of finance to [Hayden] and his explanations have always been crystal clear." *Ibid., 1951* (2nd session), p. 23.

parliamentary secretaries to the Upper House, have lost much of their earlier attractiveness. The Senate no longer needs parliamentary assistants; the individual members of the House act as so many parliamentary assistants to their leader. In this way all have benefited from the new conception of Senate leadership, which has produced an increased sense of responsibility and usefulness.

2. *The Representation of the Cabinet in the Senate*

The question of delegating some of the functions of the Government leader to his colleagues for the purpose of a more adequate handling of legislation in the Senate is only one of the problems of Senate leadership. The other, although only loosely connected with actual party organization, is the number of ministers who hold their seats in the Upper House. To complete the picture of the organization of party forces, therefore, it seems necessary to review briefly the extent to which the cabinet has been represented in the Senate.

Historically, the trend of cabinet representation in the Senate has shown a downward tendency and, unlike the United Kingdom,[72] no constitutional practice has developed in Canada to preserve a few posts in the Government for the Upper House. The result has been dismal; while at one point under the first Administration after Confederation there were five cabinet ministers in the Senate,[73] for a long time under the

[72]Cf. P. Bromhead, The House of Lords and Contemporary Politics (London, 1958), chap. VI.

[73]J. C. Aikins, Senator, October 23, 1867 to May 30, 1882, Minister without Portfolio November 16 to December 7, 1869, then Secretary of State till the end of the government in 1873.

A. J. F. Blair, Senator October 23 to December 29, 1867 and President of the Council July 1 to December 29, 1867.

Alexander Campbell, Senator October 23, 1867 to February 7, 1887, Postmaster-General July 1, 1867 to June 30, 1873, then Minister of the Interior and Superintendent-General of Indian Affairs till the end of the government.

J. C. Chapais, Senator January 30, 1868 till 1885, Minister of Agriculture July 1, 1867 to November 15, 1869, then Receiver General till January 29, 1873.

E. Kenny, Senator October 23, 1867 to April 21, 1876, Receiver General July 1, 1867 to November 15, 1869, then President of the Council till June 20, 1870.

P. Mitchell, Senator October 23, 1867 to July 12, 1872 and Minister of Marine and Fisheries July 1, 1867, till the end of the government in 1873.

Thus, for most of the period of the first Government there were four Ministers in the Senate, while between November 16, 1869, and June 20, 1870, there were five. Save Aikins, November 16 to December 7, 1869, all Senators in the Government held portfolios.

I am obliged to Dr. E. A. Forsey for drawing my attention to this list.

eighteenth there was none. The pattern set in 1878 of having at least three cabinet ministers in the Senate[74] lasted only until 1896. After the Laurier Government came into office that year usually one, and occasionally two, members of the Senate held a seat in the cabinet. The situation further deteriorated under Borden who appointed no department head from the Senate. This practice, apart from a short interval in 1921, when there were once again three ministers in the Senate,[75] survived into the years after the Great War and received a constitutional nod from Mackenzie King.

As a result, during the period of thirty-seven years under study there have been only five persons in the Senate's membership who had a portfolio. The first two owed their posts to the turbulent political situation following the election of 1925. Although the public was told before the election that there would be no portfolio in the Senate, the predicament in which the Government was involved, as the result of the election, made it advisable not to act upon that particular announcement.[76] Consequently, both Sen. Murphy and Sen. Béland, who were summoned to the Senate in 1925, retained their portfolios as Postmaster General and Minister of Soldiers' Civil Re-establishment, respectively, and Murphy was also acting minister of a few other departments from the time of the 1925 election until the Government's defeat in the House of Commons in June 1926.[77] His appointment to the Senate and the fact that he was allowed to retain his department found approval and satisfaction with a number of leading figures of the Senate. Referring to the unwise crusade of the Government against the Senate, Sir Allen Aylesworth was hopeful

[74]In that year the Speaker of the Senate, Sen. Wilmot, was made for the first time since 1867 a cabinet minister. Cf. A. Todd, *Parliamentary Government in the British Colonies* (London, 1894), pp. 48–9. As for holding the two positions at the same time, Wilmot was not the only case. Thus, Sir David Lewis Macpherson was sworn of the Privy Council Feb. 11, 1880 (as a Senator), was Speaker of the Senate from Feb. 11 to Feb. 15, 1880, then again from April 19, 1880, to Oct. 15, 1883, and Minister without Portfolio from Feb. 11, 1880 to Oct. 16, 1883; he attended Council. I owe this information to Prof. J. R. Mallory.

[75]G. Robertson (Labour); Sir J. Lougheed (Interior); P. Blondin (Postmaster Gen.).

[76]Murphy to Mrs. H. D. Petrie, Jan. 22, 1927. Murphy papers, vol. 25, no. 10616; and to W. J. Donovan, Sept. 3, 1926. *Ibid.*, vol. 8, no. 2992.

[77]This is how Murphy himself described to Sir Allen Aylesworth the circumstances of his appointment: "The only conversation that took place between the Premier and myself on the subject occurred a short time prior to our going to Richmond Hill. . . . I indicated how the change could be made from the House to the Senate in my case, and I added the portfolio was at the disposal of the Prime Minister . . . I also said that if he so desired he could have it then, or at any other time that would suit his wishes. He thanked me and asked that matters remain as they were, until after the election. . . ." *Ibid.*, vol. 1, no. 339 (Oct. 9, 1925).

that "with you in the Senate—sitting there as a Cabinet Minister—there might be less hostility to the Government. There has always—till now—been a Minister, with Portfolio, in the Senate . . . and I think there ought to be at least one. . . . It seems to me such a fatuous policy, to antagonize the Senate. It is, after all, one of the two Houses of Parliament. . . ."[78] However, it was obvious that the arrangement was merely temporary and with the return to normalcy the portfolio in question would also be returned to a member of the House of Commons. Indeed, King repeated his statement that he did not desire to have any portfolio in the Senate.[79] Consequently, as soon as he became head of the new Liberal Government in 1926, he caused the replacement of both Murphy (who was succeeded by P. Veniot as Postmaster General) and Béland (who was succeeded by J. H. King as Minister of Soldiers' Civil Re-establishment), in spite of the strong representation from Murphy himself[80] and the vehement protests of English-speaking Catholics from all parts of the country, who interpreted the withdrawal of Murphy's portfolio as an indication of the Government's hostility towards them.[81]

The next, and, no doubt, most significant, precedent since 1925 for seating the head of a major department in the Senate came with the constitutionally bold, and politically desperate, move of Prime Minister

[78]Aylesworth to Murphy, Oct. 8, 1925. Ibid., nos. 336–38.

[79]Murphy to Dr. J. Barrett, Sept. 23, 1926. Ibid., vol. 2, nos. 437–8.

[80]"Dealing with the statement that you preferred not to have Ministers in the Senate holding portfolios, I point out that the contrary had been the practice since Confederation, and that as a co-ordinate branch of Parliament, the Senate was always regarded as being entitled to have one or more members of the Government of the day holding portfolios." Murphy to King, Sept. 18, 1926. *Ibid.*, vol. 15, nos. 6051–2.

He also wrote to H. Field, Sept. 23, 1926: "This new and inexplicable move is calculated to dwarf the usefulness of the Senate and give the public generally a completely false notion of its proper function. . . . Unfortunately, the real foundations on which our constitution was built are lost sight of in these days of . . . surface thinking. . . ." *Ibid.*, vol. 9, no. 3902.

[81]See especially the voluminous correspondence between Murphy and J. J. Leddy in 1926. *Ibid.*, vol. 16. The intensity of Catholic reaction to the Prime Minister's publicized decision can be measured from the following excerpt from a letter written by Bishop M. F. Fallon of London to Mackenzie King, Sept. 17, 1926: "As I scan the list of the members-elect I can find no man who I consider worthy to be the representative of the Irish, that is of the English-speaking Catholic Liberals . . . In the circumstances we must turn to the Senate for a Cabinet representative. I know full well the prejudice that now exists against a Cabinet Minister sitting in the Senate. I have never been able to understand the prejudice. It is a departure from the custom of other days, and a departure that I have always regretted. I can understand an argument for the abolition of the Senate. But I cannot understand the existence of an amended and reformed Senate where a Cabinet Minister may not find an appropriate place." *Ibid.*, vol. 9, nos. 3617–18.

Bennett to appoint in 1930 Sen. Gideon Robertson as Minister of Labour —a portfolio which he held 1918–21 and which assumed particular importance during the time of the economic crisis. The decision was severely criticized in the House of Commons as undemocratic[82] and as a violation of the principles of responsible parliamentary government.[83] It was hailed on both sides of the Senate as an attempt, long overdue, to restore to the house "the dignity of the presence there of a member of the Cabinet in full charge of a department and with full responsibility, and having the close connection with ministerial affairs that comes only to those who have full charge of a department and sit regularly with their colleagues of the Government."[84] Robertson's record of the first year as Minister of Labour suggests that he was probably not worse than anyone else might have been under the circumstances. His achievements were defended in the House of Commons by Mr. Bennett, who stated on the closing day of the 1931 session that ". . . the onerous duties of the Minister of Labour have been discharged by the present incumbent of that office with such satisfaction to his country and such credit to himself and the Government" and that he was not willing to yield to the demands of the Opposition that Sen. Robertson should be replaced by an elected representative of the people.[85] As a result, Robertson continued as Minister of Labour during the rest of the year and for a short while in 1932. Then, exhausted by the duties of his office, he tendered his resignation on February 3, 1932, only a few days before the opening of the parliamentary session of that year.

What is of special interest for us is the fact that Sen. Robertson's appointment as Minister of Labour resulted in dividing the task of representing the Government, and, consequently, the leadership, in the Senate between himself and the official Leader of the Senate, Sen. Willoughby. Although Willoughby assured the House that the situation met with his entire approval he emphasized that as far as the leadership of the Senate was concerned it "will rest with me as representing the Government in this House and representing the House to the Government." And he added significantly: "In this position I shall have to take a share of the responsibility *even for the declarations of my Hon. friend*

[82]See St. Père's remarks, April 16, 1931. *HD*, p. 652.
[83]See King's remarks, *Ibid.*, p. 2708.
[84]*SD*, *1930*, (2nd session). p. 4. Murphy sent the following letter to Mr. Bennett, August 9, 1930: "Congratulations upon reviving the practice followed by every Administration since Confederation, save one, by giving a portfolio in your Cabinet to Sen. Robertson. This will help to restore the prestige of the Senate and regain for it the public confidence which, as a co-ordinate branch of Parliament, it should enjoy." Murphy Papers, vol. 3, no. 939.
[85]*HD*, *1931*, p. 4523.

on behalf of the Government, for while he will be accountable to it, I shall be accountable to this House; and in that respect I will not shirk my responsibility."[86] However, this proved to be little more than wishful thinking and in practice the actual leadership of the Senate shifted to a large extent from the Government Leader, who was not a member of the Government, to the man who stood at the head of the Department of Labour. Thus, all the important measures which formed part of the legislative program of the Government in 1930–31 were introduced, explained on second reading and piloted through the House by Sen. Robertson without any apparent assistance from the Leader of the Government. This seemed to establish the rule that in terms of actual leadership the Leader of the Senate will be forced into the background if there is in the Senate a full-fledged minister of the Crown as head of a government department. It is a matter of regret, therefore, that Sen. Robertson resigned in 1932, and no minister with a portfolio was sitting in the Senate during the period of Meighen's leadership; it might have been interesting to see how the relationship between the two with regard to practical leadership in the House would have developed.

Sen. Robertson's was the last important case of a member of the Senate holding an influential portfolio in the Cabinet. After his resignation some even thought that this was the last time that the Senate would have even a minister with a portfolio amongst its members.[87] Although this was not to be the case, the assignment of Sen. Macdonald to the combined office of Senate Leader and Solicitor General—a portfolio which he held from January 12, 1954, to the end of the St. Laurent Administration in 1957—could hardly be compared in importance to Robertson's position as Minister of Labour. Similarly, the appointment of Sen. McCutcheon, who was previously Minister without Portfolio, as Minister of Trade and Commerce following the defeat of the Diefenbaker Government in the House of Commons and the resignation of some of the members of the cabinet in February 1963 was in the nature of an emergency device and covered the brief period between dissolution of Parliament and the next general elections.

Apart from these five cases, none of them, except Sen. Macdonald's, extended over a year, the only form of representing the cabinet in the Senate has been by means of ministers without portfolio. It has been conventional to appoint the Government leader in the Senate as a minister without portfolio, so as to enable him to be better acquainted with the policy of the Government through attending proceedings in

[86] *SD, 1930*, pp. 10–11. Italics added.
[87] Sen. Aylesworth's remarks. *SD, 1934*, p. 162.

Council. Indeed, five Government leaders of the Senate during the last thirty-seven years bore the title of Minister without Portfolio. Dandurand was so appointed on December 19, 1921, and he held that post whenever his party was in power until he died in 1942. He was a constant attender of cabinet meetings and was even invited to the War Committee of the Cabinet, where his wide knowledge of international affairs and his strong sense of practical reality were given ample scope of usefulness.[88] Meighen himself was Minister without Portfolio from February 1932 to the end of the Bennett regime in 1935. Unlike Dandurand, however, he took only a small part in cabinet proceedings.[89] Both Dr. King, who immediately succeeded Dandurand as Government leader in the Senate, and Sen. Robertson were, in their turn, appointed ministers without portfolio,[90] and so were Sen. Haig (for the brief period October 9, 1957–May 14, 1958) and Sen. Macdonald, who was appointed Senate leader for the second time upon the formation of the new Liberal Government in 1963. There were two ministers without portfolio in the Senate during the last thirty-seven years who were not at the same time Government leaders. One was Sen. J. A. MacKinnon, who resigned as Minister of Mines and Resources on March 9, 1949 (to be succeeded by Gibson), was summoned to the Senate on the same day and continued as Minister without Portfolio in the Administration until December 13, 1950. The other was Sen. M. Wallace McCutcheon, an influential businessman, whose appointment as Minister without Portfolio on August 9, 1962, was widely interpreted as an attempt by the Government to reassure Canadian financial circles about the Government's policies and intentions, and to regain the confidence of international investors in the Canadian economy.[91]

The practice of appointing the Government leader in the Senate as a member of the Administration, either as Minister without Portfolio (Dandurand, Meighen, King, Robertson, Haig, Macdonald the second time) or under some other arrangement (Macdonald, 1954–57), was broken three times during the period under study and on each occasion by a Conservative Government. Neither Sen. Willoughby, Senate Leader from 1930 to 1932, nor Sen. Aseltine, Leader of the Government from 1958 to 1962, nor his successor, Sen. Brooks, was included in the

[88]See Mackenzie King's remarks in paying tribute to Dandurand's memory. *Ibid., 1942*, p. 102.

[89]See above p. 95.

[90]Sen. Robertson was a frequent attender of cabinet meetings. Interview with the Hon. Wishart Robertson, April 11, 1962.

[91]Montreal *Gazette*, Aug. 10, 1962; *Montreal Star*, Aug. 10, 1962; *Maclean's*, Oct. 8, 1962.

Administration of the day. However, while in the first and last case the omission was not so serious, since the Government was represented in the Chamber by Senators Gideon Robertson and M. Wallace McCutcheon, respectively, in the case of Sen. Aseltine, his exclusion resulted in the Senate's being unrepresented in the government. This arrangement caused a good deal of indignation in the Senate and was considered not only detrimental to the effective functioning of the house but an example of the Government's utter lack of respect to the Senate.[92] The Government was also criticized in the House of Commons, where Mr. Herridge (CCF, Kootenay West) suggested that if the Government Leader in the Senate was not admitted to the cabinet he should at least be appointed a sort of chief parliamentary secretary.[93] In view of the apparent reluctance of the Government to act in the matter, on January 26, 1961, Sen. Robertson put a formal parliamentary inquiry to the Deputy Leader of the Government in the Senate as to "when the Leader of the Government in the Senate will be made a member of the Administration." He repeated his question a fortnight later but all he got was a non-committal reassurance that "this matter has been brought to the attention of the Administration and when the matter is discussed and a decision reached such decision will be announced. . . ."[94]

It should be pointed out, however, that the protests made in the case of Sen. Aseltine had the modest objective to induce the Government to appoint a single minister without portfolio from the Senate; no representations have been made during the past few years for having a number of portfolios in the Senate. Indeed, there has been a marked change in the attitude of Senators in this regard. If in the late 1920's and '30's it was a constant preoccupation of members of the Upper House to complain about the practice of not seating ministers in their Chamber, in the years following the war a more realistic and more business-like attitude was adopted. With a change in the general tenor of Senate leadership and with an increase in the general efficiency

[92]*SD, 1958*, pp. 103. *Ibid., 1962–63*, p. 276. The fact that Sen. Aseltine was appointed Privy Councillor on Dec. 28, 1961, as a recognition of his services did not solve the problem of cabinet representation in the Senate. He revealed the limitations of his position when in a reply to Sen. Macdonald's request to give the Liberal group in the Senate an equitable representation on delegations at the UN, he said: "I do not suppose the hon. Senator has ever been overlooked in a matter like this, but I would point out that *this is not the first such occasion on which the Leader of the Government in the Senate has not been consulted in the way he would have liked.*" *Ibid., 1960*, p. 201. Italic added.

[93]*HD, 1959*, p. 2192.

[94]*SD, 1961*, p. 317.

rate of the House, the question as to how many ministers sat or ought to sit in the Senate became of secondary importance. The yearly average of bills initiated in the Senate reached unprecedented heights, committee work increased and the Senate's contribution to the legislative business of Parliament showed no decline despite the absence of ministers from the Chamber. Senators got used to living without ministers in their midst and calmly accepted the fact as an inevitable result of changing constitutional norms. Instead of haranguing against it, they developed new procedural rules and organized their business accordingly. Consequently, by the end of the period under review no practical-minded Senator could seriously consider the number of ministers in the Senate as a meaningful criterion for the effectiveness of their work.[95] Speaking on the question in 1959, Sen. Euler was probably expressing the majority view of the modern Senate when he said: "As a general practice, I believe that members of the cabinet should be members of the House of Commons, where they can be held to account for what they do. The precedent of the House of Lords does not appeal to me."[96]

[95]Interview with Sen. A. K. Hugessen, Dec. 30, 1961.
[96]*SD, 1959*, p. 551.

THE SENATE AND PARTISANSHIP: PARTISANSHIP AND IMPARTIALITY

4

WE HAVE FINALLY REACHED THE STAGE in our discussion where the relative degree of impartiality in the actual performance of the Senate may be considered in the light of the experience of the last thirty-seven years. What makes this question seem so important is the fact that since the Senate's right to alter or to refuse to pass legislation is constitutionally uninhibited, difference in the complexion of the majority of the House of Commons on the one hand, and that of the Senate, on the other, could, in theory, create a continuous source of frustration for the Government. Conversely, if partisan motivations played an intensely dominant role in the Senate's proceedings, congruity in the majorities of the two houses might reduce the Senate to a rubber stamp of all Government legislation.

The two factors whose interplay will in actual practice determine the extent of partisanship in the Senate are the principles governing the appointing system on the one hand, and what might be called the mellowing effect of the climate of the House, on the other. If the first is responsible for the periodic reappearance of partisan instincts in discussions and divisions, the second produces a spirit which acts, for the most part, as a sufficiently effective countervailing power. What is important to emphasize is that although Senators do not lose their partisan ties, interests, past, and traditions upon entering the Senate, they learn how to exercise enough political self-restraint to check the brute forces of partisan motivation.

As to the first, negative, aspect of these influences, we have seen that the great majority of Senate appointments are made to the active supporters of the party in power and that a considerable number of those appointed have gone through an extended period of service in the House of Commons. Besides a varying degree of personal gratitude for being appointed it would be rather naive to expect a person who is summoned to the Senate at the (average) age of fifty-eight to forget his entire political background. On the contrary, party connections remain effective after elevation to the Upper House. Indeed, many Senators continue to take part in the extra-parliamentary life of their parties after they have received a seat in the Senate. On occasion a party leader or prime minister would openly remind his appointees of the services they are expected to perform in increasing the efficiency of party organization.[1] Although such services would, in the main, be limited to speeches at party meetings and to brief appearances on the platform at election time,[2] sometimes Senators take a more prominent part in actual organizational work. For all his perfectly non-partisan manner in the Senate, Dandurand was most loyal to his party and his leaders. Although he stood in the shadow of Laurier's shining glory, he was in fact highly instrumental in bringing into being that glory. While Laurier spoke before colossal and well-organized meetings, Dandurand was constantly on the battlefield organizing and directing the Liberal forces. Typical of his unbounded resourcefulness is the story after the elections of 1908 about a Liberal saying to a leading Conservative: "I was surprised at your defeat. You had a good chief, a good policy and excellent candidates. What did you lack?" Answered the Conservative laconically: "Dandurand."[3] In 1925, after his appointment to the Senate, Murphy was asked by King to take charge of the party organization[4] and the following year he was entrusted with the task of directing the whole election campaign from Ottawa. He saw no inconsistency between such activities and membership in the Senate. "Evidently," he wrote, "my membership in the Senate did not affect the doing of that kind of work. I am glad to help the Party in the campaign and many of the strategic moves that were made, and that resulted in increasing the strength of the Party in different sections of the country, were worked out in this

[1]The main topic at the Liberal caucus, Sept. 25, 1943, was the necessity of creating an effective and up-to-date party organization for the Liberal party. After speaking to his colleagues in the Cabinet and MP's, King wrote: "I saw a number of Senators present. I would say there was not a Senator who did not owe his position for life as a Senator to the Liberal Party. That I thought they owed it to the party to help in the work of organization." J. W. Pickersgill, *The Mackenzie King Record.* vol. I, *1939–44* (Toronto, 1960), p. 578.

[2]See Solon Low's complaints, *HD*, *1954*, p. 5248.

[3]*SD*, *1942*, p. 93. See also Meighen's letter to J. Lederle, May 14, 1941. Meighen Papers, series 5.

[4]Murphy to G. N. Gordon, Oct. 30, 1925 (Murphy Papers, vol. 11, no. 4688) and to P. Bakewell, July 12, 1926 (*Ibid.*, vol. 2, no. 404).

office."[5] He was assisted by another Liberal Senator, Andrew Haydon, who was placed in charge of national headquarters, along with Mr. Campney, one of Mackenzie King's private secretaries.[6] They were generally regarded as being primarily responsible for the Liberal victory at the ensuing general election.[7]

It is true that Meighen himself consistently refrained from political speeches on the hustings and refused to take part in election campaigns during his term as Leader of the Senate.[8] However, while he tried to encourage a similar attitude amongst his Conservative followers in the Senate, several of them took a rather active part both in election campaigns and in general organizational work. Thus, Sen. C. P. Beaubien played an important part in the councils of his party particularly after the Conservative convention in Winnipeg, 1927, at which he acted as joint chairman,[9] whereas Sen. Dennis and Sen. Griesbach helped to direct the Conservative party forces in their respective provinces.[10] Sen. Jones, who was summoned to the Senate in 1935, maintained an active political life in his New Brunswick constituency, where he was credited with keeping a list of his constituents' names and personal details to help him in his efforts to organize them.[11] Among more recent examples, Sen. Lambert told the Senate in his maiden speech in 1938 that his "activities outside are identified with political organization";[12] both Sen. Murdock and Sen. Haig carried an active role in the election campaign of 1940;[13] Sen. Pirie, a King appointee from New Brunswick, was, until he died, the focal point of every election in Victoria county, New Brunswick, where "people were either for or against him and the strength of his position shifted at each party convention;"[14] both Sen. Stambaugh and Sen. Burchill were presidents of the Liberal Associations in their respective provinces of Alberta and New Brunswick,[15] while

[5]Murphy to Mrs. H. D. Petrie, Jan. 22, 1927. *Ibid.*, vol. 25, no. 10616.

[6]Murphy to Latchford, July 7, 1926. *Ibid.*, vol. 16, nos. 6351–2.

[7]See correspondence between C. W. Kerr and T. Marshall, Acting Liberal Organizer for Ontario, and between Kerr and Mackenzie King, *ibid.*, vol. 14, nos. 5811 and 5817. Also, J. C. M. German to Murphy, Sept. 16, 1926. *Ibid.*, vol. 11, no. 4608.

[8]See Meighen's letter to Lederle, Meighen Papers, series 5. Also, Mr. Nowlan's comments, *HD, 1954*, pp. 5254. Roger Graham, *Arthur Meighen*, vol. 3, p. 76.

[9]*SD, 1949, passim.*

[10]See Sen. Dennis' letter to Mr. R. J. Manion, Minister of Railways and Canals, July 21, 1933, promising support in campaigns, and Sen. Griesbach's memorandum to Manion, Sept. 16, 1930, on Conservative party prospects in Alberta. Manion Papers, personal correspondence.

[11]H. G. Thorburn, *Politics in New Brunswick* (Toronto, 1961), p. 129.

[12]*SD, 1938*, p. 13.

[13]*Ibid., 1940*, p. 64.

[14]Thorburn, *Politics in New Brunswick*, p. 91.

[15]*SD, 1951*, p. 260.

Robertson assumed presidency of the National Liberal Federation of Canada in 1943, the year of his appointment to the Senate;[16] in this post he was succeeded by Sen. Fogo, and finally by Sen. J. J. Connolly, who presided over the closed conference of members of the National Council of the Liberal party, on January 29–30, 1962, which mapped the party's strategy and organization for the 1962 election campaign.[17] At this point the corresponding position in the Conservative party was also held by a member of the Senate, Sen. Thorvaldson, who was appointed to the Upper Chamber in 1958.

However, those critics of the Senate who focused their attention on the appointing system as the dominant factor in shaping the attitude of individual members of the Senate, were bound to come up with an inadequate explanation which took no account of an equally strong stream of influence: the atmosphere of the Senate as a corporate body. For the self-consciously subordinate position of the Senate in the framework of responsible government, its remoteness from the real centre of political controversy, the relatively high average age of its members,[18] the feeling of security engendered by the life tenure,[19] the intentional laxity of its party organization and, finally, the fact that neither of the two parties that have provided its membership is a "Weltanschauung party," have had the combined effect of developing a unique sense of political self-restraint in the Senate, a mellowing or softening environment, which in the course of everyday business is as effective as, if not more than, the impact of the appointing system.

Weighing the effects of these two opposite factors of influence in the light of the actual performance of the Senate during the period under study the following general thesis may be formulated: Senators, like members of the House of Commons, do possess major premises of partisanship, which they retain after their becoming members of the Upper House. These premises, however, unlike those of the members

[16]*Ibid., 1959*, p. 1129.

[17]*Montreal Star*, Jan. 20, 1962.

[18]One of the most characteristic rituals of the Senate is performed when a member of the house dies. On such occasions tributes are paid to the memory of the departed colleague by the two leaders as well as by friends, on both sides of the house. Death is a great cementing force. In its constant shadow the Senate becomes one big family.

[19]Working together for many years of extended service both in the house and on committees, has developed strong ties of genuine friendship and comradeship, cutting through narrow party ties. The mutual respect and affection between Sen. Murphy and Sen. Meighen, based upon a common racial origin, a love of letters, and a comradeship borne of many years of parliamentary service, has become one of the most famous of such non-partisan relations in the Senate.

of the Commons, are subdued and remain inarticulate for most of the time in discharging the great bulk of the ordinary legislative business of Parliament. They are allowed to the surface of articulation only on those relatively rare occasions when a matter of great concern comes up for decision—a decision which may cast a reflection on the party as such and upon which may hinge the reputation and good fortunes of the whole group with which they have been associated throughout a lifetime. Although the Senate is a legislative body, there is much truth in the contention that its members act in a quasi-judicial fashion. Like judges, they, too, have inarticulate major premises. The only difference between those sitting in the Senate and those on the Bench is that the inarticulate major premises of the first do occasionally articulate. Senators are partisan, therefore, in the sense of being interested in the fortunes of their political parties. But the ruling spirit of the Senate is a spirit of moderation, of fair play, of due independence, of political self-restraint, with a latent determination at the bottom of all discussion and debates not to go beyond a certain limit, not to abuse the constitutional power which resides in the Chamber, giving way even when acquiescence is lacking and abstaining from pushing the course of objection to the point of obstruction.

The record of the Senate in the last thirty-seven years supports these observations. If we compare, for example, the percentage of the legislation which has been modified in the Senate, after it has passed the House of Commons, when the party complexion of the two Chambers was different with those periods during which the same party provided the majority of both Houses, we shall find no increase or decrease of any proportion. Indeed, as the following two tables (Table XV and Table XVI) show the percentage of the total amount of legislation which has been modified in the Senate during the three periods of incongruous party majorities in the two chambers (i.e., 1925–30, 1936–42, and 1958–63) was only .3 higher than the percentage during the two periods of congruous majorities in the Senate and the House of Commons (i.e.,

TABLE XV

Number of Bills Amended by the Senate under Incongruous Majorities, 1925–63

Period	Total no. of bills	No. of bills amended	Percentage
1925–30	325	46	14.3
1936–41	287	71	25
1958–63	251	16	6.2
Total	863	133	15.3

TABLE XVI
Number of Bills Amended by the Senate under Congruous Majorities, 1925–63

Period	Total no. of bills	No. of bills amended	Percentage
1930–35	282	52	19
1942–57	773	104	13
Total	1055	156	15

TABLE XVII
Number of Bills Rejected by the Senate under Incongruous Majorities, 1925–63

Period	Total. no. of bills	No. of bills rejected	Percentage
1925–30	325	12	3.5
1936–41	287	3	1.04
1958–63	251	1	0.4
Total	863	16	1.85

TABLE XVIII
Number of Bills Rejected by the Senate under Congruous Majorities, 1925–63

Period	Total no. of bills	No. of bills rejected	Percentage
1930–35	282	2	0.7
1942–57	773	0	0
Total	1055	2	0.18

1930–35 and 1942–57). While it may be true that willingness to reject legislation is greater when the majority party in the Senate is not the same as the majority party in the Commons, the absolute figures are so small and the difference in percentage is so infinitesimal that no far-reaching and meaningful conclusions can be derived from them.

Perhaps more guidance can be gained from the picture of divisions throughout this period. It is not only, as is clear from Table XIX that the formal method of recorded division[20] is very rarely resorted to (there were only 87 recorded divisions from 1925 to 1963 as against 646 in the House of Lords between 1924 and 1956[21]); what is even more important is the recurring pattern of high level of cross-voting. Indeed,

[20]On several occasions a bill is passed on division in the Senate without the names being put down. To pass a bill on division it is enough for any member of the House, when the Speaker puts the question "Shall this bill now be passed?" to shout "On division." Also divisions in Committee are not recorded.

[21]P. Bromhead, *The House of Lords and Contemporary Politics, 1911–1957* (London, 1958), chap. 7.

TABLE XIX
Recorded Peacetime Divisions of the Senate

(*a*) Number per Session, 1925–63

Year	Divisions	Year	Divisions	Year	Divisions	Year	Divisions
1925	5	1934	6	1946	5	1955	3
1926	2	1935	3	1947	3	1956	3
1927	2	1936	3	1948	2	1957	0
1928	2	1937	2	1949	0	1958	2, 0
1929	0	1938	6	1950	2	1959	1
1930	4	1939	5	1951	3	1960	1
1931	5	1940	2	1952	0	1961	7
1932	3	—	—	1953	0	1962	0
1933	4	1945	1	1954	0	1962–3	0

(*b*) Cross-voting in each Parliament, 1925–63

Period	No. of divisions	Percentage of divisions on public bills decided without cross-voting	with less than 5 per cent cross-voting	with over 5 per cent cross-voting
1925–30	15	—	27	73
1930–35	21	9	20	71
1936–40	18	11	17	72
1945–49	11	—	18	82
1950–53	5	—	—	100
1954–57	6	33	—	67
1957–58	2	—	50	50
1958–62	9	100	—	—

there were only twelve recorded divisions (five of them on the Customs Tariff bill and the Bank of Canada bill in 1961) during the whole period in which votes were cast wholly on party lines. We can learn much about the pattern of impartiality in the Senate from a detailed study of the divisions which have been held in the House over the past generation or so. However, precisely because of the small number of recorded divisions, if the atmosphere in the Senate is to be understood the evidence of voting figures must be supplemented by a closer scrutiny of the general tenor and behaviour in the Chamber.

During the period of 1925–30, throughout which the Senate was dominated by a Conservative majority, none of the fifteen recorded divisions produced solid party votes. On the Canada Temperance bill of 1925, which was defeated on the second reading, 25 per cent of the votes cast crossed party lines, more than one-third of the Conservative Senators voting with the Government.[22] The rebels included Sir George

[22] *SJ*, p. 415.

Foster who put up a valiant fight to prevail upon the rest of his group in support of the bill.[23] He also disagreed to deleting a clause from the Criminal Code Amendment bill on the rather general ground that, save some very strong reasons, the Senate should not throw out the considered conclusion of the Commons.[24] And openly defying his leader, Sir James Lougheed, he pressed for a division, which decided in favour of deleting the controversial section. There was an almost complete split in the Conservative group in voting on the second reading of the Quebec Harbour Commissioners bill; the bill was passed by a vote of 34 to 26, 16 Conservatives siding with 18 Liberals behind the measure while 26 Conservatives opposed it. Among those who broke away from the main body of Conservative Senators there were Sens. Blondin and Calder, two former Conservative Ministers, Sen. L'Espérance, Sens. Griesbach and McCormick, who were Meighen appointees, and several others.[25] On the question of insisting upon the amendments made by the Senate to the Home Bank Depositors bill, two senior members of the House decided to part company with their party fellows; while Sir Allen Aylesworth, who was appointed Senator by Mackenzie King, together with Sen. Prowse, a Laurier man, joined the Conservative majority in standing up for the Senate's right in the matter,[26] Sen. Poirier, dean of the Senate, voted with the Government side, for the reason that although the Senate amendments were judicious the Senate had no right to make them in the first place.[27]

Typically, even the intensely controversial Old Age Pension bill, which was rejected on the second reading by 45 votes to 21, produced no solid voting blocs in the Senate. Both Sen. Aylesworth and Sen. Hughes, who was summoned to the Senate a year before, voted against the bill on the ground that it violated the jurisdiction of the provinces. However, what is even more telling, sixteen of the thirty-nine Liberals in the Senate abstained from voting, although seven of them were present when the vote was taken. This apparent lack of partisanship prompted an independent member of the House of Commons to exclaim:

Have they forgotten the Liberal platform and convention called in Winnipeg in 1919, where a policy was adopted to guide the party in years to come,

---

[23]*SD, 1925*, p. 720.

[24]*Ibid.*, p. 676.

[25]*SJ, 1925*, p. 365.

[26]An action which received the following comment of genuine shock from Sir Henry Drayton in the Commons: "It is an extraordinary fact [extraordinary, that is, in the House of Commons] that Government members in the Senate took part in these proceedings and supported the action taken." *HD, 1925*, p. 4755.

[27]*SD, 1925*, p. 671.

not to be put into force in a day or a week or a year, but as circumstances warranted? . . . Was it not the duty of the Liberal Senators as henchmen or supporters of that policy, to adhere to the principles of that policy? If they had stood by their principles and by their platform [in other words, if they had followed the whip] the vote would have been 42 Conservatives against 39 Liberals for.[28]

On the other side, Sen. Robertson, who was Minister of Labour in 1917 and then again in 1931, supported the legislation, while in the House of Commons Meighen most explicitly disclaimed any part in the final decision of the Conservative Senators.[29] When the bill was reintroduced the following session carrying a mandate from the people the Senate reversed its position and passed the measure by a vote of 61:14. Although the Conservative Leader, Sen. Ross, denied that the bill had a general election mandate,[30] twenty-five of his followers who had voted against it a year before now rallied behind the Government,[31] while seven, including the two oldest members of the House, Sen. Poirier and Sen. Montplaisir, both Macdonald appointees, turned up this year and voted for the bill. On the other hand, Aylesworth, joined by Sen. Wilson, continued his opposition to the principle of the measure, "to the whole idea of pensions being paid by the state."[32] The example of Sen. Aylesworth is significant. It illustrates the high degree of personal independence which is involved in the position of a Senator. By voting against the bill, he defied the stand of his party in the House and the man who appointed him to the Senate. He did so in spite of "considerable criticism on the part of friends and not friends," because he felt that the issue brought him face to face with a conflict between his party allegiance and his "Weltanschauung," "a matter of lifelong conviction," which he breathed in "from my earliest recollection in the household at home."[33]

[28]*HD*, *1926*, p. 4422. In a reply to Mackenzie King's complaint that he, too, was absent when the vote was taken Murphy wrote: ". . . the vote stood 21 in favour of the bill and 45 against the bill. Had I been present, and voted, the vote would have been 22 for the bill, so that my unavoidable absence on the occasion . . . had no earthly bearing on the result. It is not without significance that when I was present throughout the session and discussed and voted for other bills, there was no complaint about Liberal Senators who either walked out of the Chamber to avoid voting, or who both spoke and voted against Government Measures." Murphy to King, Sept. 18, 1926. Murphy Papers, vol. 15, no. 6052.

[29]*HD*, *1926*, p. 4426.

[30]*SD*, *1926*, p. 99.

[31]Bénard, Blondin, Chapais, Crowe, Daniel, Foster (Sir G.), Gillis, Giroir, Green, Griesbach, Martin, McCormick, McDonald, McLean, McMeans, Mulholland, Planta, Pope, Schaffner, Sharpe, Stanfield, Tanner, Taylor, Webster (Brockville), and Willoughby.

[32]*SD*, *1926*, p. 167.

[33]*Ibid.*

What is important to emphasize in this connection is not the merits of this "Weltanschauung," but the fact that he was able to act in accordance with it as a member of the Senate. In a second division on the amendment by Liberal Sen. Béique to delay final decision until adequate opinion as to the practicability of the legislation could be ascertained there was an even higher degree of cross-voting, eight Liberals supporting the delaying amendment while thirty-seven Conservatives including Sen. Ross, their leader, supporting the Government's stand; the amendment was consequently defeated by 58 votes to 17.

Self-restraint on the part of the Conservative majority was evident in the Halifax Harbour Loan bill of 1928. After some lengthy discussion in committee, Sen. Ross moved an amendment to limit the power of the Harbour Commissioners to impose rates. Following the evening recess, during which Dandurand could consult the Minister of Marine and Fisheries, the Government Leader announced in the Senate that the proposed amendment was unacceptable to the Government. In a strictly partisan atmosphere this announcement would have been an invitation for the Opposition to try to embarrass the Government by insisting on their amendment. In the Senate Ross' amendment was negatived by 34 votes to 18, although he had a majority of ten in the Chamber at the time of the vote.[34] The courtesy was returned by Dandurand in the Criminal Code Amendment bill of 1930. The two contentious provisions, placed inconspicuously among the rest of the omnibus measure, for the repeal of section 98 of the Code and for restricting the sale of intelligence on horse-races, were rejected in Committee of the Whole. When the Senate was reconvened after the supper recess to adopt the Committee's report, Sen. Murdock, a fresh Liberal member, sensing that a number of Senators did not return for the evening sitting, moved to amend the Report by restoring the sections of the bill which were deleted during the afternoon. Reminded that the proper place to move his amendment was on the motion for third reading, he withdrew his motion and moved it again when the motion for the third reading of the bill was put. Although the procedure was challenged by Sen. Willoughby, Leader of the Opposition, there was nothing wrong with it, since the rules prohibiting the third reading of a bill without notice were suspended a week earlier. Therefore, had he wished to do so, Dandurand could probably have pushed the bill through the Senate at this point. Respecting the atmosphere of fair play and non-partisan attitude of the House, however, he acceded "to the suggestion of my hon. friend on the opposite side who has pointed out that some members interested in the bill are not in the

[34]*Ibid., 1928*, p. 499.

house at present."[35] He then withdrew his motion for third reading until the following day when it was duly defeated. There was a similar display of co-operative spirit in the Export Act Amendment bill, when Sen. Willoughby allowed himself to be persuaded by Dandurand and Sir George Foster to desist from his motion to delay the passage of the bill by referring it to a special committee, and when, following this, Conservative Senator Pope's amendment to postpone enactment until the conclusion of certain treaty negotiations was defeated by 40 votes to 10, ten Conservatives voting for the amendment and fifteen, including the Conservative Leader, against it.[36]

The second, special, session of Parliament in 1930 was taken up by discussions over the emergency legislation of the newly elected Conservative Government. The bills, the Unemployment Relief bill and two Customs bills, were of first-rate importance in view of the growing economic depression and the serious unemployment situation in the country. All three placed tremendous power in the hands of the Governor-in-Council, while the Customs bills and the Customs Tariff bill, which were designed to increase employment through accelerating business, also revived the historical fight over protectionism *versus* free trade. Although a number of Liberal Senators rose to criticize the bills for these features,[37] objections and criticisms remained, on the whole, isolated and individual and posed no serious challenge to the bills' passage. They were expressions of what Dandurand called the "two trends of thought" but little more. Thus, the long battle of words between Sen. Robertson, the Minister of Labour, and Sen. Murdock, his Liberal predecessor, was more of the nature of an intellectual exchange of thoughts between two persons sharing similar experiences than of a tribal war between members of the Treasury Bench and the Opposition Front Bench in the House of Commons.

This exchange largely settled the tone for the following five years. Indeed, the change of Government was almost imperceptible in the general atmosphere of the House. In his answer to Dandurand's speech during the Address Debate in 1931 Sen. Robertson agreed that Dandurand said very little that demanded a reply. He only picked the Government's tariff policy for criticism, but it was a criticism free of any partisan slanting. Congratulating him on the manner in which he spoke, Robertson added: "I consider the theme of his speech as a model of the way in which subjects should be dealt with in this Chamber at all times,

[35] *Ibid., 1930*, p. 398.
[36] *Ibid., 1930*, pp. 133 ff., 274 ff., 280. *SJ*, p. 316
[37] *SD, 1930* (2nd session), pp. 48, 55 ff.

inasmuch as the underlying motive was the welfare of Canada rather than political considerations."[38] As in the previous session, there was no opposition whatever to the Unemployment and Farm Relief bill, and although Dandurand found the terms of the bill exorbitant he expressed confidence in the honesty of purpose of the Prime Minister and in the integrity of the Minister of Labour.[39] Again, in the Tariff Board bill opposition and criticism was balanced and objective. It was supported by Sen. Graham, former Liberal Minister of Railways who had organized the original Board,[40] while it was attacked by Sen. Sharpe, a Conservative Senator of long standing, on the ground that "with conditions as they are in Canada just now, no Government would be justified . . . in going to the extra expense contemplated by this Bill,"—a position which displayed a high degree of short-sightedness and a considerable amount of independence.[41] The only recorded division that took place on the bill was on Sen. Robinson's motion for six months hoist, which he moved on his own initiative, without even consulting his leader.[42] Although not a Government-sponsored measure, the Hospital Sweepstakes bill was a private member's bill of some importance. There were a total of nine divisions on it between 1931 and 1933, when it was finally passed. In each division the split in both parties was complete; the two leaders often found themselves in the same voting lobby and a considerable number of Senators floated their votes under the impact of speeches made during the debates.

The most substantial breach of party solidarity in the session of 1932 was on the Criminal Code amendment to shift the onus of guilt with regard to cheques without funds and to abolish grand juries in British Columbia. Both these provisions came under severe and continued attacks by a combined front of Conservative and Liberal Senators, while they were defended through the joint effort of Dandurand and Meighen. On the motion for the second reading twenty Conservatives and eleven Liberals, including the two leaders, voted together for the passage of the bill, in opposition to fourteen Liberals and six Conservatives who were led by Aylesworth, Graham, and Lemieux. United, the Liberals could have outnumbered the Conservatives and defeated the Government on an important piece of legislation. On the other hand, although it *was* a

[38] *Ibid., 1931*, p. 18. [39] *Ibid.*, p. 539.

[40] Referring to his independent stand taken in this instance he said two years later that he knew he "displeased some of my friends by voting in this House for the appointment of such a Board," but he was influenced by experience "of which neither Parliament nor the Government was aware," and which convinced him of the desirability of the legislation." *Ibid., 1933*, p. 554.

[41] *Ibid., 1931*, p. 415. [42] *Ibid.*, p. 436.

Government measure, introduced and piloted through the House of Commons by the Minister of Justice who apparently felt very strongly about it, Meighen had considerable difficulties in preventing defeat of the bill in the Senate because of the merciless opposition of his own followers. In two other cases during the session there was a noteworthy degree of co-operation. One was the Radio Broadcasting bill, which was reinforced by a decision of the Privy Council and was seeking to implement the recommendations of a special committee of the Commons. Characteristically, it was hailed by Sen. Dandurand[43] while the only serious criticism came from Conservative Sen. White, who questioned the opportuneness of the legislation.[44] However, the bill was passed without division and received Royal Assent on May 26. The Relief bill was accorded similar co-operation by the Liberal side of the Senate. Although it further extended the Government's power through a number of *carte blanche* provisions, Dandurand recognized that its quick passage was vital for the Government,[45] Graham assumed "that it is our duty under the circumstances to err on the side of liberality towards those who need help,"[46] and Lemieux urged that "members of this Upper Chamber should give a helping hand to their fellow-citizens all over Canada."[47]

In the session of 1933 amendments were made to the Penitentiary bill, which placed the appointment of certain principal officers in the hand of the minister. While criticism in the House of Commons was entirely focused upon the political-patronage aspect of the legislation, discussion in the Senate was limited to the administrative and technical provisions of the bill and the amendments made were for the purpose of improving these provisions. Again, discussions between Liberal Sen. Béland, one-time Minister of Pensions and Health, Sen. Graham, a former Minister of Militia and Defence, and Conservative Sen. Griesbach on the Government's Pension bill were essentially a debate of experts whose party affiliations left no mark upon the tenor of their remarks. Indeed, it was the two Liberal ex-Ministers who wholeheartedly supported the bill and Sen. Griesbach who criticized it.[48] The pattern was repeated in the Relief bill[49] and the Tariff Agreements of the same year,[50] the Farm Loan bill and the Farmers' Creditors Arrangement bill of 1934,[51] and even in the more radical pieces of the legislative program of the year 1935. Indeed, in the division on the Convention Limiting Hours of Work, twenty-nine Conservatives voted together with sixteen Liberals, and party solidarity

[43]*Ibid., 1932*, p. 484.
[44]*Ibid.*, p. 487.
[45]*Ibid.*, p. 428.
[46]*Ibid.*, p. 429.
[47]*Ibid.*
[48]*Ibid., 1933*, pp. 532 ff.
[49]*Ibid.*, p. 377.
[50]*Canadian Annual Review, 1933*, p. 53.
[51]*SD, 1934*, p. 575.

was broken on the Employment and Social Insurance Commission bill, some of the Conservatives supporting a Liberal amendment for commencement by Proclamation after the Supreme Court has given a favourable opinion on the constitutionality of the measure, while some of the Liberal Senators voting with the Government side.[52]

Notwithstanding its majority in the Senate the Government was defeated on two pieces of legislation during this period. In 1933 the Judges bill was negatived on second reading after it was severely criticized by a number of Senators from both sides of the House, led, in the main, by Sen. Aylesworth and Sen. Beaubien.[53] Meighen, as Government Leader, urged the Senate to take a broad view of the entire problem, but made no attempt to discourage anyone to vote against the bill if he found that "the totum of good outweighed the totum of ill."[54] The actual vote was 17:11 against passage, three Conservatives, including a Bennett appointee (Sen. McRae), joining fourteen Liberals. Significantly, in terms of pure arithmetic, the Conservatives could have obtained the necessary majority if there had been no cross-voting in their ranks and if Conservative Senators Griesbach and Schaffner had not abstained.[55] Similar fate fell upon the Industrial Disputes Investigation bill of 1935, which died in the Banking and Commerce Committee.

When Meighen assumed his new role of Leader of the Opposition in the Senate at the head of a comfortable Conservative majority, he paid tribute to the co-operation and cordiality he received from the Liberals during the previous five years. "We shall receive the legislation of the Administration," he pledged, "in the spirit in which . . . hon. members opposite received ours in the years that have gone by. In this House we have made an effort, which has been common to both sides, to review carefully and to improve legislation with a single eye to the good of Canada. In that work we had the assistance and the utmost co-operation of Sen. Dandurand and of those associated with him. We owe it to them that we now reciprocate to the full. We owe it to them that we utterly abandon prejudice and deal with legislation on its merits."[56]

Accordingly, there was no Conservative opposition to the Government's National Employment Commission bill of 1936, because the Government was supposed to hold a clear mandate for it from the people,[57] and the same reasoning was applied to the bill to repeal section 98 of the Criminal Code—a proposal which had repeatedly been defeated by the Senate in the past.[58] Similar self-restraint characterized Conserva-

[52]*SJ, 1935*, pp. 203, 208. [53]*SD, 1933*, p. 507. [54]*Ibid.*, p. 505.
[55]*SJ, 1933*, p. 283. [56]*SD, 1936*, p. 20. [57]*Ibid.*, p. 174.
[58]*Ibid.*, p. 620.

tive attitudes to the National Harbours bill of 1936 and the CNR bill in the following session. Both measures were amended by the Senate, and in both instances the Government found the amendments unacceptable. Although it was plain that the Conservative majority in the Senate could cause serious embarrassment to the Government by insisting on the original amendments, the Government's recommendations were accepted in both cases.[59]

There was cross-voting on a Conservative amendment to the Government's bill to amend the Farmers' Creditors Arrangement Act in 1938, and even the rejection of the same measure in the following session produced no solid voting blocks in the Senate; the extent of cross-voting was 7 and 4 per cent respectively.[60] Even more spectacular was the split in the Conservative ranks on the Transport bill of 1938, when a last-minute motion for six months' hoist at the third reading stage was negatived by 26 votes to 12, eighteen Conservatives, including Meighen himself, voting with a handful of eight Liberals, who would otherwise have been hopelessly defeated.[61]

Apart from these demonstrations of self-restraint and cross-voting a curious pattern of "double independence" had developed among the Conservative majority in the second half of the period 1936–40. This development was closely linked with the increasingly independent course taken by Sen. Meighen in ignoring the stated policy of the Conservative party's national leadership on a number of important issues. But as the Conservative Leader in the Senate grew steadily independent of the Conservative Leader in the House of Commons, an increasing number of Conservative Senators grew steadily independent of their Leader.

At first Meighen was able to secure the support of a majority of his Conservative colleagues for giving effect to his views. Thus he could muster enough strength in 1936 to complete his determined fight against the change proposed by the Combines Investigation bill in investigational practice. The measure was emasculated not so much through differences in party policies between the two sides of the House as through Meighen's forcefully expressed views on the matter[62] and through his ability to have those views prevail among his followers.

[59]*Ibid.*, p. 625, and *1937*, p. 365. Beaubien who proposed the controversial amendment in the CNR bill summed up the case in this way: "If Government is to be carried out in an efficient way . . . both Houses of Parliament must give and take, must work together."

[60]*SJ*, *1938*, p. 27, and *1939*, pp. 119–20.

[61]*Ibid.*, *1938*, p. 367.

[62]For a possible motivation for Meighen's animosity to the proposed change see Sen. Murdock's speech. *Ibid.*, 1936, p. 592.

However, he was much less successful in the Canadian National–Canadian Pacific bill of the same session.[63] He argued vigorously that the Government had no mandate for the bill[64] and made powerful attacks upon it on both the second and third readings. "I am prepared to see the bill defeated," he said, "and to take all consequences, if by any act of mine I could bring about its defeat."[65] However, he could not, despite the great Conservative majority in the Senate and despite his clearly expressed opposition to the legislation. Here was a case of the leader of one of the parties in the Senate—and a leader whose prestige was by no means limited to the confines of that Chamber—failing to carry the majority of his followers with him. Here was a case, moreover, in which the so-called Opposition party in the Senate ignored its opportunities for causing considerable embarrassment to the Government by rejecting one of its measures. Probably many Conservative Senators did not think too much of the bill but felt with Sen. McMeans that they owed "a duty to the country and . . . realize that if the bill is not passed the road will be in a state of chaos."[66] Sen. Sauvé, a Bennett appointee, admitted that his Leader "made a forceful speech against the Bill, and it is possible that the future will confirm the wisdom of his opposition to it"; however, he felt that the Government should be allowed to "assume full responsibility for the proposed change in the administration of the Canadian National Railways."[67] Similarly, to Griesbach the important point seemed to be that "A Government has recently come from the electorate with an overwhelming majority, which implies the confidence of the people. It has deliberately chosen this step, and it must take the responsibility." And he summed up his position this way: "For the reasons I have given I cannot vote against the Bill. I must vote for it."[68] Consequently, the bill was passed on third reading on division, with Meighen being left in a minority. It was a typical case of the "quasi-judicial" attitude of Senators in matters of ordinary legislation and of a high degree of independence both in debate and in voting in the Senate.

Meighen's experience was repeated in two instances on the same subject in the session of 1939. He again opposed a bill to amend the Canadian National–Canadian Pacific Act, despite the fact that it had

[63]For his changed position on railway affairs, see Roger Graham, *Arthur Meighen*, vol. 3 (Toronto–Vancouver, 1965), pp. 39 ff.
[64]*SD*, 1936, pp. 454, 578.
[65]*Ibid.*, p. 571.
[66]*Ibid.*, p. 568.
[67]*Ibid.*, p. 587.
[68]*Ibid.*, pp. 586–7.

received the support of the Conservative party in the House of Commons.[69] But the third reading of the bill was passed by 34 votes to 24, twenty-three Liberals being assisted by eleven Conservatives. Likewise, there were seven Conservatives who joined the Liberals in voting upon the Report of the Special Railway Committee. There was also cross-voting among the Conservative Senators in the two divisions that were held on the Central Mortgage Bank bill in the same session.[70]

By this time the independent course of the Conservative Leader of the Senate was so conspicuous that *The Standard* wrote in its "Capital Comment," May 13, 1939: "The Conservative Senate Leader during the past five months has been Parliament Hill's one definite figure." The rift between Meighen and Manion, the official leader of the party after 1938, becomes clear from a "personal memorandum" which Manion wrote to Meighen in early 1939. This letter is so remarkable for its desperate tone and throws so much light on the existing relationship between the two men that it is worth quoting in full:

In view of the many years during which I was your loyal supporter, both in the House of Commons and on the election platform from coast to coast, I am venturing to write to you regarding a matter which has been causing me much concern in the last few months. . . . Many misunderstandings are occurring throughout the Dominion due to the fact that, on so many questions, I take one attitude and you take the opposite, either in the Senate or outside. This has occurred on such matters as our Empire relations, our attitude in war, various aspects of the railway question, immigration, and the Canadian-US Trade Treaty—to name some of them. On practically all of these, your attitude has been almost diametrically opposite to mine, and, indeed, to that of the Party in the House of Commons. This, of course, is your right as a citizen of Canada and as a Senator; but both in letters and in personal interviews my supporters are complaining of the embarrassing position in which they are being placed, because you, the Conservative Leader

---

[69]This is how Manion described Meighen's attitude: ". . . and now Arthur Meighen has made himself apparently the mouthpiece of the C.P.R. . . . thereby opposing the Party which did so much for him while he was leading them to defeat three times. . . . The attitude Arthur took in the Senate on railways did us a lot of damage and probably will continue to do so." Manion to Sen. W. H. Dennis, June 19, 1939. Manion Papers, personal correspondence.

[70]*SJ, 1939*, pp. 307–8. The eleven Consevatives who voted for the bill amending the Canadian National–Canadian Pacific Act were Calder, Fauteux, Green, Haig, Léger, L'Espérance, Lynch-Staunton, McDonald, Moraud, Quinn, and Robicheau. *Ibid.*, p. 234. The seven who voted with the Liberals on the Report of the Special Railway Committee were Bourgeois, Donnelly, Marcotte, McRae, Moraud, and Robicheau. *Ibid.*, p. 284.

of the Senate, take a different view from that which I have expressed on many subjects. I am even asked who is speaking for the Conservative Party. . . . With great respect, I venture to suggest that, although you are no longer the Leader of the Conservative Party, you have a grave responsibility towards the members of that Party who formerly honoured you with your leadership. When you, as Conservative Leader of the Senate and former Leader of the Party, express opinions diametrically opposed to those of the Leader of the Party, it cannot fail to add greatly to the difficulties of the supporters of the Party throughout the country. . . . [Please] "make it known publicly that *you are speaking for yourself independently of the Conservative Party and that you and I do not consult regarding political questions*."[71]

That Manion and Meighen did not consult was due to the fact that when Manion proposed it in December 1938, his offer got the following reception from Meighen:

Certainly, during the period of power [1930–35] particularly I frequently went to Council to explain the course I thought of pursuing, and to receive and discuss any suggestions that might be offered. I also went to Mr. Bennett, only I think two or three times though, in the period we were in Opposition, for the same purpose. What I was trying to emphasize was that *Mr. Bennett never sought in any way to influence our course in the Senate*. . . . I want to continue to influence the Senate to practical usefulness just as far as I possibly can, *rather than to make it a mere reflection corresponding to the respective sides of the House of Commons*. I advised Mr. Bennett of this at the very beginning and he quite concurred.[72]

Adamant in his views regarding his position as Conservative Leader in the Senate, Meighen reached the peak of his critical attitude to Government legislation in the session of 1940, when he declared war upon the Department of National War Service bill, on the ground that it was sheer propaganda, and upon the Unemployment Insurance bill, because he thought it was "inopportune," even of doubtful principle.[73] For this stand he was severely reprimanded by Sen. Dandurand, who said he was disappointed to see that Meighen failed "to shake off the prejudices and party passions that sometimes animate Commoners," and that he seemed to be speaking "as the Leader of the Opposition in the House of Commons

[71]Manion to Meighen, undated, early 1939. Manion Papers, personal correspondence. Italics added.

[72]Meighen to Manion, Dec. 28, 1938. *Ibid.* Italics added. For a confirmation of

[73]*Ibid., 1940*, pp. 285, 298, 388–91, 406–7. "He became convinced," Graham says, "that the general drift of democracy was towards self-destruction . . . that the totalitarian regimes of that day were but extensions . . . of many of the slow, socializing trends discernible in [democracies]." *Op. cit.*, p. 71.

rather than as Leader of the Conservative Party in the Senate."[74] The reason was probably that Meighen never, and especially not in the years after 1936, was truly at home in the Senate. He stood apart not only in his brilliance and mental alertness but in giving the impression that somehow his senatorship, unlike that of the others, did not mark the end of an active public career. He was first and foremost Arthur Meighen, one-time party leader and premier and then toward the end of the thirties once again a prospective candidate for Conservative leadership, and almost incidentally a member of the Senate. Even though he refused to stand at the 1938 Convention and was reluctant to accept the leadership, into which he was finally catapulted by the coming of war,[75] the fact remains that "he had never been entirely out of the picture,"[76] and it was this potential availability that separated him from his colleagues in the Senate. His amendment to defer the enactment of the Unemployment Insurance bill until the end of the war was negated by a vote of 43 to 26, several of his supporters, including Sens. Haig, Fallis, Côte, Sauvé, rallying behind the Government. In view of the repeated and consistent breaches of party solidarity if not discipline, he had to admit that "on this side of the House a measure of independence is very often in evidence. . . . For my part I have never discouraged such independence, and do not intend to discourage it. Sometimes it would even appear that the following departs while the leader heroically stands; but that I do not mind at all."[77]

Such independence was by no means an exclusive property of the Conservative Senators. Indeed, the ultimate defeat of the Farmers' Creditors Arrangement bill in 1940 was due to the decision of an eight-member rebel group among the Liberal Senators, including Senators Euler, Hayden, and Paterson (all 1940 appointees) as well as Hughes, Little, MacArthur, and Murdock, to join in insisting on the amendments

[74]*SD, 1940*, pp. 298–9.

[75]*Ibid., 1940*, pp. 285, 388. Graham describes his state of mind at the time in this way: "He became convinced that the general drift of democracy was towards self-destruction, that there was a movement of public thought, and therefore of acquiescent political action, towards some form of authoritarian collectivism, that the totalitarian regimes of that day were but extensions, horrible and frightening, of many of the slow, socializing trends discernible in the democratic portions of the world. . . . The pessimism that overtook him during those years . . . came from the realization that his philosophy of life and politics had become, not untrue and irrelevant—those things it could never be—but somehow less convincing and even less intelligible than he had ever sensed it was before to the citizens upon whose wisdom the future of democracy depended." *Op. cit.* pp. 71–2.

[76]*Ibid.*, p. 95.

[77]*SD, 1940*, p. 329.

made by the Senate to the bill, despite the announcement of the Government that it found the amendments unacceptable.[78] Their refusal to follow the wishes of the Government marked the emergence of a small and influential group of Liberal Senators with a high degree of independence and a true sense of quasi-judicial impartiality, in the best traditions of the Dandurand school. However, their role had not clearly been defined until after the end of the war and the first post-war sessions of Parliament.

As has been mentioned earlier, the turn in the party standing of the Senate came in 1942, when for the first time since a temporary ascendancy in 1931 Liberal Senators found themselves in a majority in the House, and they maintained their numerical strength ever since. This meant that from 1945 to 1957 there were corresponding party majorities in the two Houses of Parliament. According to the theories of partisanship, Liberal Governments in this period might have rested assured that their legislative programs would pass the Senate unchallenged. However, although no Government bill was formally rejected by the Senate during the twelve years from 1945 to 1957, Government measures were amended by the dozens in their principal provisions. Indeed, it was in this period beginning with the end of the war, that the substantive role of the Senate of being an auxiliary institutional check upon an ever growing executive began to take a consciously consistent shape. But what is most important for our present purposes is the fact that with the gradual widening of the gap between the party forces in the Senate, the centre of effective opposition shifted, both in debate and in amending legislation, from the "official" Conservative Opposition to a "wilful little group" of Liberal Senators, whose nucleus was made up of Senators Bench, Campbell, Crerar, Euler, Hayden, Hugessen, Kinley, Lambert, Paterson, Roebuck and Wilson, to be joined later by Senators Reid, Power, and Pouliot, to whom other members of the Liberal group were added from time to time. It is very instructive to examine some of the most characteristic cases of the operative spirit of impartiality in this period.

The one recorded division in the session of 1945 was on the third reading of the Senate and House of Commons bill, which was passed by 39 votes to 11; the whole group of Conservative Senators supported the measure while one-quarter of the Liberals voting were opposed to it. This latter group included four Senators (Crerar, McGeer, McLean, Pirie) who were summoned to the Senate that year.[79]

[78] *SJ, 1940*, p. 210. [79] *Ibid., 1945*, p. 374.

In 1946 party solidarity was broken over two important pieces of Government legislation. In the Combines Investigation bill a Government-sponsored motion to further amend the amendments made by the Senate's Banking and Commerce Committee was carried by a narrow margin of 26:15, again one-fourth of the Liberal Senators present opposing the Government's stand.[80] On Liberal Senator Roebuck's amendment to defer decision upon the Foreign Exchange Control bill until the following session the extent of cross-voting was 20 per cent and eight Liberals voted for the amendment against the Government.[81] There were also two private member's bills with recorded divisions. In the Canada Day bill, a private member's measure from the House of Commons which apparently carried the Government's approval, Sen. Ballantyne, former Conservative Leader of the Senate, was supported in his amendment by six Liberals who voted against the main body of their group.[82] On the other hand, in Sen. Bench's Dairy Industry bill, which has become a permanent feature of this period almost in the same way as had the Hospital Sweepstakes bill in the thirties, the split in both groups was complete: thirty-one Liberals and twelve Conservatives voted against the second reading of the bill, whereas twenty-three Liberals and seven Conservatives supported it; the two leaders voted in the same division.[83] Looking back on the session, Sen. Robertson, Leader of the Government in the Senate, remarked: "Any one who is under the impression that the Liberal majority in this House is a rubber stamp for the Government would soon be undeceived if he occupied my position."[84]

The Government Leader was again placed in a difficult position on the Canadian Wheat Board bill in 1948 which was amended in the Senate's Banking and Commerce committee. He gave a clear warning that the Government could not accept the proposed change.[85] However, in spite of the strong language of the warning, nearly one-third of the Liberal group, including Sen. Beaubien, Deputy Government Whip and later Chief Whip in the Senate, insisted on the Committee's recommendation.[86] The amendment was negatived by 25 votes to 17, with 25 per cent of cross-voting.

Opposition and a high percentage of cross-voting in the Liberal ranks continued in the Session of 1950 over a series of agricultural measures. The motion to exempt oleomargarine from the sales tax of 8 per cent produced a considerable proportion of non-partisan votes: five Conser-

[80] *Ibid., 1946*, p. 414. [81] *Ibid.*, p. 540. [82] *Ibid.*, pp. 412–3.

[83] The pattern was repeated almost completely in 1947 and 1948; cf. *ibid., 1947*, p. 161, and *1948*, p. 312.

[84] *SD*, *1946*, p. 776. For similar confessions, cf. *ibid., 1947*, p. 606.

[85] *Ibid., 1948*, p. 303. [86] *Ibid.*, pp. 309 ff.

vatives, including the Conservative Leader, Sen. Haig, voted with the Government majority while thirteen Liberals voted against the rest of their party.[87] Discussions over the Agricultural Prices Support bill, which sought to make the Act a part of the permanent legislation of Canada, provided the interesting spectacle of eminent Liberal Senators, such as Roebuck and Euler, attacking the measure and the Leader of the Opposition rushing to its defence.[88] The bill to extend the life of the Canadian Wheat Board Act again came under severe criticism from such Liberals as Crerar, Campbell, Lambert, Reid, and others.[89] However, the most substantial breach of party discipline in the session took place over the Canadian Grain bill which was amended in the Banking and Commerce committee to an extent unacceptable to the Government. In the ensuing division more than a third of the Liberal senators voted in support of the action of the committee. The rebel group included Crerar and Euler, former ministers of the Crown, and Sen. Hugessen, who had only recently been named Deputy Government Leader in the Senate.[90]

In the first session of 1951, apart from Roebuck's continued fight against the further extension of the duration of the Foreign Exchange Control Act,[91] group revolts took place on two important pieces of legislation. In the first place, one of the largest items of the Appropriation bill No. 2, a contemplated $65 million payment to the wheat growers of the country, was severely criticized by Liberal Senators on a variety of grounds. Yet no amendment was offered and after a stormy debate the bill was passed on the second reading on division. However, on the motion for third reading the unprecedented happened: Sen. Lambert, seconded by Sen. Pirie, moved an amendment that the controversial vote should be stricken out from the bill. "This amendment," Lambert emphasized, "establishes a precedent, the precedent of the Senate moving for a reduction in a supply bill, and therefore represents as important a question as has been presented to this House in its whole history.[92] No Conservative took part in the ensuing debate and only Liberals supported the amendment in the recorded vote which followed the Speaker's order that "the members be called in." The amendment was defeated by 27 votes to 8, eight Liberals voting for the amendment, while the two Conservatives present, including Sen. Aseltine, the Deputy Leader of the Opposition, voted with the Government side.[93]

The second and even more tumultuous defiance of party lines was occasioned by the Canada Dairy Products bill, which deserves a more

[87] *SJ, 1950*, p. 240.
[88] *SD, 1950*, pp. 172, 175, 176.
[89] *Ibid.*, pp. 456–75.
[90] *SJ, 1950*, p. 402.
[91] *SD, 1950*, p. 296.
[92] *Ibid., 1951*, p. 316.
[93] *SJ, 1951*, p. 219.

detailed analysis. The bill sought to establish national standards for dairy products and to regulate interprovincial and international trade in such products. The pith of the bill was section 6, which not only empowered the Governor-in-Council to prohibit by regulation the importation into and the exportation out of Canada or any province dairy products, but which also delegated to the Governor-in-Council the right to designate by regulation any class of products which it deemed as substitutes for a dairy product. The scope and purpose of the bill promptly galvanized the supporters of oleomargarine in the Senate who, rightly or wrongly, assumed that the real target of the measure was to provide protection for Quebec against shipment of oleomargarine into that province. The attack was led by Sen. Euler, former Minister of Trade and Commerce and an indefatigable champion of oleomargarine, who moved, seconded by Sen. Hardy, that the bill be given the six months' hoist.[94] Supporting the stand taken by Sen. Euler, Roebuck called the bill "an Act for the relief of Mr. Duplessis" and charged that its real purpose was "to facilitate the Minister of Agriculture in his political manoeuvres as between provinces." He was opposed to it "on the grounds of the deepest of principles" and accused the legislation of " 'Balkanizing' the Dominion of Canada and dividing it up into small jurisdictions of trade."[95] The same stand was taken by Sens. Vien and Lambert. Their opposition was given an important boost when Sen. King, former minister of the Crown, and former Government Leader and Speaker of the Senate, declared that despite his "loyalty to and admiration for" the Government he was "distressed and disappointed" that this bill was presented to Parliament. He warned that he was "not going to be a peacemaker and support the second reading of this bill. I am going to vote against it because I certainly think that . . . it will destroy our inter-provincial trade; it will wreck Confederation and this dominion of ours."[96] This rebel élite was joined by a dozen other Liberals while, most significantly, Sen. Haig was "disturbed about the idea of voting against any bill on second reading," and went so far as to ask Euler to withdraw his motion for six months' hoist. However, his good offices proved unsuccessful and the amendment was put to a vote in which 33 per cent of the forty-four Liberals present voted against their Leader. When the motion was defeated by a narrow margin of 21 : 15, Sen. King made another attempt to delete section 6 from the bill on third reading but he again failed. The issue was fought to the bitter end and finally the bill was pushed through the third reading on division. There had per-

[94]*SD, 1951*, p. 723. [95]*Ibid.*, p. 724. [96]*Ibid.*, p. 752.

haps never been a case in which the unhampered freedom of Senators to express their views and to take their stands accordingly was exemplified so clearly and so unmistakenly as in this instance. It was an important piece of legislation; it was a "political" measure in the fullest sense of the word; it bore the endorsement of the Cabinet and of the House of Commons and it was introduced in the Chamber and supported by the Leader of the Government. To oppose it in words and in action meant to stand up against the Government. Moreover, the opposition was carried on by people who had themselves been members of the same policy-making elite and who were in fact appointees of those whose final authority they now challenged. How convincing in the face of such performance is Dawson's statement that "the fact that they are still associating with their old colleagues only a few feet away from the thickest of the fight makes party detachment and independence little more than a fanciful aspiration which has lost contact with the fact of life?"

This case was discussed at some length because it illustrates better than anything else the *normal tone* of debates and general atmosphere prevailing in the Senate in the course of performing the ordinary legislative duties of the House. After five-and-a-half years as Government Leader in the Senate, Sen. Robertson, one of the most efficient administrator-leaders of the Senate during the last thirty-seven years, confessed "that my most difficult moments in this House have been when the fate of some piece of Government legislation which I have introduced hung in the balance. *Those difficult moments have not been occasioned wholly by the Official Opposition; they have come in large measure from Hon. senators nominated by the same Government that appointed me.*"[97] And on another occasion, after emphasizing that neither the Deputy Government Leader of the Senate, nor the Whips, were bound to support the Government, he said: "On different occasions in the last two or three years, when some contentious matter has come before the House, various Senators have suggested to me that I should stand in my place and announce that Government Senate members could exercise a 'free vote.' I have not done so for obvious reasons—*already there is nothing but a free vote.*"[98]

Although the number of formal recorded divisions has decreased after 1952, it has been no indication of any change in the pattern of the impartial attitude of the preceding years. In the session of 1953 Sen. Crerar continued his determined fight against the Canadian Wheat Board

[97] *Ibid.*, p. 56. Italic added.
[98] *Ibid., 1952*, pp. 362–3. Italic added.

bill.[99] The question of oleomargarine cropped up again during the session, but this time it had an important bearing upon party solidarity in the Senate, as it affected the Excise Tax bill and thus the balance of ways and means for the Government. The bill was amended in committee by adding oleomargarine to the list of specified food-stuffs which were exempted from the imposition of the sales tax under the bill. The Senate was told that the Government was definitely opposed to the proposed change. However, in spite of the unmistakeable crack of the whip, some of the most influential Liberal members continued to oppose the express wish of the Government. Sen. Euler was supported by Sen. Reid, one of the most outspoken Liberal Senators in the past twelve years, who simply wished "to go on record as voting against the amendment of the Leader of the Government *because of the principle at stake here*."[100] The two were joined by Sen. Roebuck, while Both Sen. Aseltine and Sen. Horner voted with the Government.[101]

In the session of 1955 party solidarity was broken to the extent of 20 per cent cross-voting upon Sen. Euler's private member's bill to amend the BNA Act regarding the filling of Senate vacancies.[102] Although it was made clear before the vote was taken that the Government was not prepared to accept the proposed amendment to the constitution, nine Liberal Senators supported the bill, while one Conservative, Sen. Marcotte, voted with the Government side.[103]

Similarly, in 1956 no less than five important pieces of Government legislation were passed over the opposition of Liberal Senators. The Canada-Denmark Income Tax Agreement bill was criticized by Roebuck and Davies;[104] a small group of Liberals, consisting of Crerar, Howden, and Pouliot, assumed the role of the Opposition over the Lands Surveys bill, by protesting against the transferring of the right to fix the number of members of the Board to the Treasury Board;[105] Crerar and Reid were instrumental in gathering opposition to the Temporary Wheat Resources bill, which was a political measure "par excellence";[106] again, on the ground of principle Sen. Lambert, supported by other Liberal Senators, delivered a bold attack upon the Government's Excise Tax bill for its provision to levy a tax on special editions of non-Canadian periodicals (section 3, part 2);[107] similarly to the Excise Tax bill, the

99 *Ibid., 1953*, p.. 456–7.
100 *Ibid.*, p. 442. Italic added.
101 *Ibid.*, pp. 438, 446.
102 See above, p. 58.
103 *SJ, 1955*, pp. 420–1.
104 *SD, 1956*, p. 524.
105 *Ibid.*, p. 745.
106 *Ibid.*, p. 224.
107 He called it "distinctly a protectionist provision and represents a bit of special privilege legislation in its most concentrated form. From the point of view both of basic principles as well as of common sense . . . this provision is reactionary and anti-liberal." *Ibid.*, pp. 1010–11.

Income Tax bill was forced to a division by no less a personage in the Liberal party than Sen. Power, who was summoned to the Senate only a year before. Consistent with his concept of senatorial independence, he succeeded in having the bill amended in committee, effecting a reduction of taxes for the Government. When the bill was reported back to the Senate, the Government Leader, speaking on behalf of the Government and the Prime Minister, tersely told the House that although constitutionally *intra vires* the Senate would be politically *ultra vires* "to substitute its judgement in this matter at this time."[108] Despite the blunt warning Sen. Power persisted in his stand. When he was told by Sen. Macdonald that the propriety of his proposed amendment was questionable, he said: "The propriety? Well, with respect to the propriety, my conscience is my own." And when he was told that it was the advisability of his action that came under suspicion, he snapped: "I have been long enough in public affairs to know what is proper or not proper, and I am not going to take any lessons from the hon. leader."[109] The bill was passed on the third reading by a narrow margin of 16 : 10; but to find such a stand one has to go to the Senate.

This attitude of the Liberal Senators was continued to the very end of the Liberal Administration. Indeed, during the session of 1957 Sen. Hugessen voted against the second reading of the Agricultural Products Marketing bill because to him it violated "the good old British principle that a man is innocent unless he is proved to be guilty. . . ." He did "not care how many Attorneys General or how many Ministers of Justice approved it. . . ." He felt the provision of the bill was not in accordance with the principles he cherished, and, therefore, he voted against it."[110] Likewise Sens. Reid and Croll found that some of the provisions of the Government Property Traffic bill represented "a process of whittling away the rights of Parliament itself," wherefore they moved that it be referred back to committee for reconsideration. In view of the advanced stage of the session this proposal was tantamount to killing the bill. Indeed, their motion having been adopted the measure died on the Senate's Order Paper.[111]

With the return to power of the Conservatives in 1957, 1958, and again in 1962 the congruity of party majorities in the two Chambers was brought to an end. However, despite the fact that the Senate was now almost entirely made up of Liberals, the tradition of senatorial self-restraint and impartiality remained effective, as far as the general tenor of the discussions and decisions respecting ordinary legislation were concerned. Sen. Haig's appointment as Government Leader in the

[108] *Ibid.*, p. 1029.
[109] *Ibid.*, pp. 1030–1.
[110] *Ibid.*, *1957*, p. 565.
[111] *Ibid.*, p. 386.

Senate in October 1957 was an obvious choice. He had not only been Leader of the Conservative forces in the Upper House for more than a decade; he held an esteemed position in the hierarchy of his party itself. However, his case proved that long years in Opposition are not necessarily an adequate training for Government leadership. Apart from his age (he was 80 when he finally became Leader of the Government in 1957), the twelve years while he was Leader of the Opposition had developed in him an "Opposition mentality" and built up a greater amount of intolerance and frustration than is desirable for constructive leadership.[112] This may explain his over-anxiety of pushing Government legislation through the Senate as quickly and as expeditiously as possible, and his suspicion that the colossal Liberal majority in the Senate had been eagerly waiting for the first opportunity to thwart the legislative program of the new Government. However, there was no Liberal obstruction during the short session of 1957–58 and no attempt to exploit the various tactical opportunities arising out of the delicate position of the Government in the House of Commons. Indeed, at the very beginning of the session Sen. Macdonald, Leader of the Opposition, set out to explain the attitude of himself and of his followers with respect to Government legislation to be dealt with during that Parliament. He said:

> In view of our numbers it will be immediately apparent that we could, under the Constitution, resist and, indeed, prevent the adoption of every piece of legislation initiated by the new Government. On the other hand, we could allow that legislation to proceed through this House without comment or criticism. I feel sure that we will follow neither of these extreme courses. There are historic considerations which would dissuade us from adopting either alternative, and which I devoutly hope would similarly dissuade others who, in the future, might find themselves in a comparable position.[113]

Apparently, his remarks left Sen. Haig unconvinced and if there was any partisan bickering during the session it nearly always originated with the Government Leader, who saw in every word of constructive criticism a veiled attempt to refuse or to delay the passage of legislation.[114] He adopted threatening tactics for the rest of the session. In trying to intimidate the Opposition he frequently overreached himself, with the result that he was ruled out of order by the Speaker on at least three

[112]See his comments, *ibid., 1957–58*, p. 434; *ibid., 1959*, p. 219.

[113]*Ibid., 1957–58*, p. 36.

[114]In particular over the Prairie Grain Advance Payments bill, *ibid.*, p. 114; Beechwood Power Project bill, *ibid.*, p. 488; Old Age Security bill, Old Age Assistance bill, Blind Persons bill, Disabled Persons bill, *ibid.*, p. 183; Buffalo and Fort Erie Bridge bill, *ibid.*, 293.

occasions during the short session—an unprecedented experience for a Government Leader in the Senate.[115]

The political self-restraint and co-operation on the part of the huge Liberal majority was continued in the session of 1958. At the beginning of the session Sen. Macdonald reassured the Senate that he stood four-square by his promise that "we should not allow narrow party prejudice and political advantage to be the overriding consideration in our attitude toward legislation which comes to us."[116] Consequently, partisan motives played no apparent role during debate and no recorded division was held; the new leadership of Sen. Aseltine carefully avoided anything that might have given rise to futile partisan bickering. When during the third reading debate of the Trust Companies bill a small group of Liberal Senators demanded that the bill be referred back to committee, they were quickly isolated by their own colleagues, without the Government representatives ever having to plead for the avoidance of further delays in the passage of the bill.[117] The real test for self-restraint and co-operation was provided by the proceedings over the Government's controversial Estate Tax bill. It was again one of those curiously hybrid situations, so typical of the Senate, in which legislation was criticized by supporters of the Government and defended by members of the Opposition.[118] By the time the committee reported back the bill to the Senate it had been made known that the Government was not prepared to accept the proposed amendment, on the ground that it was administratively unworkable and was upsetting the balance of ways and means. Nothing, therefore, would have been more understandable from a strictly partisan viewpoint than for the Opposition to make political capital out of the situation and for the Conservative side to fight to the end to defeat the amendment. Instead, one finds Deputy Government Leader Brunt and Chief Government Whip White voting *for* the amendment in accordance with their expressed views on second reading and in committee, and Sen. Macdonald, Leader of the Opposition, lending his support to the Government.[119] Although the amendment was passed, when the bill was returned from the Commons with a message that the change was found unacceptable the amendment was not further insisted on. Both Sen. Leonard and Sen. Hayden, who were responsible for the change, took the stand that harmony between the two houses was more important than the adoption of their amendment.[120]

[115]Over the Old Age Assistance bill, *ibid.*, pp. 181, 421, 282.
[116]*Ibid.*, *1958*, pp. 71–2.
[117]See in particular Sen. Hugessen's remarks, *ibid.*, pp. 373–6.
[118]*Ibid.*, p. 563. [119]*Ibid.*, p. 705. [120]*Ibid.*, 764–6.

For their attitude during the session Sen. Aseltine praised his Liberal colleagues by recalling that "at the present time there are three times as many members on the opposite side of this Chamber as I have in my party on this side; however that has not interfered in any way with getting business of the Senate properly done."[121]

Business was carried on in the same atmosphere in the following two sessions of Parliament. In the session of 1959 the Government Leader was supported by a group of Liberal Senators, among them Power, Croll, Dupuis, Kinley, Roebuck, and Macdonald, to defeat an amendment made to the Excise Tax bill by the Banking and Commerce committee.[122] In another financial measure, the Income Tax bill, the Senate did amend the bill and sent it back to the Commons for concurrence. Although the amendment did not threaten the balance of ways and means, the Minister, under pressure from all sides of the House, decided against the change and the bill was returned to the Senate a few hours before prorogation. Constitutionally, the Senate, dictated by a Liberal majority, could have insisted on its position and could either have the bill defeated or prorogation postponed until a compromise solution had been found. The Opposition chose neither of these courses. Although Sen. Macdonald protested against the practice of transmitting important pieces of legislation to the Senate in the dying hours of the session, he did not, for a moment, consider it within the practical-political jurisdiction of the Senate to block legislation of such magnitude.[123]

In the following session Sen. Euler's renewed attempts to remove the sales tax on oleomargarine from the Excise Tax bill was defeated by an unrecorded vote of 32:15, after Opposition Leader Macdonald and Liberal Sen. Golding, a former Deputy Chairman of Committees in the Commons, severely criticized the proposed amendment. Although action by the Senate respecting the resolution to amend the BNA Act for the setting of a retiring age of judges eventually yielded the same result as was fought for by the Liberal Opposition in the Commons unsuccessfully, debate in the Senate was conducted in a dispassionate and almost academically objective manner and at no point during the lengthy discussion were there two irreconcilably solid blocks facing each other. Indeed, in at least two cases there were indications of an open breach in the Liberal ranks. First, a small group of Liberal senators preferred postponing further action until the advisory opinion of the Supreme Court was available regarding the jurisdiction of Parliament in the matter and they criticized their leader for failing to move an amendment

[121]*Ibid., 1959*, p. 40. [122]*Ibid.*, p. 822. [123]*Ibid.*, p. 1139.

to that effect. An even more significant clash of opinion occurred on the question of the retroactive character of the resolution. Several Liberal senators, notably Farris, Gouin, and Leonard, accused the Government of committing a breach of contract towards members of the Bench who had been appointed under good behaviour.[124] However, in a powerful address which was full of common sense, wisdom, and a profound knowledge of constitutional history, Sen. Hugessen refuted their argument, by emphasizing that the appointment of a judge was not a contract but an exercise of the prerogative of the Crown. When the final vote came on the amendment to strike out the reference to district and county court judges from the Resolution, the vote was nearly unanimous; only the Government Leader protested in his official capacity, but it was his duty to do so.

The spirit of co-operation remained unbroken during the last year of the Conservative Administration. Although at the beginning of the session of 1962–63 Sen. Macdonald made headlines with his observation the "minority governments cast an added onus on the Senate,"[125] he also emphasized that the principles which he enumerated in 1957 and 1958 were of continuing validity.[126] Indeed, apart from a few pointed remarks during the Debate on the Address the level of discussion did not reflect the unusually tense atmosphere which prevailed in the Commons, and, similarly to 1957, the Liberal majority of the Senate made no attempt to obstruct the Government's legislative program, financial or otherwise. It followed from this attitude that Sen. Macdonald desisted from his earlier demand to refer the Atlantic Development Board bill to committee;[127] that Sen. Fournier's last-minute attempt to amend the Canada World Exhibition Corporation bill on third reading received no support from his Liberal colleagues after the Government Leader announced the Government's disapproval of the proposed change;[128] or that the repeated efforts of Senators Roebuck and Pouliot to defeat the Combines Investigation and Criminal Code bill on both second and third readings proved unsuccessful.[129]

This historical review, which dealt with only the most typical cases of impartiality in the Senate's proceedings during the last thirty-seven years, will, it is hoped, establish beyond a doubt that the aura surrounding the transaction of business in the Senate is one of co-operation and of political self-restraint. It is against this background of normalcy that the occasional flare-up of partisan feelings must be considered. The number of such occasions has been small, much smaller than is generally believed

[124] *Ibid., 1960,* pp. 978 ff. [125] *Ibid.*, 1962–3, p. 40. [126] *Ibid.*, pp. 38–9.
[127] *Ibid.*, p. 480. [128] *Ibid.*, pp. 515–22. [129] *Ibid.*, pp. 336, 342–3.

and it is probably true to say that few of them have been connected with some really important item in the legislative program of the Government of the day. What characterized them rather was the fact that the issues involved had been the subject of fully publicized and passionate partisan debates, affecting the "soft underbelly" of national party fortunes, well before they actually reached the Senate. It was in these circumstances that the partisan past of the Senators, operating through the appointing system, forced to the surface their "inarticulate major premises of partisanship," by responding to the heat and tension already generated elsewhere.

Thus, in the Beauharnois scandal of 1931–2, in which three members of the Liberal Party in the Senate were charged with using their positions for soliciting large sums of campaign contributions, action in the Senate did not start until the session of 1932, by which time the whole question was so deeply entangled in acute partisan controversy that any quasi-judicial impartiality was out of the question. The attacks were directed against the good reputation of the party and even the integrity of the party leader did not escape critical comments.[130] Accordingly, at every stage of the Senate inquiry, viz., in the Special Committee,[131] during the debate on the Committee's report, and, finally, in voting upon it, strict party lines were followed and the old partisan emotions overwhelmed any other considerations. The speeches in the Chamber bore out the character of the Report. The four-day debate in the Senate covered some 149 pages in Hansard, one-third of the Senate Debates that year; thirty-three Senators took part in the discussion, with a total of 157 interventions. The leading figures were Meighen and Tanner on the Conservative side, and Dandurand and Graham in the Liberal ranks. Meighen's passionate speech and his whole role in the affair lent substance to circulating rumours that the main reason for his appointment to the Senate in that year was that he could conclude the Beauharnois affair quickly and effectively and deliver as deeply humiliating a blow to the Liberal party and to Mackenzie King as possible.[132] Without exception, all Conservative speakers urged the adoption of the Committee's

[130]It was alleged at the time (since then proven: Blair H. Neatby, *William Lyon Mackenzie King: The Lonely Heights 1924–1932*, Toronto, 1963) that King's hotel bills at Bermuda were paid out of Beauharnois funds. See Murphy to Lynch Staunton, Nov. 17, 1931 (Murphy Papers, vol. 17, nos. 7273–4) and to H. W. Anderson, Editor of the *Globe*, July 30, 1931 (*Ibid.*, nos. 159–60); *Canadian Annual Review, 1932*, p. 31. For King's denial of the charges, see *HD, 1931*, p. 4028.

[131]The nine-member committee, consisting of five Conservatives and four Liberals, was unable to produce a unanimous report. Its final recommendations were not endorsed by the Liberal members of the committee.

[132]*SD, 1932*, p. 240. Roger Graham, *Arthur Meighen*, vol. 3, pp. 34 ff.

recommendations and all Liberals denounced them as nothing but the result of sheer politicking. In the ensuing division thirty-four Conservatives voted for the Report and twenty-seven Liberals against it.[133]

Again, the Conservative amendment to the CNR Capital Revision bill of 1937 for the purpose of tabling the CNR indebtedness in the railway's balance sheet apart from the public accounts, so that the people be given a fair picture of the railway situation, was, in fact, a continuation in the Senate of the fight which had begun in the House of Commons. Since the political repercussions of the proposed amendment had definite partisan overtones, arguments for and against the motion lacked their usual quasi-judicial objectivity and the final vote on the amendment (37:26 in favour) was wholly on party lines.[134]

The next occasion on which solid party votes were produced did not come until 1956,[135] when partisan feelings were aroused well in advance of the arrival in the Senate of the bill respecting the Northern Ontario Pipe Line Crown Corporation. Although the procedural framework of the debate was less openly stifling in the Senate than it was in the Commons,[136] the speeches during debates on the second reading, in Committee of the Whole and on the third reading, were motivated by no other than partisan considerations. The "wilful little group" of Liberal Senators who had on so many occasions rebelled against the Government was now closely behind their leader. On the other hand, all four speakers of the six-member Conservative Opposition severely criticized the Administration and urged the defeat of the legislation. The vote on the third reading of the bill (50 to 6 for passage) was cast strictly on party lines.

[133]*SJ, 1932*, p. 229.

[134]*SD, 1937*, pp. 322, 363, 365, etc. *SJ, 1937*, p. 221.

[135]Although there was no cross-voting on the rejection of the Penitentiary bill in 1938, the vote was a routine one on the day of prorogation and it was not the result of a genuine partisan battle. On the other hand, the vote on the Parliamentary Library bill in 1955, which also followed party lines, was a most unusual division. The third reading of the bill was postponed to meet Conservative Sen. Marcotte's request to be allowed to speak on the measure. When the time came on March 2, he said that owing to illness he was unable to prepare his notes. He did not indicate his reasons for opposing the bill and his four Conservative colleagues supported him from courtesy. *SD, 1955*, p. 238; *SJ, 1955*, p. 224.

[136]Charges that the rules were suspended in the Senate to meet the deadline on the bill (*HD, 1956*, pp. 4461, 4756, 5334; "The Impotent Senate," *Toronto Telegram*, June 7, 1956; "How Did the Senate Serve Canada?" *Calgary Herald*, June 9, 1956; "Sic Transit," *Globe and Mail*, June 9, 1956) ignored the fact that the rules are suspended every session in order to facilitate business. Furthermore, the bill was not read the second time until all four Conservative spokesmen (Haig, Aseltine, Horner, Hackett) had an opportunity to make their contributions to the discussion.

The unbroken party vote on Sen. Wall's motion in 1959 to authorize the Senate's Finance Committee to study the threat of inflation in Canada provided further illustration of the type of issue which is likely to awaken partisan feelings in the Senate. Although the motion was apparently not intended to seek political advantage and from the strictly scientific tenor of the explanatory remarks of its sponsor it was clear that its sole purpose was to perform a fact-finding service in a problem area of concern,[137] during the ensuing long debate (it was considered on twelve different occasions extending over two months) every speaker on the Liberal side supported the project while every speaker on the Government side was opposed to it. And by the time the motion was brought down for a vote it had become obvious that despite the original intentions, the issue had been tossed into the arena of political controversy. The vote confirmed this impression: forty Liberals voted for Wall's motion, fourteen Conservatives against it. As to the reason for this solid block formation, Conservative senators, who were not consulted before the introduction of the motion, laboured under the misconception that the motion tried to pin upon their party the responsibility for inflationary tendencies in the country. This suspicion, well grounded or not, was sufficient to arouse deep-seated party loyalties.

The last two cases in which intense partisanship coloured the deliberations of the Senate were the Customs Tariff bill and the Bank of Canada bill in the session of 1961. Although the nature of the challenge was different, in both there was an open defiance of Government policy, and the Senate became hopelessly entangled in sheer politicking. What made the whole affair thoroughly sad was the fact that in both instances the issue at stake was one in which the Senate had repeatedly claimed to have an important and historic role to play, namely, to be a protector of individual rights and a watchdog of ministerial encroachments. It would have been reassuring, therefore, to see a reasonable unanimity all through the debates and decisions. However, by the time the two bills reached the Senate in early summer the political temperature was running so high that tradition was subordinated to awakened party loyalties. Under such circumstances it would be less than fair to ascertain which one of the two parties in the Senate was more under the influence of partisan considerations. That such considerations were dominant in both parties during those months cannot be denied. Both the floor of the Senate and the floor of its Banking and Commerce committee were turned into

[137]That there was really no such motive behind the motion is borne out by Sen. Haig's congratulations after the Committee had completed its study and brought in its report. See *SD, 1959*, p. 1057.

platforms for partisan speeches while in all the divisions—twelve in number—that were held in the two cases in the Senate and in the committee votes were cast, without exception, along party lines. Such a usually objective observer as Sen. Hugessen had to admit on July 13, when all was over, that

> We have established a reputation in this House of which we are rather proud, that we do not allow political considerations or political passions to interfere with our thinking or with our consideration of matters that come before us. . . . I must admit that in the last two or three days there have been political passions aroused in this House . . . but I do hope that when the matter is finally disposed of and has gone into the realm of history our old relationships and the friendly feelings that we have for one another, whether on one side of the House or the other, will remain in undiminished force.[138]

In summary, the evidence of partisan upheavals in the Senate during the period under review indicates that such outbursts are sporadic and exceptional and are in no way typical of the general atmosphere of the Senate as it goes about performing its everyday legislative business. The fact that they do occur from time to time is a reminder of the latent potency of the principles governing the appointing system. The infrequency of their occurrence, however, is an equally strong proof of the effectiveness of the moderating climate of the House. The result is a body of men, partisan in their background but old and experienced enough to know that it would be foolish to let loose partisan passions in the Senate. Being human, however, they sometimes act foolishly.

[138] *Ibid.*, pp. 1129–30.

PROCEDURE AND ORGANIZATION OF BUSINESS

5

AS WITH THE FORMAL MACHINERY of party organization, the rules of procedure in the Senate are characterized by a high degree of flexibility. Although the Rules of the Senate contain some 152 rules, made up of an original body adopted in 1906 and of subsequent changes and amendments, including the rules governing private business and divorce, they are not adhered to with any degree of rigidity and a considerable portion of the Senate's business is in fact conducted under suspended rules. This laxity has never failed to impress newly appointed Senators, particularly those who have been members of the House of Commons. Some have acquiesced easily in the change, others have not.[1] What most of them have found difficult to grasp at once was the fact that rules of procedure invariably reflect the substantive character of an assembly's functions. They have been devised, developed, and modified so that they may suit the prevailing atmosphere of a particular legislative body. "It is well to remember," Sen. Vien, war-time Speaker of the Senate once remarked, "that the Senate's rules are made for the Senate, that the Senate is not made for its rules. Our rules are flexible, and by general consent of the House, and with leave from His Honour the Speaker, they are always interpreted in the most liberal way."[2] It may be of some interest to mention that following the tradition of the Legislative Council of Canada, the rules of the Senate were from the first based[3] upon the

[1]See, in particular, Sen. Ian A. Mackenzie's desperate attempts to introduce stringency in the application of the rules. *SD, 1948*, pp. 144, 516, 534–5.

[2]*Ibid.*, p. 144.

[3]Sir J. G. Bourinot, *Parliamentary Procedure and Practice in the Dominion of Canada* (3rd ed., Toronto, 1903), "Senate Rules," Rule. 1.

practice of the House of Lords, and respect for the precedent-setting authority of the Lords has continued in modern times.[4]

Volume of Work

One of the recurrent criticisms levelled against the Senate is concerned with its apparent idleness—its brief sittings, its short working weeks, and its long adjournments. This charge takes no account of the fact that the Senate suffers from an arrangement for which it is not responsible, and it ignores the amount of work done in the Senate's committees. It is a fact of parliamentary life that, apart from a varying number of bills initiated in the Upper House, the Senate is utterly dependent upon the House of Commons for the great bulk of its legislative business. Table XX indicates the distribution of legislation per session according to its arrival in the Senate from the House of Commons. It is apparent that the number of measures sent up to the Senate during the first two months of a session is insufficient to provide an adequate basis for the regular functioning of the House. There is nothing in the record which would suggest that the lull in the Senate's activity is in any way related to the type of government in power or to the nature of the majorities in the two chambers. An inevitable result of this "legislative frugality" on the part of the Commons in the first half of the session is a congestion of business in the Senate towards the end of the parliamentary session. There is always a varying number of bills, among them important pieces of the Government's legislative program, arriving in the Senate during the last few days before prorogation, and the experience of the 1930's shows that not even the energetic and influential leadership of a Meighen or a Dandurand could overcome this handicap; indeed, from 1932 to 1940 an average of nine government bills reached the Senate in the last ten days of the session.

It is hardly surprising, therefore, that it has become a yearly ritual for Senators to register their protests against the continuation of this irritating and humiliating practice. Indeed, no one is more sensitive to criticism on this point than members of the Senate. As mere protesting has proved ineffective, more drastic suggestions have been put forward from time to time. Recalling Sen. Dandurand's oft-repeated proposal either to refuse to pass a bill or to postpone prorogation of Parliament if the available time was found insufficient for a full consideration of the measure by the

[4]See Speaker's ruling in the Signature Loan Company bill, March 6, 1956. *SD, 1956*, p. 291.

Table XX

Arrival of Bills from the House of Commons, 1925–63

Session	Month 1st	2nd	3rd	4th	5th	6th	7th	8th	9th	10th	Last ten days	Total	No. of sittings	No. of days adjourned
1925	–	–	1	21	31						2	53	50	55
1926	–	–	–	1	12						–	13	42	85
1927	1	–	4	34	30						20	69	34	55
1928	–	–	10	25	15	1					1	51	52	35
1929	3	3	21	28	5						3	60	44	40
1930	–	4	3	40							14	47	28	40
1931	–	1	10	4	37	3					15	55	50	45
1932	1	10	12	26							14	49	42	35
1933	–	9	–	–	2	7	3	25			1	46	64	107
1934	–	4	7	4	6	31	1				13	53	59	50
1935	–	6	11	8	1	26	4				4	56	57	65
1936	–	8	6	1	28						14	43	49	50
1937	–	9	13	20							16	42	37	20
1938	–	–	17	17	16						9	50	61	50
1939	–	–	10	18	18	1					7	47	47	55
1940	3	22	17	2							2	44	42	20
1945 (2d)	1	5	14	11							9	31	44	30
1946	–	2	7	7	12	34					2	63	72	45
1947	–	5	6	4	5	18	20				9	58	59	60
1948	–	–	–	8	6	4	32				5	50	69	60
1949	–	2	5	4							4	11	39	19
1949 (2d)	–	1	9	18							9	28	43	9
1950	1	5	–	7	17						3	30	65	40
1951	–	–	5	3	12	29					13	49	62	30
1952	1	1	14	25							2	41	60	25
1953	–	–	–	5	7	17	6				1	35	59	56
1954	–	7	2	10	4	–	9	21			1	53	77	7
1955	1	–	13	–	12	17	4				–	47	79	21
1956	–	2	–	2	8	8	4	12			12	36	78	48
1957	–	4	5	16							16	25	46	–
1957–58	–	7	9	9							7	25	45	–
1958	2	2	10	19	3						3	36	59	7
1959	–	2	5	1	10	14	7				4	39	75	7
1960	2	1	3	–	6	11	5	3			2	31	87	14
1961	2	3	–	3	4	2	10	16	7	7	7	54	91	21
1962	8	8	5								3	21	40	11
1962–63	1	6	7								–	14	43	14

Senate, Sen. Farris, in his indignation over the very late arrival of the Public Superannuation bill in 1953, formally called upon the Leader of the Opposition to declare that in a similar case in the future he would hold up prorogation of Parliament until proper consideration of all legislation before the Senate has been completed.[5] Again, in the session of 1961, the Supplementary Estimates, amounting to $182 million, were brought before the Senate on March 29, thirty-five minutes prior to the time set for the Royal Assent. This time the disappointment and shock were so great that shortly afterwards a private member's bill was introduced in the Senate to provide that "the date for the Royal Assent to any bill shall not be set before the third reading of any such bill is passed by both the Houses of Parliament." The bill was described as "a revindication of the primary rights of Parliament, the rights of the Senate, to take its time to study the legislation that is before us."[6] Although the bill was not proceeded with, it was allowed to remain on the order paper as "a reminder."

In essence all protests and suggested remedies have been futile since it is not by design or through malice that the House of Commons retards the flow of legislation to the Senate. The real source of the discrepancy lies in the fact that while moving along two parallel functional lines the two houses must still synchronize their work according to an ultimately common time-table. Thus, what makes up the difference and leads, eventually, to an inevitable time-lag in the procedural stages of the two houses is that the 265 members of the House of Commons must during the session express the opinions of their electors, even though their speeches may often follow the exact trend of thought and argument contained in a dozen or more other speeches already delivered. The reason for doing so is simple; while ostensibly addressing the Commons its members in reality speaking to their constituents who have sent them and whose continuing support they constantly seek to reinforce; hence the repetitions and delays. By performing their primary political function members of the House of Commons must necessarily sacrifice some of the basic requirements of business efficiency in completing the yearly volume of legislation. Called upon to discharge an entirely different function, members of the Senate are not burdened with the responsibility of keeping one eye on the repercussions of their views in an imaginary constituency. When discussions take place in the Senate any objections raised are answered directly and no one thinks of raising them a second time once they have been answered. As a result, debate

[5]*Ibid., 1953*, p. 573.
[6]*Ibid., 1961*, p. 612.

is conducted more expeditiously in the Upper than in the Lower House. Speeches tend to be shorter and on matters of minor importance there are usually fewer senators who want to speak. According to Sen. Dandurand's estimates, in an average session of five months the House of Commons devoted at least two months to matters that were disposed of in the Senate within two days.[7]

If the Senate needs less time than the House of Commons for doing its share of legislation, and yet the two houses must still organize their business according to a common parliamentary schedule, it follows that the Senate will have to adjourn from time to time during the session. Table XIX shows the number of days the Senate was adjourned in each peace-time session from 1925 to 1963. But nothing shows better the dependence of the Senate upon the House of Commons for its legislative work than the fact that in addition to the longer periods of adjournment the Senate is often compelled to adjourn from day to day or from hour to hour, to reassemble later at the call of the bell. On Friday, May 16, 1958, for instance, four days after the opening of the session the Senate met at 12 o'clock noon and gave third reading to the Government's Unemployment Insurance bill. "This," Sen. Aseltine told the House, "completes the business for the morning. There is a possibility that the National Housing bill will reach us this afternoon. . . . Under these circumstances there is nothing to do but adjourn during pleasure. . . ." At 4 pm, when the sitting was resumed, he informed the Senate that "there is still some hope that the National Housing bill will be sent over to us in time to be dealt with today but there is also a possibility it will not." All he could suggest was that the Senate adjourn during pleasure, to resume at a later hour during the day. This is what happened and following the passage of the bill the Senate adjourned until May 19, at 8 oclock in the evening.[8] Again, on June 4 it was expected that the Senate would be able to consider the Supply bill. However, the Government Leader told the House he had simply "received a note saying that sufficient progress has not been made for that to happen. As it is unlikely that the bill will reach us before tomorrow, I have no alternative but to move . . . that the Senate do now adjourn."[9]

There has, however, been a tendency for the Senate to sit for far longer in recent years than was previously the case. In general, when we consider recent sessions in comparison with those before the war, we find that since 1945 the average length of time spent in session each year has been about twice as great as between 1925 and 1940. This increase

[7] *Ibid., 1936*, pp. 45–6.
[8] *Ibid., 1958*, p. 39.
[9] *Ibid.*, p. 136.

has also been evident in the number of pages occupied by the official report of the proceedings in the Senate Debates, Hansard having been twice as voluminous in the past few years as it used to be before.[10] Instead of adjourning for several shorter periods throughout the session the practice has been developed for the Senate to have prolonged Christmas and Easter recesses during which to allow legislation to accumulate for transmission from the House of Commons.

Times of Sitting

The days of sitting are not precisely defined. While Parliament is in session the Senate normally meets on Tuesdays, Wednesdays,and Thursdays. Sometimes, if it is found impractical to fit all the business into three days a week, additional sittings are called on Mondays or Fridays. At the beginning of the session of 1957–58, for instance, the Senate agreed to Sen. Haig's suggestion that, in view of the volume of forthcoming business, the house should adopt four-day sitting weeks, by adding to its three usual mid-week sitting days Monday nights or Friday afternoons. This course was followed throughout the session, the extra day being Monday rather than Friday.[11]

Apart from some rare occasions on which the Senate met at two distinct sittings the same day, on an ordinary day the house meets for the transaction of business at 3 o'clock in the afternoon. If at 6 o'clock pm the business is not concluded the Rules provide that the Speaker leave the chair until 7.30 the same evening. Occasionally, the Senate may bring its time of sitting earlier in the day and meet at 11 am. Again, the state of business may sometimes require that the Senate meet at 8 pm, continuing generally not later than 10 pm.

On June 4, 1940, the Senate adopted, on the suggestion of Sen. Meighen, a motion that, should a situation arise during any adjournment

[10]The pre-war record was pp. 755 in 1925; in the last five sessions the corresponding figures have been: 1959, pp. 1195; 1960, pp. 1335; 1961, pp. 1306; and for the two sessions in 1962, pp. 1194. This same trend was found by P. Bromhead in regard to the House of Lords. *The House of Lords and Contemporary Politics, 1911–1957* (London, 1958), p. 82.

[11]Senators do not like Monday sittings. When it was suggested in 1953 that the Senate meet on Monday, November 24, Sen. Marcotte said: "Usually the Senate does not meet on Monday and we can do our business with the banks on that day, but now you are trying to take that day away from us . . . I am a businessman, you are a businessman, and there are other businessmen here. Let's have at least one free day in the week in which to do business with the banks." *SD, 1953*, p. 3. Nevertheless, there was a fair attendance on Monday (58 per cent), although Marcotte failed to turn up

of the house which would in the opinion of the Speaker warrant that the Senate meet in a special emergency sitting, the Speaker should be authorized to summon Senators back to the Chamber. The Speaker acted once under the motion during that session, when on June 10 he called an emergency sitting to adopt a resolution of declaration of war against Italy. Since then the Senate regularly adopts the motion every session. It was utilized once in 1955 and twice in 1956, on each occasion for the purpose of enabling certain legislation to receive early Royal Assent, and it was for similar reasons that the Senate was called together on September 25, 1961, one day before the date set for its reconvention.

Perhaps partly because of the uncertainty caused by the Senate's dependence on the House of Commons for the fuel to its legislative engines, and partly because of the general atmosphere of the House, there is a conspicuous aura of informality in the Senate surrounding the arrangement of time. The rules of procedure do not provide any advance planning for the session, with the result that for the first five or six weeks of the session the Senate considers details of no major importance. A very characteristic practice had developed in the second half of the thirties in the form of a self-appointed committee of members from both sides of the House gathering regularly at luncheon once a week for the purpose of discussing things "which we thought we might bring before the Senate and we would agree among ourselves who should lead off and how the discussion should develop."[12] This was far more in line with the general tenor of the House than Sen. Bouffard's suggestion in 1951 that a formal steering committee should be set up to meet a few weeks prior to the opening of the session and to lay before the House a blueprint for the months ahead.[13]

Although theoretically the time-table of the House is drawn up by the Senate Leader, there is no weekly announcement of forthcoming business and changes in the schedule are made smoothly through co-operation with members across the floor. Sen. Dandurand was particularly proud of the fact that after 1935, when he resumed leadership in the Senate, he never took any action that did not have the assent of Sen. Meighen. Very often rules had been set aside, or ignored, in order that the work of the chamber might be promoted.[14] The same informality and flexibility characterize the rules governing the order of daily business in the Senate. Unlike the Commons, where in recent years government business had precedence on every sitting day except for a certain amount of time reserved for private members' days in each session, in the Senate the orders are taken in their regular order and government business is not

[12]*Ibid., 1942*, p. 149.
[13]*Ibid., 1951*, p. 203.
[14]*Ibid., 1940*, p. 329.

regularly given precedence.[15] When it is, it is by consent. But there is no distinction between government time and private members' time, no daily question period of fixed duration and no regular half-hour adjournment debate at the end of the day's business. While it is true, of course, that in fact a great part of the Senate's sitting time is occupied with the discussion of legislation introduced by the government, there is still plenty of opportunity for holding debates on all kinds of subjects according to the preferences of individual senators. Private members' motions need not depend on the chances of a ballot, and in other debates, however important, the application of rigid time-tables never becomes necessary.

Legislative Procedure

With regard to the framework of the formal procedure of legislation there is no fundamental difference between the two houses. All public bills, whether sponsored by the Government or not, and whether initiated in the Senate or brought up from the Commons, have to go through the same main stages in the Upper as in the Lower House. The first reading is usually formal and is a means whereby the House is formally acquainted of the existence of a measure.[16] The principles are discussed at the second reading stage, followed by a clause-by-clause consideration of the technical details, then a report stage, and finally by the third reading, when the House finally decides on the ultimate shape of the bill as it emerges from the meticulous examination in committee and on report. Although Rule 63 of the Senate provides that no two stages of a bill are to be taken on any one day, it has become a custom for the Senate to suspend the rules every session, so that they could, if necessary, pass a bill through all its stages on the same day.[17]

[15]In the House of Lords *SO* 35 (5) provides that on Tuesdays and Thursdays the proceedings on public bills have precedence over questions, motions, or resolutions. However, the rule is interpreted very loosely, Bromhead, *The House of Lords*, pp. 89 ff.

[16]Controversy on the first reading is very rare. In 1929 Sen. Willoughby, Leader of the Opposition, objected the first reading of the Criminal Code bill, on the ground that no copies of the bill had been distributed before the first reading. His point, however, was overruled by the Speaker, maintaining that under Rule 25 first readings do not require previous notice and that bills are distributed after the first reading for second reading. *SD, 1929*, p. 382. It is customary, however, for the sponsors of private members' bills to give, in addition to merely reading out the title, a short explanation of the nature and objectives of the measure at the first reading stage.

[17]There are always some Senators who will object to the suspension of the rules, but for the great majority such laxity would seem quite natural.

In its broad outlines, then, the Senate's procedure on bills is identical with that of the Commons. However, there are some important differences from the Commons that must be noticed. They are all related to the underlying concept of the Senate's functions and its position in the structure of Parliament. The fact that the Senate's role is essentially revisory and non-partisan in character and that the Senate is being deprived of all ministerial representation has two direct procedural consequences. First, the importance of the second reading stage, where the main political debate is supposed to take place, is greatly reduced in the Upper House, and second, as a result, the locus where the Senate performs its primary function is shifted from the Chamber to the committee room.[18] Indeed, there is a general inclination on the part of Senators to letting the second reading stage pass without very lengthy discussion. From 1925 to 1963 there were only ten bills[19] among those later amended which were debated for three days or more in the Senate on second reading, but even in these cases the debates were much shorter than the corresponding debates in the Lower House. Discussion at the second reading stage is, in many ways, a prologue to the real work in committee. It is at this point that senators may intimate the type of change they would later seek to make, and by referring to particular aspects of the bill they may also hope to prepare the minister for possible concessions at the committee stage.

An even more typical practice, which was developed in the Senate in the twenties and thirties, has been to pass the second reading of a bill "without agreeing to principle." Thus, the Home Bank Depositors bill of 1925, the Farm Loan Credit bill of 1926, the Immigration bill of 1928, or the Criminal Code bill of 1930, to pick only a few, were all passed on the second reading, referred to committee, amended and reported back to the Senate, and it was not until the third reading stage that the so-called principles were discussed. Speaking on the second reading of the Income Tax bill of 1948, Sen. Haig, Opposition Leader in the Senate, said: ". . . our consent to second reading should not be taken as implying support of the bill, because we have not had a chance to study it."[20] Consequently, he kept his "second reading speech" until the bill, returning from committee, reached the third reading stage.

[18]For a discussion of the procedural rule allowing ministers from the House of Commons to come to the Senate and move the second reading of their legislation, see chap. VII.

[19]Home Bank Depositors, 1925; Crown Debts, 1927; Export, 1930; Foreign Exchange, 1946; Canadian Wheat Board, 1947; Public Service Superannuation, 1953; Parliamentary Secretaries and the National Emergency board, 1959; Criminal Code and Customs Tariff, 1961.

[20]*SD, 1948*, p. 654.

This degradation of the second reading stage has in fact, if not in principle, had the same effect as the American and Continental practice of bringing the committee stage before the second reading. The great value of debating the "political principle" of a bill in the House of Commons before anything else happens to it lies in the fact that it provides an opportunity of criticizing the policy of the Government with respect to a specific piece of legislation. Where the executive as the highest policy-making agency is not part of the legislative assembly (USA) or where it is under the thumb of the legislature ("government by assembly") there is no reason why the two stages could not with advantage be changed. The Senate, in actual practice, is not in a very different position from Congress, in that the Government is neither represented in it directly, nor is it responsible to it. Accordingly, in 1928 Sen. Griesbach made the significant suggestion in respect of the Immigration bill that before the bill was read the second time it should be referred to committee for study, with the implication that future legislation might follow the same course. His proposal, however, was not acceptable to a majority of the Senators, who, rather than to break a new procedural path, decided to pass the second reading of the bill without giving their approval of its principle.[21] However, in 1946 in view of the importance and complexity of the Foreign Exchange Control bill, the Senate decided, on the motion of Sen. Howard, the Chief Government Whip, to refer the bill to committee before second reading, so that expert evidence on the subject could be heard. Although it was recognized that the procedure proposed was extraordinary, the Speaker gave the following ruling: "The bill is of such importance and of such character, that I can well understand the desire of members to have an opportunity of consulting the minister and officers of his department. This desire having been expressed by the leader of both parties in the Senate, and there apparently being no dissenting voice, under the circumstances I will accept the motion." He emphasized, however, that this was not good practice and hoped "it will not be resorted to except upon rare and unusual occasions."[22] Indeed, when during the following session Sen. Hayden, using the 1946 precedent, sought to have the Dairy Act Amendment bill referred to the Banking and Commerce committee before second reading, the Speaker promptly ruled against the motion, on the ground that "it would provide an easy method of bringing about filibustering in matters of parliamentary procedure."[23] In fact, there has never been a repetition of the example of the Foreign Exchange Control bill of 1946.

[21]*Ibid., 1928*, p. 515.
[22]*Ibid., 1946*, p. 640.
[23]*Ibid., 1947*, p. 232.

However, even though the Senate has not had the courage to make it a practice of upsetting the traditional stages of legislative procedure, the difficulty was circumvented by the adoption of a characteristically clever device during the war, whereby the *subject-matter* of bills has been referred to committee *before* the bills themselves have reached the Senate. The introduction of the practice was the work of Sen. King, Dandurand's successor as Government Leader in the Senate, 1942–45, who recommended in 1943, that the estimates should be referred to and considered in the Senate's Finance Committee before the bills based upon the estimates arrived in the Senate, thus enabling senators to obtain from the minister and his subordinates sufficient knowledge of the estimates, and relieving himself of the task of explaining these intricate measures to the Senate. The suggestion, so typical of the new outlook of Senate leadership, was warmly received by members of the house, and the practice with regard to the estimates has continued throughout the 1940's and '50's.

The next logical step was to try to apply the new procedure to legislation other than supply bills. In 1945 Sen. McGeer, a Liberal Senator from British Columbia, who had extensive legislative experience on all levels of government, suggested early in the session that the motion regarding the Finance Committee should be enlarged, so that all resolutions and all bills[24] laid before the House of Commons should, in advance of their arrival in the Senate, automatically go to one of the standing committees for consideration, concurrently with their consideration in the Commons.[25] The scheme, in spite of its evident practical advantages, was attacked by the traditionalists on the constitutional ground that it implied "a hole-in-the-corner method of dealing with bills by a committee, as a substitute for the open discussion of the principle of bills on the floor of this house."[26] As a result of the opposition, the motion was dropped, but the idea did not die and, if not in the sweeping terms of Sen. McGeer's proposal, it has found general acceptance. Ordinarily, the committee would briefly report back to the Senate, though not usually in support or otherwise of the resolution or bill, but rather to indicate that they had all the information they required, and thereafter the discussion would be resumed. In the session of 1945 the procedure was used on two occasions; the report of the Interim Commission on Food and Agriculture was referred to the Committee on Agriculture while the Bretton Woods Agreement to the Committee on

[24]The distinction between a bill and a resolution in this respect is that the resolution still stands on the order paper, whereas a bill, when referred, disappears from the order paper and does not re-appear until the committee has reported. See *ibid., 1948*, p. 147.

[25]*Ibid., 1945*, p. 94.

[26]*Ibid.*, p. 99.

Commerce and Trade Relations, before the bills based upon the Report and the Agreement were actually brought down in the Senate. Indeed, the procedure has proved most advantageous in considering intergovernmental agreements: in 1948 the subject-matter of the resolution to approve the Geneva Trade and Tariff Agreement of 1947 together with the complimentary agreements between Canada and the United States and Canada and Britain, the report of the Royal Commission on Transportation in 1951, and the agreement between the Federal Government and Saskatchewan respecting the South Saskatchewan River Project in 1958 were all referred to committee in advance of the arrival of the legislation built upon them. In the case of ordinary legislation the method was used only in the session of 1952, when the subject-matter of three bills, the Marine and Aviation War Risks, Currency, Mint and Exchange Fund, and Immigration, were sent to committee, simultaneously with their consideration in the Lower House.

Apart from the minimization of the role of second reading debates, the next major procedural difference from the Commons lies in the increased role played by the standing and special committees of the Senate in legislation, and in a consequent withering away of Committee of the Whole in the procedural scheme of the Upper House.[27] Tables XXI and XXII show the number of public bills referred to standing or special committees, and the appropriate stages where public bills were amended, in each peace-time session of Parliament from 1925 to 1963. They reveal that 43.5 per cent of the total volume of legislation over a period of thirty-seven years have been considered in committees. However, it is also evident that the effective utilization of the committee system has not really begun until after the war. When we compare the post-war sessions with those between 1925 and 1940 from the point of view of the number of bills referred to committees we find that in the pre-war years only 25.6 per cent of the legislation was considered in standing or special committees, with the result that on the great majority of bills in this period the Senate was put into Committee of the Whole; however, the figure has more than doubled after the war, so that from 1945 to 1963, 55.5 per cent of the total amount of legislation before the Senate have been sent to committees. Therefore, it is not surprising to find that, significantly, no more than seven bills in all have been considered in Committee of the Whole during the past eighteen years in the Senate.[28]

[27]A more detailed discussion of the committee system of the Senate follows in chap. IX.

[28]Railway, 1951; Income Tax and Pipe Line, 1956; Pension, 1957–58; Estate Tax, 1958; Excise Tax, 1960; and Halifax Signal Station, 1961.

TABLE XXI

Number of Bills Referred to Committees, 1925–63

Session	Total no. of public bills	Bills referred to committee No.	Bills referred to committee Percentage		Government Leader in the Senate
1925	56	16	28		Dandurand
1926	17	1	6		"
1927	76	25	33	27	"
1928	54	9	16		"
1929	63	31	50		"
1930	50	4	8		"
1931	60	3	5		Willoughby
1932	53	4	8		Meighen
1933	51	2	4	22	"
1934	58	24	42		"
1935	62	24	40		"
1936	49	17	34		Dandurand
1937	45	10	22		"
1938	54	19	36	33	"
1939	50	15	30		"
1940	47	14	29		"
1945	39	18	50		Robertson
1946	76	46	52		"
1947	78	39	50		"
1948	78	42	53		"
1949 I	21	10	50	55.5	"
1949 II	43	18	33		"
1950	55	32	59		"
1951	65	43	66		"
1952	55	28	50		"
1953	56	37	73		"
1954	67	40	59		Macdonald
1955	60	32	50	50	"
1956	50	21	42		"
1957	43	16	37		"
1957–58	32	14	44		Haig
1958	44	18	42		Aseltine
1959	56	43	77		"
1960	50	37	77	66.6	"
1961	66	51	77		"
1962	31	19	63		"
1962–63	18	9	50		Brooks

The reason for the sad story of Committee of the Whole and for the corresponding tendency towards an increased utilization of select standing committees has been two-fold. On the one hand, as a result of the very generous interpretation of the rules governing debates, second reading debates in the Senate are, in fact, not very different from discussions in Committee of the Whole in the Commons. Members can

TABLE XXII

Distribution of Bills According to the Stage of Amendment, 1925–63*

Session	Total no. of amended bills	In Committee of the Whole	In standing or select committee	On third reading
1925	11	5	6	1
1926	2		2	
1927	12	6	5	2
1928	8	3	4	3
1929	4	4		
1930	9	5	3	1
1931	5	3	2	
1932	5	5		
1933	7	5	1	1
1934	12	4	8	2
1935	23	2	19	3
1936	19	6	11	2
1937	10	4	6	1
1938	11	2	8	2
1939	13	4	9	1
1940	16	2	12	3
1945	7		7	
1946	12		12	
1947	14		14	
1948	6		6	
1949	2		2	
1950	1		1	
1951	16	1	15	1
1952	3		2	1
1953	4		4	
1954	5		5	
1955	5		5	
1956	0			
1957	1		1	
1957–58	1		1	
1958	4		4	
1959	7		7	
1960	1		1	
1961	2		2	
1962	1		1	
1962–63	0		0	
Total	259	61	185	25
Percentages		24	75	10

*Some bills have been amended at more than one stage.

always ask permission to question the senator who has the floor and never is such permission refused or the question left unanswered. As time goes on, Senators will even drop this pretext and interrupt the discussion whenever they wish to make a brief speech. All this is possible because of the leniency of the Speaker in having the rules kept according to the letter and the co-operative atmosphere of the House which raises no objection to such leniency. "In most of our debates," Sen. Roebuck said, "we get along much as we would if the House were in Committee of the Whole, and that is probably why the House is seldom moved into Committee of the Whole."[29]

But the second and principle cause of the replacement of Committee of the Whole by standing committees has been the inadequacy of the information obtainable in Committee of the Whole. Unlike the House of Commons, in the Senate there is no pool of ministerial authority, reinforced by parliamentary secretaries and other personnel, fully informed of the background of the legislation to be presented. The rules of the Senate contain no provision for allowing departmental officials to come to the Senate and answer questions directly. When they attend they sit in front of the Leader who consults with them on any of the questions which he cannot answer and then gives the answer to the House. The result of this elaborate and time-consuming procedure is that the Leader becomes the mouth-piece of the officials, without the advantage of the officials themselves taking an active part in the proceedings. The best way of getting round this difficulty, therefore, is to refer legislation to standing, or occasionally to special, committees where the minister or the officials of the department concerned may appear and furnish the necessary information unhampered by the rules of Committee of the Whole. Also, witnesses cannot testify in Committee of the Whole. And, finally, in a standing committee senators who are eminent members of the Bar and whose opinions are sought on points of law can freely exchange their views with the Law Clerk, right in front of the members of the Committee; this would not be feasible in Committee of the Whole.

Clearly, the substitution of standing committees for Committee of the Whole has been closely connected with the change in the pattern of Senate leadership discussed in the previous chapter. It is hardly surprising that in the heroic age of one-man leadership of Dandurand and Meighen before the war, the device of Committee of the Whole was generally preferred to standing committees; for in Committee of the Whole it is still the Leader who runs the show, precisely because he is the only medium of communication between the departmental experts and the House. As a result, during Sen. Dandurand's first period of leadership, 1925–30, only 23.5 per cent of the legislation have been referred to standing or special committees; under Sen. Meighen the percentage dropped to 19.8 per cent, and although there was some increase after 1935 it has never risen above 30.2 per cent. As the great Leaders were succeeded by great administrators, interest in the utilization of standing

[29]*SD, 1956*, p. 468.

committees, at the expense of Committee of the Whole, grew intensively. Thus, under that great innovator, Sen. Robertson, 55.5 per cent of all public legislation has been sent to standing committees, while the rest passed through the three readings without being considered in Committee of the Whole.[30] During Sen. Macdonald's four years as Government Leader (1954–57) and under Sen. Haig's short leadership in 1957–58 the percentage fell to 47 and 44 per cent respectively, but during the four years when Sen. Aseltine was Leader (who was not a member of the Cabinet!) it leaped to an unprecedented 67.2 per cent.

The disuse of Committee of the Whole and the excessive use of standing committees has been criticized on two grounds. On the one hand, it has been pointed out that the failure to examine legislation in Committee of the Whole deprives many Senators of the opportunity of participating in the detailed consideration of legislation; for although Senators who are not members of a particular committee are not precluded from attending and asking questions, they cannot vote, which discourages many Senators, particularly junior members of the House, to attend at all. To remedy this situation the practice has been developed that, in addition to the Clerk's reading out the number of the clauses and the words that have been amended, the chairmen of the committees give a short explanation of the nature of, and the reasons for, any amendment made in committee, and it is open to any Senator to ask the chairmen to further explain certain changes. Indeed, the explanations of Senators Hayden and Hugessen, chairmen of the two most important committtees of the Senate, the Committee on Banking and Commerce and the Committee on Transport and Communications, in the past decade have been, and still are, models of mastery summaries of the highlights of committee work. But the second objection is much more serious. It has been maintained, and rightly so, that transacting business in a committee room rather than in the Chamber eliminates an excellent source of publicity as to the extent of the Senate's work. Committee meetings are not attended by reporters, with the result that for the work done in committee—and the bulk of the Senate's work is done in committee—the Senate receives virtually no credit at all. The public feeling—shared by many political scientists—is that all the Senate does is what appears in the recorded proceedings of its formal sessions. It ignores the fact that the Senate's big important committees work all through the week, meeting from 10 am to 12 noon and from 8 pm to 10 pm on sitting days

[30]Indeed, there is always a varying number of bills that are passed through the three readings without being considered in committee (either standing or special or Committee of the Whole) at all.

and also on Mondays, Fridays, and Saturdays, when the Senate usually does not sit at all. Therefore, primarily for the purpose of improving the public image of the Senate there have been remarks in recent years that the consideration of certain types of legislation should be removed from standing committees and transferred to Committee of the Whole.[31] It remains to be seen whether any change would be effected along the proposed lines.

The third, and final, major procedural difference from the Commons is with regard to the third reading stage. Whereas in the House of Commons only verbal amendments are allowed at this stage, in the Senate there is no such limitation. It follows from the general flexibility of the rules of procedure in the Upper House that modifications in legislation be made at any stage, whenever it is desired that such modifications can be made. "I have never been a great stickler for rules," Sen. Dandurand once remarked, "and I have long since learned that you can twist the neck of a bill when it is reported from committee, or on the third reading, or on the question, 'Shall this Bill pass?' So we can cope with anything in the Bill at any of those stages."[32] As Table XXI indicates, 10 per cent of all amended legislation during the last thirty-seven years has been amended on the third reading. The amendments thus made have not been restricted to the final settlement of questions left open on committee. Only in nine out of the twenty-five cases did the amendments take the form of further amending changes already effected in the bill at some earlier stage.[33] In the rest the amendment made at the third reading was primary amendment, many of them moved at the request of the Government, which decided to make a last-minute change in the legislation.[34] In two cases during the period under review the Senate even decided to rescind the third reading of a bill, in order that certain changes could be made which were not brought to the Senate's attention earlier. One was the Seed Grain Loans Guarantee bill

[31]See in particular the remarks of Sen. Pouliot, *SD, 1957–58*, pp. 122, 548; Sen. Wall, *ibid., 1959*, p. 542; and Sen. Crerar, *ibid., 1960*, p. 647.

[32]*Ibid., 1928*, p. 546.

[33]Federal District Commission bill, 1927; Fertilizer bill, Gold and Silver Marketing bill, 1928; Fruit and Honey bill in both 1934 and 1935; CNR Capital Revision bill, 1937; Farmers' Creditors Arrangement bill, 1938; Central Mortgage bill, 1939; Yukon bill, 1940.

[34]Civil Service Superannuation bill, 1925; Three Rivers Harbour Commissioners bill, 1927; Department of National Revenue bill, 1928; Export bill, 1930; Bank bill, 1933; Food and Drugs bill, 1934; Dominion Franchise bill and Economic Council of Canada bill, 1935; Pension bill and Saskatchewan Seed Grain Loans Guarantee bill, 1936; Seed Grain Loans Guarantee bill, 1938; Militia Pension bill, and Farmers' Creditors Arrangement bill, 1940; Federal District Commission bill, 1951; CNR bill, 1952; Canada-Australia Income Tax bill, 1957–58.

of 1938, in which the Senate unanimously agreed to Sen. Dandurand's request that the third reading of the bill should be rescinded and an amendment proposed by the Minister of Justice be inserted in the bill.[35] The other was a private members' measure, Sen. Casgrain's Free Foreign Trade Zone bill of 1937, which, after surviving the three readings, was stopped on the Speaker's usual question, "Is it your pleasure, hon. members, that this bill be passed?" Greatly influenced by the speeches of Senators Meighen, Murdock, and Ballantyne the Senate decided to rescind the third reading of the bill and refer it back to committee for further study.[36] All this shows the ability and willingness of the Senate to tame the apparently rigid rules of legislative procedure whenever the needs of efficiency demand so.

Physical Arrangements and Vacation of Seats

In shape (if not in colour) the debating chamber of the Senate closely resembles the nearby House of Commons. In spite of demands for something more delightful both side walls are covered by paintings depicting scenes of World War I. The Chamber is air-conditioned and served by a system of sound amplifications. The proceedings in the House are conducted in either of the two official languages and since recently a simultaneous interpretation system permits the Senators, the Press, whose gallery is above the throne at the upper end of the Chamber, and the officials to follow the proceedings in the language of their choice. The benches on the floor of the House are arranged in nine blocks providing seats for 104 Senators, which is six short of a theoretical maximum of 110. Ordinarily, of course, all the seats are never filled and the size of the Chamber is satisfactory—except when, on the formal occasions of opening and proroguing Parliament and of giving the Royal Assent to bills, members of the House of Commons attend at the Bar of the Chamber; then, as Mr. Church once complained, "our members could not even enter the Senate . . . while others have to try to climb up on benches, porches and other places as porch climbers to see."[37] However, even on such occasions the situation is not nearly as bad as in Westminster.

Every new Senator, on being summoned to the House, becomes a

[35]*SD, 1938*, pp. 208–58.

[36]This was, as a matter of fact, the first occasion in the Senate for delaying the passage of a bill at this point since 1907, when a measure was rejected under the impact of a powerful address by Sen. Miller. *Ibid., 1937*, pp. 62 ff.

[37]*HD, 1939*, p. 4466.

member of the Senate after attending to the necessary formalities. Following the ceremonies of introduction, neatly described in Bourinot, the new Senator will be assigned a seat by the Speaker and will be conducted to it by the two Senators who introduced him. The seating of members may sometimes prove a delicate task, demanding considerable tact on the part of the Leader. When Meighen became Government Leader in 1932 he asked for definite rules to be framed by caucus on the subject and it was suggested that precedence and seniority were the two guiding principles in seating members of the House.[38]

Apart from the incumbent's death a Senate seat may be vacated through the resignation or the disqualification of its holder. From 1867 to 1963 there were a total of sixty-five resignations from the Senate,[39] of which fourteen fall in the period under study. Six Senators[40] have resigned their seats for apparently no other reason than their advanced age. Ill health was given as reason for resignation by Sen. Planta, Sen. J. M. Wilson, and Sen. Barnard in 1935, 1940, and 1945, respectively. In two other cases resignation was motivated by a decision to seek offices inconsistent with membership in the Senate; in 1942 Sen. Meighen resigned to accept the candidature for the House of Commons in the by-election of York South, held on February 9 of that year, and in 1951 Sen. Ferland resigned his place for a judgeship on the Quebec Superior Court.

The resignation in 1925 of Sen. O'Brien, who was appointed to the Senate by Sir Robert Borden in 1918, was a unique occurrence. It was curiously connected with parallel efforts of the Hon. Charles Murphy, then, as Postmaster General, member of the King Administration, to get into the Senate. This is how Murphy himself described what happened:

> When the Elections of 1921 were over, I had already seen the head of treachery protruding so often that I made up my mind . . . the sooner I got into the Senate the better. . . . An opportunity to put my intention into effect did not develop until December 1923, when, quite unexpectedly, I was informed by my friend, Hon. M. J. O'Brien, that he was anxious to retire from the Senate . . . and that he would resign, provided I was appointed to succeed him. He made it plain that he would not resign in favour of anyone else. Assuming that I could arrange the matter quickly, I got Mr. O'Brien's resignation from him. . . .[41]

---

[38]Correspondence between Meighen and Sen. Schaffner, Oct. 1932. Meighen Papers, series 5, no. 221.

[39]For a complete list, see *SD, 1956*, p. 232.

[40]Lavergne, 1930; McLean, 1936; Smith, 1946; Mullins, 1950; Haig and Farquhar, 1962.

[41]Murphy to Mrs. H. D. Petrie, Jan. 22, 1927. Murphy Papers, vol. 25, nos. 10615–16.

With that resignation Murphy went to see the Prime Minister on December 28, 1923. In the following he gives an account of what transpired at his meeting with Mr. King:

At that interview, I pointed out the futility of what had been under discussion, and for the sake of putting the Party on its feet again . . . I again offered to take charge of a Dominion Organization, if I were allowed to go to the Senate and retain my portfolio. I explained to the Prime Minister at length the necessity of being in the Senate and for retaining the portfolio . . . the Prime Minister was surprised to find that I could arrange for a seat in the Senate, as such a thing had previously been unheard of. . . . We discussed the matter at some length, and as I was not looking for a job and certainly not for a favour, I said I would leave the matter with the Prime Minister, and the conversation ended at that point.[42]

In fact, owing to one cause and another, it was not until 1925 that Murphy was able to have Sen. O'Brien's resignation acted upon. The resignation, contained in a letter addressed to the Governor General, was forwarded by Murphy to the Prime Minister with the following comment: "No action is necessary with regard to the acceptance of the resignation. It takes effect automatically."[43] Indeed, the resignation was accepted and Murphy was immediately appointed to fill the vacancy which he was so instrumental in bringing about. He could justly claim ". . . my appointment to the Senate did not place me under any obligation to any Party, or any individual, with the single exception of Hon. M. J. O'Brien. That fact, therefore, is the measure of my independence in the new Chamber."[44]

Although no Senator has been formally disqualified, in two cases during the period under study members were virtually forced to resign. The causes of disqualification are carefully defined in section 31 of the BNA Act. Apart from the rather remote possibilities of becoming bankrupt or subjects of a foreign power, the two, still practical, grounds on which a Senator may lose his right to sit in the Upper House are, first, failure to attend for two consecutive sessions of Parliament, and, second, conviction of felony or of "any infamous crime." As regards the first, it is the duty of the Clerk to report to the House if any Senator has failed to give his attendance in the Senate for two consecutive sessions. There has been only one recorded occasion in recent years when such action was seriously considered. On January 15, 1957, the Clerk brought it to the attention of the Speaker that Sen. Duffus had not appeared in his seat throughout the last two sessions of Parliament. Since Sen. Duffus died

[42]Murphy to C. G. Power (later Sen. Power), Nov. 27, 1925. *Ibid.*, no. 10678.
[43]Murphy to J. Ambrose O'Brien, Nov. 24, 1933. *Ibid.*, vol. 22, no. 9771.
[44]Murphy to Mrs. H. D. Petrie, Jan. 22, 1927. *Ibid.*, vol. 25, nos. 10615–16.

a few days later, the motion of referring the Clerk's report to the Standing Orders committee for consideration was rescinded on February 7.[45]

Disqualification on the ground of committing an infamous crime is a good deal more difficult and during the last thirty-seven years it was only once—in the Beauharnois scandal of 1931–32—that the Senate was brought face to face with the problem of taking drastic action in this area. On May 3, 1932, the Senate adopted on a partisan vote the report of the Tanner Committee, which upheld the charges of dishonourable conduct in manipulating campaign contributions laid against three Liberal members of the Senate by a special committee of the House of Commons the previous year.[46] While the terms of the committee's findings respecting Sen. Raymond were not considered serious enough to warrant further proceedings, and in the case of Sen. Haydon no steps were taken because of his condition of health,[47] there were no mitigating circumstances for Sen. W. L. McDougald, of whom the Report concluded that his "actions were not fitting or consistent with his duties and standing as a Senator."[48] At this point the issue raised the constitutional problem of expulsion. Although both Sen. McDougald and his counsel argued that the Senate had no legal right to expel, the fact remained that "the Senate could pass a vote of censure . . . and . . . no man would care to run that risk and dream of sitting with others who had thus expressed their opinion of him."[49] In other words, even if the Senate lacks the power of impeachment, the moral effects of a threat of censuring have been considered strong enough to be relied upon for achieving the same end. And this is what in fact happened. Although Sen. McDougald was

[45]To discourage absenteeism towards the end of the session, in 1924 a rule (105A) was adopted, which provided that to be entitled for their full indemnities Senators must attend a sitting of the Senate on at least two-thirds of the sitting days of the House, and, second, that a deduction of $25 per day should be made for every day upon which a Senator does not attend a sitting in the Senate during the last two weeks of a parliamentary session. Highly unpopular, the rule was repealed two years afterwards. It has been urged, particularly by Meighen (*SD, 1939*, p. 589) and Robertson (*ibid., 1952*, p. 361), that the rule should be re-established. However no action has so far been taken.

[46]*Canadian Annual Review, 1932*, pp. 81–3; *HD, 1931*, pp. 4261 ff.

[47]Meighen to R. A. Reid, May 5, 1932. Meighen Papers, series 5, nos. 12–13. Sen. Haydon died later in the year.

[48]The committee's report concluded with the following general statement: "Senators of Canada should not place themselves in the position of receiving contributions from or being interested in any enterprise dependent on specific favour, franchise, or concession to be made by a Government whose conduct is . . . subject to review by both branches of Parliament." This statement was a replica of a proposed new rule, recommended for adoption in 1931 by Sen. Béique but defeated on a division by 36 votes to 13. *SD, 1931*, p. 445.

[49]Murphy to Sen. Graham, Jan. 22, 1932. Murphy Papers, vol. 12, nos. 4878–79.

first reluctant to resign, at an interview with Dandurand he was bluntly told that if he refused to resign from the Senate there would be a vote of censure passed upon him. As Dandurand later said, "this seemed to shake McDougald and the latter promised to think the matter over . . ."[50] Indeed, immediately following the division upon the adoption of the committee's report, Dandurand read a letter from Sen. McDougald to which was attached another letter, addressed to the Governor General, containing the Senator's resignation from the Senate.

The nearest approach to a repetition of the precedent set by the enforced resignation of Sen. McDougald was the resignation from the Senate in 1961 of Sen. Henri Courtemanche of Quebec, former Secretary of State in the Diefenbaker Administration until his appointment to the Upper House on January 20, 1960. Similarly to McDougald Sen. Courtemanche was charged of being involved in certain financial irregularities in connection with the securing of government grants-in-aid for a Quebec hospital. Although the arrangements alleged in the charge were made before Mr. Courtemanche was made a senator, it was understood that the Government, which was severely criticized for the appointment, pressed for his resignation, and the Senator, immediately upon the publication of the report of the Chabot Commission, tendered his resignation, without waiting to face the Senate after the reconvention of Parliament.[51]

Officers of the House

Debates of the Senate are presided over by the Speaker. The Speakership of the Senate is free from the notorious anomalies connected with the political, administrative, and judicial duties which make the post of the Lord Chancellor in the United Kingdom a negation of the principles of separation of power.[52] However, like the Lord Chancellor, the Speaker of the Senate is appointed by the Prime Minister, who is not expected to consult the wishes of the Senate before deciding whom to appoint. The position is largely honorific and most of the persons who have occupied it from 1925 to 1963 held some important public office in their former careers. The appointment is usually for a Parliament, although Hewitt Bostock was Speaker from 1922 to 1930 and Drouin was reappointed

[50]Murphy to Sen. Graham, Jan. 22, 1932. *Ibid.*, vol. 12, nos. 4878–9.
[51]*Montreal Gazette*, Dec. 22, 1961. *Montreal Star*, Dec. 22, 1961.
[52]Cf. Viscount Kilmuir, "The Office of the Lord Chancellor," *Parliamentary Affairs* (1955–56).

in 1958. The practice of alternating the Speakership between English- and French-speaking persons is followed in the Senate, too.[53]

Unlike the Speaker of the House of Commons, with the Speaker of the Senate there is no suggestion of a requirement of either impartiality or aloofness from debate. On those rare occasions when the Speaker wished to address the Senate he left the chair and spoke from the floor like other members. During the second reading debate of the Trade Mark and Design bill of 1927 Sen. Bostock informed the House that he had strong protests from Vancouver, his home town, about the object of the legislation and urged the postponement of the debate, in order that all interested parties might be heard.[54] Again, in 1945 Sen. King, who, together with Sen. Moraud, represented the Senate in the Canadian delegation at San Francisco, took part in the debate on the resolution approving the United Nations Charter.[55] He was once more brought into the discussion in 1947, when he felt that as Speaker of the Senate he had to reply to an unprecedented attack by Sen. Murdock upon the report of the Senate's Internal Economy committee recommending an increase in the salary of the Gentleman Usher of the Black Rod.[56] Sen. Robertson left his chair twice during his speakership—once in 1954 to join in paying tribute to the memory of Sen. Dennis, a fellow Nova Scotian, and once in 1955 to take part in the debate on the motion to approve the Protocol on West Germany's accession to NATO. In addition to addressing the House, the Speaker in all cases has a vote; thus, Hardy participated in one division during his short term as Speaker in 1930; Blondin voted in a total of twelve divisions between 1930 and 1935, and Foster and King voted on one bill each while Speakers.

As a disciplinary officer the Speaker plays but a nominal role in the Senate. Indeed, similarly to the House of Lords,[57] the Senate contrives to run its debates without the need of a presiding officer in the traditional sense. The secret of maintaining discipline without being disciplined is to be attributed to the behaviour of the House, in which disorder and obstruction are unknown. A Senator wishing to speak is simply to rise and address himself to the rest of the Senators. The rules forbidding reference to one another by name are now not observed too strictly[58] and there is a similar forbearance towards the rather unparliamentary

[53]Thus, the line went from Bostock/Hardy to Blondin, from Blondin to Foster, from Foster to Parent/Vien, from them to King, from King to Beauregard, then to W. M. Robertson, to Drouin, and finally to White, who was Speaker of the Senate at the dissolution of Parliament in 1963, to be succeeded by Maurice Bourget.

[54]*SD, 1927*, p. 245. [55]*Ibid., 1945*, p. 123. [56]*Ibid., 1947*, p. 355.

[57]See Bromhead, *The House of Lords*, p. 96. [58]*SD, 1961*, p. 358.

practice of reading speeches in the Chamber.[59] More important still is the lack of any provision for closure, with the result that there is no formal restriction on the right of any Senator to speak at any length in any debate.[60] In case of difference between Senators the matter will be discussed by the House, with the Speaker having no more authority than any other Senator.[61] The fact is that the Speaker is not supposed to intervene, even if a rule is broken, unless a member calls his attention to the breach. As a result, some Senators may be allowed to continue to address the House while somewhat later others for the breach of the same rule may be called to order.[62] In view of his limited functions in maintaining order and in interpreting the rules, and of the circuitous way in which he goes about discharging his functions,[63] it is hardly surprising that the Speaker's rulings are practically never formally challenged.[64]

The Senate has its permanent staff under the Clerk of the Parliament, who is appointed by the Crown under the Great Seal and performs similar duties to those of the Clerk of the House of Commons. His assistant, who is also generally Deputy Clerk and sits at the Table to the right of the Clerk, reads petitions and other documents and otherwise assists the Clerk in the business of the House. At the beginning of the period under review the office of Sergeant-at-Arms was abolished and his duties were assumed by the Gentleman Usher of the Black Rod and his assistant.[65] There is no Chairman of Committees in the Senate as in the House of Lords. But in view of the important work done in the Senate's committees, special mention should be made of the Chief Clerk of Committees and his expert staff, who assist the committee chairmen in arranging and conducting the business of committees. The fact that the business of the Senate can proceed so smoothly with so little need for precise definitions indicates the value of their services.

A good deal of the work regularly carried out by the Senate and its

[59] *Ibid., 1956*, p. 732.

[60] No action was taken on the motion in 1946 "that the time has arrived when the Senate should place a time limit on the length of speeches in the Senate." *Ibid.*, 1946, p. 177.

[61] *Ibid., 1956*, p. 475.

[62] *Ibid., 1934*, p. 182.

[63] See the manner in which Sen. McMeans was declared out of order, July 13, 1940. *Ibid., 1940*, p. 322.

[64] On the only occasion, 1925–63, when the Speaker's ruling was appealed to the Senate, the ruling of the chair was upheld by 44 votes to 13. *Ibid., 1934*, p. 228.

[65] The change was particularly painful for an old-timer like Sen. Poirier, who well remembered a fight between Senators Ross and Miller, when one of them was called a toothless old serpent. "If it had not been for the interference of the Sergeant-at-Arms and the display of his sword, we do not know what might have happened." *Ibid., 1926*, pp. 89–90.

committees is such that it requires expert legal attention. For many years during the 1920's the Senate had a Law Clerk in the person of Mr. Creighton, who was reputed to have rendered invaluable service. Because he had no assistant prepared to step into his position, for years after his departure the Senate had to depend upon the help of persons sent by the Department of Justice. This arrangement, however, did not prove satisfactory, and the proposal that there should be a Law Clerk of the two Houses was rejected, on the ground that as a special officer of the Senate, a Law Clerk of the Upper House was much freer to express an opinion than would be a Law Clerk who had once approved a particular piece of legislation. The increase of work in the Senate committees after 1930 made the question of having a Law Clerk particularly acute; his absence had considerably increased the work of the Government Leader and the Leader of the Opposition in the Senate. For three years between 1932 and 1935 the Senate accepted the services of Mr. W. F. O'Connor, KC, a former professor of international law, in the capacity of draftsman and legal adviser to the Banking and Commerce committee, but this temporary solution badly needed statutory imprimatur. In 1935, therefore, noting that "without a legal adviser whose services are at the disposal of the Senate at all times we find ourselves greatly handicapped," Sen. Black, Chairman of the Banking and Commerce committee, moved that "representations be made to the Government to forthwith restore the salary for the vacant position of Law Clerk of the Senate, in order that the vacancy may be filled."[66] Indeed, on July 5 the Speaker informed the Senate that the Civil Service Commission had agreed to transfer to the Senate the right to appoint a Law Clerk and Parliamentary Counsel of its own. On the motion of Sen. Meighen the Senate then appointed O'Connor to the designated post and he held the position until his death in 1941. He was succeeded by J. F. MacNeill, KC, who occupied that post until 1956, when his appointment to the office of Clerk of the Senate and Clerk of the Parliaments vacated the post of Law Clerk. It was filled by the appointment of Mr. E. R. Hopkins, formerly Clerk Assistant of the House of Commons and latterly Secretary to the Board of Transport Commissioners. In addition to clarifying points of law during the passage of a bill in the Senate, the Law Clerk often produces memoranda upon constitutional questions of general interest.[67]

[66]*Ibid., 1935*, p. 374.

[67]See, for example, O'Connor's report in 1939 on the enactment of the BNA Act 1867; MacNeill's memorandum for Sen. Robertson *re* the reasons given by proponents of Confederation for constituting the Second Chamber (1950); and Mr. Hopkins' several contributions on questions of parliamentary procedure and the working of the Senate.

Thus, unfettered by the chains of a formal party organization and the excesses of the spirit of partisanship, untrammelled with procedural rules and assisted by an expert professional body of officers, the Senate is well placed for performing the technical and the substantive functions of a modern second chamber. It is to the performance of these functions during the thirty-seven years from 1925 to 1963 that we now must turn our attention.

Part II

THE SENATE AT WORK: TECHNICAL FUNCTIONS

TECHNICAL REVISION OF LEGISLATION: SERVICE BY A SECOND LOOK

6

BOTH THE TECHNICAL AND THE NON-TECHNICAL FUNCTIONS of the Senate are essentially derivative and complementary in character; their *raison d'être* lies in the inability of the House of Commons to discharge its legislative and checking functions satisfactorily. Whether the complementary body should take the form of a second house of Parliament or rather a system of committees or some other arrangement may be of theoretical interest; where—as in Canada—a second chamber has been adopted as a part of the evolutionary process of constitutional development it falls upon this second house to fill the gap between the ideal demands upon Parliament and the hard facts of unicameralism.

Generally speaking the technical functions of the Senate consist of two kinds of services—the revision of legislation sent up from the House of Commons and the introduction of legislation in the first place; the purpose of the first is to offer a second look at bills, while that of the second is to help the Lower House carry the burden of legislation. This chapter is concerned with the technical revision of legislation in the form of amendments made by the Senate to government bills which have already been dealt with by the Commons. These technical amendments in their turn may be divided into simple drafting corrections, administrative improvements, and last-minute changes made at the request of the Government. Their common characteristic is that they are designed to improve the legislation, or further to develop certain aspects of the legislative policy expressed in the measure, without, in fact, introducing any new principles. In that they differ from the substantive functions of the Senate, as will be seen in a later chapter.

Of the 289 public bills amended by the Senate from 1925 to 1963, including the thirty during the war, about 70 per cent fall into the category of what may be called "technical amendments" and 30 per cent into the class of "substantive amendments." Within the group of technical amendments approximately 63 per cent have been drafting corrections, 21 per cent administrative improvements, and 16 per cent changes made at the request of the Government. In many cases, of course, the Senate has amended a bill in several particulars, some of them being substantive, the others technical. In such cases I classified the amendment according to a descending scale of priority. Further, within the category of technical amendments their breakdown into a three-fold division of drafting corrections, administrative improvements, and Government-requested changes may seem to be somewhat arbitrary, as, indeed, it is sometimes difficult to draw a clear line between a drafting correction and an administrative improvement. However, it is proposed that these categories have been used merely for the purpose of facilitating a better analytical study of the technical changes made by the Senate in government bills.

Technical amendments by the Senate are among the least spectacular of the achievements of the Upper Chamber and are usually ignored by the critics and the public alike. The most that has been done in way of appreciation has been to offer from time to time some statistical data as to the number of amendments the Senate has put to a particular bill or the number of amendments the Senate has made over a certain period of time. But bare figures, although they may throw some light on the general activity of the Senate, reveal very little of the *nature* of the services thus rendered. The question is really this: how much better are the bills that are to become the laws of the country after they left the Senate as compared to what they were when they reached it? Or to put the question in the negative: what and how much would be lost if every bill were placed on the Statute Book in the form as it emerged from the House of Commons? The present chapter is a modest attempt to illustrate the type of technical improvements accorded to public legislation in the Senate.

Drafting Corrections

The most obvious form of the Senate's revisory work is to correct errors in the drafting of legislation. Over a period of thirty-seven years there have been 123 government bills (or about four per session) which have been amended by the Senate exclusively from the point of view of improving their wording.

The notion that the Senate corrects drafting errors committed by the Commons is a myth. The House of Commons does not draft legislation. Legislation is drafted by draftsmen in the Department of Justice in co-operation with officials of the sponsoring department upon instructions from the minister.[1] When it is reported, therefore, that the Senate has made certain improvements in the drafting of a bill it means that in committee, attended by the officials who sponsored the measure, often by the draftsmen who drafted it and sometimes by the minister who piloted it through the House of Commons, Senators, particularly members of the legal profession, as well as the Law Clerk of the Senate, have prevailed upon the departmental experts through a process of free discussion and intellectual give and take to accept certain suggestions for improving the text of the bill—a function which theoretically ought to be performed by the House of Commons but which the House of Commons cannot regularly perform for lack of time.

Sometimes the officials will not necessarily agree that the changes suggested by members of the Senate represent a definite improvement over the original drafting, yet they may concede to the wishes of the Senators, in order to gain a good bargaining position upon more controversial clauses yet to be considered. However, in many cases it may well happen that the original drafting is imperfect in spite of the careful and expert treatment it received before being brought down in Parliament. "Rarely is a bill prepared under ideal conditions; usually the work must be done in a hurry and under pressure," says one of the foremost authorities on legislative drafting. As a result, "draftsmen must be practical and for each bill find a place somewhere between the two extremes of the slipshod and the perfect . . . the perfect bill has never been written and never will be."[2] In consequence, although the formal process of drafting may be considered completed at the time the bill is introduced in Parliament, in actual fact the constant improvement of the drafting continues until the bill is passed by both houses, and the house which has more leisure and which is less trammelled with procedural rules is undoubtedly better placed for thinking out small perfections in the wording of legislation.[3] Even if true perfection in drafting can never

[1]This was true even before the setting up within the Department of Justice of a special drafting organization in the early 1950's. See in particular the excellent studies by E. A. Driedger in 27 *Can. Bar Rev.*, p. 291; 31 *Can. Bar Rev.*, p. 33; and *Canadian Public Administration*, vol. I (1958), no. 2, p. 14 ff.

[2]Driedger, "The Preparation of Legislation." 31 *Can. Bar Rev.*, pp. 40–1.

[3]"Besides independence to revise judicially, and the position to revise effectually," Sen. Vaillancourt said, ". . . we have leisure to revise *intellectually*." *SD, 1958*, p. 252. Italics added.

be attained, there is a great deal of difference between a good law and a bad law. What makes a law good or bad is not always the policies it seeks to implement. The best intentions may easily be distorted through the misplacement of a comma or the use of a wrong word, which may twist the whole meaning of a clause or a bill.

Typographical or grammatical errors in the drafting may be caused when the bill is reprinted in the House of Commons, and then it falls upon the Senate to spot them before the bill becomes a faultily worded law open to misinterpretation in the courts.[4] Similar confusion may arise from differences between the English and French versions of the bill, both of which have to pass through all stages in Parliament and receive Royal Assent and are of equal authority.[5]

By compressing definitions,[6] rearranging certain sections,[7] or, indeed, reorganizing the whole bill the Senate can, without actually altering the choice of words, increase the lucidity and the effectiveness of the legislation. Its care was well illustrated in the Canadian Forces bill of 1951, which proposed to amend several sections in various statutes in accordance with the National Defence Act of 1950. The bill as it came from the Commons simply listed the words that were to be added or deleted, without any attempt to relate them to the relevant sections in the various Acts. The Senate, conforming to the principles of amending legislation, struck out these solitary and unconnected phrases and substituted sections, with the result that "anyone referring to the legislation later on will not have to juggle half a dozen books on his knees while he tries to find out what the final form of the legislation is, but will have this information right before him in the one statute."[8]

The Senate prefers traditionally used and well-established phraseology, which has been tested in the courts, and tries to discourage any deviations from the norm, unless absolutely necessary,[9] It changed the word "implement" to that of "fulfil" with regard to government guarantees in the Saskatchewan Seed Grain Guarantee bill of 1936, for the good reason—overlooked in the House of Commons—that some years before

[4]See the confusion of the words "exportation" and "importation" in the Export bill of 1930. *Ibid., 1930*, p. 282. *HD, 1930*, p. 2499.

[5]Driedger, "The Preparation of Legislation," pp. 48–9. Cf. Dominion Election bill, *SD, 1929*, p. 371.

[6]See Dominion Franchise bill, *SD, 1934*, p. 660; *HD, 1934*, p. 4580.

[7]See the thirteen amendments made to the Dominion Plebiscite bill, *HD, 1942–43*, p. 1065.

[8]*SD, 1951* (2nd session), p. 196.

[9]Immigration bill, *HD, 1928*, p. 3653; Dominion Elections bill, *ibid., 1929*, p. 3446. See the Senate's cautious attitude to using the word "prime minister" in the Economic Council of Canada bill, *ibid.*, 1935, p. 2599.

on an appeal to the Judicial Committee of the Privy Council the use of the word "implement" had caused considerable and uncontemplated expense for the Government. In both the Fruit bill of 1935 and the Inspection of Sale bill of 1947 the Senate attached substantial qualifications to the word "export," for fear that the term as applied to interprovincial trade might be altogether misunderstood by the Canadian public, by visitors, and by foreign countries, and instead of consolidating Canada into a united country its effect would be to divide the country into nine separate entities.

In many instances the Senate has rendered important service by so revising the drafting of a bill as to make it more consonant with the expressed desire of the House of Commons.[10] Its action in this respect was always warmly appreciated in the Lower House.[11] The following two examples show how considerable improvements could be achieved through apparently insignificant modifications in the drafting. The Food and Drugs bill of 1935, as originally drafted, provided that "no person or company shall import . . . or sell . . . any remedy . . . as a treatment of any of the diseases" listed in the measure. On the suggestion of Meighen the Senate struck out from the above clause the words "or company." One might easily have got the wrong impression that the Senate was trying to protect companies, by excluding them from the operation of the Act. The exact reverse was the case. According to the Interpretation Act, "person" includes a company, partnership, and so forth. If the words "no person or company" were to be used together, as they appeared in the original bill, the definition of "person" would be limited in its application, because the presence of the words "or company" might be interpreted as the intention of Parliament to refer only to a human being or a company, excluding, for example, partnerships from the prohibition intended by the clause. Thus, the bill as it emerged from the Commons defeated, by its drafting, the very purpose for which the House of Commons had passed it; the deletion by the Senate of the words "or company" restored the original intent.[12] In the Railway bill of 1951 dealing with competitive tariffs the railways had to prove that the competition actually existed. The only change made by the Senate in the bill was the deletion of the word "actually." It was recognized

[10]Pension bill, *SD*, *1936*, p. 521 ff.; Toronto Harbour Commissioners bill, *ibid.*, p. 53 ff.; Natural Resources Transfer bill, *HD*, *1938*, p. 3707; Yukon bill, *SJ*, *1940*, p. 98; Northwest Territories bill, *SD*, *1959*, p. 411 ff.

[11]See, for instance, comments on Senate amendments in the Judges bill, *HD*, *1931*, p. 2813; the Dominion Companies bill, *ibid.*, *1934*, p. 4038; the Income War Tax bill, *ibid.*, *1943*, p. 2510; the Bank bill, *ibid.*, *1944*, p. 6422.

[12]*SD*, *1934*, p. 576.

that there might be cases—as in fact there had been—where competition did not *actually* exist but where the railways knew well that it might or would exist in a short while. The amendment was agreed to unanimously by the members of the Senate's Transport and Communications committee, by the solicitors representing the parties concerned, and by the government counsel who had drafted the bill.[13]

Changes at the Request of the Government

It has been noted that even in the case of drafting corrections proposals for the amendments often come from either the Law Clerk and Parliamentary Counsel to the Senate or departmental officials themselves and the Senate has no more role to play than that of the host. In the next category of technical amendments the Senate's only, though important, service is to provide a forum for last-minute changes requested by the Government to be made in a bill before it becomes law. It is action in the eleventh hour to meet the demands of the minister, departmental officials, or officers of the House of Commons, who have reason to believe that the bill, in its existing form, would not serve its purpose or would be detrimental for certain classes of people. The way to correct it is through moving an amendment in the Senate.

Frequently, on a complicated bill first introduced in the Commons many amendments are withdrawn against an undertaking by the Government to give further consideration. After further discussion the Government may be ready to make its final decision by the committee or third reading stage in the Senate.[14] On other occasions, such as in the Canada-US Tax Convention bill and the Naval Service of Canada bill in 1944, or the Income Tax bill of 1950, amendments had to be moved in the Senate to correct an earlier oversight, which might have had serious consequences.[15] In 1938 even procedural rules were set aside in order to accommodate the changes suggested by the Government to the Seed Grain Loans Guarantee bill. The Minister of Justice, unaware that the bill had been passed at the afternoon sitting, sent word to ask the Senate to amend the bill, so as to make it clear that the limitation of the

[13]*Ibid., 1951* (2nd session), p. 225.

[14]See Federal District Commission bill, *SD, 1927*, pp. 349, 380; Dominion Elections bill, *ibid.*, p. 346; Gold and Silver Marketing bill, *ibid., 1928*, pp. 368, 414; Juvenile Delinquents, Precious Metals Marketing bills, *ibid., 1929*, pp. 299, 341; Special War Revenue bill, *ibid., 1932*, p. 498; Bank Pension bills, *ibid., 1933*, pp. 457, 538–9; Criminal Code bill, *HD, 1951*, p. 4656.

[15]*HD, 1944*, pp. 5845, 4859; *ibid., 1950*, pp. 3306–7.

Government's liability, as asserted in the legislation, applied to the principal alone and not to interest—quite a difference, indeed. The Senate acceded to the motion of the Government Leader and the third reading being unanimously rescinded the amendment could be inserted as requested by the Government.[16]

In many cases it becomes necessary to postpone the coming into force of certain legislation. Under unicameral arrangements this would entail the introduction of a new bill to make the necessary changes, or, perhaps, an even wider use of delegated legislation to empower the executive to act in behalf of Parliament. With the Senate in the reserve the Government can afford to have a bill passed quickly through the Commons and then move, if necessary, an amendment in the Senate delaying the operative schedule of the bill. This has particular relevance in matters of finance, where the timing of a bill may have far-reaching effects upon both governmental policy and individual interests—as was evidenced, for instance, in the War Service Grants bill of 1944, the Excise bill in 1948 and 1953, or the Income Tax bill of 1954.[17]

But perhaps the most important function of this category of technical amendments made by the Senate at the request of the Government is to give effect to certain arrangements negotiated between the Government and various interests after the bill had left the House of Commons. It should be remembered that discussions over a bill constitute an almost continuous process, at every stage of which the Government is hearing arguments from all kinds of interested and disinterested bodies and from members of both houses of Parliament who themselves may sometimes voice the views of interests outside. The Senate, being a stage of this far-reaching political process of discussion, offers an opportunity for the Government to implement promises and undertakings without the trouble of drafting and piloting through a new piece of legislation. In 1930, for example, the Government moved an amendment in the Senate to the National Parks bill in order to meet the objections of railway companies, which protested against certain aspects of the bill as an interference with their rights and privileges.[18] Amendments had to be made in the Juvenile Delinquents bill of 1932, in response to powerful representations by some well-known authorities in the field of children's aid;[19] in the Old Age Pensions bill of 1937, to satisfy the demands of the organization of blind persons;[20] in the Toronto Harbour Commis-

[16]*SD, 1938*, pp. 208–9.

[17]*HD, 1944*, p. 6396; *ibid., 1948*, p. 5422; *ibid., 1953*, p. 4515; *ibid., 1954*, p. 6120; *SD, 1954*, p. 641.

[18]*SD, 1930*, p. 265. [19]*Ibid., 1932*, p. 83. [20]*HD, 1937*, p. 1997.

sioners bill of 1951, to implement an agreement between the Harbour Commission and the people who had been opposed to the legislation;[21] and in the Income Tax bill of 1953, to answer the objections of the Investment Dealers Association.[22] Similar pressure from Western agricultural interests against the practice of confined interpretation of the Act resulted in last-minute changes in the Prairie Farm Assistance bill of 1955. To appease the farmers in Manitoba and Saskatchewan, the Government used the floor of the Senate's Natural Resources committee to amend the bill, by striking out its objectionable features.[23]

Administrative Improvements

By far the most important category of technical amendments made by the Senate to government legislation consists of administrative improvements—changes designed to make the legislation technically better, without affecting the underlying principle. The Senate constantly endeavours to effect economies in the administration of legislative policies within the framework of accepted general principles. In the Pension bill of 1925, for example, the Senate deleted a provision which extended the grounds for appeal from a decision of the Pension Board in those cases where disability was the result not of war service but of "misconduct." Similar economies were achieved in the Soldier Settlement bill of 1926 and the Returned Soldiers' Insurance bill of 1928.[24] In the Pension legislation of 1928 the critical cause was section 25, which dealt with pensions to be paid to a widow who married a member of the forces after the appearance of the injury or disease resulting in death. The House of Commons, after forty-seven sittings of its committee, had failed to find a satisfactory formula of conferring a benefit upon a new class while guarding the state against the "designing woman" who married a soldier in the full knowledge of his having a disability from which he might die. The Senate set up a special committee for the purpose of the bill, which invited members of the Commons' committee, the Chairman of the Board of Pension Commissioners, and the Minister of Defence, Col. Ralston. In the end, the desired formula was discovered and the necessary compromise achieved.[25] Again in the Royal Canadian Mounted Police bill of 1933 the Senate, by unanimous agreement, struck out two sections which stipulated that an officer would benefit for the

[21] *SD, 1951*, pp. 261–2. [22] *HD, 1953*, pp. 4710–12. [23] *Ibid., 1955*, p. 5966.
[24] *SD, 1925*, p. 602; *ibid., 1926*, p. 144; *HD, 1926*, p. 5167; *SD, 1928*, p. 642.
[25] *SD, 1928*, p. 666; *HD, 1928*, p. 632 ff.

time served during the South African war. It was thought that in "our present condition of finances" (this was in 1933) such persons ought not to be entitled to have their extra service added to their service in the Mounted Police in the calculation of their pensions.[26]

A method often used by the Senate to effect administrative improvements in public legislation is through tightening the penalty sections in bills and increasing the rigidity of various provisions. It was in this spirit that the Senate made sometimes extensive amendments in the Bank bill of 1934, the Companies bill of 1935, the Pelagic Sealing bill of 1938, or the Naval Service bill of 1940.[27] The Senate's suspicion was again aroused by a provision in the Co-operative Credit Association bill of 1953, seeking to co-ordinate and extend the jurisdiction of the provincial co-operative credit societies and unions. The Senate, with the full backing of the Minister of Finance, amended the measure to tighten the freedom of the credit associations to invest in loans to any one member, and also established strict requirements as to publicity.[28]

The main form of administrative improvements, however, is the broadening of the scope of a bill along the line of its original intent. Amendments in this category may take the most varied forms. In the session of 1926 the Senate made twenty-five amendments to the Farm Loan bill, which improved the legislation in many areas. They enabled the borrower to have the choice between annual and semi-annual payments on the mortgage; they recognized his right to repay his loan in whole or in part at any time, instead of a fixed period of five years, as was provided in the original bill, and they prescribed a copy of the report of the accountants on the annual statement to be laid before Parliament. Most important, however, the Senate amendments recognized provincial experience in the administration of the loans. The purpose of the amendments was to get Ontario and Quebec to join the scheme, by stimulating interest in lending money to their people at a rate attractive to the farmers and by dispelling doubts about a general accounting.[29]

Likewise, while respecting the principle of the legislation the Senate found there was still room for expanding the jurisdiction of the Companies bill of 1930, by adding a clause to permit companies to establish and support associations calculated to benefit their employees and to guarantee money for charitable purposes. The amendment found support with the Government, because it was considered of "benevolent

[26] *SD, 1933*, p. 431 ff; *HD, 1933*, p. 4397.

[27] *SD, 1934*, p. *571*; *ibid., 1935*, pp. 445–6; *HD, 1938*, pp. 3968–70; *SD, 1940*, p. 218.

[28] *HD, 1953*, p. 4712.

[29] *SD, 1926*, pp. 309–10 ff.

nature."[30] To the Income War Tax bill of 1932, which levied a special income tax of 10 per cent on salaries of judges and members of the permanent force, the Senate attached a proviso that persons who were thereafter appointed to office should be subject to a deduction of 10 per cent per month; it was found that without this stipulation the Act could have been evaded altogether for the remainder of the fiscal year![31] The Minimum Wage bill of 1935 was actually rewritten by the Senate. Whole sections were entirely recast, but only to tie them more closely to the ILO conventions concerning minimum wages.[32] Again, the Senate, on the suggestion of Sen. Griesbach, who had extensive military and war experience, improved the technical quality of the Defence Purchasing Board bill of 1939, by extending the reference of the Board over all contracts between the Government and any other person with respect to the supply of equipment.[33]

The idea of widening the scope of the legislation was well illustrated by the amendments to two pieces of the "New Deal" legislation of 1935. The original version of the Employment and Social Insurance bill, as it passed the House of Commons, totally exempted from the operation of the legislation employees of banks, insurance companies, and financial institutions. After deliberating for four weeks and hearing evidence from the representatives of a wide range of interested parties, the Banking and Commerce committee decided to eliminate the exemptions and to extend the operation of the Act to every field of employment. The amendment also strengthened the powers of the Unemployment Insurance Commission, by abolishing the appeal provision to the Exchequer Court and by making the decision of the Commission final.[34] In the case of the Farm Loan bill, the Senate amendments, occupying five pages in the Senate *Journals*, produced a greatly improved piece of legislation, almost double the size of what it was when it reached the Upper Chamber. Perhaps the most important single amendment of the "broadening type" was the expansion of the total amount available and of the number of persons who would have an opportunity to participate in the scheme.[35]

In the session of 1959 the Senate amended the Parliamentary Secretaries bill, which allowed a maximum number of sixteen parliamentary secretaries to be appointed, one to each minister. While the Senate amendment did not affect the maximum number, it brought greater

[30]*HD, 1930*, p. 2500.
[31]*Ibid., 1932*, p. 3384.
[32]*Ibid., 1935*, p. 3841.
[33]*SJ, 1939*, p. 167.
[34]*SD, 1935*, pp. 294, 308, 400; *HD, 1935*, p. 2700, p. 3786.
[35]*SJ, 1935*, pp. 160–65. *HD, 1935*, p. 2698.

flexibility into the legislation, by making it possible to appoint more than one parliamentary secretary to any one minister. For this feature the amendment was praised by all parties in the Commons.[36] Two years later, in 1961, the Senate added a new subclause to the Criminal Code (Capital Murder) bill, with a view to making the technical implementation of the principle better and more practical. The bill, in the form it reached in the Senate, contained no provision for ascertaining in what manner the jury functioned in the production of its recommendation in favour of clemency or against it—whether it reached a unanimous decision or merely a decision by majority. The purpose of the Senate amendment was to empower the judge to find out how many jurors were in favour of recommending clemency and how many opposed it, and to include such information in his report to the Minister of Justice. It was thought that such information might well have an effect upon the exercise of mercy. The bill became law as strengthened by the Senate.

In many cases an amendment may be proposed in the House of Commons by the Opposition and although it does not affect the principle of the legislation and may offer a definite technical improvement, the Government would choose to turn it down rather than, by accepting it, to admit that it had escaped its attention. However, should the same amendment come back from the Senate the Government might feel more prepared to accept it, as Senate amendments are usually not looked upon as a challenge to the Government's authority. Thus, the Senate is a good face-saving device for the Government to incorporate certain technical changes in the legislation, which might otherwise never be considered for adoption. In 1952, for instance, the Senate, upon the suggestion of Liberal Senator Stambaugh, deleted a section from the CNR bill, which relieved the company of the responsibility for fencing the right of the way of the railway line and of any liabilities in damages by reason of the absence of such fencing. After conferring with the members of the cabinet, the Senate Leader announced that the Government had no objection to the amendment. However, when the bill, as amended, returned to the House of Commons, it became apparent that the Liberal-dominated Senate adopted an amendment which was suggested in vain by the Conservative Opposition in the Commons at an earlier stage. "We tried to get a similar amendment put through when the bill was before the standing committee on railways . . . but were unable to do so," Mr. Green said. And he added: "Fortunately, the Senate has been able to overcome the difficulty."[37]

[36] *HD, 1959*, pp. 4147–8.
[37] *HD, 1952*, p. 2892; *SD, 1952*, p. 359.

It seems fair to say that the services rendered by the Senate during the last thirty-seven years in form of technical amendments to government legislation have demonstrated its constructive capacity as a revisory body of great usefulness. The Senate has made a wide variety of important, though unspectacular, improvements in public bills, either on its own initiative or upon requests from the Government of the day. It is probably true that, apart from the actual operation of the "pruning hook," the knowledge that all legislation will be accorded a second look in the Senate has helped relieve the Government of too much worrying about the technical quality of legislation and enabled the House of Commons to concentrate more intensively on its primary political role.

INITIATION OF LEGISLATION: SERVICE BY A FIRST LOOK

7

1. *Initiation of Government Legislation*

THE SECOND MAIN CATEGORY of the technical functions of the Senate consists of what the Report of the Bryce *Conference on the Reform of the Second Chamber* defined as "the initiation of bills dealing with subjects of a comparatively non-controversial character which may have an earlier passage through the House of Commons if they have been fully discussed and put into a well considered shape before being submitted to it." In comparison with the technical revision of legislation, this is service by a first look, designed to alleviate the legislative burden of the Commons and thus help it to devote its energies to the fulfilment of its principal political responsibilities. However, there is also an important practical advantage from the point of view of the procedures of the Senate in having a fair proportion of government bills introduced in the Upper House in the first instance. It was seen (Chapter V) that complete dependence for legislation upon the House of Commons would deprive the Senate of any legislative work during the first part of the session and would overwhelm it with work during the last part. A better allocation of the time of the two houses can apparently be achieved if senators can spend some of their time during the first months of the session in considering bills which have been brought into their house in the first instance.

A distinction must be made between bills introduced by the Government and those sponsored by outside bodies. Special conditions attach to measures of the second type and it is proposed to defer the discussion of these measures to the second part of the chapter. For the present, then, we shall be concerned with bills brought in by the Government.

There are only two actual restrictions on the power of the Government to introduce bills for first consideration by the Senate. One is the constitutional provision that "bills for appropriating any part of the public revenue, or for imposing any tax or impost" must originate in the House of Commons;[1] the other is the unwritten rule that all important bills should start their parliamentary career in the elected Chamber. However, there is a third practical restriction, arising out of the fact that, as a rule, no department head in modern times had a seat in the Senate and no minister likes to see his bills introduced in a house where he cannot take full personal charge of their passage. As a result, the amount of legislation initiated in the Senate each session will in fact depend upon the ability of the Senate to prevail upon the Government to see that a certain number of bills are brought in in the Senate instead of in the House of Commons. In this process of persuading the Government, the pivotal role is of course played by the Government leader of the Senate. Thus, in each of the four sessions covering the period of Meighen's leadership in the Senate (1932–35), four government bills were originated in the Upper House—a high proportion as compared to the record of the immediately preceding years. There is little doubt that Meighen's personality and his prestige had an important bearing upon the increased use of the Senate as a legislative chamber of first instance. "He can impose his will on the Government," Sen. Lemieux, a Liberal, said of him with appreciation. "Much depends on [his] obtaining from the Government a fair share in the division of the legislative work of the session between the two Houses."[2] This connection between the number of public bills initiated in the Senate and the leader's ambition, or indeed aggressiveness, to have them was well illustrated by the three insurance bills brought into the Senate in the session of 1932. Meighen did not just introduce them; he took a personal command of their passage through every procedural stage. From beginning to end he was the driving force behind the bills; he really represented the Government; indeed, he was the Government, with respect to them.

However, for all his influence and eagerness no Senate leader can be successful in obtaining the desired quota of legislation for first introduction in the Senate unless he has the assistance and good will of the Government, and especially of the prime minister. Meighen was fortunate that in his efforts to secure for the Senate an adequate volume of work

[1]Sec. 53 of BNA Act.
[2]*SD, 1934*, p. 153.

in the legislative lull of the first part of the session, he was helped considerably by Prime Minister Bennett. Indeed, it was a part of the conditions of his appointment that he would be allowed a practically free hand in Senate leadership[3] and that under him the Senate's role in parliamentary affairs would materially be increased. "When appointed during Mr. Bennett's regime," he disclosed in a letter, "I made up my mind that the Senate should be of value. In our effort Mr. Bennett contributed very powerfully by initiating in the Senate nearly all measures that were intricate and involved and required intense committee study."[4] No similar co-operation, however, was forthcoming from King, with the result that, in spite of Dandurand's great personal magnetism and best intentions[5] and the intimate relationship between the two men, Dandurand's leadership in the Senate both before 1930 and following the Liberal victory in 1936 could not be compared to Meighen's resourcefulness in terms of the amount of government legislation originated in the Upper House. During the whole of Dandurand's eleven-year leadership between 1925 and 1942 only nine government measures were initiated in the Senate, six during the period 1925–30 and three between 1936 and 1942, as against the sixteen during the four years of Meighen's leadership. The truth of the matter was that King trusted Dandurand but had no confidence in the Senate, particularly when it was dominated by a Conservative majority, which was the case for the great part of Dandurand's leadership.[6]

In an attempt to find ways of increasing the proportion of public legislation originated in the Senate it was suggested at a fairly early stage that, failing the establishment of a permanent larger representation of the cabinet in the Senate, the rules of the House should be amended to allow ministers to come to the Senate and introduce their bills therein. By so doing, it was thought, the reluctance of ministers to let their measures be explained and handled by others in the first instance could be overcome and the number of government bills annually initiated in the Senate increased. This has become the story of Rule 18/A. Its

[3]Above, p. 129. See also Roger Graham, *Arthur Meighen*, vol. 3, pp. 32–3.

[4]Meighen to G. W. Nickerson, March 17, 1941. Meighen Papers, series V, no. 222.

[5]For his strenuous efforts, see, for example, *SD, 1925*, p. 110; *ibid., 1926*, p. 31; *ibid., 1938*, p. 563; *ibid., 1939*, p. 38.

[6]In a letter to Prof. Brady in 1934 Sen. Murphy wrote: "Replying to your question as to why the Senate is not used to a greater extent by having bills initiated therein, I would say that the reason is to be found in a game played by King when he first came into office, and which he has since continued when he had a chance." March 26, 1934. Murphy Papers, vol. 4, no. 1306. See also Macdonnell's (PC, Greenwood) remarks, *HD, 1954*, p. 5251.

adoption, operation, and falling into desuetude deserves to be told in some detail, as it well illustrates the processes of development of Canadian constitutional practice. As early as 1908, Sen. David moved "that it is desirable in order to increase the efficiency of the Senate, that more legislation be initiated in the House . . . and that any minister personally may introduce and defend Government measures in both Houses."[7] A similar motion was put forward by Lemieux in the House of Commons on March 21, 1921, and a year later by Sen. Dandurand, then newly appointed Senate Leader, in the Senate.[8]

Shortly after his elevation to the Senate Sen. Lemieux revived the subject in 1931. He was at a loss to understand why such measures as the Naturalization bill, the Companies bill, the Copyright bill, etc., could not be first introduced in the Senate.[9] He urged that "the only cure for the present unbalanced state of affairs between the two Houses is to be found in a change of procedure which would permit Ministers who have seats in the other House to appear here to explain their legislation, but, of course, not to vote."[10] The motion was supported by Sen. Dandurand, but it was opposed by a number of others, on the ground that it was both impractical and liable to introduce a more pronounced partisan atmosphere in the Senate.[11] Consequently, it was agreed that Sen. Robertson, as member of the Administration, should bring to the attention of the Prime Minister the discussion that took place in the Senate and test his reaction to it, and that pending the results of his mission Lemieux's motion should be withdrawn.[12]

In view of the increase in the number of bills first brought into the Senate between 1932 and 1935 the motion was not pressed further in the period covering Meighen's leadership. During the second half of the thirties, however, interest in the proposed change of the rules was revived. In 1939, a small incident took place which was widely interpreted as an encouraging sign for a closer co-operation between the two chambers in matters of legislation. On 29th May the Commons' Banking and Commerce committee, for the first time in the history of Parliament, *officially* invited the members of the Senate to attend the deliberations of the committee over the Central Mortgage Bank bill. As Meighen said, "that might lead later on to consideration of the right of ministers of

[7] *SD, 1908*, p. 187. [8] *Ibid., 1922*, p. 519. [9] *Ibid., 1931*, p. 146.
[10] *Ibid.*, p. 151.
[11] Said Sen. Bureau: "If we were to see a Minister of the Crown on the floor of the Senate, the sleeping political partisan might awake, and in putting our questions to the Minister we might undertake to teach him something. That is only human." *Ibid.*, p. 168.
[12] *Ibid.*, pp. 172–5.

either House to speak in the House on their own measure."[13] Then in 1940 proceedings in Committee of the Whole in the Senate with respect to the Department of National War Services bill almost established the long-awaited precedent. On July 12 the Government Leader was just about to ask Mr. Justice Davis, who had been designated deputy minister in the new department, to come to the floor, when he met the minister-to-be, Mr. Gardiner himself, and the latter was ready "to sit by my side and answer directly, and not through me, the questions you may ask him." Dandurand emphasized the significance of the suggested course, and it was welcomed by the House; even Meighen, despite his animosity toward Gardiner, agreed that "that is quite a change. I have no objection. It will be a precedent, though, which will likely be invoked for a long time to come." However, when the moment finally arrived for the Minister to give a direct answer to a question, unexpected opposition developed; Sen. Duff, a Liberal, rose and objected to the extension to the minister "of the privileges of a member of this House." The chairman himself, Sen. Sinclair, another Liberal, was of the opinion that "the proper procedure is for the Minister to prompt the leader of the Senate, and the leader can then reply to the question." He suggested that if the House wished to hear the Minister the proper place was at a standing committee.[14] As Sen. Dandurand's motion to permit the Minister to take an active part in the discussion in Committee of the Whole would have required a change in the rules, and since no such change could be made except by unanimous consent, this double opposition settled the matter. Gardiner was allowed to sit but not to speak.

During the war pressure was mounting in the Commons for a better balance between the two houses in the handling of legislation. In 1939 Church (Cons., Broadview) asked: "Will the Prime Minister, the Government and the House give consideration to a redivision of the work of the two houses so as to increase the efficiency of Parliament to meet modern conditions?"[15] He repeated his query every year.[16] It was pointed out that such bills as Game Export, Indians, Meat and Canned Foods, Precious Metals Marking in 1941, Petroleum and Naphtha Inspection, Toronto Harbour Commissioners in 1942, and British Columbia Indian Reserves, Canada Evidence, and Chief Justice of Canada in 1943—to cite only some of the most obvious ones—could with advantage have been initiated in the Senate. In 1944 the Leader of the Opposition, Graydon, suggested that there should be a

[13]*SD, 1939*, p. 529. [14]*SD, 1940*, pp. 304–6. [15]*HD, 1939*, p. 1471.
[16]*Ibid., 1940*, p. 1918; *ibid., 1941*, p. 1279; *ibid., 1942*, pp. 303, 4911.

conference between the Prime Minister and the Leader of the Senate "with the idea of having initiated in the other House such of the legislation . . . as may be so dealt with."[17] The following session Ilsley said on behalf of the Government that although the proposed conference had not taken place, "arrangement of the work is a matter of continued consideration."[18] At the same time Sen. Euler again urged in the Senate for a change in the rules to provide for a "standing invitation" to all ministers to come and explain their bills in the Upper House.[19]

Yet the actual adoption of the new rule in 1947 came as something of an anti-climax. Shortly after Sen. Robertson was appointed Government Leader in the Senate in 1945 he sought an interview with the Prime Minister to discuss sweeping changes in the whole constitution of the Senate. The interview ended with no concrete results and some of the Senators who knew about Robertson's mission and who were possibly more hard-boiled than the Leader, thought that King's proposal to postpone decision was "one of his characteristic, diplomatic and accomplished gestures toward shifting a hot potato to other quarters." They persuaded Robertson not to press the matter further than to present in the Senate a resolution for amending the Senate rules to permit a minister from the Commons to appear on the Senate's floor for the purpose of introducing his legislation.[20] Still, Sen. Robertson was waiting. Then shortly before the prorogation of Parliament in 1946 Sen. Ballantyne asked the Leader to use his good offices with the Government for initiating more government business in the Senate. It became apparent by 1947 that in view of the expiry of the National Emergency Transitional Powers Act on March 31 Parliament would be faced with a very heavy legislation program. In such circumstances Robertson's attempts to secure more bills for the Senate were bound to be successful, and, indeed, no less than fifteen Government measures started their parliamentary careers in the Upper Chamber in 1947. However, there was general disappointment at the scope and character of the legislation which had been selected for first introduction in the Senate[21] and perhaps this was the immediate cause that prompted Sen. Robertson to move on July 10 that the rules of the House should be amended by adding thereto as Rule 18/A the following:

When a Bill or other matter relating to any subject administered by a department of the Government of Canada has originated in and is being considered by the Senate or in Committee of the Whole, a Minister representing the Department, not being a Member of the Senate, may enter the Senate

[17]*Ibid., 1944*, p. 2282–3.
[18]*Ibid., 1945*, p. 615.
[19]*SD, 1945*, p. 292.
[20]*Ibid., 1951*, pp. 145–6.
[21]*Ibid., 1947*, p. 572.

Chamber, and, subject to the Rules, Orders, Forms of Proceedings, and usages of the Senate, take part in the debate.[22]

The change was not considered a panacea; its adoption, however, enabled the Senate to announce "to the Government, the House of Commons, and the nation as a whole, that although this may not turn out to be the most effective method of accomplishing our desire to render good service . . . nevertheless it should be given a trial." Only the Conservatives and Sen. Roebuck opposed its adoption; the Conservatives, because they were not given advance notice of the proposed Motion, and Roebuck, because he had no faith in its effectiveness.[23]

There have been seven cases in all in which ministers from the Commons availed themselves of the new rule. The rule is not clear to the effect that an invitation has to be tendered to a minister. In fact, the way the rule reads any minister can come to the Senate without an invitation. It is an equally moot question upon whose invitation, if an invitation is necessary, the minister would come; is it within the power of the leader or any other member to extend the invitation? If it is within the power of the leader does he have to consult the Senate and secure its approval before actually extending the invitation? In practice, all the seven cases occurred during Sen. Robertson's leadership and the ministers who decided to introduce their bills in the Senate all came upon invitation extended to them by the leader, who acted on his own initiative with no formal authorization from the House.

The new rule was first put to use early in the 1947 session of Parliament. On March 9 the Government Leader announced his intention to bring the minister of transport, the Hon. Mr. Chevrier, to the Chamber on the second reading of Senate bill E-5, an Act to amend the Canada Shipping Act. According to his earlier promises to the Senate, Sen. Robertson had urged his colleagues in the cabinet to permit this measure to be initiated in the Senate and also that the Minister should avail himself of the opportunity afforded by the change in the Senate Rules. However, consistent with his stand taken in the previous session Sen. Haig, Leader of the Opposition, declared himself opposed to the suggested procedure and insisted that the question was not simply one

[22]On the same day King, speaking on the Senate and House of Commons bill, said: ". . . I thought it would facilitate further co-operation between the two houses if ministers of the Crown were granted permission to appear on the floor of the Senate Chamber when important government measures were being presented and that they should have the right to participate in the debate and to answer any questions which might be asked. I believe that that reform would be most helpful and I have reason to believe that it is one which will be favourably entertained by the Senate." *HD, 1947*, p. 5366.

[23]*SD, 1947*, pp. 574, 607, 610.

concerning the rules of the Senate but one concerning the constitution of the country. "You cannot by amendment of the rules," he argued, "make a man a member of the Senate. . . . Anyone other than a Senator who appears here will be a stranger on the floor, and I will ask to have him removed."[24] As this was not only a challenge to the authority of the Senate to change the rules governing its business but also promised to cause considerable embarrassment to the Minister in case he appeared on the Senate's floor, the procedural entanglement called for a ruling from the chair. The Speaker declared that Rule 18/A was now a rule of the Senate, and "any intervention, or interference when the Minister arrives and is on the floor of the Senate would be entirely out of order, and I so rule."[25] Accordingly, when on March 16, while the Minister was awaiting word outside the Senate Chamber to be admitted on the floor, Haig rose on a question of privilege to protest, he was promptly ruled out of order by the Speaker.[26] Thereupon, the order of the day being called, Robertson withdrew from the Chamber, to return accompanied by Chevrier, whom he presented to the Speaker and then escorted to a seat on his left. The Minister was greeted by the Speaker who emphasized the historic significance of the situation.[27] This was followed by a few introductory remarks by the Minister, appreciative of the honour that was being extended to him, whereupon Mr. Chevrier quickly proceeded with the explanation of the main principle of the bill. It was a fairly short speech (occupying six-and-a-half columns in the *Senate Debates*), free from any partisan-political references and was no better or no worse than the explanations usually given by Senators who introduce legislation on second reading. The Minister's speech was followed by a lively discussion, in which many Senators from both sides took an active part and in the course of which the Minister returned to certain points in way of clarification. It is very doubtful whether members of the Senate became much better informed of the Shipping Act only because the Minister was personally introducing it; but it should be remembered that the purpose of Rule 18/A was only partly to bring the most authoritative source of information directly on the Senate floor; its main intention was to stimulate the introduction of legislation in the Senate in the first instance, by helping ministers to do what they do not like to see done by others in their behalf. If the Shipping bill could not be brought into the Senate unless it was introduced by the Minister, the appearance of the first minister in the Senate must have been considered an effective and promising sign of development.

[24] *SD, 1948*, pp. 201–2.
[25] *Ibid.*, p. 238.
[26] *Ibid.*, p. 242.
[27] *Ibid.*

On March 28, 1949, Chevrier was again invited on the Senate's floor to explain, on second reading, Bill Z-3, an Act respecting oil or gas pipe lines. The bill represented an attempt of Parliament to break new ground in the matter of general pipe line legislation and was considered by the Government a most important piece of legislation. Its immediate significance was underlined by the fact that on its passage hinged the future of five private bills for the incorporation of five companies. This time the Minister's appearance in the Senate was not accompanied by any ceremonies or introductory remarks, nor was there any attempt by Sen. Haig or others to block the smooth working of Rule 18/A. It was a most business-like and effective affair, brief, non-partisan, followed by questions by the Opposition Leader and a number of Liberal Senators and closed by the replies and concluding remarks of the Minister.[28]

The third occasion for application of the rule occurred during the second session of 1949. On November 8, the order for the second reading of the National Defence bill being called, Sen. Robertson retired from the Chamber, to return accompanied by Brooke Claxton, Minister of National Defence, whom he escorted to a seat in the Chamber. Thus, the procedure was identical with the one followed on Chevrier's first appearance in the Senate. Claxton, too, was welcomed by the Speaker and cheered by the Senators, whereupon he expressed his gratitude for the privilege of being invited to the Senate. Like his predecessor, Claxton restricted himself to the historical, technical, and legislative aspects of the measure and made no political-partisan remarks whatsoever. Upon concluding his explanation, he was closely questioned on a number of points by nearly half a dozen Senators. Claxton displayed great tact and politeness in his replies, addressed each of the Senators as "sir," and made a very good general impression upon the Senate. Whilst he was there, the bill was read the second time and referred to the Banking and Commerce committee.[29]

During the following two sessions the rule was not used and no minister was invited to the Senate. But in the session of 1952 four ministers from the House of Commons decided to introduce measures in the Upper House. The first was the Hon. Stuart Sinclair Garson, Minister of Justice and Attorney-General, who on May 13, following the same ceremonies that had greeted Chevrier and Claxton, gave an exhaustive (fifteen columns) explanation of Bill H-8, an Act respecting the criminal law. He told the Senate that one of the main reasons why the Department, the Government, and he personally decided to avail them-

[28]*Ibid.*, *1949*, pp. 258–63.

[29]*Ibid.* (2nd session), pp. 225–31.

selves of the services of the Senate was "the magnificent work which you did for us in considering the Bankruptcy Bill of 1949."[30] His explanatory remarks were followed by brief speeches by Senators, during the course of which the Minister was asked to clarify certain pertinent points bearing upon the principle of the bill. The Senate continued the second reading debate at two successive sittings; on these occasions, however, the minister was not present.[31]

The explanation of the principle of the bill to revise and consolidate the Food and Drugs Act (E-11), given by the Hon. Paul Martin, Minister of National Health and Welfare, on June 10, was a considerably shorter affair. It occupied, together with subsequent remarks from Senators, only two pages in Hansard, whereupon the bill was quickly referred to the standing committee on Public Health and Welfare.[32]

The third Minister to appear on the floor of the Senate under Rule 18/A in 1952 was F. G. Bradley, Secretary of State of Canada, who came on June 17 to explain the Trade Marks bill, which sought to revise and consolidate the Unfair Competition Act of 1932. Discussion, if possible, was even more limited than in the previous case, primarily because the bill was full of technical clauses, suitable for careful committee work, but contained hardly any principle at all.

The fourth person in 1952 to utilize the Rule was Robert Winters, Minister of Resources and Development, who, on June 23, not much before prorogation, undertook to explain his Eastern Rocky Mountain Conservation Act Amendment bill, "a very short but quite important bill."[33] The principle of the measure was exhausted in a debate not occupying more than five columns in Hansard and the remarks of Sen. Crerar were perhaps even more revealing than those of the Minister. Mr. Winters was questioned on certain technical points by at least three Senators, whereupon the bill was read the second time and promptly referred to the Banking and Commerce committee for a clause by clause consideration.[34]

Mr. Winters was the last minister to avail himself of Rule 18/A; no minister from the Commons has introduced legislation in the Senate since 1952. The reason for the discontinuance of the practice may perhaps be partly traced back to the violent protests of the late Sen. Nicol, who repeatedly stated that there was no minister who presented legislation half as well as did members of the Senate. Indeed, it should be remembered that the falling into desuetude of Rule 18/A coincided with the decentralization of the legislative functions of the Senate leader

[30]*SD, 1952*, p. 207. [31]*Ibid.*, pp. 207–16. [32]*Ibid.*, p. 404.
[33]*Ibid.*, p. 484. [34]*Ibid.*, p. 487.

among an ever widening circle of Senators.[35] Rule 18/A was essentially an aggressive device trying to enforce a practice which did not fit in the "new look" of Senate leadership. It belonged to the era that ended in 1942 and was out of line with the constitutional and political realities of the post-war period. The diffusion of Senate leadership, the minimization of the role of second reading debates, and the revitalization of the standing committee system, where ministers could be invited and cross-examined, in brief, the completion of the process of transforming the Senate from a theatre into a workshop provided no appropriate environment for the operation of Rule 18/A. Although himself responsible for the adoption of the rule, Sen. Robertson soon realized that it conflicted with his concepts of the Senate and Senate leadership, and, as he later recalled, "took the cue and I do not think I ever invited a Minister to come here afterwards."[36] On April 2, 1957, it was suggested that Mr. Pearson, then Secretary of State for External Affairs, should be invited under Rule 18/A to come to the Senate and address the House on Canada's policies towards the Middle East, Hungary, and aid to underdeveloped countries. However, the suggestion was dropped as a result of Sen. Haig's objection that the Senate ought not "to allow any Minister or other individual from the House of Commons to discuss on the floor of this House a subject that is of general interest to the whole Government. . . ."[37] There were some attempts in 1960 to revive the rule, but Sen. Aseltine, Leader of the Senate, frankly told the House that he was "not very much in favour of that system." Like the late Sen. Nicol, he believed that under Rule 18/A, even if it worked out, the Senate "would not get any more information from ministers, and perhaps not as much as we get by following our regular practice."[38] Thus, the rule, for all practical purposes, can now be considered dead.

The Senate's quick acquiescence in the demise of Rule 18/A has been, no doubt, primarily due to the fact that even without the rule the annual volume of legislation initiated in the Upper House since 1945 has been at a steady high. Compared to the thirty-one bills first introduced in the Senate during the twenty-year period from 1925 to 1945, the 220 bills between the end of the war and 1963—seven times the record of the pre-war era—represent an impressive improvement. As a result, the average number of government bills first brought in the Senate for discussion has been about ten per session, constituting nearly 20 per cent of the total volume of government legislation during the period.[39]

[35]Above, pp. 101 ff. [36]*SD, 1960*, p. 91. [37]*Ibid., 1957*, p. 457.
[38]*Ibid., 1960*, p. 103.
[39]Cf. Appendixes II and III.

Governments have invariably found the Senate a well-suited place for first consideration of voluminous, complex, and highly technical pieces of legislation, such as consolidating measures, requiring great legislative experience as well as legal and financial talent and leisurely procedure. The services rendered by the Senate in such instances have been more than simple time-saving for the House of Commons; the Senate has turned out reliable and enduring pieces of legislation, which are amongst the best framed and most competently constructed Acts on the Statute Book of Canada. The following four examples, one from the pre-war era and three from the period following the war, have been chosen to illustrate the kind of technical usefulness to be expected from the Senate as a chamber of first instance.

In the session of 1934 the Senate was entrusted with first consideration of one of the most formidable legislative products during the past thirty-seven years, the Canada Shipping Act Consolidation bill, whose aim was to revise Canadian laws respecting shipping and to provide uniformity in shipping laws in the light of the Statute of Westminster and of agreements with the other Dominions.

It is part of the history of the bill that in 1932 and in the first part of 1933 the Department of Marine undertook to formulate a shipping code. After engaging eminent counsel to assist them, the officers of the Department drafted a full revision of the Canada Shipping Act, whereupon a bill, known as Bill J, was presented to the Senate in 1933 by Sen. Meighen. However, proceedings in the Senate's Banking and Commerce committee, to which the bill was referred, had to be suspended pending clarification of certain legal points. The bill was withdrawn but copies of its text were circulated to the shipping interests in Canada and Britain, who were invited to make representations and comments. In the light of these representations, the bill was redrafted and it was reintroduced in the Senate on March 7, 1934.

After second reading on March 8 the bill was referred to the Banking and Commerce committee. The committee decided to set up a subcommittee. The subcommittee, with the help of W. F. O'Connor (later Law Clerk and Parliamentary Counsel to the Senate) and officers from the Department of Justice, made a careful study of the bill. This subcommittee sat throughout the Easter holidays and amended the bill in many respects over important points. It reduced the bill from 822 to 719 clauses by adding 16 new clauses and 51 subclauses while dropping 40 clauses as superfluous, rewriting 58 clauses, amending 279, and relocating 186; the schedules to the bill were in one case entirely changed. At the report stage on the committee the committee again heard all the interested parties, shipping associations, the grain merchants, the ship-owners, the shipbuilders, the pilots, the engineers, the labour associations, and all those who wished to be heard. Following these hearings the main committee made forty-two further principal and numerous minor amendments, at the conclusion of which the bill was reported to the Senate on May 30 and was passed the following day. Thus, when it was reported to the House of Commons after two months' study and discussion in the Senate the measure was in as complete form as possible. It contained 497 pages and comprised 16 parts, 113 definitions, and 719 sections, dealing with virtually everything pertaining to shipping. What emerged as a finished product was a bill to which "nothing in the way of legislation introduced since Confederation bears any analogy at all."[40] It prompted widespread comments and general applause from every corner of the country,[41] and having been assented to on July 3, 1934, it has been regarded ever since as one of the chief legislative accomplishments of the Upper House.

In 1949 another consolidation measure, the Bankruptcy Act Amendment bill, was first brought in in the Senate. The Act which came into force in 1919 had not been amended since 1932. Some of its provisions badly needed alteration. After three previous attempts in the preceding years, the bill was introduced in the Senate in the early part of the second session of 1949. Following second reading it was referred to the Banking and Commerce committee, whose report, containing a total of twenty-three amendments, marked the culmination of an arduous and exacting task. The bill contained 103 pages and 172 clauses; in the course of its study the Banking and Commerce committee held nineteen meetings, revised the measure twice, and made available to its extensive mailing list more than 12,000 copies of its day-to-day proceedings. Before submitting its final report the committee heard a wide and varied list of witnesses. It considered representations from the Quebec Superior Court and the Supreme Court of Ontario, from mortgage, investment and credit companies, from bank and bar associations and from boards of trade, industrial firms, and many other groups. In the 1949 session the committee heard new representations, and although interested bodies did not get all they were asking for they went away reasonably satisfied. At the same time the Superintendent of Insurance also expressed satisfaction that none of the changes made would seriously disturb the policy laid down by the Department. The Banking and Commerce committee once again proved that the committees of the Senate come very close to

[40]*SD, 1934*, p. 421.
[41]*HD, 1934*, p. 3814.

the ideal forum where all kinds of interests, representing different sections of the federal state, may appear in an attempt to influence the complex and elusive process of governmental decision-making. So numerous were the letters and briefs submitted to the committee that a subcommittee was appointed to ensure that no submission from any group, however small, was overlooked. This subcommittee, under the chairmanship of Sen. Hayden, spent a great deal of time with the Superintendent of Insurance and Mr. MacNeill, the Law Clerk and Parliamentary Counsel to the Senate, going into a digest of the various contentious parts of the bill. The main committee thus had the benefit of the subcommittee's report and was enabled to deal with the matter in an effective manner. The upshot was an improved Bankruptcy Act, which encountered no difficulty in the House of Commons.

Introduced by the Minister of National Defence, Claxton, himself, the National Defence bill was the second major piece of legislation initiated in the Senate during the 1949 session of Parliament, in addition to the Bankruptcy bill. Of the two, however, the National Defence bill was probably more national in character and more comprehensive in scope; also, it was longer. Proceedings in the Senate and in its committee and the final product that emerged showed that even after the most careful and minutest preparation by drafting experts there was still considerable room for further improvement in both form and content. The bill was undoubtedly a principal item in the Government's legislative program. Announced in the Speech from the Throne both in 1948 and in 1949 it was considered another step in the unification and co-ordination of all the defence forces of Canada and it was a clear tribute to the Senate's legislative competence that a measure of this calibre was first introduced there. The honour was doubly underlined by the fact that it was a bill in which the Minister had a keen personal interest, much greater than were the bill a mere incidence to his office.[42]

Accordingly, the bill went through a preparation of extraordinary care and circumspection. It was possibly the bulkiest measure to be placed before the Senate since the session of 1934. The 251 clauses in the bill were intended to replace 598 sections in the existing legislation. The bill represented more than two years' study by officers of the Department of National Defence, the Navy, the Army, and the Air Force as well as by the Departments of Justice and Finance. Its drafting was undertaken by a team of service legal officers under the direct supervision of the Judge Advocate-General, Brigadier R. J. Orde, assisted by a senior officer of each of the services. When the whole matter had been thoroughly

[42]*SD, 1949* (2nd session), p. 228.

explored the bill was examined by a special subcommittee of the cabinet, consisting of the Government Leader in the Senate, the Minister of Justice, the Solicitor-General, and the Minister of National Defence. On several occasions the bill was considered by the cabinet. Yet, despite all this meticulous care and conscientiousness, the Government declared itself open to any suggestions, and the Minister assured the Senate that such suggestions would be warmly welcomed. "We desire to get the best possible bill," he said, "and so we invite the co-operation of every member in this honourable House. . . ."[43]

Thus encouraged the Senate lost no time in justifying its reputation. In the Banking and Commerce committee the bill was amended on seventy-four counts. The committee had before it the Attorney-General for Canada, the Hon. Stuart Sinclair Garson, while the military delegation was headed by the Solicitor-General and former parliamentary assistant to the Minister of National Defence, Hughes Lapointe. There were also sitting through the long sessions the Judge Advocate-General, his Assistant, his Deputy and the Judge Advocate of the Fleet, who, together with the Minister, supplied the members of the committee with a large amount of information on military law and procedure. It is to be noted that each one of the seventy-four amendments was to the twelfth draft of the bill. Throughout the meetings all members of the committee, and the representatives of the Department of National Defence, evidenced a sincere desire to get into statute form something reflecting the best thinking in the interest of the defence of Canada. "It was a co-ordinated effort," said Hayden, ". . . directed towards maintaining a proper spirit in the armed forces, and making doubly sure that the rights of the ordinary service man would be protected in the same way as those of the highest officer."[44] The result?—"something rather new in military history."[45]

Encouraged chiefly by the Senate's work on the Bankruptcy legislation, in the session of 1952 the Government decided to introduce as a Senate bill its complicated Criminal Law bill. On April 7 the Minister of Justice and Attorney General tabled in the House of Commons the report of the committee which had been set up in 1949 to prepare for consideration by the Government a draft bill to amend and revise the Criminal Code which was first enacted in 1892 and had not had any major review or overhaul since that date. The bill was introduced as letter H-8 of the Senate on May 12 and the following day Garson attended in the Senate to speak on the motion for second reading. The bill was then referred to

[43]*Ibid.* [44]*Ibid.*, p. 399.
[45]*Ibid.*, p. 402. *SJ, 1949* (2nd session), pp. 263–8.

the Banking and Commerce committee, which appointed a subcommittee to consider the measure clause by clause. After twelve meetings the subcommittee reported to the main committee on June 20. The main committee held three meetings and subsequently recommended to the Senate that, in view of the amount of work still to be done, the bill should not be further proceeded with in that session. During the summer of 1952 the bill was reviewed by the officers of the Department of Justice in the light of the recommendations made by the Senate's Banking and Commerce subcommittee, and twenty-six of the recommendations were adopted. The bill was reintroduced in the Senate in the session of 1952–53 and again referred to the Banking and Commerce committee. The subcommittee had fifteen meetings, most of which began in the morning and extended over the afternoon and evening to preserve the continuity of consideration, and scrutinized minutely, line by line, even down to periods and commas, every section of the bill, which contained over 280 pages, 748 sections, and several forms. In their deliberations, both the main committee and its subcommittee continued to enjoy the assistance of officers of the Justice Department, of the Law Clerk and Parliamentary Counsel to the Senate, J. F. MacNeill, and of the entire Senate staff under Harvey Armstrong, Chief Clerk of Committees, who worked conscientiously and for long hours in their struggle to get the work through. All of these people formed a team that for a task of this kind would be hard to duplicate. In addition, the main committee heard witnesses representing interested groups in Canada. As a result, the subcommittee recommended 117 amendments, in addition to the 63 made in the previous year. Thus, in all the Banking and Commerce committee suggested 180 amendments to the Code since it came before the Senate in 1952. Not all the 180 amendments, of course, proposed major changes in the legislation. Some were purely for the purpose of clarification, but their significance should not unduly be underestimated. In condensing a Code of 1,152 sections to one of 753 sections the Senate produced a concise public document intelligible not only to those trained in the law but also to laymen—a point of considerable practical importance in an act of Parliament which was being used daily in magistrates' courts. The amendments recommended by the subcommittee were adopted without exception.[46] Due to prorogation of Parliament the measure was not passed in that session; it was enacted in 1954.

In these four celebrated examples the Senate was the scene of sustained and slowly maturing legislative efforts often spread over two, three, or

[46]*SD, 1953*, pp. 147–68 *passim*. For complimentary remarks, see *HD*, *1953*, pp. 1275–6.

four parliamentary sessions and aimed at the revision and consolidation of various statutes. But in addition to such massive contributions, the Senate has proved particularly well adapted for being the first House to deal with certain types of bills recurring annually or in short intervals. Thus, bills dealing with foreign as well as Canadian or British insurance companies or loans and trust companies are on the list of Senate bills almost every year. Similarly, railway legislation, dealing with some organizational aspect or the audit system of the CNR and CPR, is usually introduced in the Senate in the first instance. Again there is a wide range of bills affecting the Supreme Court of Canada, the Exchequer Court, the Courts of Admiralty, or seeking to amend the Criminal Code, the Canada Evidence Act, the Prisons and Reformatories Act, or the Juvenile Delinquents Act, which are submitted first to the Senate for consideration. Less frequently, but still quite regularly, legislation concerning Canadian citizenship, patents of invention, weights and measures and length and mass units, exports and imports, precious metals, national trade marks, food and narcotic drugs, national parks, natural resources, and harbour commissions are brought in in the Senate before they go to the House of Commons. These measures are of a technical and mainly non-controversial character, on which the Government is quickly able to have the benefit of the varied experience of the members of the Senate. It may be of some interest to note that about 75 per cent of the legislation initiated in the Senate during the post-war period has emanated from five government departments in the following order: Transport (18 per cent), Finance (17), Justice (15), Mines and Resources (13), and Trade and Commerce (11).

It is a proof of the technical usefulness of the Senate as a chamber of first instance that in practice even the constitutional rule that money bills must be initiated in the House of Commons may be evaded if the Government finds it convenient to introduce bills entailing public expenditure in the Senate. The usual procedure in such a case is to make the "privilege amendments" in committee in the Senate, by "omitting" the financial clauses in the bill. In fact, the sentences are never omitted; they are printed in red ink or italics and are technically supposed to be blanks. The clauses are "restored" by a financial resolution in the Commons and, when passed by the Lower House, the bill is referred back to the Senate as "amended."[47] This procedure was followed in the

[47]Sir J. G. Bourinot, *Parliamentary Procedure and Practice in the Dominion of Canada* (3rd ed., Toronto, 1903), p. 493. This does not affect pecuniary penalties incorporated in bills originated in the upper house, "provided that all such penalties . . . are only to punish or prevent crimes and offences, and do not tend

bill setting up a Department of Insurance in 1932, in the Small Loans bill of 1939 limiting the powers of money lenders, and in the National Parks bill in both 1947 and 1950, levying a tax upon the interest of any person in land in a park.

It needs hardly any emphasis at all that draft bills originated in the Senate are subjected to the same kind of scrutiny, and the same principles of technical revision are applied to them, as discussed in the previous chapter; as a result, many of them are amended, some of them extensively. The Senate made eight amendments to the Explosive bill of 1946,[48] while in the Precious Metals Marking bill of the same session it made a total of eighteen amendments before forwarding it to the Commons; to the Trust Companies bill of 1947 it put nine amendments, to the Food and Drugs bill of 1953 thirty-nine, to the Trade Marks bill of 1953 seventeen, to the Loan Companies bill of 1958 eleven, to the Bankruptcy bill of 1962–63 ten.

Whether an ordinary bill or a "money bill," the main purpose of initiating in the Senate the kind of technical and non-controversial legislation mentioned above is to save time for the House of Commons for a maximum consideration of the politically controversial issues of the day. When a bill is introduced in the Senate in the first place, the burden of the House of Commons is reduced because most of the points of detail can be disposed of in the Senate, so that the Commons has little else to do than to make a final revision without spending much time. Ministers introducing bills in the Commons after they have been considered in the Senate tend to limit their remarks to the bare essentials.[49] Members of the Commons know also that bills coming before them from the Upper House have been examined with meticulous care and attention. Speaking in the session of 1950, Mr. Carroll (Lib., Inverness-Richmond), a veteran member of the Commons, observed: "I was in this House from 1911 on, 1917, 1921 and 1925. Rarely in those days was anything initiated in the Senate. . . . I noticed that in this Parliament a great deal of important legislation has had its initiation in

---

to lay a burden on the subject, either as aid or supply to Her Majesty, or for any general or special purposes, by rates, tolls, assessments or otherwise." *House of Commons Rules*, Rule 87. A. Beauchesne, ed., *Rules and Forms of the House of Commons of Canada* (4th ed., Toronto, 1958), chap. VIII, Rule 64.

[48]Its work in this instance prompted the following comments from Mr. Diefenbaker: "The bill as it stands shows what can be done when there is proper co-operation between the two houses of Parliament. There is a care and directness in draftmanship in the bill which is too often lacking, and it indicates the desirability of using to the limit the experience and the facilities which the other house offers for considered legislation." *HD, 1946*, pp. 1687.

[49]See *ibid., 1957*, p. 3267.

the Senate, and when it comes to this House and goes into committee we can look back on the records of the Senate committees and find out exactly what happened there, and *it materially helps the work of this House*."[50] In assessing the contribution of the Senate in saving time for the Commons on such technical measures, it should be recalled that apart from the scrutiny offered by the Senate, the simple fact that a bill has already been through one house has an important bearing upon the time consumed for its consideration in the other house of Parliament. "Bear in mind," Sen. Farris said very properly, "that the news value of legislation has an influence on the time spent in discussing it. When a bill has been discussed first in this house, and the "break of the news" has taken place from here, the chances are that there will not be the same motive for long speeches in the other house."[51] Even if there are bills which take longer in the Commons than in the Senate, the point of comparison is not between the two houses, but between the time spent by the Commons on a bill already disposed of by the Senate and the time the Commons would spend on the same bill had it started in the Lower House. As Mr. Nowlan (PC, Digby-Annapolis-Kings) pointed out in 1955: "The work done in the other place certainly facilitated the work which we did here. In other words *we would have spent much longer on it had it not been for the work done in the Senate*."[52]

The effectiveness of the Senate as a house of first instance in reducing the legislative burden, and consequently the time needed for carrying such a burden, of the Commons may be evidenced from two simple sets of statistics; on the one hand, of the 208 government bills initiated in and passed by the Senate from 1945 to 1963 only 38 have been subsequently amended by the House of Commons; on the other hand, the 160 bills which have passed the Commons without amendment during the same period occupy 1,501 columns in the debates of the House of Commons, or 9.6 columns (slightly less than five pages) per bill, which is definitely much less than the space devoted by the Commons to bills which have started their parliamentary careers in the Lower House.

In addition to effecting direct time-saving for the House of Commons, Governments often initiate legislation in the Senate for the purpose of

[50]*Ibid., 1950,* pp. 2788–9. Italic added. For similar remarks, see Mr. Benidickson's (Lib., Kenora-Rainy River) comments on the Senate's work on the Canadian and British Insurance Companies bill and the Foreign Insurance bill. *Ibid., 1961,* p. 2754.

[51]*SD, 1947,* p. 616.

[52]*HD, 1955,* pp. 5934–5. Italic added. A different conclusion seems to have been drawn in the case of the House of Lords. Cf. P. Bromhead, *The House of Lords and Contemporary Politics, 1911–1957* (London, 1958), pp. 194–5.

sounding out the views of various interests before decision on the final form of legislation is made. Bills in this category are introduced in the Senate, referred to committee, and, after all interested bodies have had an opportunity to declare their stands, they are usually withdrawn to be reintroduced later in the desired form. The procedure enables the Government to combine the drafting process with the phase of interest articulation in Parliament, without sacrificing the time of the House of Commons. In the session of 1932, for example, the British and Foreign Insurance Companies Status and Powers bill and its companion, the Dominion Insurance Companies Status and Powers bill, were brought in in the Senate early in the session. The bills were designed to meet the new juridical situation in the light of a decision by the Judicial Committee of the Privy Council in the fall of 1931. However, as drafted, they were opposed by the provinces and it was feared that if enacted the bills would involve the country in renewed litigation on the question of jurisdiction. The Senate's Banking and Commerce committee tried to reach some understanding with the provinces and the insurance companies. During the process of the discussions, however, it appeared certain to the Government that no compromise was attainable except through a complete redrafting and reprinting of the bills. They were consequently withdrawn, to be reintroduced later in the session as the Department of Insurance bill, the Foreign Insurance Companies in Canada bill, and the British and Canadian Companies bill. In their new form they were duly passed and were placed upon the Statute Book of Canada.

In 1952 three bills were introduced and then withdrawn in the Senate, the Criminal Code bill, the Food and Drugs bill, and the Trade Marks bill. The last two were consolidating measures of considerable scope. In connection with the Food bill the minister hoped that "it may be possible for [the Senate] to use the mechanism of a committee to afford industry and others concerned an opportunity of making representations as to the proposals that have been put forward in this legislation. . . ."[53] Indeed, the bill was withdrawn after the committee stage in the Senate and was reintroduced next session, again in the upper house. Similar considerations applied to the Trade Marks measure whose purpose was to consolidate the Unfair Competition Act of 1932. Although the bill was drafted on the basis of the recommendation of an advisory committee the Government was aware that on a branch of the law which had so many ramifications it was unlikely that unanimity of opinion

[53]*SD, 1952*, p. 403.

could be achieved upon all points and proposals. For this reason the bill was submitted first to the Senate, so that all concerned have a final opportunity to give full consideration to, and make representations on, the draft. The Government had no intention to rush through the measure in a session. Instead, it wanted to spend a whole year hearing representations before deciding on the final form of the legislation.[54] Again, in 1957 both the Government Property Traffic bill and the Indian Reserves bill were initiated in the Senate but not proceeded beyond a certain point, whereas in the short session of 1957–58 the Government's bill to amend the Territorial Lands Act was withdrawn after the Senate's Natural Resources Committee completed its hearings and printed its proceedings, thus enabling a wide circle of interests to study the measure and air their views upon it.

2. *Initiation of Private Legislation*

ORDINARY BILLS

If lessening the work of the Commons was one of the main reasons for initiating in the Senate technical and non-controversial Government measures, the aim of originating private legislation in the Upper rather than in the Lower House is further to reduce the burdens of the popular chamber. A private bill is one that is designed to confer special powers or privileges on a person, a body of persons, or a particular area and is unrelated to general public policy.[55] As such, private bills include bills of divorce to dissolve the marriages of persons domiciled in provinces where there are no divorce courts. However, it is proposed to defer the discussion of divorce bills to the end of the chapter and to concentrate, for the present, upon private bills other than divorce.

Unlike divorce legislation which has always been considered a special jurisdiction of the Senate, ordinary private bills, for a long time following British precedent, were initiated in either one of the two houses of Parliament. Bourinot made the observation that "in Canada, the promoters of private bills are free to introduce their bills in either house. By far the larger proportion is introduced in the Commons."[56] During the twenties, however, it was urged in different quarters that the practice followed with regard to divorce bills should be extended, wholly or in part, to the rest of private legislation, thus providing more room for the

[54] *Ibid., 1952*, pp. 434–5.
[55] See Bourinot, *Parliamentary Procedure*, pp. 558 ff.
[56] *Ibid.*, pp. 578–9.

technical usefulness of the Senate and, at the same time, alleviating the growing burdens of the Commons.[57] In 1923, for instance, a Joint Committee of both Houses of Parliament recommended that the distribution of all private bills be regulated by the Speakers of both houses jointly, so that private bills be introduced one-half in each chamber.[58] A modified version of this suggestion was put forward by Sen. Dandurand, who proposed a system by which petitions concerning private bills should be received and numbered in one office, the odd numbers to be sent to one house and the even numbers to the other alternately.[59] However, no action was taken until 1934, when a penetrating and highly instructive debate took place in the Senate on the functions and powers of the House and on various methods of making the Senate's contribution more effective. As a result of the extensive discussion what emerged with universal support, namely the proposal (originated with Sir A. Aylesworth)[60] to initiate in the Senate all private bills presented to Parliament, was seized upon as likely to afford the groundwork for an advance in the desired direction. With this view, Meighen, the Government Leader in the Senate, held conferences with other members of the Administration and apparently was able to convince the Government of the desirability of the end to which common assent had been given.

As a consequence two changes were introduced in the rules of both houses; Rule 114 of the Senate was changed to the effect that private bills could from then on be introduced in the Senate at any time without previous notice, as had formerly been the case; secondly, SO 98 of the Commons was altered to increase the tax of $200 for the introduction of a private bill in the Lower House to $500, while the tax in the Senate remained the same. This, in effect, attached a payment of penalty to originating private legislation in the House of Commons. Commenting on the change, Meighen hoped that "the increase is so substantial that it will be to the interest of those who have private legislation to advance to have it introduced here." In the case of the Senate the door was more widely opened and in the case of the Commons it was more narrowly closed.[61]

The change in the rules has proved effective: since 1934 the Senate

[57]R. A. Mackay, *The Unreformed Senate of Canada* (London, 1926), p. 103.
[58]*SD, 1934*, pp. 105 ff.
[59]*Ibid., 1931*, p. 151.
[60]Correspondence between Aylesworth and Meighen, March 1934. Meighen Papers, series 5, no. 114.
[61]*SD, 1934*, pp. 254–5. In 1951 the period of publication of notices for private bills was reduced from five to four weeks to make it identical with the practice in the Commons.

has assumed a virtual monopoly over the entire field of private legislation. During the period 1925–34 inclusive, of a total of 237 private bills presented to Parliament 169 were first introduced in the House of Commons. From 1935 to 1963 altogether 440 private bills came before Parliament; of them 433 were initiated in the Senate and only seven in the Commons. Thus, over the last thirty-seven years no less than 522 private bills other than divorce have originated in the Senate, or a yearly average of about 14. Their distribution according to sponsors shows the following picture:

Banking and insurance companies	134
Railway and bridge companies	74
Religious and charitable bodies	74
Trust and loan companies	54
Pipe line companies	36
Patents	18
Telegraph and telephone companies	13
Miscellaneous other bodies	119
Total	522

Generally speaking, private bills may be introduced in the Senate for either of two purposes; first, to incorporate new companies, and second, to amend the existing incorporating act. The majority (311) of private bills over the last thirty-seven years have been petitions to amend the parent statute, whilst about 40 per cent of them (211) consist of applications for incorporation. Parliament may be asked to amend the incorporating act for a variety of reasons—changing the name of a company or organization, an extension or the construction of railway lines, an extension of the time for the completion of any work, the increase or reduction of the capital stock of any company, the extension of the powers of a company (e.g., the authorization of a charitable organization to hold real estate), and so forth.

In dealing with private bills the Senate is practically a court called upon to protect the persons whose interests are affected by the proposed legislation and who appear before the Senate as suitors and adverse parties. The fact that they must pay certain fees further underlines the analogy between the proceedings in the Senate and those of a law court. The procedure for private bills is very carefully prescribed by the rules of the Senate. The provisions governing publication and filing of petitions as well as the notification of any persons who might be affected serve the purpose of enabling all concerned to have every opportunity to present themselves before the Senate and dispute, if necessary, the bill's passage.[62]

Procedurally the three readings in the Senate have only nominal significance in the course of a private bill. Second reading is conditional or hypothetical, subject to the proof of the allegations of fact contained in the petition.[63] The essential stage, as, indeed, even in the case of public bills, is in standing committee to which every private bill is referred without exception after second reading. It is here that the petitioners and their counsels as well as any opponents are heard and the Senate examines "whether the facts are as alleged and whether a good case has been made out for the passage of the Bill. . . ."[64] The committee's findings are usually final. In contrast to the practice of the Commons a private bill reported from a standing committee is practically never committed to a committee of the whole in the Senate.[65]

In addition to being a jury hearing petitioners and adverse parties the Senate in considering private bills shows great precaution in protecting the interests of the public at large. In so doing it does not hesitate to amend or even to reject private bill petitions. This becomes particularly necessary in view of the fact that private bills are prepared by their sponsors, who may engage counsel but cannot ask for the assistance of the officials of government departments.[66]

In 1932, for instance, the Senate did not shy at taking drastic action with regard to the Quebec, Montreal, and Southern Railway Company bill, whose aim was to preserve the powers of the company to complete its railway. When the Senate learnt that it would be undesirable to permit the company to continue as a separate entity under its original charter,

[62]*Rules of the Senate*, 107, 110. Bourinot, *Parliamentary Procedure*, pp. 558–9.

[63]Bourinot, *Parliamentary Procedure*, p. 599; Sir T. Erskine May, *Treatise on the Law, Privileges, Proceedings and Usages of Parliament* (14th ed., London, 1946), p. 962; Beauchesne, *Rules and Forms*, p. 295. Cf. Hanks Patent bill, *SD, 1951*. Private bills rarely cause excitement on second reading in the Senate. Certainly an exception was the Order of the Sons of Italy bill in 1936. Italo-Canadians could hardly have chosen a more unfortunate moment for petitioning Parliament for an incorporating charter. The bill was vehemently attacked by a number of senators, who felt that "at this juncture, when Italy has overrun Ethiopia, the introduction of this bill is nothing more or less than a . . . very insolent gesture of defiance . . . against the people of Canada," and a motion for six months' hoist was promptly moved to kill the bill. Only under the influence of the measured words of Meighen and Calder was the motion withdrawn. The bill was amended in standing committee but only in its drafting. *SD, 1936*, pp. 338, 353; *SJ, 1936*, p. 224.

[64]E. R. Hopkins, *How Parliament Works* (Ottawa, 1957), p. 48.

[65]An exception was the Personal Finance Corporation bill in 1934. *SD, 1934*, p. 207.

[66]E. A. Driedger, "The Preparation of Legislation," 31 *Can. Bar Rev.*, p. 35.

the Banking and Commerce committee killed the bill, by reporting that the preamble of the measure had not been proven and the bill's passage would not be in the public interest.[67] In another case, the Mme Belle Hervey Harper Cazzani bill of 1938, the Senate stepped in to block the passage of the legislation, in order to prevent the establishment of an undesirable precedent under the Immigration Act.[68]

In several cases the Senate has amended private bill applications to ensure that the proposed project would not start until the Government has given its approval or certain conditions have been met. Thus, it amended the Detroit and Windsor Subway Company bill in 1926 to provide that the proposed amalgamation work would commence only upon approval by the Board of Railway Commissioners for Canada;[69] similar provisions for the approval of either the Treasury Board or the Board of Transport Commissioners for Canada were inserted in the bills to incorporate the Morris Finance Corporation in 1931, the Yellowknife Telephone Company in 1947, or the St. Mary's River Bridge Company in 1955.[70]

The Senate has been particularly careful in seeing to it that private bills contain no retroactive provisions,[71] while in the field of patent legislation it has tried to guard against cases of non-payment of fees[72] or against petitions which failed to satisfy the time requirement in applying for an act of Parliament.[73]

Another principle guiding the Senate in its dealings with private bills has been to attempt to bring such legislation into conformity with existing Acts or other statutory instruments. Thus, one of the amendments put to the bill to incorporate the Detroit River Canadian Bridge Company in 1928 was phrased to make the rates of pay subject to the terms of the fair wage clauses set forth in the Order of Council of 1922.[74] Again, the Discount and Loan Corporation of Canada bill of 1933 was amended for the purpose of bringing it into conformity with existing statutes relating to similar corporations.[75] Similar amendments were made in the Ottawa and New York Railways Company bill, the St. Lawrence and Adirondack Railway Company bill, and the Economical Mutual Fire Insurance Company bill, all in 1936, in the Co-operative Life Insurance Company bill of 1946, or in the Governing Council of

[67]*SD, 1932*, pp. 91–93; *SJ, 1932*, p. 252.
[68]*SD, 1938*, p. 212.
[69]*SJ, 1926*, p. 253.
[70]*Ibid., 1931*, pp. 212–14; *SD, 1947*, p. 513; *ibid., 1955*, p. 336.
[71]E.g., National Council of Women of Canada bill. *SD, 1946*, p. 132.
[72]E.g., Cobb Patent bill. *SJ, 1929*, p. 312.
[73]E.g., Towy Patent bill, *SD, 1935*, p. 338.
[74]*SJ, 1928*, p. 433.
[75]*SD, 1933*, p. 552.

Salvation Army bill of 1962, to provide that the terms of the bills were in harmony with the relevant provisions of the Railway Act, the Insurance Act, and the Canadian and British Insurance Companies Act, respectively.

The Senate received with suspicion the bill to incorporate the Export Finance Corporation of Canada bill in 1959 to assist in the financing of exports from Canada to various countries. Objections were raised to permitting a company to deal with foreign trade and to make loans to foreign governments while not being subject to the foreign policy of the government of the day.[76] What made the company's status so elusive was the fact that, since the company was not to be operating in the field of domestic trade, it did not come under the restrictions of the Small Loan Companies Act. After careful consideration the Senate made a total of ten amendments bringing the bill into close harmony with the statutory provisions of the Company Act, especially Parts I and III.

In revising private bills the Senate is consciously trying to protect or to promote Canadian interests, wherever possible. In the Detroit River Canada Bridge Company bill of 1928, already mentioned, one of the Senate's amendments stipulated that in order to encourage the use of Canadian materials a weekly statement should be submitted to the Department of Labour, giving the names and addresses of firms supplying materials and the quantity thereof.[77] Also, the bill to incorporate the Canadian Board of American Missions of the United Lutheran Church in America came under heavy criticism in the Senate, mainly on the ground that in the proposed "Canadian board" there was not a single Canadian. Meighen found it extraordinary that the Senate was asked to grant "an American corporation rights to direct the affairs of a Canadian corporation for all time." Consequently, in committee the bill was amended to provide that a certain number of the directors must be British subjects resident in Canada.[78]

As a result of all this care and precaution private bills have usually a smooth and quick passage in the Commons and take up very little of its members' politically precious time. Indeed, of the 489 private bills that were initiated and passed in the Senate over the last thirty-seven years only sixty-five have subsequently been amended by the Lower House and only ten have been rejected; of the ten rejected, nine fall into the pre-war period 1925–40.

The overwhelming majority of the Commons' amendments have been changes on points of detail, usually at the request of the department

[76] *Ibid., 1959*, p. 451.
[77] *SJ, 1928*, p. 433.
[78] *SD. 1939*, pp. 91, 136.

concerned, or, indeed, of the promoters of the measure.[79] On the other hand, it was always on grounds of policy that the Commons decided to reject a private bill petition.[80] It should be emphasized, however, that such amendments or rejection of private bills are quite exceptional, as the Senate is now given full responsibility for private legislation.

DIVORCE BILLS

Divorce legislation, over which the Senate's complete monopoly has never been questioned, is perhaps the most notorious aspect of the work of the Canadian Parliament. By section 92 of the BNA Act the solemnization of marriages comes under provincial jurisdiction and under section 91 the question of marriage and divorce comes within the powers of Parliament. There can be no doubt that divorce, which so basically affects the social organization in a community, is in the field of "civil rights" as these words are generally understood. Yet at the time of Confederation the subject-matter of divorce was lifted by the Imperial Parliament out of the general body of powers given to provincial legislatures in matters of civil rights, and was deposited amongst the powers over which the federal authority would exercise exclusive jurisdiction. If this had not been done it might not have raised a problem in Ontario, New Brunswick, and Nova Scotia. But it did raise a problem in Quebec and perhaps not so much because of the Catholic majority as because of the minority who were not Catholics.[81] On the other hand, under section 129 the courts that were then in existence, and the powers that were vested in the provinces prior to Confederation and dealing with divorce and other forms of legislation, were retained by the provinces.[82] However, Sir John A. Macdonald frowned upon the idea of decentralizing divorce jurisdiction by establishing a divorce court in Canada, for fear that it "would mean cheap and easy divorces, which would lead to great laxity in the marriage relations."[83] It was also due to his insistence that the Senate drifted into the responsibility of being the

[79]The only noteworthy expectation has been the amendments made on policy grounds to eleven bills incorporating pipe line companies in the period 1951–55.

[80]See Cornwall Bridge Co. bill, *HD, 1935*, p. 3768; Hamilton Life Insurance bill, *HJ, 1935*, p. 651; three loan companies bills, *HD, 1936*, p. 3551; Toronto Type Foundry Canada, Ltd. bill of 1947. *HD, 1947*, pp. 3040–5.

[81]For the background see the interesting debate, *SD, 1956*, particularly Sen. Bouffard's speech, pp. 492–504.

[82]New Brunswick had a divorce court prior to Confederation by 31 George III, ch. 5; Prince Edward Island, by 5 William IV, ch. 10, 1835; Nova Scotia, by 29 Victoria, ch. 13, 1866; Manitoba, according to the decision of the Privy Council in 1917, by the North West Territories Act of 1888.

[83]J. Pope, *Memoirs of Sir J. A. Macdonald*, vol. 2. pp. 235–6. For similar views, see *HD, 1875*, p. 859; *ibid., 1888*, p. 1444.

forum to deal with divorce, as indeed there is no reason why divorce bills should not originate in the House of Commons.[84]

In the early years of Parliament there were practically no divorce applications at all.[85] From 1867 to 1916 Parliament granted only 310 divorces; after the Great War the amount of divorce legislation increased and reached its peak in 1930, when the number of divorces granted by Parliament was 247. The establishment by Parliament in 1930 of a divorce court in Ontario slowed down the process, but the number of divorce petitions began to rise again after the Second World War. In all, during the period under study, 8,615 divorce bills have been introduced in the Senate, or a yearly average of 235. Since the end of the war the annual average has been 340.

When divorce bills were first introduced in the Senate after Confederation they were treated like any other private bills. The publication went to the Senate's Committee on Standing Orders and the proof of service of the documents on the respondent was made at the Bar of the House. Then an appropriate committee was struck—not as yet the Divorce Committee—and the Senator who moved the bill moved it as his own bill. Reports from the committee occupied much attention at that time and caused a great deal of discussion. When in 1888 the continuance of such a course became obviously impracticable it was necessary to create standing rules on divorce and to systematize the procedure, which has been in force since, with certain minor modifications and changes.

The most important innovation was the creation of a standing committee on divorce to which must be referred all petitions and other matters affecting cases of divorce.[86] In fact, the Senate's Divorce Committee is nearly omnipotent in matters of divorce legislation. If it decides to recommend that a divorce be granted, it makes a report. Attached to the report is a copy of all the evidence, the petition, the affidavits of service, and all other relevant documents. These are brought in by the chairman, with the committee's report. It is then necessary to have a bill, known as a bill of divorce, drawn. It is not the practice in the Senate to challenge reports of the Committee. On the contrary, the reports are usually adopted without question, and bills based upon them are passed without discussion. Indeed, the reports of the committee are not even printed until after the bill has been passed in the Senate, with the result that Senators must vote on these bills without knowing the information

[84]J. A. Gemmill, *The Practice of the Parliament of Canada upon Bills of Divorce* (Toronto, 1889), p. 63. See also Sen. Aylesworth's remarks, *SD, 1934*, pp. 162–3.

[85]1867–71, two; 1872–6, two; 1877–81, seven; 1882–6, seven.

[86]Bourinot, *Parliamentary Procedure*, pp. 628–9.

unfolded in the course of proceedings before the committee.[87] After the bill has passed the third reading in the Senate, everything, including the evidence, the report of the committee, the affidavits of service, and other papers, is sent with the bill to the Commons, where a similar procedure is followed. After third readings all the papers are transmitted to the Senate and by and by the bills are assented to and the parties are divorced.

In dealing with divorce bills the Senate follows three practical principles; first, it has taken the view that Parliament should give no relief other than divorce;[88] second, although anybody can petition Parliament for an act of divorce, now that judicial divorces are obtainable in all the provinces except Quebec and Newfoundland, a petition of a person domiciled in any province other than these two is not likely to be reported favourably out of the Senate's divorce committee;[89] finally, although Parliament has the power to dissolve a marriage on any ground or without any reason at all, the Senate, in fact, has never recognized any grounds for divorce other than adultery. Actually, there was only one case prior to 1960 in which the Senate received a petition for divorce on some other grounds. It was a petition by a husband who asked for the annulment of his marriage because of the incurable insanity of his wife. Doctors were called to testify and they discharged the wife as cured. That ended the petition.[90] In 1960 attention was stirred by the Earle petition, in which a woman resident in Quebec asked for an act to dissolve her marriage on the ground of desertion. Questioned why the petition was accepted for filing in the first place Sen. Roebuck, Chairman of the Divorce Committee since 1954, said: "because from time immemorial . . . a citizen of the country has the right to petition Parliament for anything he likes on any ground he pleases. . . . It is a fundamental constitutional law."[91] However, at a full meeting of the Divorce Committee a resolution was introduced to the effect that the petition be rejected "since this committee has no present intention of recommending a divorce on any grounds other than that which has been

[87]See *SD, 1960*, p. 237.

[88]The only exception was the Campbell case in 1876, in which Parliament gave alimony; its right to do so, however, was promptly challenged by Chief Justice Wilson of Ontario and it is a moot question as to what other relief than actual divorce, i.e., the absolute separation of the two parties, can be granted.

[89]See W. Kent Power, *The Law and Practice Relating to Divorce and Other Matrimonial Causes in Canada* (Calgary, 1948), p. 3.

[90]It is a part of the story that having been declared sane the wife applied to the Senate for a divorce against her husband and it was granted on the ground of adultery. *SD, 1960*, p. 582.

[91]*Ibid.*, pp. 581–2.

traditionally accepted as proper grounds for such action by the Parliament of Canada." The resolution was carried by 12 votes to 3, Roebuck siding with the minority. This was, as a matter of fact, the only instance during Roebuck's chairmanship in which the report of the Divorce Committee was not unanimous.[92] He summed up the Senate's position in the matter by saying:

> If a man beats his wife and deserts her, she has every cause for complaint, but as the law now stands we will do nothing . . . so, we of the committee sit there, knowing full well that the one ground that is being pleaded before us is not the real trouble between the parties. We conduct an emasculated trial, the parties knowing that it is only by their discovering or simulating adultery that we can be induced to grant relief.[93]

During the last thirty-seven years repeated attempts have been made to change the machinery of divorce legislation. According to their objectives they fall into three categories. First, attempts have been made to get a divorce act passed by Parliament for widening the grounds for divorce. In 1929 a private member's bill from the House of Commons sought to offer new rules in matrimonial domicile for married women; it was negatived on second reading in the Senate. In 1938, obviously encouraged by the so-called Herbert Act of 1937 in the United Kingdom,[94] Sen. McMeans, Chairman of the Divorce Committee, introduced a bill on Divorce and Matrimonial Causes, whose aim was to broaden the grounds for divorce by recognizing desertion, cruelty, and insanity as ample ground for Parliament to grant divorce. Having passed the Senate after a gigantic battle the bill was killed on the second reading in the Commons. In 1941 Sen. Copp, reviving the subject of domicile, brought in his Divorce Jurisdiction bill intended to give to the woman, in respect to domicile, the same privilege as was enjoyed by the man, by enabling a deserted wife to bring action for divorce in any province, provided that she had resided in that province for at least two years preceding the date of the commencement of legal proceedings. The bill passed the Senate but was blocked in the House of Commons. On the other hand, Sen. Farris' bill in 1943 dealing with presumption of death and dissolu-

[92] *Ibid.*, pp. 581–2.

[93] *Ibid.*, p. 640.

[94] In Britain the Matrimonial Causes Act of 1857, which provided for only one ground of divorce, i.e., adultery, remained in force until 1937, in spite of the recommendations of the Royal Commission in 1912. Then in 1937 Parliament passed with virtually no opposition in either house (even most of the Bishops supported it in the Lords) the Herbert Act (Herbert's book, *Holy Deadlock*, was instrumental in changing public opinion on the subject) which widened the grounds for divorce. Cf. *SD, 1955*, p. 211.

tion of marriage did not even reach the Commons. Nothing happened until 1955, when Sen. Aseltine, then Chairman of the Divorce Committee, introduced his Divorce and Matrimonial Causes bill—an exact replica of the McMeans bill in 1938. Although he took great pains to emphasize that the application of his measure would be restricted to provinces which already had divorce courts, so that it presented no threat of spreading the institution of divorce into Quebec and Newfoundland, the bill was rejected on second reading in the Senate, after a long and embittered fight, by 37 votes to 20, all Catholics (twenty-one) and sixteen others voting against its passage.[95]

No more successful have attempts been to reduce the burden of Parliament and of the Senate in particular, with regard to the handling of the growing number of divorce petitions. The reasons given in support of the various proposals have been manifold. It has been argued that the Fathers did not intend Parliament to be converted into a divorce court; that Senators should devote their time to national and international matters as distinct from domestic grievances; that Parliamentary divorce is the most antiquated divorce system conceivable; that it is cumbersome and costly; that petitions for divorce *a vinculo matrimonii* are heard by no other legislative body in the world.

In 1938 Sen. McRae introduced a resolution in the Senate urging for "the discouragement or refusal by Parliament of further applications to it for divorce to be enacted by way of private bills."[96] In moving his resolution he contended that "our divorce procedure is rapidly developing into a ridiculous business which is not in keeping with the dignity of the Senate and does not add anything to the credit of Parliament."[97] The resolution, however, was negatived, chiefly on the ground that such drastic action as proposed in the motion must be a common concern of both houses of Parliament.[98]

By way of a more constructive proposal, Sen. Haig suggested in 1944 that some arrangement should be worked out whereby the judges of the Exchequer Court or some other body should hear divorce evidence and give a decision which then, if necessary, could be sent to Parliament for approval.[99] The idea was elaborated in a proposal of Sen. Aseltine in 1946, who recommended that petitioners from Quebec should first obtain a judicial separation from the Quebec Superior Court on the ground of adultery; upon presentation of the certificate thus secured to Parliament, along with the petition for divorce, the bill of divorce would go through as a matter of course.[100] The idea was advocated by Sen.

[95] *Ibid.*, p. 352. [96] *Ibid.*, *1938*, pp. 437–8. [97] *Ibid.*, p. 438.
[98] *Ibid.*, p. 442. [99] *Ibid.*, *1944*, p. 81. [100] *Ibid.*, *1946*, p. 609.

Ross ten years later and by Sen. Bouffard in 1958, but in neither case was it seriously entertained by the Senate.

In 1947 the Senate authorized its Law Clerk and Parliamentary Counsel, Mr. MacNeill, to consider the question of dealing with divorce in Quebec by other than parliamentary action. His report[101] contained four major recommendations, two of which were novel. Under the plan either the Exchequer Court would be given exclusive jurisdiction in divorce in Quebec and concurrent jurisdiction with the provincial courts in the other provinces, or a new Dominion Divorce Court would be set up having exclusive jurisdiction in matters of marriage and divorce.[102] However, no action was taken on either of these proposals.

The idea of delegating authority to the Exchequer Court to hear divorce petitions was propagated by Sen. Aseltine, too, in 1951 but to no avail. No more successful was his alternative proposal for the appointment of an official in the nature of a King's proctor who, in a judicial capacity, would hear the evidence and decide whether or not a bill should be recommended. Under this scheme the Divorce Committee would act as a court of appeal, with power to adopt or to reject the report of the official.[103] In 1958 Sen. Pratt of Newfoundland urged the creation of a body of assessors drawn from the legal profession to decide the evidence and transmit their findings to the committee for final judgement.[104]

Not discouraged by the defeat of his Divorce and Matrimonial Causes bill in 1955, Sen. Aseltine introduced the Exchequer Court (Divorce Jurisdiction) bill in the following session for the purpose of empowering the court to hear applications for a divorce from a person domiciled in any province of Canada not having courts possessing jurisdiction to grant such divorces on the ground of adultery. Although he stressed that

[101]*SJ, 1948*, p. 419.

[102]It should be remembered that under sec. 101 of the BNA Act Parliament is empowered to provide for the establishment not only of a general court of appeal for Canada, but also "additional courts for the better administration of the laws of Canada." A Dominion Divorce Court and Dominion control of practice and procedure therein were advocated by J. Taylor, who said: "Canada has attained a stature warranting the constitution of such a Divorce Court; a court vested with jurisdiction over all persons resident in Canada wheresoever domiciled therein, ridding the country once and for all of the nice questions of domicile in these cases; a court in which the Crown on the information duly laid by the complainant would in simple procedure prosecute and take the carriage of the proceedings; a court in which conciliation and the maintenance of the home would be more dominant than the breaking up of the home." "Divorce in Canada," 23 *Can. Bar Rev.*, p. 497. See also the reference in Power, *The Law and Practice Relating to Divorce . . .*, p. 2, note (b).

[103]*SD, 1951*, p. 651.

[104]*Ibid., 1958*, p. 459.

the subject of his measure was merely a matter of procedure and that it did not propose to change the existing grounds for divorce, the bill went down on a defeat by 40 votes to 17, in face of a combined front of Catholics, those who, like Sen. Kinley, thought that legislation of this kind should properly be initiated by the Government, and those who, like Sen. Roebuck, urged that until Quebec itself has asked for a change the Senate should not push through such innovatory legislation.

Sen. Aseltine's bill in 1956 was probably the last serious legislative attempt in the Senate to modify the present divorce procedure. There are no indications that the position of the Roman Catholic Church has softened as regards enabling the courts to handle divorce cases. Since the assent of Quebec seems to be a prerequisite of any change in the matter, the question of parliamentary divorce has in fact become a political reflection of the societal problems inherent in Canadian federalism. The farthest any Roman Catholic Senator from Quebec has ever gone was perhaps the following statement by Sen. Monette in 1958: "I am not going to suggest anything that could be construed in my province as approval on my part of dissolution of marriage by the courts . . . but I think I am sincere and serious enough to admit that we are bound to come in the near future to the necessity for some modification of our present system, and that in one way or another we shall have to face the issue."[105] And he subsequently suggested that an investigating committee should be set up to study the situation with a view of bringing forward possible remedies.

In contrast with the efforts of illustrious members of the Upper House over the last three decades or so to rid the Senate of the burdens of divorce legislation, the third main group of legislative attempts has been aimed at producing exactly the opposite effect, namely, to give the Senate exclusive jurisdiction over parliamentary divorce. Originating with members of the House of Commons these direct or indirect efforts grew out of the recognition that procedures in the House of Commons regarding divorce bills serve no useful purpose at all. The Commons' Private Bills Committee, to which divorce bills are referred after they have passed the Senate, gives scant attention to these cases; rarely are there any witnesses called before the committee and members of the Commons as a rule rely almost entirely on the printed evidence as it is transmitted to them from the Senate committee. The three readings are a mere formality and the bills are usually passed *en bloc*. As a result, the Commons has rejected only thirty-one divorce bills out of 8,615

[105]*SD, 1958*, pp. 458–9.

introduced in Parliament since 1925. In 1938 Woodsworth called the procedure unsatisfactory and scandalous.[106] Things really came to a head in the session of 1960 when the parliamentary group of the CCF party determined to hold up the flow of such legislation by using the simple weapon of debating each bill. As bills were piling up awaiting passage, Sen. Monette suggested on July 21 that a way out might be found by transferring to the Senate the sole authority to hear and rule on divorce petitions. The idea was followed up in a private member's bill introduced in the House of Commons by Mr. Morton (PC, Davenport) and passed by the Lower House in 1961. It sought to permit divorce actions to be tried by the Senate without reference to the House of Commons. The delegation of authority would not, however, be unlimited in time; it would have to be renewed by annual legislation. In the Senate no one undertook to sponsor the measure, with the result that it was finally removed from the order paper. There were hints during the summer of 1961 that Sen. Roebuck and Mr. McCleave (PC, Halifax), the chairmen of the respective committees in the two houses dealing with divorce, were working away at trying to find a solution acceptable to all concerned.[107] However, the tactics of holding up the passage of divorce bills was continued by Frank Howard (CCF, Skeena) and Arnold Peters (CCF, Timiskaming) in the session of 1962, with the unfortunate result that when Parliament was dissolved on April 18 no less than 327 divorce bills died on the Commons' order paper.[108]

Apart from some undesirable features of parliamentary divorce as a system, the technical usefulness of the Senate as a house of first instance in the field of both public and private legislation is obvious. Unaided by the first look of the Senate, members of the House of Commons would have to choose between two unpleasant alternatives: either to continue to concentrate on matters of political importance and turn out technically ill-digested measures (public and private), with serious consequences in future litigation, or to devote more time on such matters at the expense of the political duties of the House. In either case the prestige and the general efficacy of Parliament would seem inevitably to suffer.

[106]*HD, 1938*, p. 3845.

[107]J. A. Oastler, "New Divorce Plan Is Combined Effort," *Montreal Star*, June 7, 1961.

[108]*HD, 1962*, pp. 3120 ff. Mr. Peters' various private members' bills on the subject were all talked out on second reading in both 1962 and 1962–63.

8 GENERAL DEBATES AND PRIVATE MEMBERS' BILLS

IT MAY SEEM STRANGE AT FIRST to discuss general debates and private members' bills in the framework of the same chapter. Viewed from their functions, however, there is much to be said for such a procedure. In essence, both serve the same purpose—to underline, and focus attention on, certain matters of general interest. As such, they both come under the heading of the technical functions of the Senate, as a valuable supplement to such services as the revision or the initiation of legislation.

The Senate, like second chambers in general, is particularly well adapted for the discussion of general subjects associated with the business of government. In the House of Commons, fettered by its rules, overwhelmed by the quantity of its work and held tightly in the grasp of the party Whips, there are always many topics competing for time, and many which cannot be debated at all. The Senate, with its comparatively elastic code of procedure and uncoerced by the ministry, or, indeed, by the chair, clearly has great potentialities as a forum for discussing questions which cannot be fitted into the crowded timetable of the Lower House. Although the Senate may lack the wealth of former ambassadors, high-ranking military men, governors general, or famous representatives of various professions, who are able to lend such an aura of authenticity to corresponding debates in the House of Lords, the great majority of the members of the Senate are persons of varied experience in public affairs who are particularly well qualified to discuss general problems in the light of the national interest as a whole. Since they need not consider party advantage or their own political careers, general debates in the Senate are characterized by a level of objectivity approaching academic detachment, full of factual information, and a leisurely consideration of the historical setting of the problem treated. It has been said that if one is really interested in a particular question one should read the debates of the Senate on the topic.

Such discussions may often be all the more useful if conducted in a chamber whose debates and divisions do not involve the fate of the executive. Indeed, the Senate's constitutional inability to dismiss a government has a wholesome effect upon its value as a debating chamber; it enables Senators, in Sidney Low's words, to "lift politics from the rust of the commonplace, and bestow some attention on those more comprehensive principles, and those remoter consequences, for which a bustling popular assembly, and a busy partisan Executive, have no time or thought."[1] For the philosopher in public affairs, if there is room anywhere, it should be, one would suppose, in the Senate.

However, as was also seen in connection with the initiation of public legislation, general debates in the Senate have a very earthly additional objective, namely, to provide work for the House while it awaits the arrival of legislation from the Commons. As the late Sen. Lewis, a journalist by profession, once said: "There is no reason in the world why we should wait for the House of Commons to send us certain legislation. . . . Even if we cannot make some arrangement with that House whereby more legislation can be initiated in this Chamber, the whole world is before us. Never before was there a time when there were so many interesting topics of discussion. Why should we not discuss them here . . .?"[2] Indeed, when one examines the timing of such debates one finds that they are nicely fitted in to fill the legislative lull caused by the irregular flow of legislation, and that a considerable portion of them are held, or at least originated, in the early part of the session, when business in the Senate is at its lowest ebb.

As we have seen above (Chapter v) the flexibility of its rules clearly enables the Senate to arrange for the discussion of general topics. When a Senator wishes to give notice of an inquiry or motion which will provide a basis for future debate, he reduces the notice to writing, signs it, reads it from his place during a sitting of the Senate and hands it in at the Clerk's table. Unlike the procedure of the House of Lords, which allows a certain category of unstarred questions that require notice and may lead to debate,[3] a debate in the Senate on a mere inquiry is not in order; although explanatory remarks may be made by the Senator

[1]Sidney Low, *The Governance of England* (London, 1919), p. 250.

[2]*SD, 1931*, pp. 59–60.

[3]P. Bromhead, *The House of Lords and Contemporary Politics, 1911–1957* (London, 1958), chap. xvii.

making the inquiry and by the representative of the Government (usually the Government leader) answering the same, observations upon any such answer are not allowed.[4] Also, unlike the Lords, where debates are usually short and restricted to one sitting day, in the Senate the discussion is very often permitted to run over several days. When the debate is over the motion is either adopted, defeated, or simply withdrawn or discontinued. However, the point is not what happens to the motion; it is the debate arising out of the motion that matters.

It would be pointless to give a list of the subjects discussed in the Senate during the last thirty-seven years. Leaving aside debates dealing with issues of sectional or local interest, the Senate has conducted some outstanding debates on such general topics as international affairs, various aspects of the country's economy, and matters relating to the constitution and, more recently, to education. The Senate's fitness to discuss Canada's international relationships was emphasized by Prime Minister King during debate of the Senate and House of Commons bill in 1947: "The Senate," he said, "is perhaps in many ways in a better position to devote a great deal of its time to international problems than is this House. Every encouragement should be given to the members of the Upper House to give a great deal of time and attention to all-important world problems."[5] Indeed, during the years 1925–40 the Senate gave close attention to the work of the League of Nations, the quickly deteriorating world situation and the pressing problems of Canada's defence policy. Most of the debates in this period were initiated by Sir George Foster, a keen observer of the functions of the world organization, as well as Sens. Griesbach and McRae, who both had extensive military experience, and they invariably drew contributions from Dandurand, Belcourt, Beaubien, and others who had established personal contacts with many of the leading figures of the epoch—such men as Sir Edward Grey, Sir Eric Drummond, Lord Curzon, etc. During the same period the Senate often found time to discuss the state and development of Canada's transportation system, and there were informative

[4]Questions play a much less important role in the Senate's proceedings than in the Lords, where there is still a semblance of government representation since Ministers sit in the chamber. It is a fair estimate that the number of questions asked in the House of Lords during an average parliamentary session is between 120 and 140 (*ibid.*, p. 224). In the Senate, on the other hand, they rarely rise above 25 or 30 and most of them are for the purpose of gathering departmental explanation upon certain technical points. The answer is printed in Hansard and may prove a valuable source of information (Cf., for example, the answer to Sen. Farris' inquiry about the Suez Canal and Israel and Egypt and the actions of the United Nations. *SD*, April 10, 1957).

[5]*HD, 1947*, p. 5350.

debates on such problems as the duplication of railway services, the unsatisfactory position of aviation in Canada, or the necessity of eliminating competition between the railways and the newer forms of transportation. In the post-war years and, indeed, throughout the 1950's the Senate's attention was concentrated more and more on the development of the Atlantic Community and its political and economic repercussions for Canada. In 1960 Sen. Robertson initiated one of the most successful debates in the Senate in recent years. Occupying the House for nine days, the discussion was on the urgency for Canada to enter into reciprocal trade with the USA and the two European trade blocks, in order to remove "the tragic possibility of Canada's becoming isolated from the great modern currents of trade and commerce."

Perhaps especial mention should be made of the subject of university education, which has received particular attention in the Senate in the form of general debates during the last few years. In 1957, for instance, Sen. Pouliot originated a discussion on the desirability of a thirty-minute free time to be granted weekly by the CBC for television broadcast to the Canadian universities. In the short session of 1957–58 Sen. Cameron, Director of the Banff School of Fine Arts, Alta., initiated a long debate on the necessity of mobilizing and expanding Canadian educational resources, while in 1960 Sen. Bouffard of Quebec introduced a debate on Quebec university subsidies; the Senate decided not to pass any resolution, but wished to draw the Government's attention to the fact that non-payment to Quebec universities of amounts voted in 1952–56 had actually placed these universities under discriminatory practices.

A satisfactory assessment of the effectiveness of these general debates in the Senate would be very difficult. On occasion, indeed, debates in the Upper House have been followed by the government's taking the course suggested. This happened, for example, after the agitation in the Senate in 1926 to have a fitting celebration of Canada's diamond jubilee. The motion was very well received by the country at large and, as a result, the Government in 1927 introduced legislation (the Diamond Jubilee of Confederation bill) for the establishment of a committee composed of a number of representative Canadians to prepare the general outlines of an appropriate program.[6] Again, it may be pointed out that the provision in the Dominion Housing bill of 1935 to assist in the construction of houses by providing loans up to 20 per cent of the cost of construction implemented an identical suggestion put forward by Sen. Michener in a debate in the Senate in 1934. In a number of other instances general debates in the Senate have resulted in the creation of special committees

[6]*SD, 1927*, p. 40.

of inquiry, which produced evidence and brought forward recommendations that gave impetus to subsequent legislative action by the Government.[7]

It is submitted, however, that even in those cases in which it does not seem possible to establish a clear causal relationship between ideas advocated in general debates in the Senate and prompt governmental action along the suggested lines, this does not necessarily imply that such debates in the Senate were without value. The political process in a constitutional democracy is composed of a vast number of pressures and counter-pressures, which the government has to balance against one another. The Senate is part of this process and debates in the Senate are one of the many channels through which public opinion is expressed. Although they do not have to pass the test of elections any more, Senators are in close contact with the currents of public opinion and with political developments in various parts of the country. Most of them have an extensive correspondence with all sorts of people, former constituents, friends and strangers and well-wishers and representatives of various organizations of interested persons, who use every available avenue of influence to the Government. It is probably fair to say that the average number of visitors who call on the Senators daily is not smaller than in the case of members of the House of Commons. Debates in the Senate are sometimes attended by members of the Commons[8] and the Senate leader, especially when he is a member of the administration, would convey the résumé of such debates to his colleagues in the cabinet, who will have to weigh them against other forms of pressures and influences that are brought to bear upon them in relation to forthcoming governmental decisions. The Senate is useful because it is a place where opinions may be expressed freely, in the form of general debates, by persons of varied experience, including former ministers who may still wield considerable influence with members of the Government.

Indeed, the same considerations can be applied to the function of public bills introduced by private members in the Upper House. Because of the more leisurely timetable and general procedural flexibility of the Senate a Senator appears to be better placed for introducing legislation than a member of the House of Commons; his chance of getting his measure enacted, however, is very slim indeed, except for agreed proposals. Only one unofficial Senators' bill has passed into law during

[7]This was the case, for instance, in the debates of 1934 on Canadian Sealing and Fishery Interests in Pacific Waters, and on Tourist Trade; in 1938 on Canada's railway problem; in 1945 on the gold production in Canada; in 1947 on chemical fertilizers; in 1949 on human rights and individual freedoms.

[8]See the remarks of Mr. McIvor (Lib., Fort William). *HD, 1955*, p. 5251.

the last thirty-seven years. Of the forty-seven that have been introduced in the Senate during this period seventeen died in the House of Commons while the rest were either dropped or negatived in the Senate itself. Indeed, since the end of the war only one private members' Senate's bill has reached the Commons, that which was subsequently placed on the Statute Book.[9]

Thus, from the point of view of actually changing the law the Senators' privilege in the field of private members' bills is really of little immediate value, unless the approval of the Government has been secured in advance. The only bill which seems to have had that support was Sen. Euler's bill in 1952 to amend the Canada Dairy Products Act. His measure was, in fact, a continuation of the fight by a small group of Liberal Senators in the previous session to delete from the Act the provision which authorized the Governor-in-Council, not merely to regulate, but to prohibit through regulations, the carrying of dairy products and their substitutes from one province to another. The provision, it was argued, was not only politically unwise but unconstitutional, violating the spirit of section 121 of the BNA Act, guaranteeing the free entry of "All articles of the growth, produce, or manufacture of any of the provinces . . . into each of the other provinces." The fact that the Act had not been implemented by order-in-council was interpreted as an indication of the Government's sensing that a mistake had been made. This assumption proved correct by the minister's admitting in the Senate's Banking and Commerce committee that the Act had not been proclaimed because after reading the debate in the Senate he had some doubt whether he needed the power which the controversial section proposed to give him. He, indeed, stated that he had intended to introduce an amendment similar to that embodied in Euler's bill, but that pressure of business had prevented him from doing so. He gave tacit approval of the objective of Euler's bill and with this powerful backing the measure, after rapidly passing the Senate and encountering no opposition in the Commons, received Royal Assent on June 18.

Although an unofficial Senators' bill may have no hope of passing within a single session, its introduction and the subsequent debate on it in the Senate may prepare the ground for some future introduction by a private member in the Commons. This was the case with Sen. Willoughby's bill in 1927 to provide in Ontario for the dissolution and the annulment of marriage. It passed the Senate in both 1927 and 1928 but was not proceeded with in the House of Commons. In 1928 there

[9]See Appendix II and III.

were efforts made in the Commons to get a special hearing for the bill and on April 27 J. S. Woodsworth moved that it should be taken up in the place of a divorce bill then before the House. This motion was not debatable and in the following division it was rejected in a non-partisan vote by 53 to 21.[10] In the session of 1929 the bill was reintroduced in the Senate by Sen. Willoughby and it passed the House against the protests of Roman Catholic Senators who were opposed to the "unqualified curse of decentralization of divorce."[11] It made, however, no progress in the Lower House. Finally in 1930 the bill was taken up by Woodsworth, a long-time protagonist of the idea, and after a stormy passage in both houses it was enacted on May 15.[12]

A third purpose which a discussion of a private members' bill in the Senate may achieve is to induce the Government to adopt the measure and introduce it as a government bill. The process of such persuasion may take a long while. In 1926 Sen. Belcourt, reviving an old idea of his, brought in his Weapons bill, which prescribed that every one who had in his possession a weapon should take out an annual licence for it. Although supporters of the bill in both houses maintained there was popular demand for legislation of this kind, it failed to make any headway in the Commons in 1926, 1927, 1928, and 1929. In 1930 the Government apparently made up its mind in favour of the idea and sections 3–7 of the Criminal Code bill of that year contained the provisions previously advocated in Sen. Belcourt's bill. As a result of last-minute representations made to the Minister of Justice, however, these sections were again dropped from the bill before third reading.[13] Sen. Belcourt did not live long enough to see the adoption of his measure. It was the Conservative Government of 1933 that introduced it as a government bill in the House of Commons and had it finally enacted. "It is very gratifying . . . to note," Sen. Tanner remarked on this occasion, "that the members of the House of Commons have at last awakened to facts of which hon. members of the Senate were fully aware several years ago. We are glad to see them following in the footsteps of this House."[14]

Even if not in the form of a bill, the Government was aroused to action in 1948 by another one of Sen. Euler's private members' bills, this time concerning the repeal of the section of the Dairy Industry Act prohibiting the manufacture, sale, and importation of oleomargarine.

[10]*HJ, 1928*, p. 309. *Canadian Annual Review, 1927–8*, pp. 106–7.
[11]*SD, 1929*, p. 50.
[12]*Canadian Annual Review, 1929–30*, p. 58.
[13]*SD, 1930*, p. 383.
[14]*Ibid., 1933*, p. 396.

He first introduced his measure in 1946, and during the month-long debate succeeded in obtaining the support of the entire Liberal "rebel-group" in the Senate; although the Leader of the Government clearly expressed himself in opposition of the measure Sen. Euler got no less than thirty Senators in the lobby on his side on behalf of the second reading; there were forty-three against.[15] The same fate fell upon the bill in the next session. In 1948 Sen. Euler brought forward the bill once again, but it was again negatived on the second reading by 35 votes to 21.[16] His enthusiasm unbroken, he then introduced a resolution to the effect that the Government immediately after prorogation of Parliament secure the opinion of the Supreme Court whether or not the part of the Act prohibiting the manufacture and sale of oleomargarine was *ultra vires* of the Dominion. The resolution was passed by the Senate and acted upon by the Government, and in the autumn of 1948 judgment was handed down by the Court declaring the prohibition clause *ultra vires* of the Parliament of Canada. On appeal the Judicial Committee of the Privy Council upheld the decision of the Supreme Court, so that Sen. Euler's private members' bill, if in a rather circuitous way, finally achieved its purpose.

Apart from these few examples, private members' bills in the Senate have had no immediate or clearly demonstrable effect upon changes introduced in the laws of the country. Indeed, there is probably much truth in the supposition that bills sponsored by private members are becoming anachronistic in modern conditions in which the Government assumes full responsibility for practically all legislation.[17] The primary purpose of unofficial Senators' bills, therefore, is not so much to effect direct statutory modifications as to offer a basis for stimulating and constructive discussions, during which views can be aired and ideas canvassed in an attempt to bring to the Government's attention some of the less patently obvious facets of the politically desirable. It is in this respect that the functions of general debates and private members' bills in the Senate show identical traits of usefulness.

As in the case of general debates, it is possible to classify unofficial Senators' bills according to their subject-matter. Thus, one finds that the forty-seven bills introduced in the Senate by private members from 1925 to 1963 actually covered only twenty-six separate topics, the same bill having often been reintroduced several times. By far the largest proportion of them dealt with proposed amendments to the Criminal Code or

[15]*Ibid., 1946*, p. 195; *SJ*, pp. 141–2.
[16]*SJ*, *1948*, p. 312.
[17]Cf. Bromhead, *The House of Lords*, chap. xv, esp. pp. 199 ff.

matters closely related to it. In 1925 Sen. McMeans of Manitoba brought in a bill whose object was to bring the Canadian practice of giving evidence into conformity with that in the United Kingdom, by allowing the accused to give evidence on his own behalf and forbidding the prosecution to ask whether or not he has previously been convicted. The bill was granted a second reading on April 30 and then went to a special committee, which recommended that no further action be taken until reports from the provincial attorneys general, the chief justices of the courts in each province, and the judges administering criminal law were made available. When all opinions had been obtained the bill was introduced in the Senate for the second time in 1926 and was passed. Although it eventually died in the Commons, its usefulness in eliciting a considerable body of valuable judicial views was not altogether lost.

In 1929 four private members' bills made their appearance in the Senate. Sen. Bureau, former Solicitor General, introduced two bills, one concerning procedures under the Criminal Code in rural areas, the other seeking to remove the handicap of a poor Quebec debtor under the Bankruptcy Act, by providing that the locality of the debtor in Quebec should be in the judicial district in which he carried out his business and not, as was the case, coincidental with the whole province. After being debated on second reading and in committee, both bills were passed by the Senate but failed to get through the Commons. Sen. Bureau made another attempt with his Bankruptcy bill in the session of 1931, but it was again negatived on second reading in the Lower House.[18] Sen. Beaubien brought forward a proposal to amend sec. 1035 of the Criminal Code, by enabling fines to be paid in instalments in cases in which there was an option between serving a prison-term or paying fines.[19] The bill was dropped because of its sponsor's absence and it was never again revived. Still in the same session Sen. Lynch-Staunton brought in another amendment to the Code, dealing with escapes by flight. After a lengthy debate, which occupied the house on two separate sittings, Sen. Lynch-Staunton reluctantly agreed to withdraw his bill, in return to a promise from the Department of Justice to give careful considerations to his proposal.[20] He made one more attempt two years later but his bill died in a special committee of the Senate, justifying an earlier warning—"how in the world are you ever going to reach an agreement among so many lawyers?"

One of the most obstinate legislative attempts during this period was the bill originated by Sen. Barnard of British Columbia in 1931, for the avowed purpose of legalizing sweepstakes of which the profit or a portion

[18] *HD, 1931*, p. 3375. [19] *SD, 1929*, p. 200. [20] *Ibid., 1929*, p. 221.

of it, was to be devoted to the benefit of hospitals. In 1931 the bill was defeated in Committee of the Whole, after it had been approved on second reading and by a special committee, largely because of Sir George Foster's devastating argument against the object of the measure.[21] In the next session the bill was again defeated in the Senate by a majority of 36:20; although Sen. Foster was no longer in the House (he died in 1931), his arguments were still ringing, as it were, in the ears of the majority of Senators. In 1933, brought in by Sen. McRae, the bill passed the Senate on division but was defeated in the House of Commons. In 1934 Sen. Barnard made renewed attempts to have the bill enacted, but it was wrecked in the Commons by a hostile vote of 105 to 57 on second reading.[22]

In 1960 Sen. Croll brought in a bill to amend the Criminal Code to abolish capital punishment. However, the bill was later withdrawn pending action in the House of Commons.

Another question often raised by unofficial Senators' bills during the period of our study was the matter of divorce and matrimonial causes. Leaving aside legislative attempts to modify divorce procedure, already dealt with in the previous chapter, there were two attempts in particular before 1939 that are worth mentioning. One was Sen. Girroir's bill in 1928 and 1929, whose aim was to make venereal disease an impediment to marriage, following the practice of certain states in the USA. The bill was ultimately withdrawn after a careful study by the Academy of Medicine of Toronto, which recommended that before such legislation is passed the public should be properly educated as to its scope and intent.[23] The other bill in this field was brought in by Sen. Hughes in 1935, for the purpose of reducing the number of divorces, by preventing the marriage of divorced persons to other than their former spouses. After a thorough and interesting discussion the bill was temporarily withdrawn. In the next session it reappeared on the Order Paper, only to be defeated on second reading.[24] The vote, Sen. Hughes charged, was a vote of non-confidence in Christ and the Bible, but there was no remedy for his plea under the rules.

In at least two instances private members' bills proposed administrative changes in existing statutes. In 1939 Sen. Hughes brought in a bill, whose object was to liquidate the remaining provisions of the Farmers' Creditors Arrangement Act with respect to soldier settlers, on the ground that in Prince Edward Island the Act had developed into a racket. He voluntarily withdrew his bill after receiving assurance from the Minister

[21]*Ibid., 1931*, pp. 274, 283, 296.
[22]*HD, 1934*, p. 3322.
[23]*SJ, 1929*, p. 422.
[24]*SD, 1936*, p. 269.

of Finance that the Act was to expire completely on a designated date.[25] Similarly, in the session of 1953 Sen. G. H. Ross of Alberta brought forward a bill to amend certain provisions of the Indian Act, under which no recovery could be made against an Indian even though a person had in fact recovered judgment. However, prompt implementation of any change in the Act was blocked by an undertaking, given to the Indians in 1951, that there would be no change affecting their rights until after a trial period of two years. Although this undertaking by the Minister did not commit Parliament, Sen. Ross was persuaded that withdrawal of his measure would save the Minister from much embarrassment.

A private members' bill may often be nothing more than a manifesto dressed up as a bill and although its promoter may know that his proposal cannot at once be enacted into law, there is much to be said for introducing and debating certain proposals in the form of a bill, rather than in the form of a motion or resolution expressing general opinions. Thus, in 1936 Sen. Casgrain brought in a bill, which provided for the establishment, operation, and maintenance of duty-free ports on the St. Lawrence, the Atlantic, or the Pacific, on the pattern of such Continental free ports as Hamburg, Stockholm, Copenhagen, Marseilles, Genoa, etc. Although the bill, after extensive discussion and inquiries in committee, passed the Senate in both 1936 and 1937, it made no progress in the Commons. Nevertheless, in view of the voluminous evidence and departmental information that was gathered together during the bill's stay in the upper house, and of the debate that was conducted on it in the Commons, the bill's sponsors could, indeed, have felt that their efforts were not altogether wasted.

Both Sen. Euler's bill in 1955 to amend the BNA Act with regard to the filling of vacancies in the Senate and Sen. Pouliot's bill in 1961 concerning Royal Assents to bills have already been discussed in other contexts.[26] In 1960 Sen. Croll brought in a bill, which required the disclosure of interest rates and finance charges when credit was extended, in order to enable the borrower or investment buyer to know exactly what rate of annual interest he was charged for a loan or purchase and what his total cost would be. In other words, what the bill attempted was to expose usury and to provide statutory checks on fraudulent lending practices. It was debated on seven separate occasions in the Senate at the second reading stage and finally referred to committee. Due to the advanced stage of the session, however, no further action was taken in 1960. In the next session the bill was again introduced in the Senate, but

[25]*Ibid., 1939*, p. 265.
[26]Above, pp. 58 and 149.

this time it was defeated on the second reading by a non-partisan vote of 35:26, for doubts about both its constitutionality and practicality. In the light of the criticisms the bill was revised and reintroduced in each of the two short parliamentary sessions of 1962 and 1962–63. On both occasions it was passed on second reading and referred to committee, but due to dissolution of Parliament it could not be further proceeded with. By the time it made its fourth appearance in the Senate in 1962–63 the bill had provoked a good deal of interest and received nation-wide support, as was evident from the number of letters sent to the members of the Senate in its support from all parts of the country, and particularly from the Maritimes,[27] and from the representations that were made by such organizations as the Canadian Association of Consumers, the Canadian Welfare Council, the Canadian Federation of Agriculture, the Canadian Retail Federation, the Canadian Labour Congress, and others. Indeed, even if it never be enacted, the least that could be said for the bill, Sen. Croll maintained in 1961, was "that it will air the problem. That in itself should make it desirable, for it cannot be denied that the problem exists and needs airing."[28]

The same could be said of the great bulk of private members' bills initiated in the Senate during the last thirty-seven years. In most of the cases prolonged and informative discussions took place, committee hearings were held and valuable opinions collected from various outside bodies of interested persons, government officials, and sometimes even from ministers, who came to give personal or written testimonies on the problem considered. Even if the press gave scanty coverage to these proceedings, every interest group which might have felt itself affected by the implications of the bill was duly notified and offered a chance to present its case before the Senate. Thus, the ultimate value of unofficial Senators' bills must not be judged in rigid Benthamite terms of measurement. Together with the general debates of the Senate they serve an important constitutional purpose, by freely ventilating various problems, thus joining the almost infinite variety of pressures and influences that are being brought to bear upon the Government with respect to every decision of any moment that it has to make.

[27]*SD*, *1962*, pp. 362, 428–41; *ibid.*, *1962–63*, p. 407.
[28]*Ibid.*, *1961*, p. 694.

THE COMMITTEE SYSTEM OF THE SENATE

9

IT HAS BEEN SUGGESTED from time to time in the preceding chapters that a considerable part of the Senate's functions is performed in committee and that in many cases what happens in the Chamber is only a preparation for, or a consummation of, what is accomplished in the committee room. It is appropriate, therefore, to devote a special chapter to the Senate's committee system in the part dealing with the technical usefulness of the Upper House, although, surely, it may be objected that such discussion would more properly belong to the chapter on procedure. As a matter of fact, the committees' role in the general functioning of the Senate, and, thus, in the whole structure of Parliament, is so important that it could well be the subject-matter of a special study. Here we can do no more than attempt to offer a summary of their organization and use.

Organization

Formally, the Senate's committees fall into two distinct categories—select standing and select special committees, the latter including special joint committees with the House of Commons. Functionally, however, neither the standing nor the special committees are exclusively to be associated with the performance of any one specific function. Their formal differentiation, therefore, must be supplemented by the notion of overlapping functionalism. Thus, a standing committee of the Senate may take the form of a committee to legislate, a committee to scrutinize, or a committee to inquire.[1] It is defined in the Senate rules as "a select committee appointed for the session." The present number of standing committees is nineteen but this number is subject to modification. Thus, to the original body of ten committees (Library, Printing, Restaurant, Standing Orders, Banking, Railway, Private bills, Internal Economy, Debates and Divorce) six new ones were added in 1918, including Agriculture, Immigration and Labour, Commerce, Civil Service Administration, Public Health, and Public Buildings and Grounds. In 1919 there was also formed, on the suggestion of Sen. Nicholls, a standing committee on Finance. Thus, at the beginning of the period under review the Senate had seventeen standing committees. Since then two additions were made; in 1934 a standing committee on Tourist Traffic was created, as the first tangible result of the recommendations of the special committee on Tourist Trade, and four years later, in 1938, it was decided (as was long ago urged by Sen. McRae[2]) that the field of External Relations be allotted a committee of its own. There have been demands for the setting up of a standing committee on defence[3] and, more recently, on land use,[4] but these suggestions have not materialized. In 1945, small changes were introduced in the committees' nomenclature; the committee on Railway, Telegraph and Harbour became committee on Transport and Communications, the committee on Commerce and Trade Relations was replaced by a committee on Canadian Trade Relations, and the committee on Agriculture and Forestry was renamed the committee on Natural Resources.

Instead of adding new ones to the existing body of standing committees it would probably be wiser to reduce their number, by simply abolishing those which no longer seem to serve any useful purpose at all. Apart from the three standing joint committees on Library, Printing, and Restaurant, which do some house-keeping work, the record of the committees on Standing Orders, on Debates and Reporting, on Civil Service Administration, and on Public Buildings and Grounds hardly warrants the continuation of these committees. The committee on Standing Orders, which had a total of nine meetings from 1950 to 1957, has no special reason to meet, because the rules of the House are satisfactory and, as we have seen, are more often evaded than observed. The same applies to the committee on Debates and Reporting, which held no meeting

[1]These and subsequent terms employed in this chapter with regard to committees are, of course, adopted from Prof. K. C. Wheare's now classic work on *Government by Committee* (Oxford, 1955).

[2]*SD, 1934*, p. 450.

[3]Sen. Griesbach's remarks. *Ibid., 1927*, p. 293.

[4]Report of Special Committee on Land Use. *Ibid., 1961*, pp. 982 ff, 1024 ff.

during the seven-year period, together with the committee on Civil Service Administration, which dates back to the time when employees of the Senate were appointed by the Senate itself. Similarly, the eight meetings held by the committee on Public Buildings and Grounds during the period indicated above suggests a paucity of opportunity for genuine usefulness; its most memorable achievement was probably its obtaining in 1956 parking space near the Library, in spite of objections from the Federal District Commission.[5]

Unlike standing committees, special committees are not set up regularly every session but appointed *ad hoc*. As the rules put it elegantly, a special committee is "a select committee other than a standing committee." Similarly to standing committees, however, special committees too can also be employed for either of the three functions of legislation, scrutiny, or inquiry. Nevertheless, the main field of their usefulness is that of making inquiries. Apart from matters related to the internal business of the Senate, special Senate committees have carried out a total of sixteen inquiries of national scope during the thirty-seven years covered in this study. In some of these cases it was quite impossible for a special committee to complete its work in a single session of Parliament; the special committee on Railway Problems in 1938, for instance, needed two years before its report was laid before the Senate, the committees on Income Tax in 1945, on Salacious and Indecent Literature in 1952, and on Manpower in 1960 also took two years each to bring their inquiries to an end, whilst the special committee on Land Use, which was appointed in 1957, sat through five sessions and did not report until 1961.

It has been suggested that interruption of extensive inquiries by prorogation of Parliament, with consequent delays in tabling the final report before the House, may result in the waning of interest in the committee's work. Indeed, in its third interim report, December 5, 1945, the special committee on Income Tax recommended that in view of the great deal of evidence to be heard the committee should be empowered to hold meetings during the recess of Parliament, so that its final recommendations might be implemented in the next budget; the rule that "no committee can sit after a prorogation"[6] may be circumvented by either of two ways; Parliament can either take a long adjournment instead of being prorogued (as was done in 1873) or the special committee can be continued in form of a Royal Commission (as was done in 1935, when

[5]For statistics and further remarks, see *ibid.*, *1957*, pp. 389–97.

[6]A. Beauchesne, ed., *Rules and Forms of the House of Commons of Canada* (4th ed., Toronto, 1958), Rule 533.

a special committee of the House of Commons was replaced by the Stevens Commission by order-in-council). In the case of the Income Tax committee in 1945 the first method was out of the question and the second, although there were strong demands for its utilization, was also dropped in the end. Confronted with the rigidity of the rules, which to his "non-legal mind . . . seems rather theoretical and technical—I might say unprogressive and impractical, and certainly not in conformity with the much-talked principles of democracy," Sen. Euler, Chairman of the committee, was compelled to withdraw the committee's report and move instead that the committee be re-appointed the following session.[7]

However, it should be emphasized that suspension of a committee's work for the duration of a parliamentary recess may not necessarily be an uncompensated loss. Such a pause, even though involuntary and annoying, may give those interested time to consider more fully what they intend to submit to the committee. This was surely the case in connection with the special committee on Salacious and Indecent Literature, which was compelled to terminate its work temporarily on June 25, 1952. Between this time and the date on which it was reconstituted in 1953 initial public interest was enabled to grow, and the demand for the continuation of the work of the committee and for some form of action became truly national in scope. Acknowledgment and appreciation of the committee's activity were shared even by foreign countries; a similar committee of the House of Representatives of the American Congress requested a complete record of proceedings of the Senate investigation and the Australian press urged their Government to follow the lead of the Canadian Senate.[8]

If special committees must occasionally retire into a state of enforced inactivity they enjoy much greater flexibility in motion. They are not tied to the capital, let alone the premises of Parliament, but are allowed to move about freely and visit experimental farms, construction works, or mines, in order to gain some first-hand information about conditions or processes pertaining to the subject-matter of their inquiry. Perhaps the most celebrated on-the-spot inquiry of this kind was conducted by the Senate's special committee on the narcotics problem in 1955. To make the scope of the inquiry as comprehensive as possible the committee decided to hold sessions over a period of three months in British Columbia, Toronto and Montreal, where the situation was most alarming. Eleven of the committee's twenty-three members attended the sittings in Vancouver during the Easter recess to hear the representatives of 150

[7]*SD, 1945*, p. 439.
[8]*Ibid., 1953*, pp. 69–70.

narcotic drug addicts at the RCMP barracks and at prison farms. This is how the Toronto *Globe and Mail*, May 7, described their achievements:

> The heroes of Vancouver's long war against the drug traffic are eleven members of the Senate's committee on narcotics. A few weeks ago, when they first proposed a precedent-setting departure from Ottawa to hold on-the-spot hearings in the heartland of the drug trade, the Senators were dubbed "tired old men who want to spend springtime in the Rockies." In five days of sessions they toured the provincial prison at Oakalla, considered a score of detailed briefs and cross-examined thirty-three witnesses . . . Doctors and investigators hailed the hearings as a major step forward . . . Impressed by the committee's vigor, they suggested that such Senate bodies might take over some of the tasks normally handled to Royal Commissions.

During the last two decades there has been a tendency for the two houses to unite rather frequently in special joint committees. The first time that such a device was resorted to was in the session of 1944, when a special joint committee was set up to inquire into the relations between the federal government and municipal authorities of the city of Ottawa. Since then special joint committees were used on eight separate occasions.[9] Unlike the Senate's standing and special committees, joint committees are uni-functional bodies; they have been used only for the purpose of carrying out inquiries into questions which usually attracted widespread public attention but which were politically of secondary importance. Strictly speaking they are outside the purview of this study, for the simple reason that they are almost completely dominated by members of the House of Commons. In every one of the nine instances when it was decided to set up a joint committee the suggestion originated in the Lower House; a disparity of two to one between representatives of the House of Commons and the Senate on the committees seems to be an established practice and although the Senate provides one of the two co-chairmen and many of its spokesmen are among the most distinguished members of the House, the show, in fact, is run by the more vigorous and more ambitious members of the elected chamber. Senators are treated very much as though they were attending a committee of the Commons in the capacity of invited guests.[10] The truth of the matter is that the Senate's only contribution to the work of these committees lies in its service of relieving the Commons of the responsibility for providing the full quorum out of its own membership. Aside from performing this

[9]National Flag, 1945–46; Indian Act, 1946–8; Human Rights, 1947–48; Old Age Security, 1950; Combines, 1951 (2nd session); Capital Punishment, 1954; Federal District Commission, 1956; Indian Act, 1959–61.

[10]See Sen. Marcotte's complaints. *SD, 1951* (2nd session), p. 332.

menial task the Senate has very little else to claim in connection with special joint committees, which, in spite of their title, are, for all practical purposes, a family affair for the House of Commons.

Although there are only two forms of committees and only three main functions performed by them, all the seven characters that Prof. Wheare has found to be associated with committee work in general—the layman, the expert, the official, the interested party, the party man, the chairman, and the secretary—appear on the Senate's committees also, whether standing or special and whether they legislate, scrutinize, or inquire. Since these committees, regardless of their forms and functions, all emanate from the same body, it seems appropriate to discuss the place and the role of the seven characters summarily, before coming to the consideration of the committees' functions.

The place for the "layman" in the structure of Senate committees is on the committee as member. This may seem to be in contradiction with the general notion since superficially the Senate's standing committees are continually reconstituted special committees and both standing and special committees seem to be patterned on the American and Continental, rather than on the British, model, where committees are specialized in the sense of being set up to deal with matters relating to particular fields of activity. Yet in fact the Senate committees provide a due mixture of specialist and non-specialist elements and considerable portion of their membership is made up of what Jeremy Bentham called the "laygent" in the British system of Government.

This combination of the two elements on the Senate's standing committees, or to put it another way, the fact that in spite of their apparent structure, these committees are not exclusively specialist in the traditional sense, is due to a number of causes. In the first place, in appointing the membership of standing committees the primary consideration is given to sectional and party ties rather than to expertness. Appointments are made at the beginning of each session by a nine-member selection committee, including the two leaders and representatives from each of the sections of the country.[11] It is a delicate task of this "striking committee" —as it is commonly called—to give to the four senatorial sections of the country fair representation on all committees and at the same time to maintain an even balance between the two parties. What happens in fact is that the Chief Government Whip in the Senate produces a list of the

[11]Rule 77. In the special session of 1950, instead of setting up the usual selection committee, a special committee was appointed to examine any legislation or other matter which might be referred to it during the brief course of the session. In its composition the special committee was analogous with the Banking and Commerce committee. *Ibid., 1950* (2nd session), pp. 1–2.

membership in the previous year, and together with the selection committee, they go over this list and arrange to fill vacancies which have been caused by death or resignation.[12] Thus, if at the opening of the session there appears a vacancy in the representation of one of the geographical groups, it is generally filled by the appointment of a member from the same section and the same political party as the departed Senator, whether he is an expert in the field or not. Similarly to other forms of business arrangement in the Senate, co-operation between the Government Whip and the Leader of the Opposition in deciding committee membership is a closely observed custom. "Every year," Sen. Haig said in 1957, "I am asked whom I wish to represent our party on the committees. Our relations could not be more pleasant."[13] Indeed, the work of the selection committee contains little else than endorsing the proposals for membership of the two leaders.[14]

Seniority rule, even if not to the same extent as in the Senate of the United States, also plays a part in the process of appointing committee membership. Members on both sides of the House approach their leaders and members of the striking committee to express preference for certain committees. But many, as a result of the seniority rule, have to wait for two or three years before securing a place on the desired committee. However, it has been a practice during the last decade for the Whip to suggest to each committee chairman that five or six seats be left vacant, for the purpose of accommodating newly appointed Senators.[15] Otherwise, once the appointments are made, whether for sectional, party or expertise reasons, membership on the various standing committees are deemed to be for life. Appointments, except in the case of prolonged illness, are very seldom disturbed. But it has been customary to drop members of the Senate from their committee seats and replace them with newcomers after they have failed to attend for two consecutive sessions.[16] This, however, is something that does not occur very often and the selection committee, in spite of its very best efforts, cannot, as a rule, satisfy everybody; the result is that several members with expert knowledge may find themselves, for the time being at least, to be excluded from a particular committee. It is not surprising, therefore, that in a letter to Meighen in 1932 Sen. McLennan complained that "... on almost every subject there are men in the house familiar with it

[12]See Sen. Haig's comments, *ibid., 1957*, p. 396.
[13]*Ibid.* [14]*Ibid., 1950*, p. 219. [15]*Ibid., 1957*, p. 396.
[16]Thus, for example, on May 3, 1933, Sen. J. M. Wilson of Quebec asked Sen. Meighen why his name did not appear on any of the committees. He was then told the reason simply was that he had been absent for most of the time during the sessions of 1930, 1931, and 1932.

who would only by chance be on the appropriate committee. If these committees are to be continued, . . . some arrangements should be made by which they could have power to add *pro tempore* to their number, choosing men especially qualified to discuss whatever the subject might be, who at its conclusion would retire."[17] The Senate has never adopted such a plan and although on occasion Senators, not officially members of a particular committee yet possessing special interest or knowledge in the matter before it may attend the meetings of such a committee, the provision which prevents them from taking part in the final decision has, on the whole, militated against that practice.

In the second place, the size of the important standing committees of the Senate is certainly not conducive to producing small specialized units consistently working in demarcated areas of interest. The Senate's committees are too big for that. Before the war, when the use of the standing committees was not yet so well developed,[18] many of them were of reasonable size. The committees on Agriculture, Immigration, Commerce and Health, for example, consisted of nine members each. The committee on Tourist Traffic had a membership of fifteen, the committees on Private Bills and External Relations twenty-five each, the committee on Finance thirty-five, and the Banking and Commerce committee forty-two; only the committee on Railway, Telegraph, and Harbour had as many as fifty members, more than fifty per cent of the total membership of the Senate that time. Immediately after the war, however, almost the same time that the membership of the corresponding committees of the US Congress was reduced for the purpose of increasing their expert competence, the membership of the Senate's committees was increased. Now there were two committees, in addition to that on Transport and Communications, which had fifty members each (Banking and Commerce, Finance); the membership of the committee on Natural Resources was increased from nine to forty; those on Private Bills, Immigration, Trade, Health and External Relations to thirty-five each; the committee on Civil Service and the committee on Tourist Traffic were each allotted twenty-five members, whilst the membership of both the Standing Orders committee and the committee on Public Buildings and Grounds was raised from nine to fifteen.[19]

Realizing that specialization was highly unlikely to be achieved under a system of oversized committees, which were attended not only by those whose knowledge or interest coincided with the main lines of the com-

[17]Meighen Papers, series V, no. 221.
[18]Above, pp. 157 ff.
[19]*SD, 1945*, pp. 374–5.

mittees' terms of reference but also by quite a number of others who had no such specific interest, Sen. Robertson suggested in the second session of 1951 that the size of half a dozen standing committees of the Senate (Transport and Communications, Finance, External Relations, Natural Resources, Trade, and Immigration) should be reduced in two stages; first to carry out the reduction in the committees on Transport and Communications, Finance, and External Relations and then, if the experiment has proved successful, to implement it in the rest of the six chosen committees. The membership of the committees in the first group was to be seventeen, so as to ensure equal representation to each traditional area, four members being appointed from each of the four main geographical divisions and one member from Newfoundland. Under the completed scheme the total membership of the Senate (102) would have been divided among six committees, each being responsible for giving specialized consideration to matters referred to them. In drawing this plan it was clear that Sen. Robertson was influenced by the modern structure of committees in the US Senate, which was practically of the same size as the Senate of Canada and whose committees had an average membership of fifteen. Sen. Robertson, for whom the question of committee specialization was only one aspect of increasing the general efficacy of the Senate, was attracted by the US experience, where "because of its small membership each member has become a specialist and enjoys an enviable reputation for his wide knowledge of the subject that comes within the committee's purview."[20] Although there was no unanimity, Robertson's motion was carried and the first part of the scheme was put into effect. The experiment, however, lasted only a year; it did not bring the desired results and under pressure from the chairmen of the three committees affected by the change Sen. Robertson suggested in 1952 that the old arrangement should be reverted to.[21] The Senate agreed to his motion and never again since this brief flirtation with American practice was it seriously contemplated that the Senate's standing committees should be small nuclei of specialists without a large body of laymen attached to them.[22]

In addition to their size and the principles governing appointments to them, the third factor responsible for the non-specialist nature of the Senate's standing committees is the phenomenon of overlapping

[20]*Ibid., 1951* (2nd session), p. 221.
[21]*Ibid., 1952*, p. 82.
[22]On March 20, 1957, Sen. Pouliot urged that the memberhip of the standing committees should be considerably reduced. After debate the motion was withdrawn. *Ibid., 1957*, p. 389.

membership. In the first post-war session of Parliament the situation was as follows:

2 Senators were members of every committee;						
6	"	"	"	"	7	committees;
6	"	"	"	"	6	"
16	"	"	"	"	5	"
19	"	"	"	"	4	"
15	"	"	"	"	3	"
14	"	"	"	"	2	"
17	"	"	"	"	1	committee.

Therefore, one of the main objectives of Sen. Robertson's motion in 1951 for reducing the size of the standing committees of the Senate was to eliminate overlapping in the committees' membership and to produce a system in which no one Senator should serve on more than one committee. The failure of his proposed scheme meant failure of the attempt to curb overlapping. Thus, ten years later, in 1961, one Senator was a member of as many as 15 committees; one was on 13, two on 11, three on 10, seven on 9, fifteen on 8, twelve on 7, fifteen on 6, fifteen on 5, seventeen on 4, five on 3, and three on 2.[23] In all, 77 per cent of the Senate's membership in 1961 were on committees ranging in number from four to eight. Surely, in these circumstances it is difficult to speak of the Senate's standing committee system as a network of specialized centres of activity carefully differentiated according to parallel spheres of interest. Rather, the Senate's standing committees seem to occupy a halfway position between the American and the British practice; if in the United States the various subject-matters go to the members with special knowledge and interest, and in Britain the members with special knowledge and interest go to the various subject-matters, a continuous process of fluctuation is built in to the whole committee system of the Canadian Senate by seating members of the House on more than one committee. However, it should be emphasized that while the system of overlapping (like that of fluctuation) may have the effect of enabling people with special knowledge or interest in the subject treated to attend the meetings of a committee, it may equally well have the opposite effect of bringing together a large number of laymen round a committee table, who may sit there simply because it happens to be one of those committees of which they are members through overlapping.[24]

[23]These figures include membership in three special committees but exclude the two leaders who are *ex officio* members on all standing committees of the Senate under Rule 78/A, which was adopted in 1951.

[24]Another result of overlapping membership and of simultaneous committee meetings is that the average rate of attendance is around 50 per cent.

As a result of the above-mentioned factors the Senate's standing committees, whether they function as committees to legislate, committees to scrutinize, or committees to inquire, are never wholly specialist or wholly non-specialist. On the committee on Finance, for example, whether it considers a piece of legislation, or looks into the estimates of a department, or conducts a special study of the problem of inflation, there will be persons who at the same time may be members of five or six other standing committees of the Senate. This makes the committee on Finance, together with the other standing committees, less a group of people who devote their attention every session to essentially the same type of questions and more a body of men whose attention is evenly divided among many questions and many committees.

In the case of standing committees to legislate, however, there is one additional reason why these committees differ so markedly from their American counterparts and resemble, rather, the standing committees of the British House of Commons. When we look at the actual distribution of public bills among the various committees (Table XXIII) we find that more than one half (507) of the total number of bills referred to committee (828) in peacetime sessions during the years from 1925 to 1963 were committed to the Banking and Commerce, and a much less, but still impressive, 149 to the Transport and Communications committee. When we add to this that even of the 380 private bills which later passed the House of Commons without amendment during the same period 142 were considered in the Banking and Commerce committee, 82 in the committee on Transport and Communications, and no more than 152 in the committee on Miscellaneous Private Bills[25]—the body whose sole function would be to discuss private legislation—the absolutely dominant position of these two committees, and particularly that of the Banking and Commerce committee, becomes evident.

The role of the Banking and Commerce committee, the "queen" of the Senate standing committees, and its effect upon the operation of the whole committee system, deserves especial mentioning. The rules of the Senate contain nothing defining the jurisdiction or the purpose of any of the committees of the Senate. Although in some cases the name of a committee indicates reasonably well what its purpose is, a committee's jurisdiction is determined by the order of reference from the Senate. The Senate, acting as a Senate, can refer any matter to any committee, since nowhere—not in the BNA Act, or the rules of the Senate, or the Senate and House of Commons Act—can one find anything to determine the

[25]There were also three referred to the committee on Health and one to the committee on Natural Resources.

Table XXIII

Distribution of Government Bills among Senate Committees in Peace-time Sessions, 1925–63

on	Banking and Com-merce	Transport and Commu-nications	Natural Resources	Immi-gration and Labour	Public Health and Welfare	Canadian Trade Relations	External Relations	Finance	Miscel-laneous Private Bills	Internal Economy	(Se Ad tr
	4	1	6								
	1										
	10	15									
	1	1	1						2		
	2	27	1		1						
	1	1									
	1								1		
	2	1	1								
	1		1								
	12	3	5		2				1	1	
	19		3	1							
	13	4									
	4	3	3								
	7	5	2	1	1	2					
	12		2		1						
	9	2	1								
	11	3	2		1			1			
	38	4		1	1	1		1			
	19	2	7		1		2	6			
	21	2	11	3			1	4			
(1)	6	1	3								
(2)	12	3	3								
	29	2	1								
	35	2	3	2					1		
	18	4	3	1			2				
	26	6	2	1	2						
	25	7	4	1	2		1				
	16	7	7	2							
	10	8	2	1							
	10	4	2								
–8	11	2	1								
	11	3	3		1						
	32	4	6				1				
	24	9	2			1	1				
	34	10	3		3						
	13	3									
–63	7				2						
otal	507	149	91	14	18	4	8	12	5	1	

jurisdiction of any particular standing or special committee. Therefore, at least until the rules are changed, it is in order for the Senate to refer any matter in its discretion to any committee.[26]

The Senate in its wisdom has found it convenient and desirable to make an ever growing use of its Banking and Commerce committee in the functional sphere of legislation. If before the war it was urged that because of its large membership the Banking and Commerce committee was better adapted for examination of witnesses[27] and for percolating down general information to as many members of the House as possible, the same could hardly be argued after 1945, when most of the committees were considerably enlarged in size. However, by this time the custom of referring the great bulk of annual legislation to the Banking and Commerce committee had become relatively established[28] and, thus, the change in the size of the other standing committees caused no corresponding change in the practice. This arrangement of sending every second bill to the Banking and Commerce committee has resulted in the rather odd practice of employing the committee for the consideration of a great many measures which were only remotely, if at all, related to the field of banking and commerce. Such bills as Veterans' Land, Explosives, Canadian Citizenship, Feeding Stuffs, Food and Drugs, Agricultural Products, Canadian Wheat Board, Canada Dairy Products, and many others of this kind have usually been referred to the Banking and Commerce committee rather than to some seemingly more appropriate standing committees. Similarly, everything pertaining to the Criminal Code or to legislation affecting prisons and reformatories, juvenile delinquents, the RCMP, statute law, judges, etc., has automatically been sent to the Banking and Commerce committee. At one point in 1947 Sen. Copp recommended the creation of a standing committee for bills involving law practice and procedure, but the suggestion was not acted upon.[29] The proper jurisdiction of the Banking and Commerce committee has been as generously interpreted as the meaning of property and civil rights in the constitution. As a result, the committee has become an overburdened body, a reduced Committee of the Whole, with rules even more elastic than those of Committee of the Whole. On the other hand,

[26]See Speaker's ruling, *SD, 1943*, p. 203.

[27]See, for example, the arguments in the Canada Grain bill, *ibid., 1926*, p. 266, and in the Agricultural Poisons bill, *ibid., 1927*, p. 319.

[28]Thus, when the committee on Finance, which had been moribund for years, was authorized in 1943 to look into the war financial measures it was regarded by some Senators as an affront to the Banking and Commerce committee and its chairman personally. *Ibid., 1943*, pp. 204, 218.

[29]*Ibid., 1947*, p. 350.

the character of the Banking and Commerce committee as a "general purpose committee," consuming 50 per cent of the legislative output of a session, has tended to bring the committee system of the Senate closer to the ABC committees of the British House of Commons, and away from the specialized committees of the American system, upon which the Senate's standing committees were ostensibly modelled.

Although it might be expected that when special committees are set up in any of the three main functional areas they are entirely made up of specialists, in fact their composition shows much the same features as we have seen in the case of standing committees.[30] Under the rules of the Senate (Rule 83) the Senators to serve on a special committee are either nominated by the mover, or, if three Senators so demand, they shall be elected by the whole House taking a vote on the membership. The second method has never been used, for the simple reason that there never were three members to insist. What happens in practice is, of course, that the motion for committee being passed the committee is selected by the two leaders, after consultation with their followers. However, in choosing the members of the committee, they must have regard for sectional and party considerations. The two parties are represented on the committee proportionately to their strength in the House. It happened only once, in the case of the Manpower committee in 1960, that the thirty-two members were equally divided between Liberal and Conservative Senators, irrespective of the parties' actual stand in the Senate. As a result, such illustrious members of the house as Sen. Crerar, Sen. Farris, and others were not included in the committee.

Surely the ratio of expert and lay elements on a special committee is also dependent, to a certain extent, upon the subject of the committee's inquiry. There are matters on which the good sense of the layman is the best type of expertness. Who is an expert on salacious literature, for example, which was inquired into by a Senate special committee in 1952? Or, indeed, on human rights? On the committee which was set up to study the latter in 1950 there were seven lawyers, seven businessmen, and one doctor. Of the eighteen members of the special committee to look into the Income Tax legislation at the end of the war nine were

[30]It should be pointed out, however, that the size of special committees tends to be smaller than the size of most of the main standing committees. The biggest special committee to be set up was the committee on Reconstruction in 1943, which consisted of thirty-eight members. One other committee had a membership over thirty: the Manpower committee in 1960 with thirty-two members. Otherwise, the average size of special committees is twenty to twenty-two. The smallest one during the period under study was the committee on Tourist Traffic in 1934, which had six members.

members of the legal profession, but the nature of income tax laws is probably such that lawyers might be considered experts. Such topics as sealing and fishery or land use, which formed the subject-matter of Senate inquiries in 1934 and 1957, respectively, were much more concrete and palpable issues; yet we find that even on them there was a fair proportion of the lay element, those whose background and professional experience had no direct bearing upon the subjects under consideration.

This combination or mixture of the expert with the layman on the membership of Senate committees is a fortunate arrangement, indeed. While the first brings special knowledge to the work of the committee—and there are always many members of the Senate who have wide and varied experience in matters that are referred to committee—the second is able, with a penetrating, probing, and questioning attitude, "to check the excesses of bureaucratic and expert nonsense by the application of his own common sense."[31] Evidently, the most obvious source from which to draw this type of layman in the Senate is the large number of businessmen, whose skilled practical sense Prof. Wheare considered the best material for effective laymanship. A good portrait of such men in action is provided in the following description by Sen. Murphy of what took place at the meeting of the Railway, Telegraph, and Harbour committee in 1927 during consideration of the application of a group of Quebec promoters for permission to build a railway in the Northern wilds of the provinces of Quebec and Ontario.

> It was advocated before the committee by gentlemen of such eloquence, many gestures, a surfeit of "politesse" and all the other earmarks of the fellow of Gallic ancestry who is constantly described to you as a "splendid speaker." Consequently, there was much bunk and a minimum of facts. Eventually, it was dragged out of some of the orators that the railroad was to be built for the purpose of affording an outlet for the paper to be manufactured at a pulp-mill that would be built in the dim future. Thereupon, Sen. Curry loomed large. First, he quietly asked what the output per day of the mill would be. The reply was about 200 tons. Then, Sen. Curry remarked, even more quietly, that such an output was insufficient to pay the running expenses, of the proposed railroad for ten miles of its length, to say nothing of the 135 miles which it was proposed to build. The eloquence and the railway charter died right there. Now, that is the kind of service constantly rendered to the country by practical men like Sen. Curry.[32]

Indeed, precisely because of the high percentage of businessmen and lawyers in the Senate's membership and in the "active element" both in

[31]Wheare, *Government by Committee*, p. 23.

[32]Murphy to Miss M. Sheridan, March 11, 1927. Murphy Papers, vol. 27, no. 11473.

the House and in committee[33] the lay talent is more than adequately represented on the Senate's committees. Even when we come to those Senators possessing specialized knowledge we find that apart from some specific instances where the experience of the lawyer,[34] the businessman, the agriculturist, or the doctor nicely fitted the exact nature of the subject before the committee, most of the Senate's specialists are general practitioners rather than experts in the strict sense of the word. This is borne out also by the fact that so many of them had been active politicians and members of various elected legislatures in their former public careers.

The "real" expert on the Senate committees is either a representative of a Government department or a non-government expert, and in both cases he may be either a witness or an adviser attached to the committee. Like the committees of the American Congress but unlike those of the Parliament of the United Kingdom, committees of the Senate may invite and hear expert witnesses and benefit from their testimonies placed *directly* before the committees. The special committee on Human Rights in 1950, for example, heard such academic authorities as Professor F. R. Scott and Dr. R. S. K. Seeley, Provost of Trinitiy College, University of Toronto, and received a submission from Professor Lower of Queen's University—a very illuminating statement on the whole question of human liberties and democratic rights in Canada, which was subsequently published in the committee's proceedings.[35] In the case of the Finance committee's inquiry in 1959 into the problem of inflation in Canada the first expert witness to be heard was Professor Knox of Queen's University, who presented an explanation and broad analysis of the nature of inflationary forces, which formed the basis of the committee's line of questioning subsequent witnesses. Again, during the course of the long inquiry of the special committee on Land Use, 1957–61, non-government experts included academicians from the Macdonald College of McGill University, the University of Saskatchewan, and Waterloo University College.

On occasion the Senate committees may appoint some of these experts as their advisers. The most notable example in recent years was probably that of Professor J. J. Deutsch, whose knowledge and experience first invoked comments of appreciation in the Senate in 1955–56 when he

[33]Above, pp. 65, 72 ff.

[34]The nine lawyers on the eighteen-member special committee on Income Tax in 1946 were particularly useful when they were confronted with another member of their profession, the Deputy Minister of National Revenue, Mr. Elliott, K.C., who represented the Income Tax branch before the committee. It was suggested that his cross-examination was very much a case of fighting the devil with his own tools.

[35]*SD, 1950*, p. 612.

appeared as witness before the Finance committee to give evidence on the Estimates in his capacity of Secretary to the Treasury Board. In 1959, therefore, when the same committee decided to study the problem of inflation, he was invited on the committee as adviser. His assistance proved so effective and helpful in assessing accurately the evidence of forty-four witnesses drawn from every field of the country's life that in 1960, by then at Queen's University, he was again offered the same post on the special committee on Manpower and Employment. He consequently organized a small research team[36] and while the committee itself could not function during the time Parliament was prorogued, no such limitation handicapped the research team, whose members started a series of six research projects before prorogation, in order to provide the committee, when reconstituted, with all the background that could be obtained.

Advisers attached to Senate committees may be drawn from the ranks of government experts also. Thus, the success of the inquiry of the special committee on Income Tax in 1945, for example, was due in no small measure to the assistance of Mr. Stikeman, a high-ranking official in the Taxation Branch of the Department of National Revenue, who brought to the committee the benefit of his experience and knowledge and displayed great skill in examining the witnesses and in obtaining from them valuable information. Also, much of the credit for the drafting of the committee's final report went to him.[37] Similarly, the special committee on Land Use in 1959 secured the assistance as its technical adviser of Mr. R. Stutt of the Economic Division of the Department of Agriculture, who helped the committee in reaching a conclusion in the proposed study. Likewise, legal officers of the Department of Justice who drafted a bill may appear in a quasi-advisory capacity before Senate committees, answering questions with regard to the wording and giving legal advice to members of the committee in drafting amendments.

However, when departmental officials attend the meetings of Senate committees as witnesses they are there in a double, indeed triple, capacity. They combine the characteristics of the expert, the official, and, to a certain extent, the interested party, and which character will be dominant in a particular case depends on the kind of committee they attend and the nature of the question before the committee. Although no hard and fast rules can be laid down, it may be suggested as a general principle

[36]It included Mr. Frank Denton, a Toronto economist, Prof. Wm. C. Hood of the University of Toronto, Mr. R. W. James, Department of National Defence, Prof. Sylvia Ostry of McGill University, Prof. S. Judek of the University of Ottawa, and a number of officials from the Economic Branch of the Department of Labour.

[37]*SD, 1946,* p. 335.

that when departmental witnesses give evidence in relation to such general topics of inquiry as mining or sealing, tourist traffic or narcotics, human rights or land use, which are not primarily concerned with departmental policies, they function as experts. When, however, the committees' terms of reference have a direct bearing upon departmental matters, as in many cases before committees to legislate, in almost all cases before committees to scrutinize, and in some cases before committees to inquire (e.g., the special committee on the Government Annuities Act in 1936), government witnesses are first and foremost officials of a particular department and should only secondarily be regarded as experts.

When they represent their department, explaining or defending its policies to a senatorial committee, government officials also exhibit certain features of the "interested party" or the "partisan." Nevertheless, they must be distinguished from the interested party proper—those individuals or, usually, organizations who are regularly invited to put their case before the Senate's committees, either on a piece of legislation or on a matter of special inquiry. The task of inviting such bodies is mainly the responsibility of the Senate leader and the chairman of the committee concerned, assisted by the chief clerk of committees of the Senate, who are guided in their decision by the single criterion of who are those whose interests will most likely be affected by the contemplated action. It is proposed to say more of the role of the interested party in the second half of this chapter. What is important to emphasize here is that the only role in which the interested party appears before Senate committees is that of a witness. They are never supposed to be on the committees as members. Indeed, Rule 84 of the Senate clearly states that "no Senator who has any pecuniary interest whatsoever . . . in the inquiry to be entrusted to any Select committee, shall sit on such committee."[38]

The same can be said, to a great extent, of the presence of the "party man" on the Senate's committees. Although party label is a determining factor in appointing committee members,[39] it has no direct bearing upon the way in which business is conducted in the committees of the Senate. Indeed, the proposition which has been put forward in Chapter IV regarding partisanship and impartiality in the Senate's proceedings in

[38]Thus, for example, when Sen. Foster was unanimously selected chairman of the Banking and Commerce committee in 1925 he immediately resigned the directorship of the Canadian Bank of Commerce, lest even a suspicion of partiality could be appropriated to him in his rulings as chairman. *Ibid., 1931*, p. 47.

[39]Sen. Dandurand once suggested that it was "in this instance only that party affiliations appear on the surface and impose themselves on our attention." *Ibid., 1933*, p. 459.

general applies with added force to proceedings in committee, where principles are never at stake.[40] Indeed, except when partisan passions are already running high at the second reading stage, usually as a result of tension generated outside the house, and then brought into the committee room, party differences are practically imperceptible in the functioning of the committees. As a result, the only consistent "party man" in the Senate's committees (apart from the Government leader who is *ex officio* member of all committees) is the minister, who may appear as witness. Of course, Senate committees have no power to subpoena any member of Parliament;[41] however, they can and do indicate that they are conducting a hearing and if ministers like to make representations they are welcome. The frequency and willingness with which members of the cabinet avail themselves of this opportunity and attend the meetings of Senate committees to take part in the consideration of matters technical seems to suggest that they lack similar opportunities in their own Chamber.

The last two of Wheare's seven characters, the chairman and the secretary, are important figures of all Senate committees of whatever complexion. Although the chairman of the Senate's committees lack the executive power and somewhat theatrical prestige of their US counterparts, they, in a more modest way, perhaps, still provide the *leitmotiv* of their respective committees. According to the rules, after the members of a committee are appointed, an organization meeting is held by the committee and it is here that, in theory, nomination for chairman takes place. In practice, however, the custom has developed for the Senate Leader to nominate the chairman for every committee, with the exception of the Divorce committee which chooses its own chairman.[42] Although the practice of nomination of chairmen by the Senate Leader had been criticized as undemocratic the special committee which was set up in 1950 to study the constitution of the Senate's standing committees recommended no change in this regard.

In making his selection the Senate Leader is certainly influenced by various factors, particularly by geographical location, experience[43] and

[40]See, in particular, the comments of Sen. Ballantyne, *ibid., 1936*, p. 47; Euler's remarks, *ibid., 1946*, p. 335; Haig's remarks on the handling of the Manitoba Natural Resources bill by the Natural Resources committee, *ibid., 1948*, p. 646; his and Crerar's remarks on the working of the Finance committee respecting the Estimates in 1950, *ibid., 1950*, pp. 571–2, etc.

[41]See chairman's ruling in *Proceedings* of the Banking and Commerce committee on the Bank of Canada bill (1961), p. 8.

[42]*SD, 1939*, pp. 62–3.

[43]Thus, of the five chairmen of the Banking and Commerce committee between 1925 and 1963, two were businessmen and three lawyers; of the five chairmen of the Transport and Communications committee two were lawyers and one a

seniority. The most important tradition for the Senate Leader, however, has been to renominate the same chairman year after year until he dies or resigns from his post. Sen. Robertson believed this was a bad practice, but he also realized that it was "difficult for a Leader to say to a chairman who is known to all of us as a man of high calibre, wide experience and good judgment, that he should relinquish his office."[44] As a result, the chairmen of the Senate's standing committees enjoy a practically undisturbed continuity of status, irrespective of the party in power and of any change that may take place in the Government. It is not surprising, therefore, that the number of persons who have held the position of chairman of the Senate's standing committees in these thirty-seven years has been small. Thus, both the Banking and Commerce committee,[45] the committee on Transport and Communications,[46] and the Natural Resources committee,[47] had five chairmen, while the Canadian Trade Relations committee[48] and the committee on Health[49] only four—to pick just a few examples.

Although the practice of permanent chairmanship may be open to

---

businessman, Sen. Robertson was former vice-president of a railway union, Sen. Graham an ex-Minister of Railways and Canals; two chairmen of the committee on Canadian Trade Relations (Foster and Euler) were former Ministers of Trade and Commerce; all the five chairmen of the Natural Resources committee were agriculturists and one of them, Crerar, a former Minister of Agriculture; similarly, each one of the four chairmen of the committee on Health and Welfare were members of the medical profession, while one of them (Béland) was a former Minister of Soldiers' Civil Re-establishment and Health.

[44] *SD, 1950*, p. 217. Both he and Crerar advocated a system of rotating committee chairmanship among members of the house. Consistent with this view the latter resigned as chairman of the Finance committee in 1956, after so many years of successful chairmanship, to allow room for others. *Ibid., 1956*, p. 158. The continuation of chairmanship poses of course no similar problems in the case of *ad hoc* special committees set up usually for a short duration. Change in the chairmanship, even when the inquiry of a special committee extends over more than one year, is rare; Sen. Davis succeeded Sen. Doone as chairman of the special committee on Salacious Literature in 1952 after the latter died; also, Sen. Pearson took over the chairmanship of the special committee on Land Use in 1959 after Sen. Power had occupied the post in the first two years of the committee.

[45] Foster (C. 1925–7); Black (C. 1927–44); Beauregard (L. 1945–9); Farris (L. 1949–50); Hayden (L. 1951–).

[46] Blain (C. 1925); Robertson (C. 1926–30); Graham (L. 1931–40); Copp (L. 1941–9); Hugessen (L. 1950–).

[47] McCoig (L. 1925–7); Donnelly (C. 1928–47); Crerar (L. 1948–50); McDonald (L. 1950–51); Vaillancourt (L. 1952–).

[48] Foster (C. 1925–31); McLennan (C. 1932–9); Euler (L. 1940–52); McLean (L. 1952–).

[49] DeVeber (L. 1925); Béland (L. 1926–35); Bourque (C. 1936–48); Veniot (L. 1948–).

criticism on several grounds it has certainly one commendable feature: it has produced some outstanding committee chairmen, precisely by enabling them through long years of service to accumulate superior knowledge and vast experience in the respective fields of their committees as well as in the difficult art of presiding over committee meetings. This is particularly significant in the case of the big committees on Banking and Commerce and Transport and Communications, which, as we have seen, have to deal with the great bulk of legislation each session, and whose large membership requires special fitness from their chairmen to maintain an aura of efficiency and informality. As Sen. Black, who was chairman of the Banking and Commerce committee from 1927 to 1944, once said, if any one thought it was "an easy job to keep things running smoothly in such a large committee, with numerous witnesses and members in attendance . . . a closer acquaintance with the work would quickly dispel the illusion."[50] The success of the chairman is often a guarantee of the success of the committee as a whole. Thus, the work of such chairmen as Black, Beauregard, Hayden in the Banking and Commerce committee, Hugessen in the Transport and Communications committee, or Crerar in the committee on Finance has been in great measure responsible for the effectiveness with which these committees have discharged their functions.

In addition to performing the basic duties connected with the organization of committee work, the chairmen of the Senate's committees have a special responsibility towards the large number of witnesses who appear before the committees to make representations. On the one hand, they must see to it that the witnesses are at ease and are not cross-examined at undue length;[51] on the other hand, they must guard against any attempt on the part of the members of the committee to put questions on policy to a departmental official. "That type of question," Sen. Robertson warned, "should be put to a minister only or . . . his parliamentary secretary. . . . A committee chairman who knows his business will definitely rule out any question on policy. . . . That is a factor of great importance."[52] With regard to ministers appearing as witnesses before Senate committees, it

[50]*SD, 1936*, p. 359.

[51]A good example of this occurred during the deliberations of the committee on Health on the Food and Drugs bill in 1953, when one of the witnesses, Dr. Shute of London, was so excited when he started that Senators around him feared he might collapse at any moment; however he soon cooled off, thanks to the great skill of the chairman, Dr. Veniot, and gave a fine presentation. Afterwards, he expressed his gratitude for the way in which he was received and treated and admiration for the conduct of the committee and that of the Senate generally. *Ibid., 1953*, pp. 105–7.

[52]*Ibid., 1960*, p. 63.

sometimes falls upon the chairman, particularly in the case of a complicated piece of legislation, to brief the minister in advance of his attendance in committee on the nature of the amendments suggested and the reasoning behind them.[53] Moreover, the decision of a minister to appear before a Senate committee may be greatly influenced by the chairman's prestige and reputation. It was pointed out for instance in connection with the effective scrutiny carried out by the committee on Finance in 1952 that "what makes the committee's report so valuable . . . is the co-operation that he [Crerar] and he alone received not only from civil servants but from members of the Government whom he asked to assist us by giving us information."[54] A powerful chairman like Sen. Crerar can carry the whole committee with him. The reports of the committee on Finance during the term of his chairmanship bore the unmistakable stamp of his personal views and read like a series of letters from Cassandra warning against undue government expenditures.

This function of a chairman to animate or galvanize the whole work of the committee was manifest in the case of several committees of inquiry during the past thirty-seven years. Thus, the success of the lengthy inquiry conducted by the Senate's committee on Immigration into the operation and administration of the Immigration Act from 1946 to 1948 was the result of the agitation and enthusiasm of the committee's chairmen, Sen. Murdock and Sen. (Mrs.) Wilson. Similarly, the special committees on Human Rights in 1950, on Salacious Literature in 1952, or on Narcotics in 1955 were called into existence, organized, kept together, and brought to a successful close by the men who became their chairmen,[55] and who had a life-long interest in the problems which formed the subject of the committees' inquiries.

In many cases the chairman is assisted by a deputy chairman or a vice-chairman and a small steering committee drawn from the membership of the committee itself.[56] The steering committee helps the chairman

[53]Thus, Hayden communicated with Finance Minister Fleming before the latter's second appearance in the Banking and Commerce committee in connexion with the Estates Tax bill in 1958. He enumerated for the minister the sections that were stood and the arguments for the proposed changes. *Ibid., 1958*, p. 765.

[54]*Ibid., 1952*, p. 566.

[55]Roebuck, Doone, and Reid, respectively.

[56]Thus, e.g., the committee on Finance scrutinizing the Estimates appointed a five-member steering committee in 1952; the same committee in 1956 set up a steering committee of four and elected Sen. Turgeon as Vice-Chairman; in the case of the special committee on Land Use in 1959 the steering committee consisted of seven members and Sen. Bois was chosen Deputy Chairman. This practice is followed in most of the cases where the number of the witnesses to be heard is large, the subject-matter before the committee is complicated and the committee's Report is likely to be a complex and lengthy document.

to decide upon the list of witnesses to be invited as well as on the general timetable of the committee and it may also give assistance in preparing the committee's report. In addition to the steering committee the main committee may set up subcommittees to concentrate on specific aspects of the issue before the committee as a whole. The subcommittees have their own chairmen, they hear representatives and report to the main committee. The place for the most consistent use of such subcommittees is in the standing committee on Divorce, which usually sits in four or even five "sections," each section or subcommittee hearing the evidence and then reporting its findings to the general committee.[57] However, the most efficient and most systematic assistance for the committee in general and for the chairman in particular comes from the Law Clerk and the officers of the permanent staff of the Senate's committee branch who act as "secretaries" on the committees of the House. The contribution of the Law Clerk and Parliamentary Counsel in advising the chairman and the members of the committee on points of law, in arguing out difficulties of drafting with departmental officials and the law officers of the Crown on behalf of the committee and very often in recommending actual changes to be inserted in a bill, is invaluable. If the Law Clerk is the "intellect," officers of the committee staff are the "memory" of the Senate committees; it falls upon them to notify members of the committee as well as witnesses about forthcoming business, the time and place of committee meetings, and the subject to be considered by the committee; they keep the minutes and compile the statistics and in the case of the Divorce Committee they look after the papers, payment of fees, advertising of notices, etc., which in the ordinary courts are left to the judge.[58] In sum, their services, together with those of the Law Clerk, the chairman, the steering committee and the subcommittees, are among the prerequisites of the effective functioning of the Senate's committees.

Having discussed the organizational aspects of the Senate's committee system, we can now move on to consider the use to which the Senate's committee are put, or, in other words, consider their functions. The place allotted to committees in the present study does not allow us to give a detailed analysis of the services rendered by the committees of the Senate. The most we can do is to indicate in a summary way the functions they regularly perform as a part of the machinery of Parliament. There are, it is suggested, six such functions, three of which are termed main or principal and three derivative or incidental. The principal

[57]The arrangement was instituted by Roebuck upon assuming the chairmanship of the committee in 1954.

[58]*SD, 1955*, pp. 644–7.

functions are to legislate, to scrutinize, and to inquire; the incidental ones are to educate Senators, to provide an institutional forum for the articulation of interests, and to form a liaison between Parliament and government departments.

Principal Functions

TO LEGISLATE

Perhaps the primary and most obvious role of Senate committees lies in the field of legislation. We have seen the two-stage development that took place in this area—first a shift from Committee of the Whole to standing and special committees[59] and, next, concentration on standing committees and the disuse of special committees,[60] with the result that after 1930 and particularly during the period following the Second World War the functional field of legislation came to be dominated entirely by standing committees.[61] We have seen, furthermore, that even within the group of standing committees, two committees, the Banking and Commerce and the Transport and Communications, have controlled the great majority of bills selected for committee consideration. To put it somewhat bluntly, the legislative functions of the Senate during the last two decades have been performed in the committees on Banking and Commerce, and Transport and Communications. It was here that the services of the Senate as a revisory body and as a chamber of first instance have been rendered most convincingly. It has been shown[62] that, an insignificant percentage aside, all the technical amendments made by the Senate to government measures on the lines suggested in Chapter VI have been put in committee. It may be added that modifications effected by the Senate in Government legislation from the point of view of safeguarding certain principles, as will be seen in the next two chapters, have been made in committee also. In brief, all important changes in legislation, whether technical or substantive, were moved, weighed, and finally inserted when the bill was before a standing committee. Similarly, all celebrated cases of introducing important items of the Government's legislative program, such as the Canada Shipping bill in 1934, the National Defence bill and the Bankruptcy bill in 1949, the

59Above, pp. 157 ff.

60Above, Table XXIII, p. 244.

61The last occasion when the device of a special committee was resorted to in the field of legislation was in 1940, when a special committee was set up to consider the Debts Due to the Crown bill.

62Table XXII above, p. 159.

Criminal Law bill in 1952–53 and many others cited in chapter VII, were handled by one of the Senate standing committees and the final product rarely required further improvement by the Lower House. Whether revising legislation sent up from the House of Commons, or introducing it, and irrespective of the nature of bills before them, the Senate's standing committees to legislate follow a standard pattern. In giving a skilled and leisurely consideration to the technical provisions of a bill they invariably pose the following three-fold question: What does the clause mean? How will it operate? And what will it cost? A combination of experts and laymen, assisted by a body of trained advisers and assessing the evidence of government and non-government witnesses, the Senate's committees will usually come up with a satisfactory answer to these questions, before deciding upon the desired improvements. The result is better legislation. On the basis of the Senate's legislative services during the period under review it might be said that the value of the Senate's contribution to parliamentary legislation can be measured almost solely in terms of the accomplishments of its committees.

TO SCRUTINIZE

Less systematically than in the field of legislation, Senate committees have been used also for the purpose of financial scrutiny regarding the public accounts and departmental estimates. The Senate has no select committee in either of these two areas,[63] with the result that whenever it was decided to consider the accounts or the estimates it was necessary either to set up a special *ad hoc* committee or to use one or more of the Senate's select standing committees. The select committee whose scope of jurisdiction comes closest to that of a Public Accounts Committee or an Estimates Committee is surely the Committee of Finance. Indeed, two exceptions apart, the function of scrutiny has been performed by this committee. Regardless of the intrinsic value of its services the use of the Finance committee as a committee to scrutinize has been important also as a device of saving its life from the slow attrition which faced it as a committee to legislate, due to the continued practice of referring to the Banking and Commerce committee every bill having to do with finance.

As regards the Public Accounts the Senate has never really got beyond the first tentative attempts. In 1934 a special committee was appointed under the chairmanship of Liberal Senator Robinson to investigate

[63]Sen. Hughes' proposal in 1928 for the creation of a Public Accounts committee was rejected, mainly on the ground that the terms of reference of the Finance committee were wide enough to include the Public Accounts. *SD, 1928*, p. 570.

federal expenditures and the Report of the Auditor General.[64] Although the committee heard the auditor general of Canada, the comptroller of the Treasury, the superintendent of government annuities, and the secretary of state, it had no time to examine all witnesses whose evidence would have been of value, and, therefore, it made no report to the Senate.[65] Its suggestion that a similar committee should be reconstituted the following session was not acted upon. The next occasion that it was decided to study the Public Accounts did not come until 1951, when by an order of reference, October 19, the committee on Finance was empowered to examine and report upon the Public Accounts. However, since the Public Accounts did not become available until only two weeks before prorogation, the committee was unable to accomplish anything during the session.[66]

Much more successful have been the attempts to deal with the Estimates in committee. Not only has it been urged that because of the rich professional, political, and business experience of its members the Senate could be of real help for the Commons, without derogating from its prerogatives, in studying the details of expenditures, but it has also been realized that under the practice of receiving the Supply bill shortly before prorogation the Senate could not hope to discuss the main estimates effectively. Consequently, on March 3, 1943, the Senate adopted, on the motion of Sen. King, the Government Leader in the Senate, a resolution authorizing the committee on Finance "to examine expenditures proposed by the estimates laid before Parliament and by resolutions relating to war and other proposed financial measures of which notice has been given to Parliament, in advance of the bills based on the said estimates and resolutions reaching the Senate."[67] Although Sen. King had some difficulty in convincing Dr. Beauchesne that the Senate had the right to review the Estimates at all, the committee began its consideration of the Estimates after the Minister of Finance had delivered his speech on the Budget.[68] The same resolution was adopted in 1944,[69] 1945,[70] 1946,[71] and in 1949.[72] Then in 1950, exploiting the rare opportunity of having the estimates brought down within eight days of the opening of Parliament, the Senate adopted, on March 16, Sen. Robertson's motion that the Estimates should be distributed for consideration among the follow-

[64]In choosing the committee's sixteen members Sen. Robinson deliberately ignored, with the exception of Senators Lacasse and L'Espérance, the members of the Finance committee. He admitted he might be "treading on the toes of the Finance committee." As it turned out, he was not only treading on their toes but "tramped them into the mire." *Ibid., 1934*, p. 576.

[65]*SJ, 1934*, p. 337; *Canadian Annual Review, 1934*, p. 111.

[66]*SD, 1951*, p. 221.

[67]*Ibid., 1934*, p. 72.

[68]Actually what the Senate received was the subject-matter of the Estimates rather than the Estimates themselves. I owe this piece of information to Professor Norman Ward.

[69]*Ibid., 1944*, p. 57.

[70]*Ibid., 1945*, p. 66.

[71]*Ibid., 1946*, p. 488.

[72]*Ibid., 1949* (2nd session), p. 205.

ing nine standing committees: Transport and Communications, Health and Welfare, Tourist Traffic, Public Buildings and Grounds, External Relations, Trade, Immigration and Labour, Natural Resources and Finance. This arrangement was clearly extraordinary and although it proved a success it has never again been repeated. In 1951 the Estimates were tabled in Parliament one-and-a-half months after the session began. In these circumstances the Senate decided to return to the pre-1950 practice of referring the Estimates to the committee on Finance in advance of the actual arrival of the bills based upon the Estimates. However, the advantages of the multiple-committee study of 1950 did not pass unnoticed; the estimates were allocated between five subcommittees of the Finance committee, each having its own sphere of reference. In 1952 the usual order of reference was extended, so as to enable the Finance committee to study the incidence of federal, provincial, and municipal taxation and their effect upon different income groups.[73] In 1953 the committee on Finance received no order to study the Estimates, the official explanation being that Parliament completed its work at an earlier date than usual in view of the forthcoming coronation, the unofficial explanation being that "with a general election coming on within the next six months it might be argued that our committee was gathering information" which might have involved members of the Senate in political controversy.[74] No explanation was given for omission to authorize the committee in 1954. But in 1955 and in 1956 the committee again acted under its traditional order of reference. Although it was maintained that the setting up in 1955 of a select committee on Estimates in the House of Commons (which three years later became a standing committee on Estimates) did not diminish the value of the work done by the Senate's Finance committee,[75] in the last five years the committee has made no study of the Estimates. Instead, in 1958 it was entrusted with the task of considering the report of the Central Mortgage and Housing Corporation for the fiscal year ended December 31, 1957, whilst in 1959, 1960, and in 1962–63 it was authorized to review the report of the Canada Council, together with the Auditor General's balance sheet for the Council. Thus, after a decade or so as a virtual committee on Estimates the Finance committee may now be headed towards a new role of being the Canadian counterpart of the standing committee on Nationalized Industries in the British House of Commons.[76]

[73]*Ibid., 1949*, p. 87. [74]*Ibid., 1953*, p. 354. [75]*Ibid., 1955*, p. 296.

[76]For the desirability of the Senate to examine systematically the annual reports of Crown corporations see the interview given by Professor J. R. Mallory to the *Montreal Star*, May 29, 1961.

Apart from such "incidental" functions as educating Senators and encouraging co-operation with departmental officials, which will be discussed later, the primary object of the Senate's committees to scrutinize in general, and of the committee on Finance in particular, has been to take an intelligent and politically unbiased look at the Estimates or the accounts, with a view of discovering abnormalities and of recommending economies. Indeed, the annual report of the Finance committee, even during Sen. Crerar's chairmanship, has never set out specifically either to praise or criticize the Government for the manner in which it conducted its business. That has never been the purpose of the committee, which has merely essayed to gather and present facts regarding government spending. This could be done either through a comprehensive study (as was done, for example, in 1950, when nine standing committees worked on the Estimates) or through concentrating on selected areas (as, e.g., in 1955 and in 1956, when the Finance committee only dealt with the Estimates of certain chosen departments of the government). Thus, in so far as the usefulness of the committee has depended primarily on its reports, functionally the Senate's committees to scrutinize have been also committees to advise.

Whether the Senate has a right, constitutional or otherwise, to reduce Estimates is a problematical but practically not a very important question. It has been customary for members of the Senate to claim to have such a right but never to exercise it.[77] The proper way for the Senate's committee to recommend economics is, indeed, not so much through moving direct cuts in the current estimates as through suggesting improved methods of administration of the department in future.[78] Thus Sen. Robertson urged in 1950: "If at any time after a study of the public accounts and estimates we found that much smaller expenditures could be made in a certain field without harm to the public interest, we should not reduce any specific items, but rather should make a report setting out our conclusions and the reasons for them, and urging the Government to reduce them in the following year's estimates." He was convinced "that a carefully prepared report of that kind from the Senate would carry great weight."[79] It has been pointed out also that "too often

[77]"To move to reduce the amount of the estimates," Sen. Robertson advised, "is a matter of detail. Certainly it has never happened in my time . . . But I do not think there is any question about our right so to act if we see fit." *SD, 1949* (2nd session), pp. 173–4.

[78]This, as a matter of fact, seems to have been the policy of the select, and later standing, committee on Estimates in the House of Commons as well. S. P. Singh, "Canadian Committee on Estimates," unpublished MA thesis, McGill Univ., 1962.

[79]*SD, 1950*, p. 255.

busy ministers are the prey of civil servants for continuation of excessive and needless expenditure." If the suggestion to do away with them comes from the Senate it can be accepted and implemented without the danger of losing face.[80] Accordingly, there has been an abundance of valuable and practical observations accumulated in the reports of the Senate's committees to scrutinize. Such ideas as to centralize all publicity undertaken by the Government through the establishment of a central publicity bureau;[81] to table separate Estimates covering arsenals and the activity of the Research Council for the purpose of educating public opinion about the country's total defence expenditure;[82] to compel each government department to furnish a statement with its Estimates showing its revenues in the preceding year and the sources from which these revenues came;[83] to put an end to the practice of government departments of bypassing the Department of Public Works and building up miniature public works branches of their own;[84] or to set up an organization under the Central Mortgage and Housing Corporation to study the problem of the flow of mortgage funds with a view of extending greater lending opportunities to the low-income housing residents[85]—to pick only a few of the many examples available—such ideas have not been without their practical value. Coming from men with considerable administrative and business experience, the reports of the Senate's committees to scrutinize have been an important, although generally not too well-recognized, element of Parliament's control over departmental administration. It is, therefore, a matter of regret that there have been lapses in the continuity of the operation of the Senate's committee on Finance.

TO INQUIRE

The third main function performed by Senate committees is the conducting of non-partisan inquiries into some problem area of concern. It is usually pointed out that, since the employment of judges on royal

[80]See remarks of Sen. R. W. Gladstone of Ont. *Ibid., 1951*, p. 189.

[81]Report of Natural Resources committee and External Relations committee. *Ibid., 1950*, pp. 505, 562.

[82]Report of Trade committee. *Ibid., 1950*, p. 557.

[83]Report of Finance Committee, *ibid.*, pp. 530 ff. It is to be noted that the large sheet—the summary of Government expenditures by departments—which accompanies the annual Blue Book of Estimates each year was introduced into that volume as a result of the suggestion of the Finance committee in 1950. See Sen. Lambert's remarks, *ibid., 1955*, p. 668.

[84]Report of Finance Committee, *ibid., 1952*, p. 537.

[85]Report of Finance Committee, *ibid., 1958*, p. 501. Although the proposed organization was not set up, the CMHC carried out the recommended inquiries and it was as a result of them that the National Housing Act (1954) Amendment bill was introduced the following session. *Ibid., 1959*, p. 275.

commissions is open to serious objection, committees of the Senate could handle much of their work. The assumption is that a Senate's select committee, if given adequate research assistance, is capable of a more leisurely, expert, and detailed inquiry than a similar committee of the Lower House, while being a less cumbersome device of investigation and public instruction than a royal commission.[86] Also, both Parliament and the administration would enjoy greater freedom of action in dealing with a matter on the basis of a report from a Senate committee than a report from a Royal Commission.

From a formal point of view there is no particular committee or system of committees (as is in the case of committees to legislate or to scrutinize) primarily associated with the function to inquire. Inquiries may be carried out either by special or by standing committees and, although the device of special committees has been used more frequently than that of standing committees, some of the most important investigations have, indeed, been conducted by standing committees of the Senate. Of the twenty-nine inquiries (not counting joint ventures with the House of Commons and inquiries restricted to some aspects of the internal business of the Senate) organized during the period 1925–63, sixteen have been handled by special committees and thirteen by standing committees, in the following ratio: four by the Natural Resources committee, three by the committee on Tourist Traffic, two by the committee on Trade Relations and one each by the committees on Finance, Railway, Banking and Commerce, and Immigration and Labour. Although it might be urged that Senate committees could undertake more inquiries than they actually do, it is fair to point out that due to the length of many of the inquiries there has hardly been a year when some inquiry was not under way and there have been many sessions in which more than one inquiry was going on simultaneously.

From the point of view of the nature of their subject-matter, Senate inquiries have covered three main areas of concern; economic matters, whether relating to some broad questions of economy or dealing with some particular facet of the economic life of the country, formed the

[86]For pertinent comments, see Solon Low's speech, *HD, 1954*, p. 5249, and an illuminating article by F. Flaherty, "The Senate Could Take a Hand in Control," *Saturday Night*, March 3, 1945. Speaking of the role of the royal commissions in Canadian Government Prof. Hodgetts, too, urged that a much neglected device was the "wasted assets in the Senate. Good work has been inconspicuously carried on by committees of the Senate, but for problems of long-term implications . . . we could make much more use of these committees than we do at present." *Proceedings* of the 3rd Annual Conference, 1951, Inst. of Public Administration of Canada (Toronto, 1951), p. 365.

subject of inquiry in eighteen out of twenty-nine cases;[87] the second biggest group (eight) concerned matters of sudden incident and of an *ad hoc* nature demanding prompt inquiry;[88] while in three cases the object of Senate inquiries was some aspect of government machinery, usually the operation and administration of certain statutes.[89]

Although nearly all committees to inquire during the period under study have produced a final report,[90] it is possible to make a functional distinction between committees whose chief value lay in the concrete *recommendations* contained in their reports and those whose main contribution lay in the *exposition* of a situation or problem and in the publication of the evidence gathered during the course of the inquiry, rather than in putting forward some specific suggestions. Accordingly, like committees to scrutinize, committees falling into the first category combine the features of committees to inquire and committees to advise; whereas those with an emphasis upon exposition tend to underline the educative role of committees to inquire.

In the first group of committees to inquire, i.e., those which were set up to study a situation, hear the evidence of experts and of interested parties, and draw up proposals to meet the problem, some have indeed

87CNR (Special, 1925); St. Lawrence River (Special, 1928); Trade (Trade, 1932); Cattle Industry (Agriculture, 1933); Sealing and Fishery (Special, 1934); Tourist Trade (Special, 1934); Agriculture (Agriculture, 1934); Railway (Special, 1938); Tidal Power Development in N.B. (Railway, 1944); Tourist Trade (Tourist Trade, 1946); Mining (Natural Resources, 1946); Fertilizers (Natural Resources, 1947); Trade (Trade, 1953); Tourist Trade (Tourist Trade, 1954); Land Use (Special, 1957); Inflation (Finance, 1959); Tourist Trade (Tourist Trade, 1959); Manpower (Special, 1960).

88Copies of Provincial Legislation of Prospectuses . . . (Banking and Commerce, 1929); Judges (Special, 1931); War Co-operation (Special, 1940); Reconstruction (Special 1943); Immigration (Immigration, 1946); Human Rights (Special, 1950); Salacious Literature (Special, 1952); Narcotic Drugs (Special, 1955).

89Canteen and Disablement Funds (Special, 1925); Government Annuities Act (Special, 1936); Income War Tax Act and Excess Profits Tax Act (Special, 1945).

90Apart from interim reports both the special War Co-operation committee in 1940 and the special committee on Post-war Reconstruction in 1943 were brought to an abrupt end; the first because of the allegedly partisan motivations behind the work of the Bureau of Public Information, which prompted Meighen and his colleagues to withdraw from the committee (Meighen to Col. J. Mess, Sept. 7, 1940, and to Sen. Beaubien, Sept. 11, 1940. Meighen Papers, series V, no. 263); the second because it was regarded as being merely a duplication of the work carried out by the House of Common committee on social security and on reconstruction and research. The committee on Trade, which conducted an extended inquiry from 1953 to 1956 on Article 2 of the North Atlantic Treaty, tabled no final report because of failure to obtain the assistance of an economist to help summarize the evidence. *SD, 1956*, p. 352. Similarly, no report was forthcoming from the committee on Tourist Traffic in 1959, which inquired into the activities of various governmental agencies concerned with promoting tourism in Canada.

admirably performed their task. Their success may be measured by the effect of their recommendations upon consequent government action. Thus, for example, both the main suggestions of the committee on Trade in 1932, respecting Canada's trade commissions and the country's cattle export trade, were adopted in subsequent regulations. The committee's report also proved to be the turning point at one of the discussions before a subcommittee of the Imperial Economic Conference, which was meeting in Ottawa the same time.[91] Two years later, in 1934, a special committee on Tourist Trade, under the enthusiastic leadership of Sen. Dennis, urged the appropriation of $150,000 for the establishment of a travel bureau. Within two months the Government set up the Canadian Travel Bureau (which later became a branch of the Department of Trade and Commerce), consisting of a director and an advisory council, as suggested by the Senate's committee. Also, gradually, the committee's recommendation that the Canadian system of national parks be extended to embrace all the provinces had been generally implemented throughout the years.[92] In a similar way, although not immediately upon their presentation, the recommendations of the Natural Resources committee examining into the economic value of metalliferous mines in Canada in 1946 found their way into the Government's legislative program; they formed the basis of the Emergency Gold Mining Assistance bill of 1948, which aimed at keeping the gold mining industry productive.[93] In the same session the committee on Immigration and Labour, on the motion of Sen. Roebuck, began its inquiry, extended over three parliamentary sessions, into Canada's immigration policy. Apart from its services of educating public opinion, it brought in a great number of practical suggestions, the most important of them concerning the adoption of a selective immigration policy consistent with Canada's economic and absorptive capacity.[94] Indeed, in the light of the committee's report and of the sympathetic reception which was accorded to it throughout the land[95] the Government decided to widen the classes of admissible persons, and open the door in the years 1946 and 1947 to twice as many people, including the Polish soldiers and the war brides with their children, as reached the Canadian shores during the previous six years.[96]

[91]Report, *SJ, 1932*, pp. 258 ff. *SD, 1933*, pp. 386–7.
[92]Report, *SJ, 1934*, pp. 205–13. *SD, 1934*, pp. 400–4. *Canadian Annual Review, 1934*, p. 111. *SD*, 1946, p. 651.
[93]Report, *SJ, 1946*, pp. 283 ff.
[94]*SJ, 946*, p. 503.
[95]*SD, 1947*, p. 99.
[96]*Ibid., 1947*, p. 588. For congratulatory remarks upon the committee's accomplishments see *inter alia* the comments of Mr. Castledon (CCF, Yorkton) and of Mr. Hlynka (SC, Vegreville) in the Commons on April 28 and May 2 respectively.

Still in 1946 one of the most successful special committees of the Senate in recent times presented the results of two years' extensive inquiries into the operation and administration of Canada's income tax legislation. The effects of its far-reaching and widely publicized work under Sen. Euler were borne out in the Income Tax bill of 1948, which admittedly resulted from the committee's three principal recommendations; it simplified and clarified the law (Part II of the committee's report); it set up the Income Tax Appeal Board for a cheap, easy, and expeditious machinery of appeal with powers over both law and fact (Part I of the report);[97] and although it did not entirely adopt the committee's recommendation for an elimination of ministerial discretion, it carried further the work of reducing the number of discretions vested in the minister to a few minor instances relating to departmental mechanics.[98]

Sometimes it may take several years for a committee's recommendations to be adopted by the Government, but if they are sound and properly substantiated they will be put into effect sooner or later. The interval was probably longest in the case of the Senate's special committee on narcotic drugs, which brought forward its well-documented recommendations in 1955 for increased penalties for trafficking in narcotic drugs on the federal level and for more humane treatment of drug addicts on the provincial level. The committee's recommendations were accepted *in toto*. The Government of British Columbia, where the problem was perhaps most acute, soon made arrangements along the lines suggested in the committee's report.[99] On the federal level the desired legislation was brought down in 1957 as a Senate bill, but owing to the early dissolution of Parliament it died on the Commons' order paper after receiving first reading. With the change of government the measure was temporarily shelved and was not proceeded with until 1961. In that session the Narcotic Control bill, a replica of the 1957 bill, was introduced in Parliament and quickly passed both houses.

In the second group of committees to inquire the emphasis is not on the short-term practicability of the committee's reports. They may or may not contain recommendations, but their real value lies in the long-term educative effect produced by the accumulated evidence and information of their proceedings. Instead of being a cure-all, they are rather a contribution to the study of the subject and form the basis of further discussions in Parliament, in the departments of government concerned,

[97]The record of the Board in the first six years fully justified its establishment. Of a total of 2,463 appeals launched from 1949–55, 40 per cent were allowed in whole or in part. Cf. *ibid., 1956*, p. 976.

[98]*Ibid., 1946*, p. 556.

[99]*Ibid., 1955*, p. 730.

and in the public at large. Their most obvious use is in areas where the problems are either still too rudimentary, or too controversial, or too elusive and big for simple and straightforward solutions. Thus, for example, the special committee that inquired into "the matter of the development and improvement of the St. Lawrence River" in 1928 made no recommendations whatsoever; its work was confined to compiling all the information bearing on the project, and the report, printed in Blue Book form, became one of the most authoritative works on the subject. Similarly, in the case of the special committee studying the highly controversial railway situation in 1925 and again in 1938–9, the actual recommendations of the committee were certainly overshadowed by the significance of its bringing together the relevant views of the country's leading business and railroad experts.

Surely the value of the work of the special committee on human rights and fundamental freedoms in 1950 went beyond the committee's tentative suggestion for the adoption of a declaration of human rights as an interim device until the time when a national bill of rights could be incorporated in the Constitution.[100] The committee's primary concern was to do something to educate opinion, "to 'keep the ball in the air,' to have people continually thinking on this subject of human rights, of respect for the individual, and of the importance of maintaining those right inviolate."[101] From this point of view the inquiry was successful: the spontaneous and quick response to the call of the committee for representations by ethnic and religious groups, civil liberties societies, churches, labour and welfare organizations, newspapers, etc., the calibre of these representations and the high-pitched interest that continued all through the committee's proceedings demonstrated how the idea of a bill of rights had caught the imagination of the people.

In each one of the three big economic inquiries organized by Senate committees during the last five years the idea was again the exposition of the problem rather than its solution. Clearly, neither the problem of inflation, nor the problem of unemployment, or, for that matter, the complex question of land use was likely to be susceptible of an easy and ready-made answer. On the contrary, what was needed was a full, fair, and penetrating analysis of the situation, and this was what the three Senate committees produced. The committee on Finance, studying the threat of inflation in Canada in 1959, considered its primary duty "to get . . . farmers from the West, people from the Maritime provinces, manufacturers, union men, and members of different kinds of organizations across Canada to tell their story."[102] The evidence placed before

[100]Report, *ibid., 1950*, p. 589. [101]*Ibid.*, pp. 97–8. [102]*Ibid., 1959*, p. 1056.

the committee was published in the eleven volumes of the committee's proceeding and constitute a most valuable contribution to the discussion and elucidation of a problem of great economic and social significance. The special committee on land use, 1957–61, which conducted the lengthiest Senate inquiry in modern times, produced a number of interim reports before it brought down its final report in the session of 1961.[103] Although the committee shifted the area of its inquiry every year, by breaking down, through a narrowing process, its general orders of reference to more manageable proportions, and although some of its "incidental" and more technical suggestions were gladly adopted by the Government,[104] it was clear that its real service, like that of the Finance committee, consisted in educating whoever cared to be educated by publishing its more than thirty-four volumes of findings and proceedings, or, as Mr. St. Laurent said in 1957, in bringing "about an atmosphere in which the Canadian public in their threefold capacity of municipal electors, provincial electors and federal electors are going to want to have something done to bring about an improved situation."[105] The Senate's special Manpower committee in 1960–61 went further than any of its predecessors in staying in the background as an adviser to the Government. As Sen. Croll said very succinctly: "The more we considered this unemployment problem in committee the more frightened I became, and the less hopeful I was of our being able to reach a quick solution. Whether this committee, after its study, will be able to suggest a solution, I do not know, but . . . if we cannot suggest a solution, at least we shall be able *to make known the problem which will have to be faced by the country*."[106] To achieve this goal and to avoid duplicating the work of the Gordon Commission on Canada's economic prospects in 1956–57, a good deal of the actual inquiry was entrusted to a five-man research team, each of its members having a particular area to study and report on. The committee's recommendations were, in fact, a summary of the evidence offered to them by this group and by a multitude of interested witnesses who appeared before the committee to make representations. The method of delegating so much of the committee's

[103]*Ibid., 1957*, p. 443; *ibid., 1958*, pp. 634 ff; *ibid., 1959*, pp. 1078 ff; *ibid., 1960*, pp. 1060 ff; *ibid., 1961*, pp. 982 ff, 1024 ff. The committee was reappointed on February 7 and, again, October 18, 1962.

[104]Both the Farm Credit bill of 1959 and the ARDA legislation in 1961 were based on the recommendations contained in the committee's report and evidence. *Ibid., 1962*, p. 88; *ibid., 1962–63*, p. 102. Also, following the recommendation of the committee, a four-man committee of the Department of Agriculture was formed in 1960, which studied and reported on rural development programmes in the USA.

[105]*HD, 1957*, p. 34.

[106]*SD, 1960*, p. 1136. Italic added.

work to a body of experts revealed a new aspect of the usefulness of Senate's committees to inquire. Instead of digging up the material themselves they can act as the centre of a whole system of researchers, experts and other parties, who come and go, bringing their knowledge, findings, and complaints before a body of sympathetic laymen who will examine them, ask questions, and probe further until they get the point and ultimately draw up a report which will be intelligible to the country. They are the vehicle through which the work is done and the work can be done because they give birth and shape to it. This service of animation is perhaps no less important a function than the gathering of the information itself.

Incidental Functions

In addition to the three main functions discussed above, there are certain "incidental" functions regularly performed by committees of the Senate. The term "incidental" is not used in a qualitative sense—the functions that fall under this heading may be just as important as the functions to legislate, to scrutinize, or to inquire. It simply means that during the process of performing their main or principal functions Senate committees perform at the same time, "incidentally," other functions too which are not directly related to the main function but derive from the procedural structure of the Senate's committee work. More light will be shed on the nature of these functions if we add that they can be defined also through a permutation of the chief "characters" on Senate committees. Thus, the confrontation of the "interested party" with the "party man" (i.e., usually the minister) and the "official" will determine the first incidental function performed by Senate committees, that is, to provide an institutional forum for interest articulation within the framework of Parliament. The confrontation of the "layman" (i.e., members of the committees) with the official and the minister will, on the other hand, yield two further incidental functions—the function of educating Senators and the function of forming a liaison between Parliament and government departments.

FORUM FOR INTEREST ARTICULATION

The first of these incidental functions, which is performed by all Senate committees, whether they legislate, scrutinize, or inquire, is to arrange a rendezvous between interested persons or groups of individuals on the one hand, and those who prepare and make legislative policy on the other. As has been suggested earlier, it is a part of the procedure of Senate committees to send out invitations to all those who are known to have an interest in the subject to come before a Senate committee, be it a piece of legislation or a question under inquiry. They can then make representations, either in person or through counsel or through the submission of briefs, letters, or memoranda, in an attempt to influence departmental officials, the deputy minister, the responsible minister, and ultimately the cabinet, before decision is made one way or the other. "It is our part," Sen. Meighen wrote in 1937, "to make sure that conflicting interests from every end of this country have an equal hearing, so that everyone concerned has opportunity to express his view and tell us that this or that provision is not going to work, and why. Thus, all contentions and all arguments are advanced before a Bill takes its final form. This system has been developed very successfully with the full co-operation of both sides of the House. . . ."[107]

Ordinarily, of course, Senate committees are only one of the many media of communication between organized interests and the Government. On occasion, however, they may prove to be, if not the only, at least the main opportunity for various interested bodies to state their case before representatives of the government. It was noted, for example, in the important Estate Tax bill of 1958 that although written representations had been distributed amongst the members of the Commons committee which studied the bill, no one was permitted to present his views in person, and the written representations were not included in the committee's reports.[108] Therefore, when the bill was brought in in the Senate it was of especial significance that such bodies as the Canadian Chamber of Commerce, Sun Life, the Royal Trust Company, the Montreal Trust Company, the Toronto General Trust Company, the Canadian Federation of University Women, the Canadian Committee of the Status of Women, the Canadian Life Insurance Officers Association, and the Imperial Life Company were allowed to appear before the Senate's Banking and Commerce committee, which held two-session daily hearings on five separate occasions.[109]

What can such interested bodies regularly appearing before Senate committees hope for? In many cases the confrontation of the interested party with officials and/or ministers has had a direct effect upon government policy. In the session of 1934, for instance, members of the Agriculture committee, inquiring into Canada's cattle trade, were so much

[107]A. Meighen, "The Canadian Senate," *Queen's Quarterly* (1937), p. 161.
[108]*SD, 1958*, p. 568.
[109]*Proceedings*, nos. 1–5.

impressed by the evidence of a witness trading between Canada and Great Britain that they arranged to have him meet the Minister of Agriculture, who admittedly received useful suggestions from him.[110] The immigration policy of the government in respect of the problem of Chinese residents in Canada separated from their families abroad, on the one hand, and of Estonians then in Sweden, on the other hand, was considerably affected by the report of the Senate's Immigration committee examining Canada's immigration policy in 1948, which, conversely, was based upon the submissions from representatives of these two ethnic groups in Canada.[111] In the case of the Bankruptcy bill of 1949, which was first introduced in the Senate and considered extensively in the Banking and Commerce committee, the two principal amendments inserted in the bill were the direct consequence of hearing the representations of the Canadian Authors' Association and the solicitors for certain banking interests.[112] Similarly, in 1954 the Government quickly acquiesced in the amendments made by the Senate in the Public Service Superannuation bill in response to the representations made before its Banking and Commerce committee by a considerable number of civil servants, who were opposed to the compulsory features of the contemplated group insurance plan.[113] The bill was brought in in the House of Commons only one month before prorogation of Parliament, with the result that there was not adequate time for civil service officials to ascertain the views of rank-and-file members of the staff associations. The Senate amendment, incidentally, was similar to the suggestions put forward by the Opposition in the Commons unsuccessfully.[114] Again, the arguments advanced before the Transport and Communications committee by representatives of the Western Union Company and the Commercial Union Cable Company against certain provisions of the Telegraphs bill in 1956 were effective; after a full morning and afternoon session the Minister conceded to the unusual method of having a statement included in the committee's report as to the way in which certain regulations were to be administered if the bill became law. Although the appearance of such a statement on the record was a matter of good

[110]*Canadian Annual Review, 1934*, p. 113.

[111]*SD, 1948*, pp. 663–6.

[112]*Ibid., 1949* (2nd session), pp. 206 ff, 219.

[113]See Saul J. Frankel, *Staff Relations in the Civil Service* (Montreal, 1962), pp. 100–1.

[114]*HD, 1954*, p. 6705. "There is one very interesting lesson from this event," Mr. Macdonnell (PC, Greenwood) said. "It is interesting to realize that this shows that there is one deliberative body of Parliament, namely, the Senate . . . They weighed the evidence. They considered the interests of those affected, which does seem a reasonable course." *Ibid.*, p. 6700.

faith rather than a question relating to the law, it gave some assurance to the parties concerned and dispelled doubts about the intentions of the Government.[115]

Indeed, even where interested parties failed to produce a direct effect upon government policy, they could at least feel they had had their day in court. Most of them seem to appreciate this official hearing at the eleventh hour and leave satisfied with the objectivity, informality, courtesy, and attention which they received at the hands of the members of the committee.[116] Moreover, they can always hope that in the long run their views will be brought to bear upon the policy of the Government and find their way into some form of legislative action. The main characters in the performance of this function, it is to be noted, are the interested party and those speaking on behalf of the Government, with Senators discretely keeping in the background. The stage, it should be emphasized, however, is set in the Senate committees, whose role as a host forms an important element of the political process.

EDUCATION AND LIAISON

The other two incidental functions performed by Senate committees are to educate the Senators themselves and to contribute to the harmonious relationship between Parliament and the civil service. This double function flows from a single confrontation of the "layman" on the one hand and the official and the minister, on the other. One might say that the regular meeting of the two educates both at one and the same time in different ways.

It has been noted earlier[117] that one of the main reasons for an increased utilization of the Senate's standing committees in modern times has been the inadequacy of the information, both political and technical, obtainable on second reading and in committee of the whole. It is in the Senate's standing committees that such information can be gathered from the minister and departmental officials, who are invited to attend and permitted to take a *direct* part in the proceedings.

Indeed, Senators are equally eager to enlarge their knowledge on the political as well as on the technical aspects of legislation. Political information, however, can only be furnished by the political head of a department. Hence the insistence of the members of Senate committees

[115] *SD, 1956*, pp. 987 ff.

[116] See D. S. Robertson, "Business and the Senate," *Canadian Business*, Feb. 1954, and Sen. Roebuck's article "Tinkering with the Senate of Doubtful Value." *Saturday Night*, vol. 27, no. 2 (1954).

[117] Above, pp. 157 ff.

to secure the attendance of ministers as frequently as possible. The work of the Senate's Finance committee over the Estimates during the war is a case in point. The reason for their reference to the committee in anticipation of the Appropriation bills to follow was not so much to suggest economies (the amount of the military estimates was practically fixed and no change could be made in them) as to set up machinery whereby much useful information could be gained from ministers appearing before the committee. Thus, in the session of 1943, for instance, the witnesses included the Minister of Agriculture, Mr. Gardiner; the Minister of Labour, Mr. Mitchell; the Minister of Munitions and Supply, Mr. Howe; the Minister of Defence for Air, Mr. (later Sen.) Power; and the Minister of Naval Affairs, Mr. Macdonald. Each of them was very co-operative and informative. When some piquant questions were put to him, Mr. Power simply turned to the press and said, "This is off the record," then answered the questions. "After hearing him," Sen. Ballantyne, Leader of the Opposition in the Senate, commented, "we could not but feel a greater confidence than ever in the Air Force."[118] Such a galaxy of political star performers has perhaps never again gathered before the same committee in a single session. However, Senate committees, especially the Banking and Commerce and the Transport and Communications committee, have been successful, on the whole, in securing the attendance of members of the Government, particularly on politically contentious pieces of legislation.

Although aware of the rules respecting the political neutrality of civil servants, Senators, especially in the absence of the responsible minister, often try to squeeze out political information from departmental officials. It is the duty of the chairman to foil such attempts. Failure to do so will invariably result in a politely firm rebuff on the part of the officials. Asked, for example, to clear up some difficulty arising out of a provision of the North West Territories bill in 1959, Mr. Driedger, the Deputy Minister of Justice, said: "Perhaps I might state my position here, that I am a civil servant and I could not as a civil servant undertake at the request of the committee of either House to make an amendment that I know is contrary to Government policy. I would have to take my instructions from the Minister of the Cabinet."[119] Similarly, in 1961, replying to a question from Sen. Molson in the Banking and Commerce committee during consideration of the Customs Tariff bill, Dr. Annis, Director of Tariffs, Department of Finance, said evasively: "This in-

[118] *SD, 1943*, p. 403.

[119] *Proceedings* of the Banking and Commerce committee, 1959, p. 33.

volves the quest for an expression of opinion, and as a civil servant I am pretty hesitant in doing that in a matter so controversial as this."[120]

What civil servants can and do answer are questions relating to either the history or the technically involved aspects of the proposed measure. A typical opening question was the one put to Dr. Leaney, a high-ranking expert from the Department of Agriculture, before the special committee inquiring into land use. "Can you tell us," he was asked, "in a very broad way what has been done in the way of soil surveys in Canada up to the present by the Dominion Government."[121] This enabled the witness to present a well-considered and logical summary, which, conversely, helped the members of the committee to proceed with their cross-examination of successive witnesses. The catalogue of government officials appearing before Senate committees during the past three decades indicates that Senators have no reason for complaining about the range and the calibre of government witnesses. They usually include the deputy minister, or at least the assistant deputy minister, and a few other officials immediately connected with the matter before the committee, in addition, of course, to the draftsman representing the Department of Justice. The competence of these people to satisfy even the most probing curiosity on points of detail or administration has never failed to show itself. Even such a well-recognized expert of tax laws as Sen. Hayden had to admit in 1950 with regard to the Income Tax bill that "the only way in which we are going to learn and appreciate just what is intended by these amendments is to have them explained by the proper officials."[122] Apart from their sheer educative value the explanations offered by departmental officials may often have the effect of withering opposition and forestalling proposed amendments. "After listening to the splendid explanations given by the officials in committee," Sen. Macdonald thought "it was advisable to go along with the bill as it is now worded" despite earlier attempts to amend it.[123] Similarly, although one of the sharpest critics of the Combines Investigation bill in 1960 on second reading, Sen. Hayden felt quite satisfied after the committee meeting. "As far as I am concerned," he said, "I have had my

[120]*Proceedings* of the Banking and Commerce committee, 1961, p. 127. In another case, in 1960, noting that no minister was present when the Old Age Security bill was considered in Banking and Commerce committee, Sen. Reid complained: "It is true that there were two highly qualified and skilled servants of the Government there . . . but there were one or two questions we raised with regard to matters of policy which should have been answered by a minister, and which the officials could not answer." *SD, 1960*, p. 842.

[121]*Proceedings* of the Special Committee on Land Use, no. 1, p. 7.

[122]*SD, 1950*, p. 337. [123]Agricultural Stabilization bill, *ibid., 1957–58*, p. 544.

day in court. . . . From the indications we had in committee there certainly appeared to be a full and complete understanding of the scope and effect of the bill," and he let the bill pass as drafted.[124]

But the confrontation of the official with the layman, the civil servant with members of the Senate, has other beneficial effects than simply educating the legislators on points of technical and historical detail. It contributes to the harmonious relationship between Parliament and the departments in two distinct ways. On the one hand, through a day-to-day contact, continued session after session in the informal atmosphere of the committee room, with the spokesmen of practically all government departments, and, consequently, through a firsthand knowledge of the working and the policy of these departments, the problems of administration and the mentality of the administrator, Senators have gradually adopted a new attitude towards civil servants, discarding the romantic fears of the *New Despotism*. Voicing the sentiment of the Senate, Sen. Fraser of Ontario said after the nine standing committees had completed their study of the estimates in 1950: "it is incumbent upon this honourable body to recognize the fact that in this Dominion we have the highest type of senior civil servants to be found in the Commonwealth."[125] Similarly, so much impressed were the members of the Senate's special committee on Manpower with the competence of civil servants and their genuine concern about the problems confronting the country that the committee's 1961 report made special tributes to their services.[126]

On the other hand, this meeting of the "lay sense" with the "official sense," which Bagehot considered to be so important for effective democratic government, has something very definite to offer to departmental officials also. Indeed, they welcome every opportunity to appear informally before the Senate committee and to tell that committee about their duties and problems. After eight years of experience as chairman of one of the Senate's most important committees, Sen. Hugessen found "that the departmental officials were only too glad to have the opportunity of appearing before a committee of this House and explaining to the committee the work that they were doing. *They do not often get that opportunity*. The [House of Commons], for reasons of its own, has not sufficient time to devote to these things. . . ."[127] When they come, officials must be prepared to answer such questions as: "Why is it necessary to enact this particular amendment? What are the circumstances which give rise to this amendment? Illustrate by example what you are intending to cover here." Through the ensuing exchange of thought

[124]*Ibid., 1960*, p. 1196.
[125]*Ibid., 1950*, p. 558.
[126]*Proceedings*, p. 7.
[127]*SD, 1958*, p. 57. Italic added.

around the committee table they not only can learn that members of the Senate are not *a priori* enemies of executive departments—a belief no less fallacious than the one about conspiring bureaucrats; in the course of question and answer, while trying to explain the reasons for, and the scope of, the different activities of their departments and of justifying the expenditures of public funds needed for the purpose of carrying on these activities, officials of the government will also have to plead and argue and reason in order to persuade a group of sympathetic laymen, many of them lawyers and some having extensive administrative experience. In brief, they are compelled to think—a virtue that so often tends to be overlooked in the routine of government. The upshot, it is hoped, will be a more intimate relationship between Parliament and bureaucracy.

Part III

THE SENATE AT WORK: ITS SUBSTANTIVE ROLE

THE SENATE *VERSUS* THE EXECUTIVE

10

THE TECHNICAL REVISION OF LEGISLATION, the initiation of public and private bills, and the organization of general debates—the three functions discussed in Part II—have been grouped together under the heading of the technical role of the Upper House, because their discharge required no principle or ideological stand on the part of the Senate. Indeed, their success could be measured by the effectiveness of the Senate to render the expression of the principle, as formulated by the Government and (in case of revision) endorsed by the Commons, more consistent without effecting or deviating from the principle itself.

In contrast, in its substantive role the Senate influences legislation from a distinct ideological standpoint. We have seen[1] that the modern substantive function of second chambers in countries adhering to the cabinet system has been shaped by the changed relationship between Parliament and the executive, which, conversely was simply a constitutional reflection of the economic and social changes brought about by the transition from the *laissez-faire* state of the nineteenth century to the positive state of the present one. Although antagonisms towards these two sides of the new situation very often go hand in hand, in fact a distinction must be made between policies reasserting nineteenth century Whiggism in its entirety, including its economic and social tenets, and policies reasserting only its political values—between antagonism towards the economic/social achievements of the positive state and antagonism simply towards cabinet preponderance. Accordingly, one can discern various degrees of conservatism in the attitude of political institutions towards policies emanating from the new *status quo*. Perhaps the two

[1]Above, Introduction.

best known examples of virulent opposition to such policies were the consistent stand taken by the United States Supreme Court in its "activist" period of "substantive due process" on the one hand, and the emasculating by a still powerful House of Lords of the progressive legislation of the Liberal Government during the first decade of the present century, on the other hand. Since in both cases the target of the obstruction was the principles of "collectivism" the attitudes of the institutions concerned could justly be considered reactionary, for in their resistance to the new they were doggedly trying to uphold the obsolete elements in the old.

The question that must here be faced is whether the conservatism which is usually associated with the Senate has been aimed at arresting or retarding the movement towards the "positive" state in Canada during the last thirty-seven years, or, to put it bluntly, whether the Senate has been a reactionary institution in the Canadian political system. Often the mode of composition may be a fairly accurate indication of the ideological preferences of a second house of legislature. While direct election by the people will in all probability produce a body with sympathies identical with those of the Lower House, a system of indirect election through various intermediary associations generally tends to introduce an element of conservatism into the character of the house. So does, indeed, the method of heredity. On the other hand, appointment by the Government is not necessarily conducive to any particular "Weltanschauung," as the people responsible for the appointment are free to choose whatever type of persons they wish to. Radical critics of the Senate have repeatedly warned, however, that because of the overrepresentation of vested interests in its membership the Senate was likely to prevent the enactment of "popular legislation."[2] Thus, speaking on the question of Senate reform in the House of Commons in 1925 the Rev. A. J. Lewis (Progressive, Swift Current) asked: "How can you expect that when any democratic government wished to bring forward legislation for the well-being of the Canadian common people that these men will not nullify it?"[3] And writing in 1935 the authors of *Social Planning for Canada* concluded:

> . . . in recent years, the real function of the Senate has been to act as a bulwark of property interests, i.e., of the interests of large property owners, individual or corporate. The remarkable number of company directorships

[2]See "Canada the Siren," *Forum*, Sept. 1938; "Ottawa's House of Lords," *Saturday Night*, Sept. 10, 1938. Also Woodworth's speech in the House of Commons in 1927. *HD*, p. 1036.

[3]*HD, 1925*, pp. 434–5.

held by Senators is the most significant fact about our upper house . . . the real motive is, of course, the services they are expected to render in throwing out bills of which these corporations do not approve. The Senate has, in fact, become one additional line of defence for the real ruling classes in this country.[4]

Although these expectations and fears have never really materialized it is true that during the years preceding the great depression the Senate showed an unfriendly sensitivity to legislation implementing "collectivist" principles. This attitude was detected in its initial stage by Professor Mackay, who studied the Senate prior to 1925 and found that in the matter of government ownership of railways and in the construction and control of other public works the Senate did not hesitate to use its power of amending or vetoing legislation.[5] It needs be emphasized, however, that from the point of view of composition the really decisive factor was not so much the number of directorships held by individual Senators as the sociological fact that the membership of the Senate in this period still represented the pioneer psychology of individualism characteristic of the pioneer phase of Canadian history. We have seen[6] that at the beginning of the period under study the largest single element in the Senate's membership was made up of manufacturers most of whom had made their fortunes as self-made men in the pioneer era of Canada. In addition to them, there were many, appointed by both Conservative and Liberal governments, who had moved in the early days from Ontario, Quebec, and the Atlantic provinces to the West to play the role of the pioneer in the settlement of the provinces of Alberta, Manitoba, and Saskatchewan. Some of them were farmers, others were merchants. But they were all self-made men. The Turriffs, the Lessards, the Willoughbys, the Rosses, the Kents, the Burnses, the Rileys, the Johnstons, the Calders were all rugged individualists, imbued with the spirit of the expanding frontier, who from humble circumstances by dint of native ability and concentrated effort fought every inch of the way and marched steadily to posts of distinction both in the professional and in the political life of the country. They assumed heavy responsibilities and occasionally sustained tremendous losses, but they had the unbreakable spirit of the pioneer and a complete confidence in the efficacy and power of self-reliance. As a result of their presence, the Senate represented not so much the rich as the successful. Politically, surely, they had a genuine aversion to socialisms of all brands or anything that smacked of socialistic

[4]*Social Planning for Canada* (Toronto, 1935), p. 500.
[5]R. A. Mackay, *The Unreformed Senate of Canada* (London, 1926), p. 137.
[6]Above, p. 67.

ideas. Because of its attempts to apply the "Weltanschauung" of an earlier epoch to the conditions of the late 1920's the dominant element in the Senate's membership was bound to come into conflict with some of the legislation presented to Parliament in the years 1925–30. Indeed, during this period the Senate acted in rather reactionary manner, not altogether different from the behaviour of the House of Lords some twenty years earlier. In 1925 it killed the Canada Temperance bill, whose object was to empower the provinces that had control of the sale of liquor to prohibit its importation by any private citizen or any export house. Led by Sen. J. D. Reid, the majority of the Senate rushed to the rescue of the export warehouses, whose only motive was "the greed for lucre that they wish to put into their pockets, and who do not care a tinker's damn how they do it so long as they make the money."[7] In the following session the Senate committed its most notorious act of defiance of popular policies in modern times by rejecting the Government's Old Age Pensions bill, which was to supplement (after a means test) the income of people of 70 years of age or over up to $365 a year. Although the grant was not to be made direct to the pensioner by the Dominion Government but was to be subject to an agreement with the provinces whereby they would contribute one half of the pension and provide the machinery for administration, all those who spoke against the measure on second reading posed as the champions of provincial rights. The federal argument thus once again proved an effective weapon in the service of Whig policies. But the real motivation behind the obstruction can be gathered from Sen. Beaubien's anticipatory remarks in 1925: "The very same people who are now demanding the removal of the Senate are the people who are asking for legislation to fix the scale of wages, the control of labour contracts, unemployment insurance, and old age pensions. . . . How could they ever expect to get this country to pass such legislation . . . so long as this House remains in existence? No, they know it, and therefore, not being able to surmount the obstacle, they want to blow it out of the way."[8]

Typical also of the Senate's attitude during this period was its uncompromising stand towards two pieces of Government legislation aimed at offsetting the exceptional legislation arising out of the excitement accompanying the Winnipeg strike of 1919, and at restoring normalcy in Canadian penal legislation. One was the bill to repeal section 41 of the Immigration Act, under which British subjects, not

[7]The remarks of Sir George E. Foster, who supported the measure. *SD, 1925*, pp. 720, 726.

[8]*Ibid.*, p. 63.

Canadian citizens, could be deported without trial. It was rejected by the Senate in both 1926 and 1927, for fear that its passage would encourage Communist infiltration in Canada.[9] The other was the measure to repeal section 98 of the Criminal Code enacted in 1919 to deal with "unlawful associations." Although organized labour considered the section of the Code prejudicial to its interests and the Trades and Labour Congress made annual representation to the Government for its repeal, and although the desired legislation was passed every year by the House of Commons, the Senate consistently refused to consent to it in 1926, 1927, 1928, 1929, and 1930. The majority of the Senate held that communism was still making headway in Canada and if the clause were repealed there would be no provision in the Code to deal swiftly with agitators seeking to overthrow the government.[10] In 1930 Sen. Murdock, a former Minister of Labour and for many years Vice-President of the Brotherhood of Railroad Trainmen, made a determined attempt to change the mind of the majority of the Senate and in an eloquent speech pleaded "on behalf of the tens of thousands of reputable and upright Canadian citizens belonging to labour organizations. . . ."[11] However, it was to no avail. Sen. Willoughby, one of the most stubborn opponents of repeal, threatened to talk out Murdock's amendment; but it was negatived by 18 votes to 14, without his taking the trouble.

Never again did the Senate embark upon such an unpopular and retrogressive course of policy. The Whiggish sentiment, so effective in rousing the Senate to action before 1930, has been restricted to isolated and individual occurrences after that date. Whilst individual members of the house may have continued their animosity to the phenomenon of expanding state services the Senate *as an institution* has never again tried to retard or obstruct that trend. The continual emergencies caused by the economic crisis of the thirties, the war, and the problems of post-war reconstruction have certainly had an awakening effect upon the attitude of the Upper House as regards the necessity of various social welfare measures and of increasing state intervention in the economic and social sector of the nation's life. Thus, in 1930, only four years after the rejection of the Old Age Pensions bill, the Senate passed without dissent the War Veterans' Allowance bill and the Pension bill, although

[9]*Ibid., 1926*, pp. 237–52; *ibid., 1927*, p. 390.

[10]*Ibid., 1926*, pp. 270 ff; *ibid., 1927*, p. 389; *ibid., 1928*, p. 507; *ibid., 1929*, p. 388; *ibid., 1930*, pp. 411–2. Its attitude is hardly rendered more creditable by the fact "that the government and many members of the House of Commons welcomed or at least acquiesced in" the rejection of the legislation. Mackay, *The Unreformed Senate* (1963), p. 125.

[11]*Ibid., 1930*, p. 409.

it was brought home to the members that the measures were not pension legislation in the narrow sense but rather represented an advanced step in social legislation.[12] In the same session the Senate gave its unreserved approval to the Fair Wages and Eight-Hour Day bill, which sought to establish statutory authority for the observance of fair wages and hours on all contracts for federal works.[13]

In 1931 two private members' bills, reminiscent of the ill-famed provisions in the Immigration bill and the Criminal Code, were introduced in the Senate in rapid succession by Sen. Casgrain, one of the most consistently outspoken Whigs in the House. The bills, the Registration bill and the Identification of Aliens bill, required the registration of all alien subjects in Canada, on the ground of communist danger in the country. Significantly, however, they were unable to make any progress in the Senate this time. Speakers from both sides of the house rose one after the other to warn against "becoming a little hysterical on the subject of Bolshevists and Communists." Sen. Logan found the measures "mysterious," Sir G. E. Foster called them "inquisitive," while to Gordon they appeared "absurd and ridiculous."[14] Sen. Hughes of Prince Edward Island, whose views came closest to what might be called Christian socialism, reminded the Senate that "revolutions were inevitable unless drastic changes were made in the economic condition of the world. . . . If this country and the other nations of the world can make conditions better for their people than they are in Russia, Soviet propaganda will have no effect. If conditions are not made better, these registration cards will not give much protection."[15] And when Sen. Casgrain and his confrère Sen. Beaubien,[16] called him a communist, he gave the following reply: "My hon. friend is opposed to what would really help. . . . I am afraid he belongs to that class of people who are opposed to doing anything that will really assist in making the people satisfied and prosperous, and thereby preventing revolution. We cannot have true prosperity so long as a great many of our people are bordering on a state of destitution while on the other hand we have hundreds of millionaires who are rolling in wealth."[17] These were hard words to be

[12]*Ibid.*, pp. 328–9.

[13]*Ibid., 1930*, pp. 244, 287.

[14]*Ibid., 1931*, pp. 101, 102.

[15]*Ibid.*, p. 253.

[16]He supported the bill by saying: "This measure was intended for people of a very different kind from those with whom you and I associate. It is all very well for you or for me to stand up in this House and say: 'I should not like to displease the excellent company in which I move.' But what about the slums?" *Ibid.*, p. 456.

[17]*Ibid.* In a similar vein Sen. Murdock said during a debate on the League of Nations in 1934: ". . . I hold here and now that the capitalist and the capitalistic institutions of this and other countries of the world are alone responsible for the

uttered in the Red Chamber, but they revealed the great impact made by the exigencies of the time upon the outlook of a growing number of Senators. The Registration bill was negatived on second reading by 20 votes to 12; the Identification of Aliens bill was withdrawn soon afterwards. Their defeat marked an important victory of the progressive element in the Senate.

The attitude displayed by the majority of the Senate in 1930 and 1931 set the tone for the years ahead. When in 1933 a small group of Senators, including Calder, Aylesworth, and Beaubien (two Conservatives and one Liberal), moved an amendment to strike out Part III of the CN-CPR bill providing for compulsory arbitration by a tribunal in cases of conflict between the two railway systems, on the ground that "why should we as a Parliament intrude in the affairs of a corporation which is privately owned," they were bluntly told that "it is time that they divested themselves of those ideas and realized that the rank and file of Canadian citizens are looking at things through different spectacles today, that most of them are . . . sick and tired of this never-ending catering to the rich or nearly rich, and the big fellow."[18] Thereupon the amendment was negatived on an unrecorded division.[19] No more successful was Sen. Casgrain with his private members' bill in 1935 aimed at deleting section 498 from the Criminal Code dealing with unlawful agreements. He found himself completely isolated and his argument that the anti-combine law was unfair to those who wanted to establish combines brought loud protests of "Oh, Oh" from his colleagues. Finally, Sen. Dandurand, his own Leader, after urging that the Senate "must see the signs of the times and recognize them," moved that the bill be given a six months' hoist, which was adopted without division.[20]

The Senate's attitude was equally impeccable with regard to the contentious "reform legislation" introduced in the last session of the 17th Parliament. Despite shocked protests from the usual quarters, there was no attempt on the part of the Senate as a whole to challenge the legislative program of the Government. In replying to the traditional die-hards who denounced "at the drop of the hat" all forms of public ownership, whether municipal, provincial, or federal, as an absurdity and contrary to the law of nature,[21] Meighen was speaking on behalf of the whole House when he said that "with respect to enterprises of a national

---

wars that have taken place heretofore; and that if another war comes it will be largely, if not entirely, the result of either their activity or their inactivity in this matter." *Ibid., 1934*, p. 327.

[18] *Ibid., 1933*, p. 288.

[19] *Ibid.*, p. 305.

[20] *Ibid., 1935*, p. 252.

[21] *Ibid.*, pp. 15 ff., 27, 425.

or state character, particularly where the amount of capital is great in relation to the labour required, it is very probably that in these days public ownership and operation will be the better."[22] He also stated in solemn terms that there were "in this country to-day tens of thousands suffering, through no fault of their own, the consequences of the industrial evolution of the last twenty-five years. That they will continue to suffer unless new steps are taken, we must all admit. That they should not suffer under a properly regulated economy, we must also all admit."[23] Voicing the sentiment of the "official opposition" in the Senate, Sen. Dandurand said that although he had been brought up in the liberal school of economy, "by studying the situation of the labourer," he had gradually come to the conclusion that unemployment insurance and other aspects of social legislation were an absolute necessity.[24]

Accordingly, all the six ILO conventions were passed by an impressive vote of 45 to 3, only Senators Lemieux, Lacasse, and Aylesworth protesting against what they considered to be a violation of the Constitution, "as it was given to us by the Fathers of Confederation."[25] The three bills that followed (Minimum Wage, Limitation of Hours of Work, and Weekly Day of Rest) as well as those springing from the recommendations of the Price Spread Committee (including the Companies bill, the Fisherman's Loan bill, the Combines Investigation bill, the Dominion Trade and Industry Commission bill and the Fair Wages and Hours bill) and the many others that were designed to improve the situation of the farmer (Canadian Wheat Board, Farmers' Creditors Arrangement, Farm Loan) or to meet problems of a general nature (Dominion Housing, Public Works Programme, Employment and Social Insurance) encountered no serious opposition in the Senate either on second reading or in committee or on third reading. Indeed, where amendments were made they were all intended to improve the administration or to broaden the scope of the principle involved.[26]

It is probably true to say that the Senate, or, at any rate, the majority of its members (which practically means the same thing), came out of the period 1930–35 with a matured and considerably changed outlook on the problem of the role of the state in the twentieth century. The Senate's Conservative majority made no attempt to block or to amend in principle the Bank of Canada bill in 1936, which established a predominance of public ownership in the share of the Bank and gave sufficient voting power to the Government to control the majority of the

[22]*Ibid.*, p. 29.
[23]*Ibid.*, p. 32.
[24]*Ibid.*, p. 185; 428.
[25]*Ibid.*, pp. 83–5.
[26]Above, p. 184; *SD, 1935*, p. 415.

board of directors. Similarly, when in 1937 Sen. Duff, of the same school that had so adequately been represented by Casgrain, Beaubien, and Aylesworth, earlier, criticized the Home Improvement Loans Guarantee bill as "that kind of legislation which tends to inculcate in the minds of the people the idea that whenever anyone gets in difficulty . . . he can turn to the Government and have his affairs straightened out," he was told by Meighen that "extraordinary circumstances justify extraordinary measures," and that the depression and its aftermath were such extraordinary circumstances.[27] He received another rebuke in the same session from Sen. Dandurand for his unbridled attack upon the bill to set up the TCA. Rigidly hostile to the principle of government ownership he was opposed to what he called "the rate-payers of the country being saddled with another white elephant," and urged that the services contemplated in the legislation should be entirely left to private enterprise. Told that "in the past a vast majority of the people have voted for state ownership, and we must bow to the will of that majority,"[28] he began "to think I was perhaps losing my grasp on social and financial matters and . . . was getting to be old-fashioned,"—a statement which no one took up to challenge.

Although in 1939 and in 1940 there was some hostility to such measures as the Farmers' Creditors Arrangement bill, the Central Mortgage Bank bill, and the Unemployment Insurance bill, the core of the opposition in each case was Meighen, whose growing bitterness and conservatism had partly been caused, no doubt, by "his measureless contempt" for Mackenzie King and partly by a more general pessimism over the direction in which things seemed to be developing.[29] Commenting on the popularity of these legislative measures, he remarked: "They may be popular, it is true, but if popularity is to be the final test of a measure's merits, then good-bye to democracy, good-bye to liberty."[30] On another occasion, speaking of the Central Mortgage Bank bill, he said that the legislation was no more nor less than "an election measure . . . a sell-out of this country's integrity for a mess of ballots."[31] It should be added, however, that in spite of his stand all these bills were duly passed into law.

The tradition which seemed to emerge during the 1930's survived into the post-war years, and remained the dominant attitude of the Senate throughout the 1950's. Although individual voices continued to be raised against the by now established practices of the "positive state," and although such objections, as a rule, were very ably articulated, they

[27] *SD, 1937*, pp. 99, 100. [28] *Ibid.*, p. 295.
[29] See Roger Graham, *Arthur Meighen*, vol. 3, in particular, pp. 71–2 and 95.
[30] *SD, 1939*, p. 578. [31] *Ibid.*, p. 589.

never succeeded in carrying the majority of the Senate with them. In view of the ever diminishing size of the Conservative group in the House the clash of ideas occurred within the Liberal camp itself between the liberal wing and the conservative wing of the party. On the one hand, there was a handful of those who were bewildered by their Party's adopting legislative programs so contrary to the traditional Liberal-Whig principles and moving steadily and gradually towards the Left. Referring to the bill to extend the application of the Canadian Wheat Board Act to oats and barley in 1948 Sen. Vien said that it was "opposed to the fundamental principles of the Liberal Party." And he charged that "during the past few years due either to war or other emergency conditions, the Government of this country has placed upon our statute books a great deal of socialistic legislation. But none of it has been more socialistic than the measure establishing the Wheat Board itself. . . . Therefore, I hate the Wheat Board and the legislation under which it operates just as much as I hate this particular feature of the bill now before us."[32]

Probably the most representative and most distinguished member of this group has been Sen. Crerar. A former Progressive, who later joined the Liberal party, he has fought unremittingly against everything that went beyond the nineteenth century concept of the state. If it had been for him to decide, there would be no crown corporations,[33] no state interference of any kind, no unemployment insurance, no old age pension, no family allowances, or similar benefits. Speaking on one of the favourite targets of his attacks, the Canadian Wheat Board, which he regarded as inimical of man's natural rights, he stated in 1950:

> This is not the kind of legislation under which this country has been developed. It has been the self-reliance and initiative of our individual citizens which in the space of eighty years has developed our vast resources. If our forefathers or even our fathers had been asked in their day to contemplate legislation of this kind . . . they would have trampled it into the dust. This is not the way by which Canada has developed, and it is not the way in which its greatness can be preserved.[34]

He had the same Whiggish misgivings about social legislation in general. The reports of the Finance committee during the term of his chairmanship were turned into his personal messages, in which he cautioned, warned, and admonished against government spending for social

[32]*Ibid., 1948*, p. 311.

[33]Cf. his remarks on the Research Council bill and the Government Companies Operation bill. *Ibid., 1946*, pp. 400–1.

[34]*Ibid., 1950*, pp. 461 ff. For similar views on the same subject see in particular *ibid., 1948*, p. 310; *ibid., 1953*, pp. 456–7.

purposes.[35] In 1955 he summed up his opinion on the matter in this way: "The more the idea grows in the mind of the individual that in some beneficient fashion the state is going to aid him and look after him the more you undermine his concept of freedom and liberty and his concept of responsible government."[36] With the passage of time his views hardened; in 1958 he virtually equated the welfare state with totalitarianism[37] and two years later, on the occasion of setting up a special committee on manpower, while repudiating the notion of the state taking care of the jobless, he gave the following classic formulation of his Whig philosophy: ". . . we are creating conditions which in the end, if they continue to develop as they have over the past fifteen years, will make democratic government an impossibility. I think that country is best governed which has the least government necessary to maintain law and order, to maintain defence and to see that equity and justice is done. . . ."[38]

In him, then, we have the recognized spokesman of the group of Liberal Senators whose unyielding stand on economic and social questions has repeatedly brought them into conflict with the official policy of their party and government. Implicit in their attitude was the notion that since their party had abandoned its traditional principles they were absolved from serving it with the same old loyalty. They formed a link with those Liberal Senators who directly or indirectly helped to defeat the Old Age Pensions bill in 1926 because it was a negation of all the ideas they cherished and stood for.[39] However, unlike 1926 they were now in a minority. Despite the sincerity and forcefulness of their argument they failed ever to dominate the Senate. A new "Senate generation" had grown up, conscious of the need of positive state action and progressive in its outlook on economic and social policies. "Canada is marching on," Sen. Farquhar said in 1951, "and I feel that . . . some of the older members in this Chamber have not kept pace with Canada; possibly some of us have held too strongly to the old school of thought and have not kept up with changing conditions. . . . As Canada develops and goes ahead we cannot always obtain guidance by looking back to the old days when we were boys. What we did then is not necessarily what should be done today. Sometimes we hear people say that they are Liberals of the old school. Well, I think that Liberals, too, are changing, in keeping with the spirit of the times."[40] Similarly, Sen. Hugessen, one

[35]See in particular the Reports in 1951, 1952 and 1955 in *ibid., 1951*, p. 716; *ibid., 1952*, p. 532; *ibid., 1955*, pp. 627–8.
[36]*Ibid., 1955*, p. 451. [37]*Ibid., 1958*, p. 57. [38]*Ibid., 1960*, p. 559.
[39]Above, p. 120. [40]*SD, 1951*, pp. 306–7.

of the leading figures in the Senate during the past two decades, warned against the tendency "to go back, as it were, to the days of our youth . . . and to think that things were so much better when we were younger than they are today." And addressing his words to Sen. Crerar, he urged: "Let us not become old mossbacks together, but let us keep abreast of the times."[41] With the change in the chairmanship of the Finance committee the tone of the committee's reports has changed significantly. In a posthumous report in 1958 the new chairman, Sen. Hawkins, gave the following succinct résumé of his views: "There is a concept of government with which I most heartily agree and it is that, after the maintenance of law and order [here is where Crerar stopped] their next responsibility should be the creation of conditions wherein each citizen would have an opportunity to help himself, improve his own position and participate with his fellows in achieving a satisfactory standard of living."[42] This "new look" on the role of the state and the Senate's attitude to it was well summed up by Sen. Hayden, chairman of the all-important Banking and Commerce committee, in 1960. Arguing for the desirability of a special inquiry into employment conditions in Canada he maintained that the association between private enterprise and government had acquired a new character after the war and that it "must continue developing, because in our economy we have a changing situation. Our approach to it, and the policies that we adopt from time to time to deal with, *must be flexible as the changing situation itself*. . . . Government . . . must be fully informed at all times so as to be able to move in and deal with particular circumstances that are disturbing the economy and leading to unemployment."[43]

Views put forward during the same period concerning social legislation reveal a similar understanding on the part of the majority of the Senators. Strongly in favour of the family allowance system, Sen. Roebuck, one of the most outstanding individual rights men in the Senate in recent times, rejected fears that the scheme might rob employers of occasional child labour. "Now is not that sad!" he exclaimed. "I find it very difficult to be sympathetic to those estimable citizens who wish to rob the playgrounds for messengers to ride bicycles through dangerous streets delivering parcels for a pittance, or to sell newspapers on busy corners or sweep floors in factories. I say that if Family Allowances have made it impossible to use children in this manner I am strongly for family allowances."[44] Speaking on the Old Age Security bill in 1951 Sen. Reid reminded his colleagues of the sad

[41] *Ibid., 1954*, pp. 280–1.
[42] *Ibid., 1958*, p. 754.
[43] *Ibid., 1960*, pp. 614–15. Italic added.
[44] *Ibid.*, 1949, p. 206.

fate of a similar measure a quarter of a century before. "Today, however, we see all parties agreeing with the Government in this forward legislation. . . . Today we are on the march, and social welfare is inevitable." Thrift, he said, "is outmoded, out of date . . . and today our people are looking to the state, to the government to take care of almost every phase of our life."[45] Contributing to the same debate, Sen. Petten of Newfoundland greeted the measure as "the tangible expression of a growing awareness on the part of the Government of its social responsibilities." Then he added: "Fifty years ago, in a much simpler society, there was little need for old age pensions, but in today's urban and highly industrialized society *there is an urgent need for organized social action to correct the imbalances and inequalities of our system.*"[46] And convinced of the absolute necessity of all welfare legislation enacted in Canada during the previous two decades Sen. Davis, a recent appointee, summed up the views of himself and of the Senate's majority by stating in 1953:

> All these measures are of a similar pattern, and their effect is to make Canada a welfare state, a social democracy. . . . It is ridiculous to advocate today the old theory of the Manchester School . . . we have been subjected long enough to some of these ancient fallacies, without registering protest, and I take this opportunity to say that I do not believe in them. . . . If the welfare state continues to develop, as today's Order Paper indicates it will, we shall never abandon the co-operative functions of modern government.[47]

A fine demonstration of this matured outlook was provided by the Senate's stand in the Excise Tax bill in 1959. The bill, seeking to replace the practice of taxing the export of electricity through executive discretion under the Exportation of Power and Fluids and Importation of Gas Act with a fixed specific amount under the Excise Tax Act, amendable only by an act of Parliament, came under the attack of powerful business interests, including the British Columbia Electric Company, the Peace River Development Corporation, and the Consolidated Mining and Smelting Corporation, who wished to defeat the legislation and maintain the *status quo*, in which they had more room for bargaining for favourable rates. As a result of their lobbying the Senate's Banking and Commerce committee decided by a vote of 13:12 to reject the controversial clause of the bill. Back in the Senate, the committee's action was severely criticized. Speaking in favour of the original draft, Sen. Croll[48]

[45] *Ibid., 1951* (2nd session), p. 94.
[46] *Ibid.*, p. 102. Italic added.
[47] *Ibid., 1953*, p. 471.
[48] Said he in 1956: "I belong to the public ownership school. I believe in public ownership. I have urged it and I have counselled it." *Ibid., 1956*, p. 678.

told the house: "We are entering into an era in this country where the great debate will be on public ownership and public control of natural resources. If we accept this recommendation of the committee . . . we will have committed a colossal blunder, bad in principle and worse in practice, and subject to abuses."[49] And accusing big business of not respecting the idea of the supremacy of Parliament, Sen. Roebuck thundered: "Big business has never liked doing big business in public. Publicity deprives them of that elbow room which they would like . . . for secret bargains. Secrecy in the past has always enabled some people to get away with something big in a hurry."[50] They were joined by a number of other influential Liberal Senators, such as Golding, Power, Dupuis, Kinley, and Macdonald, the Leader of the Opposition in the Senate. In the end the committee's amendment was negatived and the bill passed in its original form.[51] Compared to the performance over the Canada Temperance bill in 1925 the Senate's stand in this instance was surely a considerable improvement.

In the light of this tradition Sen. Roebuck emphatically protested against the impression that "we in the Senate are subject to the dictates of men of large accumulations of capital . . . that we are the pliant servants of the House of Have." Instead, "my experience which is now considerably over a decade in this Chamber, is that the Senators of today are not defenders of property as such, but rather represent the people of the dominion of Canada."[52] Indeed, when we compare the attitude of the Senate during the short period 1925–30, or, for that matter, in the first part of the 1920's, with its actual stand since the world crash in 1930, the difference becomes obvious. The example of the Old Age Pension bill in 1926 has never been repeated again, while acts have been placed by the hundreds on the Statute Book of Canada, carrying the country further and further on the road of economic and social progress, with the approval and consent of the Senate. In looking for an explanation of this adaptability and sympathetic disposition two important things have to be remembered. In the first place, politically, during its "reactionary" period 1925–30 the Senate was dominated by a Conservative majority and it is difficult to ascertain just how much the rejection of such a measure as the Old Age Pension bill, for example, was due to partisan considerations and how much to certain economic and social principles. On the other hand, both in 1930–35 and during the years following the war, when Parliament was presented a heavy

[49] *Ibid., 1959*, p. 829.
[50] *Ibid.*, pp. 636–8.
[51] *Ibid.*, p. 844.
[52] *Ibid., 1958*, p. 369.

dose of forward-looking legislation, there was a congruity in the party forces of the two houses of Parliament. Similarly, it should be noted that the Senate has never been confronted with a socialistic government advocating a truly radical program of economic and social legislation. However, although the fears of the Left concerning the ultimate fate of such a program in the Upper House should not be dismissed too lightly, it must be emphasized that such fears appear rather futuristic as long as effective political power remains in the hands of the traditional parties. Whether and to what extent the Senate would oppose some far-reaching socializing legislation is problematical. In view of the Senate's tradition of political self-restraint, however, it is unlikely that it would in fact reject a program carrying the mandate of the electorate.

In the second place, the change in the composition of the Senate's membership has had an equally important bearing upon the Senate's attitude towards economic and social legislation in recent times. The gradual withering away of the pre-1925 "Senate generation" has had two consequences. Occupationally, it meant the replacement of the "manufacturer class" in 1925 with the "lawyer class" in successive appointments as the dominant element both in the total membership and in the active nucleus of the Senate. Also, in a more general sense, it meant the weakening of the pre-take-off mentality to a point where it could no longer dictate the actions of the Senate in concrete instances. The Senate may have continued to provide in its membership for an undue representation of men of substance, but it has ceased to be the House of ruggedly successful old pioneers.

The upshot of all this is that the Senate as a parliamentary institution has made no articulate attempts in the last twenty-five or thirty years to erect a defence for certain economic and social principles in contradistinction with the express wishes of the elected representatives of the people. Since the replacement of the pioneer by the lawyer the emphasis has shifted from the economic/social aspects to the political/legal values of nineteenth century Whiggism. The conservatism of the Senate became the conservatism of the common law and of the idea of the supremacy of Parliament.

Stated simply, the policy of the Senate during this period has been to check the political extremism of the "positive state," without obstructing its economic/social implications. We have seen that the idea of the Senate as a check upon the executive was advocated by no less a personage than Sir Clifford Sifton at the early date of 1917.[53] Since

[53]Above, p. 18.

then the notion has gained acceptance by a growing number of people.[54] Shortly after his appointment to the Senate in 1951 Sen. Power, whose active political career suggests that he is not a sophisticated theorist, remarked that as an ardent believer in liberal traditions he could not bring himself to "support a tenet which practice and usage may elevate into a doctrine—that of the infallibility of the Cabinet." He was, therefore, delighted to find that "a cursory study of some of the functions admittedly within the authority of the Senate leads to the belief that perhaps this assembly may exercise a salutary and effective restraint on an otherwise omnipotent ministry, . . . there may be, through the instrumentality of this Chamber, a means to bring about greater expression of individual liberty and greater freedom from the exigencies of party discipline."[55] Indeed, if more leisure and greater flexibility in the rules of procedure have contributed to the Senate's success in its technical functions, the laxity of party organization and the operative principles of independence have enabled it to fulfil its substantive role.

Generally speaking, this role has had two broad objectives. First, to prevent the practice of government by decree, whenever it could be done without jeopardizing the underlying legislative policy. And second, to see to it that in the course of legislation the interests and the rights of the ordinary person were not brushed aside to any unreasonable degree. Thus, whereas the first objective has been aimed at restating the supremacy of Parliament (with special regard to delegated legislation), the second has been aimed at restating the case of the individual. In the following pages it is proposed to illustrate the working of these principles in a few concrete examples.

1. *Restating the Supremacy of Parliament*

Unlike those of Britain and Australia the houses of the Canadian Parliament have no select committees to scrutinize the great variety of subordinated legislation by executive agencies. Although it has been suggested time and again[56] that a committee of the Senate would be

[54]Cf. *inter alia* the remarks of Mr. White (PC, Middlesex East), *HD, 1954,* p. 274, and of Mr. Dinsdale (PC, Brandon-Souris), *ibid., 1955,* p. 5486. Also Mackay, *The Unreformed Senate*, p. 136; J. N. Turner, "The Senate of Canada, 1924–48," unpublished BA thesis, University of British Columbia, (1949), pp. 196–7.

[55]*SD, 1956,* pp. 130–2; *ibid., 1950,* p. 251 (for remarks of Sen. Reid).

[56]See, e.g., J. E. Kersell, *Parliamentary Supervision of Delegated Legislation* (London, 1960), *passim*; and an interview given by J. R. Mallory to the *Montreal*

exceptionally well qualified to review all forms of statutory instruments now covered by the Regulations Act in 1950,[57] no action has so far been taken on these lines. We have seen that in the course of performing their ordinary business the committees of the Senate regularly come into contact with ministers and departmental officials. However, no Senate committee is specifically authorized by its order of reference to scrutinize orders-in-council or departmental legislation. Post-natal supervision being unfeasible, the Senate's chief method of restating the supremacy of Parliament has been through built-in restrictions effected by amending the parent legislation, for the purpose of circumscribing the use of delegated legislation. Its policy in this respect was well summed up by Sen. Croll in 1959: "Orders in Council are necessary. They are necessary for administrative purposes, for the day-to-day business of the country, for housekeeping. They are necessary in case of emergency when Parliament is not in session. . . . In other words, Orders in Council have their place in government. It is their abuse we are opposed to. . . . *Our main important task in this Senate . . . is to return government to Parliament. . . .*"[58] Judging by this attitude, the Senate has not been opposed indiscriminately to the practice of delegated legislation; it has simply tried to ensure that such a practice was not resulting in a greater evasion of Parliament than absolutely necessary.

This objective has been pursued on five levels. In the most extreme cases the Senate has prevented the delegation of authority altogether. In 1935, for example, it struck out section 26 from the Dominion Trade and Industry Commission bill, which authorized the Secretary of State to hold up Dominion Companies' issues. Apart from duplicating the work of the provincial commissions, the Senate felt the clause was increasing the power of the Secretary of State to an undesirable extent, particularly since it contained no time-limit within which the Secretary of State was to act. In view of the Senate's insistence the Government reluctantly accepted the amendment.[59] Similarly, in 1938 the provision in the Radio Broadcasting bill empowering the governor-in-council to exempt receiving stations in cars owned by tourists in Canada was

---

Star, May 29, 1963. During a Bill of Rights debate in the House of Commons in 1955, Mr. Diefenbaker recommended that each year a joint committee of the Senate and the House of Commons be appointed to act as a watchdog over civil and human rights. *HD, 1955*, p. 903. He repeated this idea, when Leader of the Government, on Aug. 3, 1960, but action was still not forthcoming.

[57]See J. R. Mallory, "Delegated Legislation in Canada," *Canadian Journal of Economics and Political Science*, vol. XIX (1953), pp. 462–71.

[58]*SD, 1959*, pp. 828–9. Italic added.

[59]*Ibid., 1935*, pp. 481–2; *SJ, 1935*, pp. 313–14, 374; *HD, 1935*, p. 4312.

criticized in the Senate's Railway, Telegraph, and Harbours committee as an unnecessary addition to the powers of the cabinet. Thereupon the bill was amended, to the effect that instead of an order in council the parliamentary Act itself should provide for the desired exemptions.[60] In a rather similar case, in the Food and Drugs bill of 1953 doubts were raised as to the wisdom of giving the governor-in-council a *carte blanche* legislative authority to define the meaning of "adulteration," a key term in the bill. Instead, after careful consideration and hearing various representatives, the Senate's committee on Public Health produced a satisfactory definition, which was incorporated in the bill.

The Senate has been particularly sensitive to attempts to transfer to the Executive the right to control the internal business of Parliament. Its prompt action in the Publication of Statutes bill of 1925 and in the Public Service Superannuation bill of 1953 is a case in point. In the first instance the Senate was thoroughly shocked by the idea of conferring to the cabinet the right to establish by order-in-council the number of copies of the statutes members of the two houses of Parliament were entitled to receive. Unmoved by the argument that the bill was merely trying to formalize a practice that had been in existence since Confederation, the Senate objected to the relinquishing of "this little right." The amendment unanimously adopted in Committee of the Whole substituted joint resolution of Parliament for order-in-council, thus preserving "the present rights of Parliament under the existing law."[61] In the second case the bill, which sought to establish a universal superannuation scheme for the public service, took away the saving clause from the existing Act respecting the ancient prerogative of both houses of Parliament in matters of controlling and removing their own officers. The attempt to leave it with the discretion of the governor-in-council to determine by order-in-council the retiring age for the higher officials of Parliament was regarded by the Senate as just another sign of "the tendency of the Government through this post-war period . . . to grasp for itself every power it could." Consequently, an amendment was adopted in the Banking and Commerce committee reserving the right for each house of Parliament to decide whether any of its officers be continued in office after he reached the retiring age.[62]

On the next level the Senate has not stopped delegation of legislative authority but inserted safeguards against the conferment of unlimited "blank-cheque" powers upon the executive. In the Beauharnois Company bill of 1940, for example, this took the form of incorporating in

[60] *HD, 1938*, p. 4433.
[61] *SD, 1925*, p. 299; *HD, 1925*, p. 3493.
[62] *SD, 1953*, p. 568; *HD, 1953*, p. 5106.

the bill directory words on the basis of which subsequent orders-in-council were to be drafted.[63] The National Emergency Transitional Powers bill of 1945 was received with mixed feelings in the Upper House. While, on the one hand, it was recognized that in the period immediately following the war the Government was entitled to certain emergency powers, it was noted, on the other hand, "that a lot of government officials in Ottawa think they are not only the Government of Canada, but also the House of Commons and the Senate. . . ."[64] The most disturbing aspect of the measure, and the one which caused the greatest storm in the Senate, was the fact that although the bill terminated the War Measures Act it nevertheless empowered the governor-in-council to continue in force by an order *any* orders-in-council or administrators' orders passed under the War Measures Act during the Second World War, even including some whose lawfulness might well have been in doubt. To eliminate as much as possible the objectionable features of this blanket provision, the Senate put an amendment to the bill, making it certain that only those orders and regulations could be continued under the new legislation which had been made *lawfully*.[65]

Again, in a somewhat different context in 1958 the Senate felt impelled to place limitations upon the powers of the executive. As it emerged from the House of Commons, the Broadcasting bill provided that all the officers of the BBG and all the nine directors of the CBC should hold office during good behaviour removable only upon a joint address of the Senate and the House of Commons. However, for the President and the Vice-President of the CBC the terms were for seven years during pleasure. Influenced by the representatives of various outside bodies, including the Canadian Broadcasting League, the Senate's Transport and Communications committee amended the bill by placing the two officers in the "good behaviour" category, removable for cause, lest any undue political influence be brought to bear upon them by the executive. The Government accepted the amendment, although it had rejected it on a previous occasion when it was proposed by the Opposition in the Commons.[66] Much the same consideration applied to the provision of the Feeds bill in 1960, which gave a "blank-cheque" authority to the minister to appoint *anyone* as an inspector for the purpose of the Act. The Senate's Natural Resources committee amended the bill, by inserting a statutory limitation to require that the person to be appointed by the minister must be a qualified individual either under the Civil Service Act or under a provincial act.

[63] *HD, 1940*, p. 1162.
[64] *SD, 1945*, p. 407.
[65] *HD, 1945*, p. 3496.
[66] *Ibid., 1958*, p. 4761.

On the third level the Senate tries to prevent further subdelegation, taking the ground that important regulations in a bill should be safeguarded by being made subject to order-in-council rather than to mere ministerial order. The idea behind this policy is that a minister may be actuated by a certain "departmental angle" of the argument presented, whilst the governor-in-council looks at things from all angles. Sen. Graham, who had some experience with ministerial duties, maintained it was an error to suggest "that a Minister's recommendation is always adopted by Council. . . . sometimes the sponsoring of a recommendation is a wearisome experience. It is a common thing for a department to focus its attention on one objective, and the minister usually takes the advice of his departmental experts. But when he brings his recommendation to Council, other ministers may have entirely different ideas and the recommendation may be seriously amended before it is adopted."[67] It was in this spirit of precaution that the Senate amended the Dominion Elections bill in 1925, which gave the secretary of state the right to appoint the returning officer. The Senate amendment provided that the appointment should rather be made by the governor-in-council.[68] Similarly, in the case of the Militia bill of 1947 there developed a view in the Senate that the wording of the measure implied that it was rather the exception than the rule for the governor-in-council to make regulations. Accordingly, the Senate's Banking and Commerce committee redrafted the bill to make it clear that it was for the governor-in-council to make regulations and that any exception to that rule, empowering the minister of defence to issue regulations, would have to be made by the governor-in-council. Thus the regulatory powers of the individual minister were restricted.[69]

The same policy has been applied with added strength to administrative authorities below the level of a minister. In 1936 the Senate insisted on its amendment to the centralizing National Harbours Board bill, requiring all tenders to be submitted by the board through the minister to the governor-in-council, for the purpose of awarding the contract under his authority.[70] To the Foreign Exchange Control bill of 1946, whose sweeping terms provided statutory authority for orders-in-council passed under the War Measures Act, the Senate attached a whole series of amendments designed to substitute the authority of the Governor-in-Council for that of the Foreign Exchange Control Board regarding regulatory powers over a vast number of subjects. Again, in the St. Lawrence Seaway Authority bill in 1951, establishing an authority

[67]*SD*, *1934*, p. 373; *HD*, *1934*, p. 2763. [68]*SD*, *1925*, p. 752. *HD*, *1925*, p. 5064.
[69]*HD*, *1947*, p. 1707, *SD*, *1947*, p. 186. [70]*SD*, *1936*, p. 625. *HD*, *1936*, p. 4029.

to construct a deep waterway between the port of Montreal and Lake Erie, the Senate found that the powers of the president were too arbitrary. In committee, therefore, it amended the bill to cut down those powers, by providing that they should be defined in the by-laws subject to the approval of the Governor-in-Council; it also eliminated the right of the president, established by the draft bill, to delegate his powers further down.[71] The idea that responsibility was better guaranteed when collectively held was expressed in an amendment made by the Senate to the War Service Grants bill in 1948. The bill, as originally worded, sought to abolish the five-man board of review, which heard the cases of dishonourably discharged servicemen, and to transfer its duties to a single reviewing officer. The Senate was opposed to giving too much power to any one individual and, on the suggestion of Sen. Haig, adopted an amendment enabling the committee to carry on.[72]

The fourth method used by the Senate to circumscribe executive law-making power has been through inserting provisions in the delegating statute for the publication and reporting of the exercise of such power. Although parliamentary supervision will scarcely be effective until the establishment of select scrutiny committees, compulsory publication and reporting still offers the advantage of mitigating the most disturbing aspect of executive law-making—the idea of "secret ordinances secretly arrived at." Indeed, long before the Regulations Act of 1950 the Senate has realized the value of forcing statutory instruments into the open and directed its revisory work accordingly. In 1927, for example, the Senate found the Crown Debts bill, empowering the Governor-in-Council to regulate the adjustment of indebtedness incurred for advances of seed grain and other relief, "a general jubilee remission of debts," and although it approved of its principle it disliked placing almost unlimited power in the hands of a department.[73] Therefore, it put an amendment to the measure requiring the minister of the Interior to lay before both Houses of Parliament within fifteen days of each session a list giving particulars of his activities under the provision of the Act.[74] Again, three years later, in the session of 1930, whilst supporting the principle of the Fair Wages and Eight-Hours Day bill the Senate adopted an amendment to the effect that regulations passed under the Act should have statutory effect only after the elapse of fifteen days following their publication in the *Canada Gazette*. Shortly afterwards an identical amendment was inserted in the Maple Sugar bill, which authorized the minister to make any regulations prescribing "any means deemed by him

[71]*SD, 1951* (2nd session), p. 264.
[72]*Ibid., 1948*, p. 337.
[73]*Ibid., 1927*, p. 117.
[74]*SJ, 1927*, p. 280.

to be necessary for the carrying-out of the provisions of this act." In the Combines Investigation bill of 1935, which transferred to the Dominion Trade and Industry Commission the functions previously administered by the minister of Labour, the Senate, by adding a new clause, compelled the commissioners to report to the minister, and through him to Parliament, annually.[75] The same principle was implemented in the bill to establish a Veterans Affairs department in 1944. The Senate's amendment required the minister to lay annually "before Parliament, within fifteen days after the meeting thereof, a report and statement of the transactions and affairs of the department during the year . . ."—an idea which was advocated unsuccessfully by members of the House of Commons also.[76] Again, the Senate made one amendment to the National Trade Mark bill in 1949, initiated in the Senate, providing that every regulation made under section 4 of the Act should be laid before Parliament within thirty days after it was made. The measure was withdrawn in 1949; when it was reintroduced in the second session of that year it contained the amendment incorporated by the Senate the previous session.

Even after the Regulations Act of 1950 there was still room left for the Senate to exercise its traditional restraining influence. In the session of 1959, for example, the Government brought down its National Defence bill, which established a universal code of rules of evidence to apply in all proceedings before military courts. The Senate found no fault with that. However, it opposed giving "blank-cheque" authority to the Governor-in-Council to formulate regulations with regards to the rules of evidence. Chiefly under the impact of a powerful address by Sen. Roebuck, the Senate's Banking and Commerce committee amended the bill to provide, first, that the rules of evidence would become effective only upon publication in the *Canada Gazette*, and, second, that they must be tabled in Parliament within fifteen days after they are made.[77] Also in the same session, the Senate found it desirable to amend the RCMP bill dealing with contracts between the RCMP and a province with regard to policing within the province. The Senate amendment required that "the minister shall lay before Parliament a copy of every arrangement made within fifteen days after it is made."[78]

This policy of compulsory reporting to Parliament has been applied

[75]*Ibid., 1935*, pp. 357, 447.

[76]*HD, 1944*, p. 4382.

[77]*SD, 1959*, p. 336. *HJ, 1959*, p. 226.

[78]It is only fair to mention that the amendment was made in accordance with the undertaking the minister gave the House when the matter was under discussion in the Commons. *HD, 1959*, p. 6409.

with equal vigour to Crown corporations. The Senate's position in the matter was well summed up by Sen. Hayden in 1946; he said: "If Crown companies are necessary and are to be set up, they should be required to bring in statements of their operations directly to Parliament, so that Parliament may pass upon the necessity of the work they are doing, and the efficiency with which they are carrying it on."[79] Thus, similarly to its policy towards orders-in-council and ministerial orders the Senate's stand on Crown corporations has been one of toleration and understanding, yet always with a view of trying to foster the notion of parliamentary supremacy. It, therefore, amended the Central Mortgage and Housing Corporation bill in 1945, by adding a new subsection to section 34, to the effect that as soon as practicable after the end of each calendar year the Board should prepare a report about the administration of the affairs of the corporation during the preceding year and lay it before Parliament, together with the auditors' reports.[80] Still in the same session the Senate amended the bill to increase the authorized capital of TCA and to empower the Governor-in-Council to create new companies as subsidiaries of TCA. Disturbed by the prospects of erecting "screens and barriers between responsible ministers of the Crown and the public business which has to be carried on,"[81] the Senate's Railway, Telegraph and Harbours committee, upon the suggestions of Sen. Hayden, amended the bill in three particulars: that orders-in-council made under the act should be laid before Parliament; that the company should submit an annual report to Parliament, summarizing "the results of their operations and such other information as appears to them to be of public interest or necessary for the information of Parliament"; and that the annual reports of both the board of directors and the auditor should be tabled in Parliament through the minister.[82]

The Senate applied the same principle to the Canadian Commercial Corporation bill and the Government Companies bill in 1946. In both cases the amendments were to the effect that the corporation should furnish financial statements and such information as was required to be furnished to shareholders by a company incorporated under the Companies Act.[83] Similarly, in the Agricultural Products Board bill in 1951, which sought to give statutory form to a board that had been in existence by virtue of an order-in-council, the Senate drafted a new clause requiring the minister to prepare an annual report "with respect

[79]*SD, 1946*, p. 401.
[80]*Ibid., 1945*, p. 320; *HD, 1945*, p. 2843.
[81]*SD, 1945*, p. 239.
[82]*Ibid.*, pp. 303 ff; *SJ, 1945*, pp. 240–1; *HJ, 1945*, p. 340.
[83]*HD, 1946*, p. 3719.

to the administration of this Act during the preceding calendar year," and to lay it before Parliament.[84] Asked about the nature of the amendment, Mr. Gardiner said in the Commons: "It is just that once a year we make a report to the House. . . ." This "just once a year" represented just about the only safeguard for the authority of Parliament.[85]

The fifth, and last, form of restating the supremacy of Parliament has been the placing of a time limit upon certain types of legislation. This method proved most effective in the years immediately following the end of the war, when the emergency-dictated "control complex," which so many civil servants and boards developed during the war, was still very much in the air and influenced the drafting of legislation. The Senate viewed with apprehension the trend of concentrating in peacetime too much power in the hands of politically non-responsible individuals. It was feared that "if Parliament fails to criticize and restrain legislation of this character, undoubtedly the institution of Parliament will fall into disrepute."[86]

The Senate's constitutionally constructive stand was well exemplified on three important pieces of legislation during this period. In 1946 the Government brought down its Foreign Exchange Control bill, whose purpose to put in statute form the extraordinary powers of the Foreign Exchange Control Board was criticized in the Senate, on the ground that it "confers the kind of authority given to individuals over other individuals that Schacht enjoyed in pre-war Nazi Berlin."[87] They found alarming the government proposal granting a board unlimited authority to remake the laws of Parliament to suit its own purposes, to discriminate in favour of groups or individuals at the expense of others, to declare a resident of Canada, as defined by statute, a non-resident, or *vice versa*, indeed, even to "make a man a woman,"—powers, "which, exercised by civil servants, would be almost sufficient to cause the kind of annoyance that would induce a monk to commit the sin of violent anger."[88] Although the necessity of continuing a modified form of foreign exchange control was not questioned, in order to retain for Parliament authority in the matter it was agreed in the Banking and Commerce committee to make the legislation effective for only a comparatively short period of time, until Parliament could again consider it and decide whether or not it should be re-enacted.[89] The idea was supported by the Acting Minister of Finance, Mr. Abbott, and after two days' hesitation it was approved

[84]*HJ, 1951* (2nd sesion), p. 341.
[85]*HD, 1951* (2nd session), p. 2194.
[86]*SD, 1950*, p. 512.
[87]*Ibid., 1946*, p. 601.
[88]Sen. McGeer's remarks. *Ibid.*, p. 759.
[89]*Ibid.*, p. 757.

by the Government.[90] Accordingly, the life of the bill was limited, making it expire sixty days after the opening of the first session of Parliament in the year 1949.[91]

Exactly the same stand was taken with regard to the Canadian Commercial Corporation bill, which was aimed at enabling the corporation to continue to operate in the interests of international trade, embracing both the export and import fields. Again, it was not so much the principle of government entering into manufacturing or processing that was criticized as the practice "to enter into trade and commerce, to import, export and process *without any supervision by Parliament as to what it will import or export*."[92] Although the minister stated in the Commons that the legislation was not permanent legislation, the bill, as passed by the Lower House, contained no time-limit upon the duration of the corporation.[93] Therefore, to surround its operation with the necessary safeguards for retaining some measure of parliamentary control, the same amendment was put to it as in the Foreign Exchange Control bill, so that if its continuance was deemed necessary the measure could again be brought before Parliament to review.

In the session of 1947 the Canadian Wheat Board bill offered another opportunity for the Senate to bring administrative action under periodic supervision by Parliament. The aim of the bill was to give the Board by statute some of the powers which it had previously enjoyed by virtue of orders-in-council under the National Transitional Powers Act, for the purpose of fulfilling the wheat contract with the United Kingdom. Although the bill contained a time-limit for the pool period, there was no similar limitation upon Parts II and IV, which gave the board an all-embracing power to control elevators, mills, railway transportation as well as interprovincial and export trade in the field of the grain industry. The Senate found the powers not only excessive but absolutely unnecessary for carrying out its obligations under the United Kingdom wheat agreement.[94] It was observed as a general rule that "if it is sought to give some board or other authority certain powers by Act of Parliament . . . there is a tendency to make these powers as all-embracing as possible, instead of restricting them to what is necessary for carrying out the immediate purpose."[95] Consequently, it was decided in the Banking and Commerce committee to insert a new clause, clause

[90]Sen. Haig's comments. *Ibid., 1951*, p. 296.
[91]*HD, 1946*, p. 5670. *HJ, 1946*, pp. 802–6.
[92]Sen. Roebuck's remarks. *SD, 1946*, p. 574. Italic added.
[93]*Ibid.*, p. 572.
[94]See Sen. Paterson's remarks. *Ibid., 1947*, p. 261.
[95]*Ibid.*, p. 262.

19/A, providing that Parts II and IV of the legislation were to expire on August 1, 1950. As in the previous instances the minister was quite agreeable to the change.

In all these cases the Senate was confronted with the double task of allowing the Government to retain certain of the powers vested in it as a result of the war emergency, on the one hand, and of trying to prevent the executive from running away with its newly acquired powers, on the other hand. In its substantive capacity the Senate has certainly helped facilitate the process of returning to pre-emergency constitutional normalcy. Such a return, experience shows, is never complete and a post-emergency situation can, at best, only approximate the pre-emergency level of constitutionalism. However, what is possible is not always what is desirable, and the Senate, through its amendments, played an important role in crystallizing certain normative principles.

2. *Restating the Case of the Individual*

If the first objective of the Senate's substantive role has been to circumscribe executive action for the purpose of restating the supremacy of Parliament, the second objective has been to circumscribe executive action for the purpose of safeguarding the "procedural rights" of the individual in the course of every-day legislation. This idea has been followed both in cases for general application and in cases in which the interests or the rights of some specific person were involved.

IN GENERAL

This section covers both Criminal Code legislation and bills giving police powers and/or quasi-judicial powers to executive authorities. The methods used by the Senate in the protection of individual rights have been varied. It is proposed to indicate the most regularly occurring ones as applied in particular cases during the thirty-seven years from 1925 to 1963.

The Senate never hesitated simply to reduce the penalty provisions in bills when it considered them unreasonably strict for the objective to be attained. Thus, for example, it made the penalty clause less severe for the first offence in the bill on Interprovincial and International Traffic in Intoxicating Liquors in 1928[96] and it considerably reduced a similar section concerning thefts of cultivated plants in the Criminal

[96] *HD, 1928*, p. 3118. *SD, 1928*, p. 538.

Code bill of 1938—a decision inviting comments that Senators were not such lovers of horticulture as members of the House of Commons.[97]

The Senate has been consistent also in providing for ministerial or judicial discretion where the legislation seemed to be too inflexible to the disadvantage of the individual. Thus, to counterbalance the very heavy penalties for smuggling under the Customs bill in 1925, the Senate inserted a new clause to keep the power of remission in case of seized and forfeited goods of smugglers in the hands of the minister.[98] Interestingly, the same problem arose in connection with the Canadian Agriculture Products Standards bill and the Meat Inspection bill in 1955, which contained provisions dealing with violation of any regulation made under these Acts. The Senate was again opposed to the idea of automatic forfeiture by executive order. To prevent Parliament from taking out of the offence any question of intent or knowledge, the Senate amendment provided that forfeiture of the vehicle must be preceded by a direction of the court.[99]

In the Criminal Code (Offensive Weapons) bill in 1933 the Senate struck out the provision for one year's imprisonment as a minimum penalty for anyone carrying a weapon concealed upon his person and, on the suggestion of Senators McMeans and Griesbach, substituted another enabling the judge to exercise his discretion with regard to the length of the sentence within a five-year limit.[100] In the same session the Government brought in another amendment to the Criminal Code respecting the protection of children. Opposing the rigid definition of what constituted an "irrebuttable presumption" the Senate prevailed upon the Government in a free conference to leave it to the discretion of the court to decide whether the circumstances in the home of a man and his common-law wife were such that the morals of the child were likely to be corrupted.[101] Similarly, the Senate struck out section 7 of the Criminal Code in 1943, regarding the definition of a common betting house, and made it a matter of judicial decision to discover the subjective intention of the person doing the thing with which he was charged.[102]

The Senate amended the Dominion Companies bill in both 1934 and

[97]*HD, 1938*, p. 4487. *SD, 1938*, pp. 575 ff.

[98]*SJ, 1925*, p. 352. *HD, 1925*, p. 4527.

[99]*HD, 1955*, p. 5044.

[100]*SD, 1933*, p. 405.

[101]"In deleting this subsection . . . ," Mr. Lavergne, Deputy Speaker of the House of Commons, commented, "the Senate showed more common sense than was shown by this House and conformed to the traditions of British justice." *HD, 1933*, p. 5083.

[102]*Ibid., 1943*, p. 5295.

1935 to provide for greater judicial discretion than was contemplated in the original draft. In the first instance the change made by the Senate brought the measure into conformity with the provisions of the English Companies Act of 1929, allowing a certain discretion for the court in respect of the extremely severe penalties laid down by the legislation. "The Senate," the Solicitor General told the House of Commons, "were unanimous in support of that provision. Personally I think that under the circumstances it is just and should be accepted."[103] In the second instance the Senate left the penalty clause itself unaffected but brought judicial discretion into play for determining the existence of speculative practices.[104]

Again, the Senate amended section 68 of the Criminal Code bill in 1954 to invest discretionary powers in a justice, mayor, or sheriff, enabling these officers to satisfy themselves that a riot was in fact in progress before proceeding to read out the riot act. By so doing the Senate implemented a suggestion that was put forward unsuccessfully by CCF members in the House of Commons at an earlier stage.[105]

In the third place, the Senate has employed various devices to circumscribe the techniques of prosecution as provided for in bills drafted by government departments. Thus, it unanimously amended both the Indian bill and the Excise bill in 1927, to the effect that a mere certificate of a departmental analyst was not to be accepted as conclusive, but only as *prima facie*, evidence, thus enabling the party complaining to contradict the evidence by some other testimony and to cross-examine the analyst.[106]

It amended the Combines Investigation bill in 1935 and again in 1936 to guard against simultaneous prosecution, on the same set of facts and for the same offence, under the Criminal Code and the Combines Investigation Act. "This practice," Meighen said, "is not permitted anywhere in any other British country, nor is it the practice in Canada in any other connection. We do not say 'You cannot prosecute under both laws,' but we say 'You must not place a man in the position of being prosecuted under both at the same time.' "[107] For the sake of the same principle it amended the Weights and Measures bill in 1935, lest proceedings could be taken against a person for the same offence under that legislation and the Food and Drugs Act.[108]

[103] *Ibid., 1934*, p. 4039. *SD, 1934*, p. 500.
[104] *HD, 1935*, p. 4255.
[105] *Ibid., 1954*, p. 5979.
[106] *SD, 1927*, pp. 85, 120; *HD, 1927*, pp. 2210, 2313.
[107] *SD, 1935*, p. 447; *ibid., 1936*, pp. 524, 548, 595, 623.
[108] *HD, 1935*, p. 3692.

Often the Senate has seen fit to make the commencement of prosecution contingent upon the grant of special leave by a superior authority. This was the case in the Criminal Code bill in 1931, which was aimed at checking certain practices among the Doukhobors. The measure, which was introduced at the instigation of the Women's Christian Temperance Union and similar organizations, prompted comments in the Senate that almost any particular group of people seemed to be able to get through the Commons a bill to make a crime of an action that never before had been regarded as such, for the simple reason that MP's preferred that it should not be said on the hustings that they approved of such an action. The amendment made by the Senate provided that no prosecution under the Act could be set off without the leave of the attorney general for the province.[109]

In the Combines Investigation bill in 1937, while the Senate conceded that the administration of the Act should be transferred from the Trade and Industry Commission to a single commissioner under the minister of Labour, it inserted an amendment, to the effect that a certificate from the president of the Exchequer Court or the chairman of the Dominion Trade and Industry Commission was necessary for the commissioner to exercise his compulsory powers with respect to the summoning of witnesses and the production of papers as well as the holding of other than a preliminary investigation.[110]

In the Department of Reconstruction and Supply bill in 1945 the Senate amendment provided that to authorize any police officer to enter and search, the investigator needed the approval of a judge of the Exchequer Court or the superior court, or a county court, of any province.[111] Similarly, to mitigate the severe restrictions placed by the Foreign Exchange Control bill of 1946 upon tourists coming into the country, one of the Senate amendments (No. 43) divested customs officers of the power to search a person without going before a magistrate if the person did not wish it done.

Procedural safeguards of a miscellaneous character have been applied on a number of occasions. The Senate stepped in to save honest-minded persons from prosecution under the Weights and Measures bill in 1935, by providing that a single pre-packed article underweight did not constitute evidence of a practice punishable under the Act.[112] In the Fish Inspection bill of 1949, which empowered inspectors to arrest without a warrant and to seize fish on mere suspicion and detain it for two months, the Senate inserted an amendment, requiring departmental

[109] *SD, 1931*, p. 531.
[110] *HD, 1937*, p. 2496; *SJ, 1937*, p. 240.
[111] *SJ, 1945*, pp. 347–9.
[112] *SD, 1935*, pp. 400–1; *SJ, 1935*, p. 330.

inspectors, before assuming their duties, to take an oath that they would not engage in trading in fish or fish containers. "Officials who accept responsibility . . ." Roebuck said, "sometimes get a little over-zealous. They are very serious about the performance of their duties, and may go a little too far if the bill provides them with more power than is strictly necessary. The Senate is here for the very purpose of keeping that kind of thing in check. . . . Looking after the rights of the individual is our special province, and we should give it every consideration."[113] In 1951 the Senate reduced the period for which merchants' books could be held up by an official in case of "suspected infraction of the regulations" under the Consumer Credit Act from ninety to thirty days; the minister gladly acquiesced, because he had forgotten that there were such things as photostats.[114] Two years later, in the session of 1953, the Senate was confronted with section 21 of the Food and Drugs bill, which sought to authorize an inspector to enter anybody's *home* at any time if he thought, on reasonable grounds or not, that there was on the premise some article which was in any way a contravention of the Act. The Senate amended the clause, making it sure, first, that an inspector might not enter a private house but only a "place of manufacture, preparation, preservation, packaging or storing," and, second, that he could enter only if there were reasonable grounds for his suspicions. Again, the National Harbours Board bill of 1954 received a good deal of criticism in the Senate for its provision empowering a police officer to take a person charged with an offence upon National Harbours Board property before *any* court in any area in which property under the administration of the Board was located. It was pointed out during second reading debate that under the bill as drafted a person charged with having committed such an offence in Montreal could be tried on that charge in Vancouver. "This is a type of legislation," Roebuck again reminded the house, "with respect to which the Senate has a peculiar function to perform, namely to make certain that the rights of the individual are not infringed upon by those to whom infringement of rights seems most attractive."[115] Consequently, the Senate's Banking and Commerce committee, with the assistance of the Law Clerk and the counsel for the Board, amended the bill, limiting to fifty miles the jurisdiction of a court to deal with an offence defined in the bill.

The fourth chief method for the Senate to restate the case of the individual has been by means of inserting appeal provisions in the law. In 1934 it stood fast on its action upon the Excise bill, the effect of

[113]*Ibid., 1949* (2nd session), p. 354.
[114]*HD, 1951*, p. 3587.
[115]*SD, 1954*, p. 382.

which was to give protection "to an absolutely innocent party" whose only chance to recover his forfeited property would otherwise have been only through the leniency of the department officials themselves or an action by the Exchequer Court. In view of the fact that the latter sat only seldom in the outlying provinces the Senate amended the bill to ensure that action might be taken in a superior court as well.[116]

In the session of 1945 the Government brought in its bill to transfer to a new department the functions of the Department of Reconstruction and the Department of Munitions and Supply. The bill not only empowered the minister to cause an inquiry whenever he deemed it expedient and the investigators to authorize any police officer to enter and search by force, if necessary, for the purposes of the inquiry, but, by section 12, it also enabled departmental "fishing expeditions" to be organized even with no specific ground for suspicion at the outset. Criticism came from members of the Liberal majority in the Senate, especially Senators Bench, Hayden, and Campbell, who called the legislation "an all-time high in star chamber methods," and warned that "Parliament would be going a very long way if it clothed any Minister . . . with these powers." While it was felt that there might be reasons for the Government to carry out inquiries envisaged in the bill, it was also felt that "the subject should have some right in matters of this kind."[117] The amendment which finally emerged empowered the Exchequer Court to review upon the hearing of an appeal any direction or decision of the minister and to confirm his order or direction or vary it, and the decision of the Court was final and conclusive. As soon as the amendments were printed the Government Leader, Sen. Robertson, went to ascertain the view of the Minister as to whether or not they would handicap him in carrying out the intention of the legislation. The Senate was assured that the amendments did not handicap C. D. Howe or his Department in any way.[118]

The Senate amended the Post Office bill in 1951 to authorize the Board of Review, hearing appeals against an interim order of the Postmaster General prohibiting the use of the mails, not only to report but also to make recommendations to the Postmaster General as to what should be done. "In view of what happened," Sen. Haig said referring to the proceedings in the Banking and Commerce committee, which were attended by the Postmaster General, "I have no doubt that those recommendations will be carried out. The Minister has an over-

[116]See the appreciative remarks of Mr. Stewart, former Liberal Minister of the Interior. *HD, 1934*, p. 4377.

[117]*SD, 1945*, p. 337.

[118]*HD, 1945*, p. 3416.

riding power, but I doubt very much whether he will exercise it."[119] In the same session the Senate put amendments to the Customs bill and the Excise Tax bill, extending the time limit from six to twelve months within which an appeal could be launched for the remission of overpaid taxes. As Mr. Fleming said in the House of Commons, "It is obvious that the Senate has made an amendment which should have been made in this House."[120]

There were two aspects of the Criminal Code bill in 1954 which promptly galvanized the Senate into action. Consistent with its stand a year before[121] it induced the minister of Justice in committee to adopt the view that no leave of the court of appeal was necessary for an appeal from conviction and sentence in the case of contempt of court.[122] The amendment also covered cases of contempt of court not committed in the face of the court. But perhaps even more important, the Senate flatly rejected sections 690 and 691 of the measure aimed at abolishing the right of the individual to apply for an order of habeas corpus to all judges available, or to as many as necessary, in lieu of the much narrower right of appeal from the first judge's decision, should he refuse to grant the application. The proposal to grant an appeal to the Crown against a habeas corpus order was even graver, for it meant that authorities might continue the imprisonment of an individual after a judge has granted a writ of habeas corpus, until the matter finally came before a court of appeal. The Senate agreed that this was a decided and important restriction upon the historic right of habeas corpus, and devised an amendment putting the law back in the position in which it was prior to the introduction of the bill in the House of Commons. "We think that is a good idea," remarked Mr. Knowles, who was fighting unsuccessfully for the same, "and we are glad the Senate has made that change."[123]

In the light of this tradition there was hardly anything surprising about the action of the Senate, or at least of its Liberal majority, concerning

[119]*Ibid., 1951*, p. 4681. *SD, 1951*, p. 661.

[120]*HD, 1951*, p. 4137.

[121]The Criminal Law bill, a Senate measure; cf. *SD, 1953*, pp. 147–68 *passim.* Its provisions, here under discussion, were altered by the House of Commons.

[122]*Ibid., 1954*, p. 585. Commenting on the Senate action Mr. Drew said in the Commons: "There is that broad question of contempt of court by the press, by writers, either in the court or outside the court, which is yet undefined by statute and in respect of which we are still carrying on with the inherited common law practices . . . which leave to the judge the responsibility for deciding what the penalty will be, as well as deciding whether the person charged is guilty of the offence . . . The right of appeal from such decision . . . will undoubtedly be a substantial improvement." *HD, 1954*, p. 5975.

[123]*Ibid.*, p. 5974; *SD, 1954*, pp. 459, 586.

the Government's Customs Tariff bill in 1961, which sought to give absolute power to the Minister of National Revenue to fix the rate of customs duty. What caused widespread resentment was the abrupt discontinuation of the practice under which a taxpayer, if he felt aggrieved by any decision regarding the rate of duty, could appeal to the Tariff Board, with further appeals lying to the Exchequer Court and to the Supreme Court of Canada. Supported by a considerable public opinion[124] the Senate amended the bill to make ministerial rate-fixing appealable to the Tariff Board. It is to be noted that in order to facilitate speedy administration, the amendment made no provision for continuing appeal beyond the board to the highest federal courts, as was previously the case, and it also should be borne in mind that since the membership of the Tariff Board has been increased from five to seven earlier in the session there was no reason to fear long delays in the handling of future appeals. Rigidly stuck to its original position, the Government rather let the whole bill die than to compromise on what was surely a highly unpopular item of policy.

It is worth mentioning that the Senate has always held a friendly and sympathetic attitude to members of the armed forces when legislation involving their rights and interests were under consideration. Apart from the National Defence bill of 1959, which has already been mentioned,[125] the National Defence bill of 1949 might be cited as another good example. The bill, a Senate measure, was thoroughly considered in committee and was amended on seventy-four scores. The purpose of the substantive amendments was to give full protection for individual members of the armed services who might at any time find themselves under some disability before a court martial or other official disciplinary body. More specifically, they established the right of an accused person to be represented before a court martial, eliminated various formalities in the preparation of a statement of appeal, and gave officers and men ample and clear protection in relation to anything done by them in the execution of their duties.[126]

IN THE CONCRETE

Consistent with its traditional stand on individual rights in general, the Senate reacted quickly on those relatively few occasions when it felt that the rights or the interests of some particular person or group of

[124]See, e.g., the editorial in the *Globe and Mail*, March 13, and the Toronto *Telegram*, May 4, also the views of the Charlottetown *Guardian*, a Conservative Paper of long standing, in *SD, 1961*, p. 617.

[125]Above, p. 300.

[126]See amendments nos. 25, 26, 28, 31, 45, 49, 54, 60.

persons were being dealt with harshly or unfairly by the proposed legislation. It was largely on these grounds that it rejected the Judges bill in 1933, which sought to retire superior court judges at the age of 75, by providing that judges would be entitled to retire on full pension at 75 while those who did not elect to retire should receive by way of salary no more than the amount of the pension. Influenced by the arguments of Senators from both parties, led in the main by Sen. Beaubien, a Conservative, and Sir Allen Aylesworth, a Liberal, the majority of the Senate took the view that, by seeking to achieve its aim in a circuitous route, the bill was both unworthy of Parliament and violated the rights of the incumbent judges. Consequently, the bill was negatived on second reading, in spite of Meighen's last minute attempt to save it.[127]

Five years later, in the session of 1938, the Senate rejected another piece of legislation, the Penal Reform bill, which planned to replace the administration of the superintendent of penitentiaries by a commission with sweeping powers under the minister of Justice. The Senate felt that the bill dealt very harshly and in some respects unjustly with the then Superintendent, General Ormond, and on third reading it threw it out by 25 votes to 9.[128]

The next opportunity for the Senate to interfere on behalf of the interests of a person was provided by the bill to amend the Exchequer Court Act in 1957. In an effort to pattern the Act more closely upon the Judges Act in relation to the Supreme Court of Canada, the Government inserted a provision in the bill to make it compulsory for the Registrar of the Exchequer Court to reside within five miles of the city of Ottawa. It was pointed out in the Senate that such a limitation, while understandable in the early 1900's, was utterly unrealistic in 1957 and that there was nothing inherent in the position or work of the Registrar that would warrant such a restriction. On the contrary, it was the Senate's unanimous opinion that the main consideration was that he attend to his job and that, within those limitations, where he might choose to live was entirely for him to determine. Accordingly, the five-mile-limit clause was stricken out of the measure as nothing but a nuisance and bother to the person whose interests were involved.[129]

Viewed against this background, the reception by the Senate of the Bank of Canada bill in 1961 was no more extraordinary than that of the

[127]*SD, 1933*, pp. 509, 531.

[128]*Canadian Annual Review, 1937–8*, p. 82; *SD, 1938*, p. 596. The bill was passed the following year with some important amendments. *HD, 1939*, p. 1991.

[129]*SD, 1957*, pp. 332 ff.

Customs Tariff bill in the same session concerning the question of appeal. We have seen that in both cases the Senate was unfortunately caught in a political controversy, which prevented it from taking a unanimous stand on the issues involved. However, it should be emphasized that, although the motivation of the Liberal majority in the Senate may have been coloured by partisan considerations, the *effect* of its action, and thus, that of the Senate, was strictly in line with the Senate's tradition during the last quarter of a century.

Briefly, what constituted the pith and substance of the case is this. Mr. James E. Coyne was appointed Governor of the Bank of Canada in 1954 for a period of seven years under the Bank of Canada Act, 1934, which contained no specific provision for removal of the governor from office. His appointment would have expired in the normal course of events at the end of 1961. Although the relationship between the Government and the Governor was never ideal and it had deteriorated since the end of 1959, when the Governor adopted the practice of making public statements ranging outside his own sphere of monetary policy into fiscal policy, it nevertheless came as a surprise when on May 30, 1961, with little more than six months of his term remaining, he was summoned, without warning, to a private interview with the Minister of Finance, where he was requested to tender his resignation within twelve days. When he refused the Government introduced in the House of Commons the Bank of Canada bill, one of the shortest public measures ever before Parliament, whose three lines and twenty-five words provided that "the office of Governor of the Bank of Canada shall be deemed to have become vacant immediately upon the coming into force of this Act." Passed by the House of Commons the bill then came before the Senate on July 8.

The attitude of the Senate, or at least of its Liberal majority, showed the usual signs of understanding. Whether or not the reasons given by the Government for the immediate resignation of the Governor were correct, what emerged from all the politicking was the possibility that in the process of controversy, conducted in the full view of concentrated public attention, the integrity and the reputation of *an individual* might be endangered. The question, rightly or wrongly, was no longer treated by the Senate as a conflict between a public servant and the Government; it was viewed as a fight of a single individual, harassed and powerless, against the executive. In a sense the measure was looked upon as a bill of attainder, unique in Canadian parliamentary history, with the venerable tradition of the House of Lords in the background, sitting, as it were, as the highest court of the land and delivering a verdict according to the consciences of the individual peers hearing the case. Indeed, there were many even among the Liberal Senators who disagreed with the stand of the Governor in economic policy.[130] But it was a question of *how* he should go. "Here we have a man," Sen. Hugessen said, "an individual, attacked in his honour, in his reputation, in his position by the whole enormous force of a Government with a huge majority in the House of Commons behind it, and I think that rather naturally, *regardless of what we may feel about the merits of the controversy, our sympathies must go out to a man who finds himself in that position.*"[131] Therefore, after the bill was given second reading it was referred to the Banking and Commerce committee—a step not accorded it in the Commons—where the Governor, assisted by his officials, appeared as the sole witness in the case and had his day in court through seven sittings lasting for a total of thirteen-and-a-half hours. By simply allowing him to appear before a parliamentary committee and to state his case the Senate performed a valuable and useful function. It is probable that in spite of the Governor's efforts to justify his conduct the Senate would have passed the bill, for it was fully realized that the abnormal relations between the Governor of the Bank of Canada and the Government of the country could not be continued. However, in view of the implied promise at the end of the Governor's dramatic summary that he would resign the following day, the committee decided by a vote of 16:6 to recommend "that this bill should not be further proceeded with." And it added: "the committee finds that the Governor of the Bank of Canada did not misconduct himself in office." The Senate, thus, was again true to its tradition—the individual was able to leave with his head erect.

In all these cases throughout the years, whether of general or specific application, the Senate has acted in the capacity of a sort of institutional Ombudsman in the Canadian parliamentary system. Through performing its substantive functions on behalf of the supremacy of Parliament and of the interests and rights of the individual the Senate has helped preserve what is worth preserving in the progressive ideas of nineteenth century Whiggism, without in fact implementing its social/economic principles. Its efforts to put a brake upon an all-powerful executive, but not to obstruct the "positive state" which gave rise to the all-powerful executive, may prove to be a quixotic fight. The fact, however, that none of its actions in this regard has been seriously challenged by the

[130]See Hugessen's remarks. *Ibid., 1961*, p. 1069.
[131]*Ibid.*, p. 1130. Italics added.

Government of the day[132] may indicate that the Senate in its substantive role has acted as the "subconsciousness" of the House of Commons, or, for that matter, of the Government. Indeed, not only has the Senate effected substantive modifications in government bills; its consistent stand in matters of parliamentary supremacy and individual rights has served as an effective guide for civil servants at the stage of drafting legislation, by constantly reminding them of the pitfalls their measures may fall into in the Senate[133]—a gratifying example of the "rule of anticipated reactions."

[132]It is significant that no mention was made of the Senate's action on the Customs Tariff bill and the Bank of Canada bill in 1961 during the 1962 election campaign, in spite of earlier rumours that the Government might go to the country on the issue.

[133]Interview with Mr. E. A. Driedger, Deputy Minister of Justice, April 11, 1962.

11 THE SENATE AND SECTIONAL INTERESTS

DURING THE DISCUSSION of the "substantive" functions of the Senate it should constantly be borne in mind that we are talking about a second house of Parliament, which, by its essence and position, is never supposed to be more than a second-line defence within the framework of the political system. We saw in the preceding chapter how the Senate, through effecting changes in government bills, could be a useful expedience for safeguarding the time-honoured principles of parliamentary supremacy and individual rights. It should be stressed, however, that there has been nothing dramatic about its role as a moderating influence on the executive, for the simple reason that there has been nothing dramatic about the attempts of the Executive to tread upon Parliament or the individual. There was no suggestion of a requirement for the Senate to check some genuinely dictatorial forces in the last few decades. It seems rather that the true source of existing dissatisfaction lies in certain general trends and tendencies and the Senate, in its revisory capacity, has been like an index-finger pointing to "those more comprehensive principles, and those remoter consequences" which have tended to be overlooked in the popular house so effectively dominated by the cabinet. As such, the Senate has been an *auxiliary*, rather than a primary, check upon the executive—one of the many control devices provided by the political and social forces of a federal state. Therefore, the word "substantive" in relation to its functions is not to suggest any politically decisive character; it is used simply to contrast those aspects of its work which have a principal undertone with those which are merely for technical usefulness. These qualifying statements by no means try to belittle the services of the Senate; they simply clarify their exact nature.

This auxiliary character and "second-linedness" has a particular relevance in considering the Senate's historic role as a defender of provincial rights. There has been a good deal of misunderstanding and confusion on this point from the outset, the popular notion often being as though the Senate were the main and principal institutional protector of the federal units. The Senate, it should be laid down as a general thesis, is not and could never be destined to play such a role, for the good reason that a "senate-type" of second chamber, such as the Senate of the United States or the old Bundesrat, built into the constitution as a citadel of states' rights, is incompatible with the fundamental principles of the British cabinet system, upon which the political regime of Canada was constructed. The assertion of the federal function of the Senate at the time of Confederation, therefore, was rather a well-calculated political device used as a constitutional tranquillizer to palliate the sectional fears of the weaker partners to federalism from the numerical majorities of the House of Commons. In order that such fears might not endanger the ultimate outcome of the bargain, the value of the Senate as a reliable safeguard of provincial rights had to be stressed. Sen. David, who was sixty years of age at the time of his appointment to the Senate in 1903, could still well remember in 1925 how Sir George Etienne Cartier proclaimed "in his loud voice, in order to induce the French Canadians to accept the article of the Constitution which condemned the province of Quebec never to have more than sixty-five members: 'Do not fear: there will be a guarantee, a compensation, in the fact that the province of Quebec will be represented in the Senate by one-third of its members.' "[1] Another eye-witness of those days, Sir Allen Aylesworth, who was thirteen years old at the time of Confederation, reaffirmed that the "subject of the continuance of a second chamber or upper house was, during the time of the Quebec Conference, not only a matter of daily reading in the household from the columns of the Toronto Globe, but was a matter of daily, I might say almost hourly, discussion between themselves [his father and grandfather, who were "fairly representative of what I call the rank and file of the electors of Upper Canada at that date"] and with neighbours about the farm—in the fields or in the barn, wherever they might be working. . . ." Thus, "to the members of the Clear Grit party in Canada West at the time of the Quebec Conference and at the time of Confederation, it was stated

[1]*SD, 1925*, p. 65.

by George Brown as their leader, not merely in his public speeches or in the columns of his newspaper, but by personal letter, by personal conversation, by intercourse between man and man, that no opposition on their part ought to be offered to the creation of a Senate as an integral part of the Constitution of this country; that it was the price of representation by population, that it was part of the bargain, and that it ought to be accepted—and accepted it was."[2]

Indeed, when after spending nearly half the time of the Quebec Conference on the constitution of the Senate agreement was reached upon the principle of equal sectional representation, George Brown could claim that it was "the very essence of the compact. Our Lower Canadian friends have agreed to give us representation by population in the lower house, on the express condition that they could have equality in the upper house. On no other condition could we have advanced a step."[3] In the same vein Sir Alexander T. Galt declared during the discussions of the London Conference that "to the Legislative Council all the provinces look for protection under the Federal principle," and Sir Charles Tupper reasserted that "in the Maritime provinces we felt that the great preponderance of Canada could only be guarded against by equal representation in the Legislative Council."[4] Thus, the stratagem to present the Senate as the bastion of provincial rights appears to have succeeded in dispelling the original fears of those who felt themselves to be in a numerically disadvantageous position.

Yet, in spite of the confident statements of the time the provision by which appointments to the Senate were to be made by the federal government, and the arrangement under which the numerically weak, when isolated, continued to be numerically weak in the Senate also,[5] cast doubt upon the apparent naivety which greeted the Senate as a real and effective remedy for provincial anxieties. Indeed, Cartier's reference to his sixty-five supporters in the House of Commons and Sir Narcisse Belleau's reassuring words that "the elective principle as applied to the Legislative Council becomes unnecessary in view of the numerical strength of Lower Canada in the Federal Parliament, for the House of Commons is the body that will make and unmake ministries,"[6] indicate that there was ample awareness of the nature of responsible parliamentary government and of the relative importance and scope of its respective

[2]*Ibid.*, p. 506. [3]*Confederation Debates* (Ottawa, 1951), p. 88.

[4]J. Pope, ed., *Confederation Documents* (Toronto, 1895), pp. 117 ff.

[5]See the interesting figures in the article "Let's Stir up the Senate" by J. B. McGeachy in the *Financial Post*, vol. LII, Aug. 2, 1958, about the Senate as it now is and as it would be under representation by population.

[6]*Confederation Debates*, pp. 571, 181.

elements. There must have been awareness that the role of the Senate in this scheme was not to be that of a prime political force, yet allusions continued to be made to it as though it were. From these contradictory attitudes and statements it seems clear that the theme of the Senate as a bulwark of provincial rights was essentially a rhetorical device, a psychological rather than a political remedy.

The federal function of the Senate has proved to be one of the most enduring myths of political demagogy in Canadian history. Whenever attention has been called to its function as a protector of the provinces it was not on the basis of what the Senate "had done when," but rather what it "might do if." While the Senate's effect on the changing patterns of federal-provincial relations has been undetectable, its bare presence has allowed pleas and references to be made to it ostensibly on behalf of the provinces. Thus, for example, the veiled threats directed against the Senate in the Throne Speech in 1925 were interpreted by Quebec Senators as a constitutional attack upon their province. "For the first time since Confederation," Sen. Beaubien said, "we see a Government aiming a blow . . . at the fortress of minority rights in the Dominion. Indeed, there is no doubt that the Senate was created by the Confederation pact the trustee of the rights of minorities."[7] He was strongly supported by Rufus H. Pope, another Senator from Quebec, who assured the House that "the protestants or English-speaking minority of that province stand shoulder to shoulder with the majority in Quebec in declaring that there shall be no alteration made in the constitution of this Senate by any Government of Canada, that will deprive us of the right of appealing to this honourable body for protection from any infringement of the rights of minorities, whether French Canadian or English speaking."[8] Not surprisingly, it has been mostly Opposition members in the House of Commons who have been appealing to the Senate as the saviour of the provinces from an ambitious federal executive. During their long stay in the wilderness Conservative members of the House of Commons often turned to a Liberal-dominated Senate as the bulwark of provincial rights. During a debate in 1955, for example, both Mr. Green and Mr. Diefenbaker spoke of the Senate as the chief constitutional instrumentality of preserving the rights of the provinces.[9] And Mr. Drew, summing up their position on the matter, said:

. . . the primary reason for the setting up of a second chamber was the protection of our federal constitution and the rights of the provinces under

[7]*SD, 1925*, p. 57. [8]*Ibid.*, pp. 79–80. [9]*HD, 1955*, pp. 5339, 5347.

the constitution. . . . It is a guarantee against the invasion of the rights of smaller provinces by the larger provinces; but above all, at a time when there is a greater and greater concentration of financial and political power in the hands of the central government, it may well be the only protection of the provinces against an increasing strength of the central government.[10]

During the same debate Mr. Hansell (SC, Macleod) re-emphasized that ". . . from the constitutional point of view Senators, appointed . . . by the Governor in Council, represent in a sense Her Majesty, and one of their prime functions constitutionally is to guard the rights of sovereign bodies. One of their functions is to protect and guard the rights of the legislatures of the provinces. To me that is . . . perhaps the most important constitutional function of the Senate."[11] This was closely in line with the views expressed by Solon Low during a debate on Senate reform the previous session; ". . . at least until we have built up something like a different political concept in its application to the federal system by the safeguarding of provincial rights," he said, ". . . the Senate can continue to perform a very useful function, in addition to being a check on hasty legislation."[12]

Thus, the Senate, to paraphrase an old saying, has become the opiate of the provinces. Although nobody has been quite certain as to how and when the Senate could intervene on their behalf, provincial governments kept looking to the Senate as a reliable protector of their rights and privileges. At the 1927 Dominion-provincial Conference, which discussed, amongst other things, various reform proposals for the Senate, no provincial premier supported the idea of abolition of the Senate, while all emphasized the right of the provinces to be consulted about any plan of reform. Similarly, although Senate reform was not on the agenda of the 1950 Conference, it is clear from the report that the general opinion of the provincial authorities was that some of the sections of the BNA Act concerning the Senate should not be amended without the consent of Parliament and of all the provinces. It is interesting to compare the stands of the provinces in this regard. Section 17 of the BNA Act, which provides for the existence of the Senate, was classified by New Brunswick in group 5, i.e., amongst the fundamental rights, the so-called entrenched provisions, forming the cornerstone of federalism; Ontario, Nova Scotia and Alberta placed section 17 in category 4, i.e., amongst the provisions to be amended with the consent of all the provinces. Concerning section 21, which establishes the number of Senators, Ontario, Nova Scotia, British Columbia, Prince Edward Island, Alberta, and Newfoundland submitted that the number of Senators should not be changed without

[10]*Ibid.*, pp. 6009–11. [11]*Ibid.*, p. 5337. [12]*Ibid., 1954*, p. 5249.

the consent of all the provinces. With regard to representation of provinces in the Senate, as laid down in section 22, Ontario, Nova Scotia, Prince Edward Island, Alberta, and Newfoundland were opposed to any change in this area without the consent of all the provinces. The same opinion was held by Prince Edward Island and Alberta of section 23 affecting the qualifications of Senators. Sections 26–28 inclusive provide for the addition of Senators; section 29 fixes the tenure for life and section 31 determines the grounds for disqualification of Senators. (Sections 32–36 deal with procedure.) With regard to sections 26–29, Alberta held that these sections required the unanimous consent of the provinces for their amendment. Prince Edward Island maintained that the life tenure as well as the reasons for disqualification should be modified only if all the provinces approve such a change. In their briefs Manitoba and Saskatchewan took the position that the provisions of the BNA Act relating to the Senate concern Parliament only.[13] The Quebec brief itself did not make any specific reference to the Senate; however, the province's historic stand is to be found in the appendices of the report of the Attorneys General. Accordingly, Quebec considered sections 24, 29, 31, and 32 as concerning all provincial legislatures; it classified sections 33, 35, and 36 in groups 1 and 4, while it put in categories 5 and 4 sections 22, 26, 27, and 28. What emerges from these recorded views reflects the traditional psychological attachment of Quebec and the Maritime provinces to the Senate. "Over the years," Sen. Robertson of Nova Scotia remarked in 1959, "there has been a curious friendship and common interest between Quebec and the Maritime provinces . . . that springs from the thought that one was a minority of racial origin and the other a minority based on economics. I would be quite prepared to believe that the West is not as interested in the Senate as are Quebec and the Maritime provinces."[14] And he probably offered the most candidly accurate expression of the "psychological approach" to the Senate's federal role when he held that although the Senate had never really fought for provincial rights in face of federal encroachment he felt *instinctively* that the Senate had that role and that "should the occasion arise, any attempt on the part of any Government to encroach on the rights of the minorities in Canada would be fiercely resisted in this Chamber."[15]

The misconception behind this curious blend of bluff and wishful aspirations regarding the Senate's role in the field of provincial rights has probably been caused by the unfortunate choice of the word

[13]*Proceedings* of the Dominion-Provincial Conference, 1950, 2nd session.
[14]*SD, 1959*, pp. 588–9. [15]*Ibid.*, and *ibid., 1950*, p. 204.

"defend." Somehow the Senate has been pictured as a body whose function is to shield the provinces from the deliberately vicious onslaughts of a central government. However, similarly to its substantive functions in connection with parliamentary supremacy and individual rights, any dramatization of the Senate's role in the federal field is bound to misplace the emphasis. The Senate has never had to deal with an encroaching executive wilfully violating the sacred domain of provincial rights. Rather, the danger has been posed by general, historical, and universal trends, which the Senate has been too fragile a force to resist. The movements and counter-movements that so fundamentally transformed Canadian federalism in the last two generations or so have clashed outside the Senate. In spite of the grandiloquence of the Confederation debates and the lip service that has continually been paid to the Senate ever since, the provinces have found the guardians of their rights elsewhere. During the period of classical federalism it was the judicial process, in the present phase of co-operative federalism, characterized by nation-wide enterprise and a nationalization of sentiment, it has been the political process.[16] The direct connection between provincial premiers and the federal government, the use of Dominion-provincial conferences as clearing-houses for all sorts of disputed questions, the closely observed constitutional convention that the federal cabinet must mirror in its composition all the provinces of the country, and the political fact that no democratically sustained government can afford to ignore the provinces are certainly more reassuring bulwarks of provincial rights than the Senate. If it be objected that all these political and constitutional instrumentalities are inadequate to meet the complex problems that plague French Canada, it is equally difficult to see how the Senate, as a legislative forum, could be of much help. Indeed, already on the basis of its first fifty-seven years of history, Prof. Mackay could ascertain that the Senate was a centripetal, rather than a centrifugal, force in the structure of Canadian federalism.[17] "Senators," said Sen. Turgeon, an Acadian, in 1925, "should look after the policies of the country at large, and their secondary or more local functions are not so insistent as those of members of the House of Commons."[18] Indeed, the notion that the

[16]For a lucid summary on this changing pattern, see Prof. J. A. Corry's study on "Constitutional Trends and Federalism," in R. M. Clark, ed., *Canadian Issues, Essays in Honour of Henry F. Angus* (Toronto, 1961).

[17]R. A. Mackay, *The Unreformed Senate of Canada* (London, 1926), pp. 144–5. His conclusion seems to be maintained in the revised (1963) edition, p. 121.

[18]*SD, 1925*, p. 163.

Senate has been essentially a nationalizing force (partly because of the appointing system and partly because of the former careers of its members) has never lacked strong advocates in the House itself.[19] The understanding on the part of the majority of Senators of the meaning of co-operative federalism and of the Senate's place in it received perhaps its most concise and mature definition in the following statement of Sen. Lambert:

> Whatever may have been expected to happen in this Chamber following Confederation is very different from what happened. . . . the historical reasons for the beginnings of our Confederation have been overshadowed by the realities of political growth. . . . In considering the broad political situation in this country, both domestic and international . . . it is important to avoid any suggestion that "dominion" and "provinces" are mutually exclusive terms. The dominion and the provinces are complementary to each other; indeed, they are more essential to each other today than ever before. . . . *Senators must remember that they are members of an integral part of the federal parliament.* We cannot approach any of our duties apart from the standpoint of what is in the broad federal or national interest. This does not imply the exclusion of provincial interests. The provinces have a vital federal interest: it exists in the common ground of mutual relations in trade and commerce, in taxation, in defence, in social standards and security. In short, it exists in the sphere of all-around national welfare. *Our duty is to see that matters of concern to the provinces are clearly and definitely presented here . . . that emphasis is put in the right place, and that unity of democratic purpose shall be promoted throughout this land, regardless of language, race or creed.*[20]

Indeed, it is difficult to see how the Senate during the last thirty-seven years could have defended provincial rights in the classical sense without exposing itself to the charge of protecting outmoded economic and social principles. It should be remembered that the *argument* (if not the reason) for defeating the Old Age Pensions bill in 1926 was that it violated provincial jurisdiction over property and civil rights. Yet, few would regard the Senate's action in that instance as a proper exercise of its protective responsibilities towards the provinces. Using the same argument as in 1926 the Senate could, if it had wanted, have thrown out a considerable portion of the Government's program in 1935, thus relieving the courts of subsequent litigation. However, the Senate did not do so and there was no suggestion on either side of the House that it should do so. Similarly, it was pointed out that the Senate

[19]See, e.g., Sen. Roebuck's article, "Tinkering with the Senate of Doubtful Value," *Saturday Night*, vol. LXIX, Feb. 27, 1954.

[20]*SD, 1950*, pp. 500 ff. Italic added. See also his article, "Reform of the Senate," reprinted from the *Winnipeg Free Press*, April, 1950.

failed to take "a proper attitude" on the Family Allowances Act—"the most flagrant encroachment of provincial rights," in which "from the title to the last clause, the Government dealt with matters which belonged to the provinces and against the principles given in the judgement . . . in re the Unemployment Insurance Act."[21] Even Sen. Lambert had to admit "that the Senate would have been justified in refusing to pass the bill at that time because it was presented to us on the eve of an election and without any appreciable demand for it from any part of the country."[22] The Senate was accused also of neglecting its duties in the case of the Redistribution Act, which did away with the provision that the number of seats in Quebec should be fixed at 65 and that this number should be used to establish a population quotient for determining the number of seats in all other provinces.[23] In the Canadian Wheat Board bill of 1947, which declared all grain elevators and mills mentioned in the schedule to the bill to be a work for the general advantage of Canada, only Sen. Farris objected to taking away, by "a solemn statutory declaration" a provincial jurisdiction under subsection 10 of section 92 of the BNA Act and substituting Dominion jurisdiction, without the leave or consent or sanction of the provinces involved; the Senate made no attempt to interfere.[24] It remained passive in the Dairy Industry Act, too, with the result that it was left to the courts "to arrive at a decision in that matter, and results were achieved which apparently were not possible in the Parliament of Canada . . . such instances affect the entire function of the Senate in its relation to provincial rights."[25] Likewise, Sen. Roebuck's cautiously phrased dubiety as to the absolute constitutionality of the Canada Council bill in 1957 was not even entertained by the Senate, whose members were, instead, engaged in hailing the measure as a sign of Parliament's forward-looking attitude in the field of education.[26] Surely, it would have been difficult for the Senate with its new look on the "positive state" to substitute itself for the judicial committee of the privy council. Not unlike the United States Supreme Court after 1940, the Senate's "activism" has been concentrated on the fields of parliamentary supremacy and individual rights, while removing all effective opposition to the economic/social policies endorsed by the elected representatives of the people. As such, the Senate could not possibly live up to the expectations of the Fathers—that is, if the Fathers had, indeed, any expectations at all.

[21]Marcotte's remarks. *Ibid.*, p. 419.
[22]*Ibid.*, p. 503.
[23]*Ibid.*, pp. 419, 504.
[24]*Ibid., 1947*, pp. 328–9.
[25]*Ibid., 1950*, p. 503.
[26]*Ibid., 1957*, pp. 341 ff. For other instances, see Mackay, *The Unreformed Senate* (1963), pp. 118–21.

The fact, however, that the Senate is not a primary safeguard of provincial rights should not be taken to imply that it has no useful function to perform as a reinforcement of provincial or sectional interests. Indeed, there appear to be four ways of attaining this end. In the first place, since the Senate's concurrence is necessary for amending the BNA Act, the Senate can make it sure that the device of formal amendment of the constitution is not used lightly or to the detriment of the provinces. This function, while important today, will certainly gain in significance if and when the process of "domiciling" the constitution of Canada has been completed. As Sen. Robertson, that keen observer of the functions of the modern Senate, said, the Senate had a useful and acceptable role to play "in the relations between federal and provincial authorities, now that we are in the process of acquiring the right to amend our own constitution . . . When the time comes that we have power to deal with this important matter in Canada, the responsibilities of the Senate will be even greater than they are today. The protection of minority and territorial rights will, I suggest, be one of the duties of the Senate. . . ."[27]

There have been two occasions during the period under study on which the Senate has exercised its inherent power in constitutional amendments. On May 19, 1936, a Joint Address, already approved by the House of Commons, reached the Senate to amend the BNA Act, by limiting the rights of provinces to borrow money and widening the field of taxation available to them. In the ensuing long debate, which was extended over five sittings, the amendment was criticized in the Senate for its effect of empowering the provinces to levy indirect taxes. Consequently, the recommendation of the Banking and Commerce committee for removing the provision of conferring on the provinces certain powers of indirect taxation was concurred in by the Senate by a vote of 49 to 10, three Liberal Senators, Hardy, Hughes, and Little, voting against the official stand.[28] A conciliatory amendment moved by the Government having failed to pass[29] the main motion was finally defeated by 40 votes to 15. The Address was not subsequently revived.

The second case occurred in 1960 over an amendment of section 99 of the BNA Act, providing for a retirement age of 75 for judges on superior courts as well as on district and county courts. Some isolated instances of opposition aside, centred on the retroactive character of the amendment, the main line of criticism in the Senate was directed against the "expensive constitutional superfluity" of dealing with district and county court judges in an amendment to the BNA Act through the

[27]*Ibid., 1951*, p. 55. [28]*SJ, 1936*, p. 205. [29]*Ibid.*, p. 227.

instrumentality of the Parliament of the United Kingdom, when such judges had been retired at 75 since 1913 under the Judges Act. This unnecessary degeneration of the method of formal constitutional amendment was denounced also as a backward step, "an attitude of colonial dependency and of a national inferiority complex which it was hoped that we in this country had outlived."[30] Accordingly, an amendment was adopted, removing district and county court judges from the Senate resolution, and it was passed unanimously, only Sen. Aseltine opposing it in his official capacity as Government Leader in the Senate.[31] Since in this instance, unlike the 1936 case,[32] identical addresses were submitted in each chamber, the Government could choose between two alternatives; either to transmit two different resolutions to the Queen or to bring the House of Commons resolution into harmony with the amended version of the Senate Address.[33] The Government decided to choose the latter; on July 29 the Minister of Justice, on behalf of the Prime Minister, moved that the House resolution be rescinded and a new one be substituted therefore, identical in language with that of the Senate. "This change," the minister said, "is made necessary . . . by the fact that the other place . . . came to the conclusion that they should delete the reference to district and county court judges." And he added in an afterthought: "The determination of the retiring age of county court judges might . . . still be made in accordance with the present provisions of the Judges Act."[34]

As a second form of looking after the interests of the various regions of the country, the Senate has often made modifications in government legislation. Sometimes such changes were aimed at promoting the interests or claims of the provinces in general. Thus, for example, in the Canteen Funds Distribution bill of 1925, which provided for the disposition of a sum of $2,300,000 amongst returned soldiers, the Senate inserted an amendment, to the effect that instead of a central

[30]*Ibid., 1960*, p. 1022. [31]*Ibid.*, p. 1058.

[32]Of course, the Government might have chosen the procedure of introducing a resolution in one House to be transmitted to the other. But the Minister of Justice said he had found that the procedure followed in this instance was "the procedure that has been followed with respect to addresses regarding amendments to the Constitution since 1940." He had "not been able to find authority as to why this course began to be followed and has been consistently followed since 1940 whereas previously it was not the course followed." *HD, 1960*, p. 7203. The Government simply accepted the procedures worked out by the officials of the two Houses. As a procedural consequence of the method of two identical resolutions, the device of a free conference between the two Houses in case of disagreements was no longer feasible under Commons Rule 22. See below, p. 360.

[33]See remarks of Mr. Argue (CCF, Assiniboia). *HD, 1960*, p. 6343.

[34]*Ibid.*, pp. 7193–4.

agency the existing machinery of the provinces be used for distribution of the fund. The change, incidentally, also met the demands of the ex-servicemen who appeared to be hostile to the idea of a Dominion Veterans' bureau.[35] Perhaps the one case in the last twenty-five years in which a Senate amendment was based purely on the ground that the provision infringed upon "property and civil right" was the amendment made to section 6 of the Criminal Code bill of 1935; paragraph (*f*) of the said clause made it an offence to deduce "from any employee's wages for any purpose not warranted by law unless such deduction has been approved first by a competent public authority." The Senate's Banking and Commerce committee deleted the provision from the measure for fear that "there, if anywhere, you are definitely on the ground of civil rights."[36] The amendment was accepted by the Government. In the same bill the Senate made another amendment at the request of law officers of the provincial governments to render the law more definite in regard to gambling devices found in stores and places where the public resorted.[37] Similarly, the Senate made it sure, through amending the RCMP bill of 1940, that before the Minister of Justice exercised his authority under the Act to enter into agreements with municipalities for the taking over of the policing of them he had the approval of the provincial governments.[38]

The amendments put to the Northwest Territories bill of 1940, on the other hand, were intended to satisfy Western pride. The measure, which sought to extend to superior courts of Ontario jurisdiction in civil matters within that portion of the Territories lying east of the 80th meridian, came under the concentrated attacks of Western members of the House, who argued that if the bill became law certain parts of the Northwest Territories, including some mining centres, would come under Ontario jurisdiction. Instructed by the Senate, the Banking and Commerce committee amended the bill, giving jurisdiction in civil matters to the courts of the provinces of Ontario, Quebec, Nova Scotia, New Brunswick, and Prince Edward Island with respect to all parts of the Territories lying east of the 89th meridian, and to the courts of the provinces of Manitoba, Saskatchewan, Alberta and British Columbia over the parts lying west of the 89th meridian.[39]

In some rare instances individual Senators were able to secure changes in government legislation favourable to their own districts. Thus, for example, Sen. Bureau, a former Minister of Customs and

[35] *SD, 1925*, pp. 258, 592 ff. *HD*, *1925*, pp. 4799–800.
[36] *SD, 1935*, p. 466.
[37] *HD, 1935*, pp. 4297–8.
[38] *Ibid., 1940*, p. 2249.
[39] *SD, 1940*, pp. 264–5.

Excise, successfully intervened to prevent the cutting off a part of the city of Three Rivers from the harbour limits—as was proposed by the Three Rivers Harbour Commissioners bill in 1927. A Senator from Three Rivers, Sen. Bureau obtained the advance approval of the Minister of Marine before introducing his amendment.[40]

Perhaps the Senate's most effective interventions have been on behalf of Maritime interests. It amended the Bank bill of 1934, whose purpose was to permit the banks to advance money for the purchase of seed grain upon the security of the crop to be grown. It was recognized in the Senate that the farmer in the Maritimes would be handicapped under the Act, in that if he wanted to obtain a loan from an organization with which to buy fertilizer, he was compelled to mortgage his product to that organization. Therefore, on the suggestion of its members representing agricultural communities, the Senate amended the bill, so that fertilizer and seed grain were placed on the same basis. The amendment, explained in the Commons by the Prime Minister himself, was greeted as an important improvement by members of the House.[41]

Agricultural interests were again advanced by the action of the Senate in connection with the Transport Board bill in both 1937 and 1938. Introduced as a Senate measure in the session of 1937 the bill was sharply criticized both inside and outside Parliament for its provision to empower the Transport Board to license truck operations and fix tariffs on intra-provincial traffic. Opposition was strongest on the part of the Maritime Senators, who demanded in the Railway, Telegraph and Harbours committee that their section should be exempted from the operation of the bill. Although their motion was defeated by a narrow margin, the intensity of their representations induced the Government to move an amendment to meet Maritime demands. Encouraged by the success of their Maritime colleagues, Senators from the West asked for similar concessions at the third reading stage. They saw in the bill an attempt "to improve the situation of the railways . . . by imposing an extra charge upon the grain producers . . ., for the application of this principle [i.e., the one embodied in the bill] is tantamount to giving a free right of way to individuals or companies in order that they may establish transportation lines without competition."[42] That the opposition was primarily sectional was shown by the fact that Conservative Senators other than from the prairie provinces supported the regulatory provisions of the legislation.[43] However, in the end sentiment was strongly against the bill and it was defeated by 30 votes to 18 on third

[40]*Ibid., 1927*, p. 391. [41]*HD, 1934*, pp. 4251 ff. *SD, 1934*, pp. 508, 571.
[42]*SD, 1937*, pp. 183–4, 210.
[43]See, for example, Sen. Beaubien's (Quebec) remarks. *Ibid.*, p. 203.

reading, with Dandurand and Meighen abstaining.[44] The following session the bill reappared in the Senate after it had been passed by the House of Commons. This time responding to representations from British Columbia, which had been largely ignored by the Commons, the Senate amended the bill to exempt shipments from that province to Atlantic ports *via* the Panama Canal; it also exempted certain classes of freight on the Great Lakes from agreed charges, for the purpose of preventing an increase in the cost of transport to the primary producers of Western Canada.[45] The Government, after a "good deal of consideration," concurred in the Senate amendments, which were passed into law.[46]

Similarly to its moves on behalf of farmers, the Senate has often stepped in in the interest of Maritime fishermen. The Salt Fish Board bill of 1939, for example, was stopped at the third reading stage by Sen. Tanner of Nova Scotia, who requested the bill to be referred back to committee and amended to make it perfectly clear that it was intended to assist the fisherman rather than the middle-man. Indeed, urged by Fisheries committees of various Boards of Trade in the Maritime Provinces, the Senate's Banking and Commerce committee made three substantive amendments; by amending the preamble of the bill it clearly set out as the objective of the legislation the obtaining of better prices for their products by the fishermen-producers; by modifying section 2 it provided that all members of the board should be representatives of the fishermen-producers; and by deleting section 9 of the bill, it freed the board of the tutelage of the Governor-in-Council. The amendments were approved by the Minister of Fisheries and the Minister of National Revenue, who had both appeared before the Banking and Commerce committee, and greatly pleased some members of the Commons who had fought for the same results without success.[47]

[44]*Ibid.*, p. 225. "Aimed definitely at an increase in the existing rates for grain carriage on the Great Lakes," R. Banks commented in the *Saturday Night*, "it [the bill] met the stormy protests by the wheat-growers of the prairies. The bill was killed in the Senate and the Senate has appropriated for itself the popular side of a controversy over legislation. It also served to weaken the reputation of the Senate as the champion of the so-called big interests among which the transportation companies rank fairly close to the top." March 27, 1937. It was because of the fate of this bill that C. D. Howe decided not to initiate more legislation in the Senate.

[45]*Ibid., 1938*, p. 483.

[46]*HD, 1938*, p. 4446.

[47]"This is an excellent illustration," Mr. Stevens said, "of the value of having legislation from this House pass through another sphere before becoming law." Mr. Neill (Ind., Comox-Alberni) congratulated Stevens, Cahan, and himself "upon having been upheld by the wisdom of the Upper House in giving us so much of what we fought for so unsuccessfully just a few days ago." *HD, 1939*, pp. 4914–5.

In the Canada Shipping bill of 1948, which was first introduced in the Senate, the House of Commons changed the definition of a "sailing ship," with the result that the small fisherman, operating a boat of over ten tons, was required to have a certified master for taking his fish to market in his vessel. Arguing that the new limitation would be a hindrance to the traffic of small vessels in minor or coastal waters, Sen. Kinley of Nova Scotia moved an amendment in the Transport and Communications committee to restore the original provision of the bill. His motion having failed by a majority of one, he resumed the fight when the bill reached report stage in Committee of the Whole in the Senate. "As one closely connected with the people who live along the coasts of this country," he considered it his duty "to bring to the attention of Parliament what I regard as their right and what I believe should be retained in their interests. . . . Whatever we do, I feel that our people along the coast should know that we who represent them here are looking after their interests. . . ."[48] This time his efforts proved successful. Having discussed the matter with the law officers of the department and having secured the support of a considerable number of people in the House of Commons he was able to prevail upon the Government to accept his amendment. Indeed, his knowledge of the trade and his interest in the conditions of people who made a living out of it in the Atlantic provinces were so well recognized that the Government let it be known through its representative in the Senate that it was favourably "predisposed towards any suggestion that he may make in their interests . . . and shall be happy to concur."[49] And so it did.

The same measure came up again in the session of 1956 with the provision to empower the Governor-in-Council to make regulations requiring masters and mates of fishing vessels to hold certificates of competence. This suggested departure from traditional administrative practice was promptly attacked by Senators from the Maritime provinces, who urged that before the bill was enacted full consideration of the views of the fishermen must be given. Instead of regulations, they demanded an educational program to be launched to prepare the fishermen for the contemplated change.[50] Consequently, after hearing all interested parties the Transport and Communications committee came to the conclusion that the time had not arrived for compelling masters and mates of small vessels to obtain licences, wherefore it struck out the relevant section of the bill. The Government quickly acquiesced in the amendment, and members of the Commons praised the Senate

[48]*SD, 1948*, pp. 547, 578.
[49]*Ibid.*, p. 578.
[50]*Ibid., 1956*, pp. 370.

for the circumspection and care it displayed in behalf of Maritime fishermen.[51]

The third method available for the Senate to protect provincial interests is in the field of private legislation. The forms in which this can be done depend on the nature of the bills that seek to promote the interests of private bodies.[52] In case of railway lines the Senate has been watchful that the promoters had the consent of municipalities for the construction and operation of lines along highways or public places, establishment of connections and offices, regulation of tolls and charges, protection of crossing, drainage of lands, etc. A more substantial issue arose in 1956 in connection with the bill to authorize the Grand Falls Central Railway Company to enter into the highway transportation business under the relevant provisions of the Dominion Railway Act. Objections were raised that as the bill stood the new company would not be made subject to the jurisdiction of the provincial authorities. These suspicions were reinforced by the testimony of the Minister of Transport, Mr. Marler, who told the Senate's Transport and Communications committee that it was a matter of Government policy for trucking business to remain under the jurisdiction of the provincial authorities. Thereupon the Senate quickly moved in and amended the measure, by striking out the reference to the Railway Act and securing the predominance of the provincial authorities.[53]

There is a similar precaution with regard to telegraph and telephone companies. In the session of 1957–58, for instance, a bill was introduced in the Senate to increase the capital stock of the Bell Telephone Company from 500 million to 1,000 million dollars, for the double purpose of expansion and payment of commission on stock sales. Since the bill contained only one condition as to the validity of the issue and the sale of capital stock, namely, that such issue and sale must have the endorsement of the Board of Transport Commissioners for Canada, Senators feared that the effect of the provision would be to interfere with provincial legislation, especially as regards the securities commissions which operated in practically every province for the prevention of fraud. There was no doubt in the minds of the Senators that the authority of the provinces would be maintained by the courts; but it was recognized also that this would have entailed litigation and certain difficulties and

[51]See in particular the comments of Mr. Bell (PC, St. John-Albert). *HD, 1956*, p. 5560.

[52]See the letter of Mr. Creighton, Law Clerk of the Senate, to Sen. Béique. *SD, 1925*, p. 500.

[53]*Ibid.*, *1956*, pp. 530–1.

that innocent parties might have been put to expense. Therefore, the Senate amended the bill to reinforce provincial authority.[54]

In the case of power companies, protective clauses similar to the provisions in the Railway Act had occasionally to be inserted to frustrate attempts to establish monopolies or to obtain control of provincial resources.[55] The Senate was on its guard also in the case of bills respecting religious, educational, charitable, and benevolent corporations and associations, as well as miscellaneous organizations for patriotic, professional, artistic, scientific, trading, etc., purposes, to make it sure that there was no interference with the exclusive powers of the provincial legislatures under section 92 and 93 of the BNA Act, particularly subsection 13 of section 92.[56]

In all these cases the action of the Senate to protect provincial interests had some immediately visible effect, usually in form of modifications effected in the legislation before the house. As a fourth, final, method the Senate has provided a forum, both in the Chamber and in committee, for its members to intervene on behalf of their respective provinces or sections either in general debates or through contributing to the discussion of a particular measure. Such interventions (even if not resulting in prompt remedies) suggest that Senators do have the problems of their localities at heart and, in spite of their interest in national affairs, are ready to speak out for the provinces they come from. Thus, a New Brunswick Senator, Thorburn says, "sees himself as a spokesman for his province, and the Maritime region generally. Many references are made to the troubles faced by fishing, forestry, and potato growing industries. Much is made of the tendency of young New Brunswickers to migrate to other provinces. . . ."[57]

While Maritime Senators have certainly been in the foreground as champions of their section, willingness to plead the cause of one's province or region has been a fairly general phenomenon in the Senate during the years from 1925 to 1963. Thus, for example, in 1925 three Senators from Manitoba, Senators McMeans, Sharpe, and Watson (a Laurier appointee) put up a chivalrous fight to block the passage of the Railway Freight Rates bill, which they considered detrimental to their province. Their amendment, however, was not acceptable to the Government and it lacked the support of the majority of the House too.[58] In

[54]*Ibid.*, *1957–58*, pp. 62, 77–81, 124–8.

[55]E.g., Gatineau Transmission Company bill. *SJ*, *1926*, p. 296.

[56]E.g., the Pharmacy Examining Board of Canada bill, *SD*, *1962–63*, pp. 424–5, 442–4.

[57]H. G. Thorburn, *Politics in New Brunswick* (Toronto, 1961), pp. 45 ff.

[58]*SD*, *1925*, pp. 616, 640.

the same session provincial considerations cut across party ties on the bill to construct a new branch line between Sunnybrae and Guysborough, Nova Scotia. Ignoring Sen. Loughheed's opposition to it, Conservative Senators Girroir, McLennan, and Tanner from Nova Scotia rallied behind the measure, because "the districts on their own merits are deserving of railway communication . . . for the people who live away down in the far eastern part of Nova Scotia, where they have been waiting and waiting and waiting for thirty and more years for the sound of the railway whistle."[59]

Still in 1925 Sen. Willoughby of Saskatchewan initiated a general debate on rural credits, well in advance of the introduction by the Government of its Rural Credits bill. Thus, the debate, Sen. Dandurand told the House, "may have some influence on the action of the Government."[60] It was for similar purposes that Sen. Robertson introduced a debate on the conditions of Nova Scotia coal mines, or that in the session of 1927 Sen. Hughes of Prince Edward Island brought up the question of a potato warehouse at George Town, PEI. In the following session he again rose to call the Senate's attention to the marked discrimination against King's County, one of the three counties in Prince Edward Island, with regard to public works, public service, or public appointment. He was anxious to place this complaint before Parliament prior to the preparation of the Supplementary Estimates, "in order that at least a measure of justice might be done to that county."[61]

Maritime interests were advocated in the debate, originated by Sen. Black of New Brunswick in 1929, on the necessity of building the Chignecto Isthmus Canal to connect the Northumberland straits with the Bay of Fundy and, thus, to facilitate direct shipment of Atlantic products by water as far west as Port Arthur and Fort William. Maritime Senators participating in the discussion were promised by the Government Leader that the matter would be looked into by the cabinet.[62] Sen. Hughes was once again instrumental in raising the question of Prince Edward Island's financial situation in comparison to the other provinces of Canada. Speaking on behalf of his province, the Liberal Senator said:

> It would be hard to find in the history of the modern world a more pronounced example of discrimination. . . . Prince Edward Island has now reached what might be termed almost a crisis in her history. Notwithstanding economy in every department of the Government service, and the levying of all the local taxation the people can bear, we cannot make ends meet.

[59] *Ibid., 1925*, pp. 644–6.
[60] *Ibid.*, p. 150.
[61] *Ibid., 1928*, p. 147.
[62] *Ibid., 1929*, p. 129.

We are going deeper into debt all the time. . . . Our population is dwindling . . . with our revenue we cannot make anything like adequate provision for the sick and the poor. . . . We cannot think of introducing the old age pension scheme . . . our educational system was on the eve of disorganization—perhaps disruption—lately, and a crisis was narrowly averted.[63]

There was some uneasiness on the part of Senators of Alberta and British Columbia with regard to the National Parks bill of 1930, for fear that certain "choice areas" might be acquired by private interests and they wanted to make it sure that "the Provincial Government will be protected in the transfer of those lands."[64] They were not satisfied until Belcourt, the Acting Government Leader of the Senate, brought authorized information from the Government that the areas in question were to remain under the administration of the federal government, and that no privileges of any kind would be granted by the government until the whole transfer of the national resources was consummated.[65]

Even the special committee on Tourist Traffic in 1934, despite its best efforts to take a national view, could not completely refrain from favouring sectional interests, and both in its report and in the summary of its chairman, Sen. Dennis from Nova Scotia, special attention was given to the importance of tourist trade to the Maritime provinces. The committee looked "to the tourist trade as one of our greatest sources of revenue and the means through which we may bring back to their native land those sons and daughters of the Maritimes now living in another country." It was pointed out also that "if at the moment we lack adequate industrial development in Maritime Canada, we have a priceless asset in our unmatched scenery and climate . . . and as members of the family of confederated provinces we urge that special considerations be given the Maritime situation in the provision of better highways and transportation services, particularly the development of steamship traffic tapping the great centres of population which lie on or near the American seaboard."[66]

The question of Nova Scotia coal mines again formed the subject of a general debate (initiated by Sen. Tanner of Nova Scotia) in 1936, in which the Government was strongly urged to consider measures for the purpose of enabling the Nova Scotia coal mining industry to expand its markets within Canada. Sen. Dandurand, Leader of the Government in the Senate, said at the conclusion of the debate that he would convey its résumé to the minister of mines. In the same session the debate, occupying the Senate for nine sittings, over the problem of setting up a

[63]*Ibid.*, p. 133.
[64]*SD*, *1930*, pp. 253–4.
[65]*Ibid.*, p. 259.
[66]*Ibid.*, *1934*, p. 401.

Canadian amending process of the BNA Act offered an opportunity for French-Canadian Senators to restate the rights and claims of Canadians of French descent and the position of the province of Quebec in the scheme of Canadian federalism.[67]

In the first post-war session of Parliament Senators from the Maritime provinces raised a general discussion on the question of hydro-electric development in New Brunswick, which was being studied by the Government along the lines of the recommendations of the Senate's Railway committee in 1944. Contributors to the debate wanted quick action, for "the lack of hydro-electric energy in the Maritime and Prairie provinces has been a serious handicap for their industrial growth, and leaves them at a marked disadvantage in the home market when their manufacturing products come into competition with those of Central Canada."[68] It was urged that there was "a moral obligation on the part of the more fortunate provinces to come to the rescue of the ever willing but always handicapped Maritime provinces."[69] A few sessions later Sen. Burchill of New Brunswick introduced a debate on the Maritime lumber industry,[70] while three of his colleagues, Senators McLean, Veniot, and Léger, have consistently stressed the case of fishermen and canners in New Brunswick and the Atlantic region as a whole.[71] Even such a broad topic as Sen. Robertson's motion in 1957 to create a free trade area with the United Kingdom and the United States had its sectional-provincial aspects; it was urged during the three-day debate that one of the main objectives of such a policy would be to provide an opportunity for the less prosperous areas of Canada to attain a degree of economic development comparable to that enjoyed by the "have" areas.

In assessing the value of such interventions, the same principles that were laid down in connection with the indirect effects of Senate debates in general[72] should be borne in mind. However, it is to be noted that because of the paramount importance attached to federal considerations in the political process Senate debates ventilating real provincial or sectional grievances will probably be listened to by the Government more carefully than are discussions of a more general character. Indeed, it is the duty of the Leader of the Senate to indicate to the members of the cabinet the opinions expressed in the House, and in view of the

[67]See in particular the contributions of Senators Casgrain, Bourgeois, Chapais, Turgeon, Marcotte, Beaubien, and Dandurand.

[68]*SD, 1945*, p. 152.

[69]*Ibid.*, p. 154.

[70]*Ibid.*, 1949 (2nd session), Dec. 2 and 8.

[71]Thorburn, *Politics in New Brunswick*, pp. 168–9.

[72]Above, pp. 224 ff.

sensitivity of any Government to provincial or sectional interests it is unlikely that such opinions would be ignored studiously or systematically.

In sum, the Senate's federal record during the years 1925–63 suggests that in spite of rhetorical references to the contrary, it has acted in full understanding of the nature of cabinet government and of its own place and role in the system. The sheer fact that there is a Senate may still have some psychological value for those who conceive federalism in terms of mutually exclusive spheres of power. However, in actual practice the Senate has been not so much a bulwark against an unidentified foe, as an additional line of representation of provincial or sectional interests. Through its revisory work, its committees and its debates, reminding the Government of some failure or shortcoming, it has been a distinguished spokesman of the component parts of Canadian federalism. Thus, what the Senate may have lost in drama as a "citadel of provincial rights," it has regained in constructive effect as an auxiliary form of protection of the provinces in Parliament.

12 THE POWERS OF THE SENATE AND RELATIONS BETWEEN THE TWO HOUSES

IT SEEMS APPROPRIATE to wind up the factual discussion of the Senate's work and functions with a statement of its powers and the way in which they are exercised. Although party discipline and the ascendency of the cabinet have rendered somewhat anachronistic the traditional notion which conceived Parliament in terms of two opposing chambers, it is still possible in a technical sense to speak of the powers of the Senate as a corporate entity in its relations with the House of Commons. The two main criteria of assessment are the Senate's power over money bills and its power of delaying and rejecting legislation. In both, the Senate's prerogatives remained unchanged since Confederation. Unlike the House of Lords, which has suffered considerable curtailments in its powers on two separate occasions in the last fifty years, the power and position of the Senate has never been seriously threatened. The reason for this relative security has been that, although the legal powers of the Senate are unparalleled among second chambers in parliamentary regimes, so has been the Senate's moderation and discretion to use them. Curiously, both the scope of these powers and the caution with which the Senate has used them have been closely connected with the principles governing the Senate's federal role. Whereas the granting of the powers was prompted by the original theory concerning the Senate's function to protect the provinces, the exercise of the powers has been shaped by the Senate's understanding of the practical limits of that function.

1. *The Senate and Financial Legislation*

In the case of financial legislation the conflict of views between the two chambers has centred around the question whether the Senate has a right to amend money bills as that term is generally understood. Since our discussion is concerned with current political realities it seems sufficient to describe the relevant rules as briefly as possible. The written part of the Constitution, by virtue of sections 53 and 54 of the BNA Act, provides that bills for appropriating any part of the public revenue or for imposing any tax or impost have to originate in the House of Commons and that appropriation measures must be preceded by a royal recommendation. Convention requires, however, that taxation measures must also be preceded by a royal recommendation and that both supply and taxation bills have to be founded on a resolution that has been considered and recommended by a Committee of the Whole House in the Commons. These provisions, clearly, make it impossible for the Senate to revise financial legislation upward, because it would be tantamount to introducing a money bill.[1] While the right to refuse or reject is admittedly within the legal powers of the Senate, for the reason that public money cannot be spent or taxes imposed except under the authority of an act of parliament, which implies the consent of the Senate, the House of Commons has taken the view that the provision in section 53 of the BNA Act which requires that the entire bill on which the ultimate law is founded must originate in the Commons prohibits the Senate even to amend money bills downward; for if the Senate amends, then the bill passed by the Senate is not the one that originated in the House of Commons. This attitude, which is incorporated in SO 63 of the Rules of the House of Commons, in effect equates the financial powers of the Senate with those of the House of Lords at the time of Confederation, when the Lords were restricted by constitutional conventions but not as yet by the statutory provisions of the Parliament Act. In contrast, the Senate's stand, crystallized in the so-called Ross Report of 1918,[2] which served both as a summary of past practice and as a guide for future action, has always been that of the two restrictions on the rights of the House of Lords which the House of Commons by its Resolution of 1678 tried to impose, namely the denial of the right to

[1]Thus, an amendment to the Civil Service Superannuation bill of 1927 to provide for the entrance into the scheme of an additional class of about 7,000–8,000 persons was ruled out of order by the Speaker, on the ground that the provision by imposing upon the Treasury an expenditure of at least half a million dollars, created "a charge which will have to be borne by the Government, and which therefore will be a charge on the revenue." And he added: "There is no doubt that the Senate has a right to amend a money bill, but it has no right to increase a charge upon the public." *SD, 1927*, pp. 416–22.

[2]The *Report* of the Special Committee under the Chairmanship of Sen. W. B. Ross re Rights of the Senate in Matters of Financial Legislation (Reprinted Ottawa, 1957).

originate and the denial of the right to amend money bills, the BNA Act adopted the first in section 53 but did not mention the second and that this proved that the Fathers did not intend the Senate to follow the practice of the House of Lords and not amend a money bill. Thus, the Senate has repudiated all suggestions for equating its powers with the Lords' and the Ross Report declared "that the practice of the Imperial Houses of Parliament in respect of money bills is no part of the Constitution of the Dominion of Canada." Indeed, the cardinal point of the Report's argument was that the Senate was a different kind of second chamber from the House of Lords, in that the Senate was a second chamber in a federal state, with duties and powers peculiar to a federal environment. The Senate's power to amend money bills, the Report said, "was given as an essential part of the Confederation contract," for "if the Senate has not the power to amend money bills it has no practical power to see fair play to the Provinces in finance, or to protect an interest unfairly used financially."[3] However, the history of the Senate's federal role, as we have seen in the previous chapter, has been so much at variance with the original expectations regarding that role that the federal argument no longer seems to be able to support the Senate's theoretical claim to the power to amend money bills. Moreover, while at the writing of the Ross memorandum it might still have been urged that such questions as provincial subsidies, public lands in the western provinces, or the rights of the provinces in connection with pending railway legislation and the adjustment of the rights of the provinces thereunder required the Senate to have revisory power in the field of financial legislation,[4] it is difficult to see how the Senate in the post-war period of federal-provincial relations could have been of great value for the provinces through exercising its right to amend money bills downward.

But these arguments and counter-arguments respecting the Senate's financial powers, although theoretically interesting, are now-a-days little more than examples of academic pedantry and to discuss the Senate's

[3]The federal argument was repeated, for apparent political reasons, by Meighen in the controversy over the Senate's amending the Home Bank Depositors bill in 1925; speaking in defence of the amendment he maintained: ". . . here in this Dominion, in view of the fact that Confederation is a compact which all the provinces came into, the Senate may quite naturally exercise, indeed was given, powers beyond the powers exercised by the Lords of England, because the Senate was looked upon as destined to be the repository of minority rights." *HD, 1925*, p. 4765.

[4]For the salutary effect of the Senate's amendments to railway bills in the period following the Great War, see R. A. Mackay, *The Unreformed Senate of Canada* (London, 1926), pp. 111 ff. (1963), pp. 102–4.

right to revise the Government's financial program in terms of conflict is really to present a very misleading picture of its functions in the modern state. On the contrary, the Senate has acted in full understanding of the meaning and the implications of responsible government and accepted as binding upon itself the proposition that it should not unduly disturb what has come to be called the "balance of ways and means"; or, as Hopkins says, "that it would be inadmissible to tamper with the overall financial program submitted by the Government in its budgetary proposals in such a way as to effect a material change in the budgetary surplus or deficit envisaged therein."[5] Indeed, we have seen in connection with the work of the committee on Finance that the Senate has never considered it politically or practically proper for itself to move, or even to recommend, reductions in the Estimates.[6] Even the Ross Report, while condemning the practice of tacking other matters to a bill of aid or supply,[7] concluded that "a Supply Bill should be passed as a matter of course by the Senate in almost any conceivable circumstances if it contains nothing but Supply." Similar views have been expressed by leading figures of the Senate throughout the years. Regarding the amendment made by the Senate to the contentious Home Bank bill of 1925, Sen. Robertson, later Minister of Labour, in a letter quoted in the House of Commons expressed the view that ". . . if the Government is earnest in its professed desire to provide a measure of relief for Home Bank depositors it should include in the estimates of the present session of parliament whatever amount it desires to contribute for that purpose. Estimates . . . are wholly within the jurisdiction of the House of Commons and are not subject to revision or modification by the Senate."[8] Both Dandurand and Willoughby have maintained that "on the members [of the House of Commons] lies the principal responsibility for the levying and expenditure of the amount necessary to carry on the affairs of the country. . . . Our power is limited to the approval or rejection of Bills for these purposes. . . . Of course we would not exercise our power of rejection except under very unusual circumstances,"[9] while Meighen, speaking of the Income War Tax bill of 1936, asserted that "it might be quite proper to make an amendment and submit it to the

[5]E. R. Hopkins, "Financial Legislation in the Senate," *Canadian Tax Journal* (1958), pp. 320–5.

[6]Above, pp. 260–1.

[7]Senate Rule 71 declares: "To annex any clause to a Bill of Aid or Supply, the matter of which is foreign to, and different from the matter of the Bill, is unparliamentary."

[8]*HD, 1925*, p. 3975. See also his remarks, *SD, 1925*, p. 672.

[9]*SD, 1930*, pp. 413–4.

other House, but if it is not accepted there this House should retreat forthwith from the position. We could not seek to press any amendment to a money bill which we did not consider vital to the state—and so far we never have considered any money bill to be such."[10] When the Senate was faced with Euler's amendment to the Excise Tax bill of 1953 to add oleomargarine to the list of specific foodstuffs exempted from the imposition of the sales tax and thus to deprive the Government of an approximate sum of two-and-a-half million dollars per year, Sen. W. M. Robertson warned that "the Senate, by attempting to reduce the rate of taxation, the incidence of taxation, or the estimates, would be setting itself up as a second budget-making authority," leading to the intolerable situation of "that of 'two kings in Israel'."[11] His successor, Sen. Macdonald, has been consistent also in urging moderation in amending revenue legislation. He opposed from the first the attempts to amend the Estate Tax bill in 1958 because in his opinion "the money to be raised by the Government is a matter peculiarly and strictly in the hands of the Government. The Government has drawn up a financial scheme for carrying on the business of the country, and the revenue to be received from this bill is included in the money which is to be required by the Government."[12] He expressed similar views regarding the Income Tax bill in 1959[13] and took the same stand as Robertson before respecting Euler's proposed amendment to the Excise Tax bill of 1960; "the balance of ways and means," he said on this occasion, "should be preserved and . . . the Senate should not upset the calculations of those charged with the making of them,"[14] whereupon the amendment was rejected by 32 votes to 15, in a House where the total number of Government supporters was 22.

The acceptance by the Senate, despite theoretical claims to the contrary, of the consequences of responsible government has, however, been only one aspect of the practical flexibility characterizing the operation of its financial powers. Equally important has been the fact that on those occasions when the Senate did exercise its power and amended money bills, whether it was with the express approval of the Government or with the concurrence of a reluctant House of Commons, its action was in fact upheld, and each time there has been established an important precedent for the tacit recognition by the Commons of the Senate's actual power in the field of financial legislation.

Indeed, the usual way for the House of Commons to give its consent to Senate amendments on money bills has been through the "waiving

[10]*Ibid., 1936*, p. 535. [11]*Ibid., 1953*, p. 433. [12]*Ibid., 1958*, p. 705.
[13]*Ibid., 1959*, p. 1139. [14]*Ibid., 1960*, p. 952.

of its privileges under protest."[15] At the beginning of our period, in the session of 1925, the Senate made drastic amendments in the Home Bank Depositors Relief bill, by reducing to less than three-fifths the estimate passed by the Commons for relief of the creditors of the bank; by extending the class of persons not eligible for relief to directors of the bank, governments, corporations and MP's; and by changing the principle upon which distribution was to be made.[16] In its first indignation the House of Commons decided, by 131 votes to 19, to reject the Senate's stand and it sent the following message to the upper house: ". . . the House of Commons, adhering to the BNA Act and the fundamental principle embodied in rule 78 [now 63], cannot renounce its inalienable right to initiate and regulate the voting of all aids and supplies granted by Parliament, and it has never acknowledged the right of the Senate to make amendments to money bills."[17] Standing to its guns, however, the Senate persisted in its position and after a free conference the Commons, on the motion of the Prime Minister, gave up fighting. King added, nevertheless, that ". . . while agreeing to the amendments . . . the Government still maintains its position and reserves its right to discuss at some future time the constitutional question that may be involved with respect to the right of the Senate in the matter of money bills."[18]

In 1939 the Senate amended the Income War Tax bill to eliminate some retroactive features of the legislation. Although the amendment was probably a meritorious one[19] it was certainly beyond ordinary modifications, as it altered periods during which certain income taxes were to be levied. Supported by all sides of the House, the Government first contemplated refusal, but in view of the advanced stage of the session, promising little hope of a free conference, it finally moved "that this House concur in the said amendments, and while doing so it does not think it advisable at this period of the session to insist on its privileges in respect thereto, but that the waiver of the said privileges in this case be not however drawn into a precedent. . . ."[20] Two years

[15]There is even a form (59) in Beauchesne, *Rules and Forms of the House of Commons of Canada*, provided for such occasions: "that the clerk do carry back the bill to the Senate and acquaint their honours that this House hath agreed to their amendments, the Minister of Finance accepting the said amendments with a protest against the right of the Senate to make amendments to money bills."

[16]*SD, 1925*, pp. 606–7.

[17]*HD, 1925*, p. 4754.

[18]*Ibid.*, p. 5056.

[19]"There is," Ilsley said, "something to be said for the amendment, on the merits . . . and the Government have decided that they do not particularly object to the merit of the Senate amendment. . . ." *Ibid., 1939*, p. 4846.

[20]*Ibid.*, See Lapointe's remarks, p. 4845.

later, in 1941, the Commons again conceded to the amendment made by the Senate in its Special War Revenue bill, delaying the coming into force of the legislation until its constitutionality has been decided by the Supreme Court of Canada, with the usual phrase added—"that this House, while disapproving of any infraction of its privileges or rights by the other House, in this case waives its claims to insist upon such rights and privileges."[21]

In the case of the Estate Tax bill of 1958 the Senate, in a fine example of party co-operation,[22] did not insist on its amendment to eliminate double taxation of superannuation and pension benefits. However, the interesting thing in this connection was not so much the Senate's retreat as the fact that what the House of Commons objected to in the Senate's action was the merits of the change rather than its constitutionality. The Minister of Finance, in his rebuttal, was concerned with the impracticability of the Senate's proposal, while Mr. Argue, summing up his argument on behalf of the CCF group in the House (which supported the Government in this instance), made the following significant remarks: "I do not for one moment question . . . the constitutional right of the other place to do such a thing, but I do not think it should be done."[23] The omission of the usual constitutional argument in the Commons' reasoning prompted Mr. Hopkins to say: "It thus appears that the House of Commons no longer takes the rigid view . . . that the Senate cannot amend a money bill in any particular, but must either accept it or reject it *in toto*. However, the recent action by the Commons does not mean that the Commons might not in future resist on Constitutional grounds a Senate amendment which would materially disturb the balance of ways and means during a fiscal year."[24] The last part of the prophecy came true when the following year the Senate amended the Income Tax bill to delete from it section 19 aimed at discontinuing the traditional designation of "foreign business corporation." Since the deleted section "was not a provision of leading importance," as it did not threaten to affect the revenues of the treasury, the Government decided to accept its deletion and waive the Commons'

[21]*Ibid., 1941*, p. 3854. [22]Above, p. 139. [23]*HD, 1958*, p. 4465.

[24]E. R. Hopkins, "Financial Legislation in the Senate," *Canadian Tax Journal*, vol. VI (1958), pp. 320–5. See also two articles in the *Financial Post*, Sept. 6, 1958: "Senate Proposals Point up 'Unjust' Estate Tax Angles" by J. G. McDonald and "Senate's Status to Get a Test?" by L. Wilson. It should be mentioned that the controversial amendment which was not accepted by the Government in 1958 was implemented two years later in the Estate Tax bill and the Income Tax bill of 1960, as a result of additional representations made by the Canadian Bar Association and other organizations. *SD, 1960*, pp. 820–1.

claims to insist upon its rights and privileges.[25] Although the motion was severely criticized by members of the Opposition,[26] it would certainly have been carried in view of the large majority enjoyed by the Government. However, unexpectedly, it was blocked by the Speaker's ruling that since the waiver of the asserted privileges of the House of Commons in effect amounted to a waiver of SO 63, "unless that order is suspended I do not see how I can permit alternations of a money bill by the Senate to be brought before the house for approval."[27] As proper notice had not been given the only way of suspending the standing order would have been through unanimous consent, which was evidently lacking. Therefore, the Government, despite its best intentions, was unable to get concurrence in the Senate's amendments and to waive the privileges of the Commons. The matter was dropped there, but on the day of prorogation Mr. Fleming introduced a new motion declaring that the House disagreed with the Senate's amendment, the reason given being that the amendment *inter alia* "infringes the sole and undoubted right of the Commons to impose taxation; it alters the application of taxes and interferes with the public revenue."[28] The Senate did not insist on its amendment, lest the whole legislation be jeopardized.[29]

A third factor which underlines the flexibility and further obscures the constitutional aspects involved in the exercise of the Senate's financial powers has been the evolution of the pragmatic, one might say opportunist, notion that if the Senate acted at the request, or with the approval, of the Government the Senate was *intra vires* in amending money bills. In addition to securing modifications in the timing provisions of financial measures,[30] the Senate has been requested also to make changes affecting the revenue principles of such legislation. Thus, in 1932 Meighen assured the Senate that it was constitutionally proper to reduce the tax payable on insurance premiums by outside mutuals

[25]*HD, 1959*, p. 5978.

[26]Taking a somewhat different view from his stand in the previous session, Mr. Argue now said that "If it is assumed that the Senate has the right to amend money bills, then they can use the right to amend money bills to circumvent the rule that they cannot initiate money bills." And Mr. Benidickson (Lib., Kenora-Rainy-River) warned that "precedents build on each other and get increased strength from repetition." *Ibid.*, p. 5980.

[27]*Ibid.*, p. 5984. The Speaker, by his ruling, broke with a precedent in 1917, when in an almost identical case the Speaker made the following ruling regarding the question whether or not Rule 78 (the predecessor of present SO 63) prevented the Commons from waiving its rights: "while this rule is an affirmation of what this House considers its powers and prerogatives, there is nothing contained in it or any of our rules which prevents this House from adopting as its own, amendments such as this. . . ." *Ibid., 1917*, Sept. 7.

[28]*Ibid., 1959*, p. 6402.

[29]*SD, 1959*, pp. 1139–41. Above, p. 140.

[30]Above, p. 181.

under the Special War Revenue bill, because the Government wanted them to do so.[31] There was a similar reasoning respecting the amendments made by the Senate at the request of the Government in the Income Tax bill of 1953, the effect of which was to remove the provision for the deduction by Canadian purchasers of tax on sales by non-residents and to restore the situation as it was before the introduction of the legislation. It was pointed out in the House of Commons that, no matter how negligible, the Senate amendments did have some effect on the balance of ways and means. "If the Senate," Mr. Knowles (CCF, Winnipeg North Centre) said, "can make a change involving a few dollars merely because the amount is small, when the Minister of Finance requests it, then they could make a change that would be quite substantial in nature;" and he asked: "What section of the BNA Act gives the Minister of Finance the right to request the Senate to do something which they are not permitted to do by the terms of the BNA Act?" Pressed, Mr. Abbott had to admit that "the question of the right of the Senate to deal with money bills is . . . a very difficult one and very controversial in some respects. . . . There are differing opinions as to what the Senate can do to a money bill after it gets there. However, custom and usage over a great many years have determined that they can reject a money bill but that the House of Commons will not accept amendments to money bills made in the Senate *except when made on the request of a Minister of the Crown.* That is the practice."[32] The same principle was invoked in the case of the Income Tax bill of 1960, of which three clauses were struck out by the Senate. Although, strictly speaking, the amendments originated with members of the Senate's Banking and Commerce committee and not with the Government, they were all approved by the Minister of Finance before they were passed in the Senate.[33] As a result, Mr. Fleming could argue in the Commons that there was no constitutional question at stake in accepting the Senate's amendments.[34]

[31]*SD, 1932*, p. 498. Cf. Rhodes' remarks, *HD, 1932*, p. 3423. What made Meighen's attitude vulnerable under the circumstances was the fact that, as he was now reminded by Dandurand, when the Senate made similar amendments to an income tax bill in 1921 it was Prime Minister Meighen who moved a resolution in the House of Commons declaring that the Senate's action should not be taken as a precedent. "As he now sits in this chamber, and as he will be obliged to look at things from a different angle," Dandurand wished to draw "his attention to the solemn declaration, known as the Ross resolution . . . in which we asserted our right to amend all money bills." "I agree to this extent," an uncomfortable Meighen replied. *SD, 1932*, pp. 498–9.

[32]*HD, 1953*, pp. 4710–2. Italic added. (The amendment was accepted on division.)

[33]*SD, 1960*, pp. 1035–6.

[34]*HD, 1960*, p. 6412.

On the negative side of this governmental attitude to the Senate's financial powers, when the Senate has made amendments in money bills contrary to the desires of the administration, governments have been apt to argue that the Senate was constitutionally *ultra vires*, even if the amendments had no direct effect upon the "balance of ways and means." Thus, the Government meekly accepted nineteen of the twenty amendments put by the Senate to the War Risk Insurance bill of 1942 but refused to adopt one which sought to enable the minister to enter into an agreement with provincially registered insurance companies also. After debate Mr. Ilsley told the house on July 29 that the Senate amendment in fact "contravenes constitutional usage and practice," because "the alteration of that scheme in any important particular . . . is the alteration of what is essentially and soundly considered a financial bill."[35] While the Senate did not insist on its amendment in 1942 it did so in 1961 when its action on the Customs Tariff bill was emphatically disapproved by the Government. Although, clearly, the Senate was not in this instance opposing a revenue principle, but rather one provision of a revenue bill which dealt with a minister's discretionary power, the Government's motion said that the Senate amendment "infringes the sole and undoubted right of the Commons to impose taxation; it alters the application of taxes and interferes with the public revenue." The Minister of Finance, who in the previous year had no objection on constitutional grounds to the Senate's amendments in the Income Tax bill because it was done with his approval, now charged the Senate with violating the Commons' ancient prerogatives in matters of financial legislation. The bill, he said, "is a fiscal measure. It was one of the budget bills. It is clearly a revenue bill. It is no answer to say that the particular amendment does not expressly relate in its terms to particular tax rates. The bill itself is a revenue measure. The main statute, which it purports to amend is by any standard a revenue measure, a fiscal enactment."[36]

Thus, instead of clarifying it, these contradictory attitudes and policies have considerably confused the exact constitutional position of the Senate in the field of financial legislation. What emerges from the experience of 1925 to 1963 is the fact that the Senate's financial powers

[35]*Ibid., 1942*, p. 4911.

[36]*Ibid., 1960–1*, p. 7611. Unlike some other occasions, the Government was not supported in its position by any one of the Opposition groups in the Commons. "In our opinion," the CCF houseleader said for example, "on this occasion the Senate has performed a service for the Canadian people. Hon. Gentlemen of the other place have protected the rights of the Canadian people in . . . taking this second look and finding out the weaknesses in the legislation. . . ." *Ibid.*, p. 7633. The Government's motion to reject the Senate's amendment was carried by 134 votes to 39, strictly on party lines.

are limited by the considerations of practical politics rather than by fine legalistic arguments. While the Senate has wisely acquiesced in the limitations flowing from the wide interpretation that is generally attached to the idea of responsible government, the House of Commons and successive governments have found it equally desirable to have amendments made to money bills in the Senate. The extent to which the Senate may go in revising financial measures is, therefore, a part of the general self-restraint which the Senate has evidenced throughout the years. As long as the Senate adheres to its policy of moderation there seems to be little reason why it should not be spared of the fate of the Lords.

2. *The Veto Power and Legislative Deadlocks*

Constitutionally, the Senate has absolute power to modify legislation (public and private) by any mode and in any particular. The power of veto over legislation sponsored by the Government and passed by the House of Commons is only the most extreme form of the exercise of the legally unrestrained powers enjoyed by the Senate. In view of this unique constitutional position the Senate would seem to be eminently able to perform what the report of the Bryce Conference, qualified by the Churchillian concept of the "deepening of the shadow,"[37] considered the most important function of a modern second chamber, i.e., to delay, if necessary, legislation passed by the Lower House "until public opinion shall have had an opportunity of expressing itself." The difficulties about such a role under the conditions of responsible cabinet government are obvious. Even if the proposition is accepted that the people ought to be protected against wholesale innovations manifestly at variance with the record and the program of the Government which the people had placed in office at the last general election, and if the Senate is to have power to provide that protection, it must then have power to force a dissolution of the House of Commons, or at least to compel the Government to hold a referendum on each controversial issue. However, the assumptions on which such a role is founded are in conflict with the assumptions on which the theory of governmental responsibility is founded, especially in the extreme form in which it is generally accepted today.[38] Significantly, similarly to its moderation in matters of financial

[37]Above, pp. 19–20.

[38]For more on this question see, e.g., C. S. Emden, *The People and the Constitution* (2nd ed., Oxford, 1933), p. 226; P. Bromhead, *The House of Lords and Contemporary Politics, 1911–1957* (London, 1958), pp. 12 ff.

legislation, the Senate never, during the thirty-seven years studied here, took upon itself the task of re-interpreting the popular will, and by developing a conveniently flexible theory of the mandate it has in fact repudiated the suggestion of the Platonic function envisaged in the Bryce-Report. On the one hand, it has always been a guiding principle for the Senate to respect what might be called an open or clear mandate, that "once the people have clearly registered their verdict on a question of public policy, whether we consider that verdict a wise or unwise one," the Senate should not "stand in the way of passing such legislation."[39] Even Meighen, for all his partisan furies during the years as Opposition Leader in the Senate, refrained from rejecting a Government measure either after a general election or in any case where, through the recommendations of a Royal Commission or otherwise, it was proved to his satisfaction that the measure was rationally founded or had an undisputed mandate behind it. "He would thunder against it," a contemporary remarked, "and leave the matter to the responsibility of the House of Commons."[40] But the Senate has gone farther than that. In addition to honouring an open or clear mandate, it has in fact also abided by what might be termed "mandates by default," that is to say, questions in a party's general platform which, even though not discussed publicly during the election campaign, were not seen fit by any other party or individual to be made a definite issue.[41] This liberal interpretation of the mandate, which has been closely linked to the partisan self-restraint of both the Senate as a body and its individual members, suggests that the Senate has in practice accepted the notion that "when the people vote in favour of a particular party at a general election they do not show themselves in favour of every single item of that party's program; they show simply that they prefer to be governed by that party rather than any other party during the ensuing five years."[42]

[39]See Sen. Crerar's remarks. *SD, 1955*, p. 452.

[40]*Ibid., 1951* (2nd session), p. 244. Above, chap. IV, *passim*.

[41]See Sen. Farris' remarks in connexion with the bill to abolish appeals to the Privy Council. *SD, 1949* (2nd session), p. 149.

[42]Bromhead, *The House of Lords*, p. 14. Surely, these views only cover the constitutionally normal situation in which the Government has a clear majority behind it in the House of Commons, while in the extraordinary circumstances of minority governments it might be argued that the Senate should offer more positive resistance to the Government's legislative proposals, precisely on the basis of the mandate-theory. It is proposed, however, that even in such circumstances the Senate should refrain from regulating or accelerating the process of the Government's appealing from the legal to the political sovereign, for two reasons; on the one hand, the Government's primary responsibility lies to the House of Commons and not to the electorate and as long as it retains the confidence of the Commons it is entitled to remain in office; on the other hand, any decisive interference on

This does not mean, of course, that the Senate has never rejected a Government bill during these thirty-seven years. But in those cases, some fourteen in number, when it did so its action could hardly be said to have been based upon the idea of giving public opinion time to express itself. In other words, *the method of rejection has never been elevated to a function.* When it was used as a last resort it was always in the service of some other functions or principles. Most of the cases have in fact already been mentioned in other contexts. However, it seems appropriate at this point to present a summary of the legislative measures which the Senate has negatived during the years from 1926 to 1963 either by a vote on principle on second reading (or perhaps on third reading) or in the form of an unfavourable committee report, recommending against further proceedings. Thus, we have seen how the Senate in advancing certain conservative principles has rejected the Canada Temperance bill of 1925, the Old Age Pensions bill of 1926, the Immigration bill in both 1925 and 1927 and the bill to repeal section 98 of the Criminal Code on four separate occasions.[43] On the other hand, in the case of the Judges bill of 1933, the Penitentiary bill of 1938, and the Bank of Canada bill of 1961, which have failed to pass the Senate, the guiding principle seems to have been the safeguarding of the rights and interests of particular individuals.[44] As has been mentioned also, in some cases the final decision of the Senate may have been influenced by political considerations. Such motives, surely, played an important role in the rejection of the Farmers' Creditors Arrangement bill of 1939, whose defeat was mainly due to Meighen's awakened belligerance.[45] Apart from these cases already referred to under previous headings, the Senate has rejected government measures in six other instances—all during the pre-war period. In the session of 1925 three bills, in addition to the Canada Temperance bill, failed to pass the Senate; the Canada Evidence bill was stopped on third reading with the full approval of the Government Leader in the Senate[46] and referred to a special committee, which later recommended that the enactment of the bill be postponed until expert information from the Bench and the Attorney General has been secured;[47] in the case of bill no. 210 to

---

the part of the Senate would inevitably lead to a strengthening of partisan passions in the House, which is not consistent with its modern functioning. The Senate's behaviour in the sessions of both 1957–58 and 1962–63 was impeccable in this respect (above, pp. 138 ff). For further argument, see Mackay, *The Unreformed Senate* (1963), pp. 171–3.

[43]Above, pp. 282–3.

[44]Above, pp. 312–14.

[45]Above, pp. 130, 287. *SD, 1939*, pp. 196–7.

[46]*SD, 1925*, pp. 452–3.

[47]*SJ, 1925*, p. 336.

construct a CNR branch line between Sunnybrae and Guysborough, NS, the Senate simply repeated its action of a year previously, when by a unanimous vote it rejected the same measure on grounds of economy.[48] This time the bill was given a second reading but was reported out unfavourably of the Railway Committee, which found that the preamble of the bill was not proven and that its passage would be detrimental to the public interest;[49] finally, the Senate threw out the Dominion Farm Loan bill, because it arrived on June 26, on the eve of prorogation of Parliament. Even the Government Leader had to admit that his mind was "not made up as to the best scheme. Unless the majority of this Chamber feel that they are sufficiently informed on the question and ready to endorse the bill after a few hours' study in committee, which we could give it, I will not insist upon pressing the bill to a second reading." The Senate then decided unanimously that the bill should not be further proceeded with during that session.[50] In 1928 it refused to pass the Naturalization bill, which sought to abolish reference of applications for naturalization to the courts. Criticized on the double ground that its passage would unduly enhance ministerial powers and introduce an undesirable element of secrecy into the proceedings, the bill met its end in Committee on the motion that "the chairman do now leave the chair."[51] In the session of 1935 the Conservative Government suffered its second defeat (the first one having been the loss of its Judges bill in 1933) in a Conservative-dominated Senate, with the rejection of the Industrial Disputes bill aimed at enabling the minister to effect a settlement in certain cases of discriminatory action. Apart from constitutional reasons, the Senate's Banking and Commerce committee, heavily relying on the evidence submitted to it by representatives of labour organizations, found that the legislation was superfluous as the Act already gave the minister ample powers in all cases where there might have been any reason for the exertion of efforts at conciliation. It therefore recommended that the bill be not proceeded with.[52] Finally, the Senate, again in form of a hostile committee report, killed the Soldier Settlement Act Amendment bill of 1940, which sought to lift the reservation restriction from minerals under formerly private lands, in contrast to lands acquired by soldier settlers through the Soldier Settlement Board, and to make it retroactive to 1919. Opposition to the measure was led by Meighen, but the sincerity of his indignation upon the discriminatory aspects of the legislation[53] must be viewed

[48]*SD, 1925*, p. 644.
[49]*SJ, 1925*, p. 392.
[50]*SD, 1925*, pp. 745, 748.
[51]*Ibid., 1928*, pp. 625 ff.
[52]*Ibid., 1935*, pp. 363–4.
[53]*Ibid., 1940*, p. 362.

against his generally antagonistic attitude towards government legislation in this period.[54] In any case, he remained unconvinced by a special memorandum prepared by the Department in defence of the bill, and so did the majority of the Senate.[55]

Looking back on the list of rejected measures and the issues involved in each instance, two things emerge. First, despite the fact that in most of the cases the Senate's action occurred in the second half of a parliament's life, the exercise of the Senate's veto power was never based on the argument that the Government had no mandate for a particular piece of legislation or that the Senate was better placed for ascertaining the state of public opinion than were members of the elected Chamber. Second, equally important, none of the measures negatived by the Senate during the period 1926–63, with the possible exception of the Old Age Pensions bill of 1926, was really of first rate importance or closely connected with the Government's over-all legislative program.[56] Accordingly, no Government has seriously argued that the Senate by rejecting any of those measures has thwarted the will of the people, and, therefore, such an action by the Senate never constituted a definite issue in the ensuing election. In other words, the exercise by the Senate of its constitutional power to reject legislation passed by the House of Commons never amounted to obstructionism in the same way as did the behaviour of the House of Lords or the Legislative Council of New Zealand in their respective periods of history. Consequently, no retaliatory action has been considered necessary by successive governments in Canada, either for the purpose of curbing the powers of the Senate (as did the two Parliament Acts in 1911 and 1949 in England) or for the purpose of abolishing the whole institution of second chambers (as happened under the Legislative Council Abolition Act of 1951 in New Zealand[57]). Perhaps the one case in which the Senate, in a limited sense, came close to parallel the Lords' conduct in the years 1906–11 was its unfortunate decision to throw out the Old Age Pensions bill in 1926. Indeed, had it not been for the development of an even greater constitutional crisis involving the Governor General's prerogatives, the Senate's action might not have passed unpunished. But Lord Byng, quite unintentionally, saved the Senate

[54]Above, pp. 126 ff.

[55]*SD, 1940*, p. 416.

[56]It is probably true to say that, in spite of its immediate effect, even the highly controversial Bank of Canada bill of 1961 will in retrospect appear of relatively little import.

[57]H. J. Benda, "The End of Bicameralism in New Zealand," ***Parliamentary Affairs*** (1950–51).

from the wrath of the Government, in the only instance in its modern history where it failed to observe the delicately drawn line between what is legally permissible and constitutionally proper.

To complete the record of the Senate's veto power, a brief discussion of the public measures introduced by private members in the House of Commons and rejected by the Senate seems to be in order. The purpose of this discussion is not so much to contrast the stands of the Senate and the Government as to point to the peculiar procedural difficulties, flowing from a lack of adequate co-operation between the two chambers, in matters of private members' bills. Indeed, although in most cases when the Senate refused to pass a private members' bill it was a defiance of the unanimous will of the House of Commons, rejection of a private member's bill does not involve a conflict between the two houses in the usual sense, for private members' bills are not the concern of the Government, even if their passage through the Commons implies at least the tacit approval of the cabinet.[58] As for the principles involved, in the majority of cases (all falling into the pre-war period) the Senate's decision to reject a private member's bill stemmed from its traditional concern for the interests and rights of the individual, as discussed in chapter x.[59] Procedurally, however, a special difficulty is created by the problem of arranging responsibility in the Senate for private members'

[58]Thus, in the United Kingdom "if the Lords should reject a private member's bill, it is not likely that the procedure of the Parliament Act would be able to ensure the passage of the bill in the next session unless it were taken over by the Government." Bromhead, *The House of Lords*, p. 212.

[59]Thus, it rejected Neill's (Ind., Comox-Alberni) bill to amend the Criminal Code in 1925, which proposed to make the printer liable in case of libellous or false publications (*SD*, *1925*, p. 136; *SJ*, *1925*, pp. 339, 392); Church's (Cons., Toronto North-West) persistent Post Office bill on no less than five separate occasions, as a threat to "anonymous and impersonal journalism" (*SJ*, 1928, p. 163; *ibid.*, *1929*, pp. 420–1, and *Canadian Annual Review*, *1928–29*, p. 67; *SD*, *1930*, p. 321; *ibid.*, *1935*, p. 368; *SJ*, *1938*, p. 308); the Electricity and Fluid Exportation bill (or "Stewart bill") in 1929, after extensive committee study, on the ground that its provision for an act of Parliament rather than a mere licence as a requirement for the right to export power unduly impeded prospective exporters in comparison to the companies already established. (*SD*, *1929*, p. 298); the same measure, when it returned in 1938 under the title of Electric Power Exportation bill, after having been sponsored in the House of Commons by the Prime Minister (it was first introduced in the Commons as a "private bill" but later, upon Bennett's insistence, its status was changed to that of a private members' bill) (*HD*, *1938*, p. 361; *SD*, *1938*, pp. 220 ff, 564. *Canadian Annual Review*, *1937–38*, p. 82); and Brunelle's (Lib., Champlain) Lord's Day bill in 1939, which proposed to make officers of a corporation personally liable to imprisonment for violations of the Act (*SD*, *1939*, p. 105). This was the second debut of the bill in Parliament; in 1938 it was amended by the Senate, replacing the imprisonment penalty with substantially increased fines for the corporation; the amendment was unacceptable to the bill's sponsors (*SD*, *1938*, pp. 228–9).

bills brought up from the House of Commons. Some Senator must be found willing to look after the bill and pilot it through all its stages in the Upper House. He will have to be instructed beforehand by the sponsors of the bill in the Commons and properly forearmed against all the arguments which he may find himself to be faced with during the course of the discussion at the second reading, committee, and third reading stages.[60] Failure or carelessness to do so may seriously imperil the fate of the measure. Thus, for instance, the Divorce Jurisdiction bill of 1929, which sought to give a separate domicile to a married woman deserted by her husband, was simply left on the doorstep of Sen. McMeans, without any instruction at all, because he was chairman of the Divorce committee. So inadequately prepared, he was unable to withstand Aylesworth's powerful attack on the principle of the bill and to muster enough support, which would have carried it through over the motion for six months' hoist.[61] Similarly, in the case of the Post Office bill in the same session, Belcourt, who fathered the measure in 1928, admitted that he "received no instructions of any kind at the time and have none now, when the waif is again deposited at my door." He did "not know what I can say about the bill except to refer to its terms."[62] This was a rather spiritless introduction on second reading, and, although the Senate would probably have killed the measure in any case, it only helped to accelerate the process. When the same bill made its fifth re-appearance in the Senate in 1938 it was in Sen. Murdock's care. Although he in general seemed to be in agreement with the objective of the measure[63] there was a curious lack of enthusiasm in his saying that he only took up the bill because "it would seem discourteous to the House of Commons if a bill passed by that House were not given an opportunity to run the gauntlet of the Senate of Canada." But he quickly added that he had "no special remarks to make as to the propriety or necessity of the bill and I am not sure how it would be worked out for the benefit of the Canadian people if it were passed."[64] His reluctance to render more positive assistance signalled the end of the parliamentary career of the measure.

The situation in which private member's bills from the House of Commons may find themselves in the Senate is even more embarrassing if no sponsor is available at all. Mr. A. P. Côté's (Lib., Matapédia-

[60]For similar problems in the United Kingdom, see Bromhead, *The House of Lords*, p. 211.

[61]*SD, 1929*, pp. 373 ff.

[62]*Ibid.*, p. 76.

[63]See his remarks in 1935, *Ibid., 1935*, p. 321.

[64]*Ibid., 1938*, p. 403.

Matane) rather controversial Canada Day bill in 1946, which proposed to substitute Canada Day for Dominion Day, was given first reading in the Senate on April 9, with Sen. Copp, Deputy Government Leader in the Senate, put down as its sponsor. The Senator, however, disclaimed the bill and so did Sen. W. E. Foster, who was named as sponsor for the second reading stage. It was promptly argued by opponents of the measure that it should never have appeared on the Senate's order paper until someone in the Senate was ready to take charge of it. While this suggestion was in accordance with the proper parliamentary formula, over a period of years there had grown up a practice that when a Commons bill was presented to the Senate, with a message stating that the bill had been passed by the House of Commons and requesting the concurrence of the Senate, it was, as a matter of course, read for the first time by the Clerk *on the assumed motion* of the Leader of the Government. The proper procedure for the mover of a private member's bill in the Commons is, of course, to secure a sponsor in the Senate. This was apparently not done in this instance. The bill was placed on the order paper in the name of Sen. Copp *without his consent.* Since the Government Leader, too, was unwilling to sponsor it, he suggested that the order be allowed to stand in his name for a "reasonable length of time" to enable Mr. Côté to secure a sponsor in the Senate. The bill was almost dropped on this point of technicality and was only saved by the common sense of Foster, who felt that since it was passed by a substantive majority in the House of Commons, "this orphan must be looked after."[65] Nevertheless, this was certainly an ill-omened beginning and the bill has indeed ultimately failed to receive Royal Assent. The stage reached by Morton's (PC, Davenport) private member's bill to change divorce procedure in 1961[66] was even less advanced before meeting its final fate. Although it was granted first reading in the Senate on December 19, the order for second reading was stood over on four occasions, until it was finally removed from the Order Paper by an order of the Speaker for lack of sponsor. There was not a word of discussion on it and the bill was not even accorded the privilege of being negatived on its merits. At one point Sen. Pouliot volunteered sponsorship, but only on the express condition that he be given assurance that the bill will be defeated on second reading! The Senate, however, was not in a mood for making use of such good offices, and the measure died a dismal death.

These examples point to a lack of continuous co-operation between the two chambers, which is probably in part a result of the strong

[65] *Ibid., 1946,* p. 146.

[66] Above, p. 220.

feelings of separate identity held by each House. Indeed, apart from joint standing and joint special committees, the only modes of official communication between the two houses consist of messages and conferences.[67] The houses almost constantly during sessions send and receive messages in regard to bills which require the assent of each House. However, unlike the cases of concurrence and amendment, there is no channel whereby the House of Commons can receive official information of the rejection of any of its measures by the Senate. "If a bill does not come back from the Senate," Mr. Neill reminded the Commons in 1926, "there are several reasons that might account for it. It might have been lost in transit,[68] or one of the papers, when a clerk was collecting a number to send here from the other place, might have slipped out from the folder, have been picked up by the char woman and by her, in ignorance of its value thrown into the waste basket."[69] In any case, the only way for the Commons to find out what has happened to its bill is through a motion authorizing the Clerk, under the rules, to search the *Journals* of the Senate and "to conclude by some Sherlock Holmes methods that something has happened to it, and that it has been thrown out." The only instance in which this ridiculously awkward device was applied during the last thirty-seven years was in connection with the Old Age Pensions bill in 1926, whose rejection probably caused greater storm in the Commons than any subsequent instance of the exercise of the Senate's veto power.[70] However, Mr. Neill (Ind., Comox-Alberni), who was responsible for the motion, emphasized that "it is not desirable, it is wholly undesirable, that this haphazard method of communication should prevail," and urged that instead, "this House should be informed when any bill so important as this has been rejected or whenever any action whatever with respect to it has been taken by the Senate." The need of changing the procedure was supported by Meighen, who said that "it is a motion which I have never seen made in this House until to-day, and which I fancy is a relic of antiquity having as much place in our modern practice as would some procedure adopted at the Norman Conquest."[71] The suggestion, so opportune in 1926, has lost nothing in opportuneness since then.

[67]A. Bourinot, *Parliamentary Procedure and Practice in the Dominion of Canada* (4th ed.), p. 271.

[68]Thus, in 1929 Adshead asked: "the leader of the Government in the Senate apparently has complained that certain news was lost in transit between the House of Commons and the Senate. Can the Prime Minister give us any information as to how it was lost?" To which King replied: "I am afraid I have no information. My hon. friend will have to judge for himself, as I will have to do." *HD, 1929,* p. 3747.

[69]*HD, 1926,* p. 4420. [70]*HJ, 1926,* p. 418. [71]*HD, 1926,* pp. 4421, 4426.

Messages apart, both Houses may appoint "managers" to meet in a conference upon any subject which, by parliamentary usage, is considered appropriate for such a proceeding.[72] A special category of such conferences, called the Free Conference system, is preserved for resolving legislative deadlocks between the two chambers over a particular piece of legislation. A legislative deadlock may be caused by either house, but we are only concerned here with those precipitated by the Senate. When a bill is returned from the Senate with amendments[73] the Commons may concur in them, it may reject all or any of them or it may put "consequential amendments"[74] to them. If the Senate's amendments are accepted, the bill goes for the Royal Assent. If any of the Senate's amendments is rejected or further amended by the Commons, the Commons passes a resolution stating reasons for its disagreement and the resolution is communicated to the Senate. On each of these amendments the Senate has then to decide whether to "insist" on their former stand or not. If the Senate insists on any amendment or produces

[72]See Bourinot, *Parliamentary Procedure*, p. 274.

[73]It may be mentioned in passing that members of the House of Commons often complain about the way in which Senate amendments are presented in their Chamber. Usually it is entirely at the discretion of the minister concerned or (particularly in 1930–35) of the prime minister, to move the adoption of Senate amendments, or to suggest non-concurrence in them (unlike the United Kingdom, where the reasons for disagreement are drawn up by an *ad hoc* committee of members from both sides of the House. Bromhead, *The House of Lords*, p. 132). The House does not go into committee unless it is so desired by unanimous consent. It has often been complained that copies of the Senate's amendments have not been printed and distributed, with the result that MP's did not know what they were expected to vote upon. (Cf. proceedings on the Canadian Farm Loan bill of 1935 or on the Civil Service Superannuation bill of 1940. *HD, 1935*, pp. 2762–3; *ibid., 1940*, p. 1721.) On other occasions the minister, making the explanatory remarks was himself unprepared or poorly briefed as to the content of the Senate amendments. Thus, for example, on the Wheat Co-operation Marketing bill of 1940 the minister said: "I have no explanation why they [i.e. the Senate] desire the change. I was not at the meeting of the committee when the change was made." (*HD, 1940*, p. 830) The situation is even worse when the minister is away and the task of explaining Senate amendments is delegated to his parliamentary secretary. In 1946, for example, on the Excess Profits Tax bill, the parliamentary assistant to the minister of finance admitted he was "not in a position to give the necessary information. The Minister is not here today, and I do not think the parliamentary assistant should be required to make the explanation." (*HD, 1946*, p. 5359) The amendments were verbal corrections.

[74]The rules require that a "consequential" amendment must be consequent upon, or relevant to, the original Senate amendment. (Bouriot, *Parliamentary Procedure*, p. 535; Beauchesne, ed., *Rules and Forms*, Form. 589) Thus, it cannot be a change simply proposed in an afterthought (cf. Meighen's inability to effect changes in the Foreign Insurance Companies bill of 1932. *SD, 1932*, p. 463) or amendments that are consequent, not upon the original amendments, but upon the consequential amendments (cf. Speaker's ruling in the amendments proposed by Gillis, Roebuck, and Wright to the Dominion Elections bill of 1944. *HD, 1944*, p. 4938.)

a new amendment in place of the old one or still further amends the Commons' consequential amendments, the Senate sends a message informing the Commons of the fact. At this point the Commons may either give way or insist on their disagreement. In the former case, the matter is settled and the way is open for the Royal Assent; in the latter case, a legislative deadlock arises.

It is in the absence of any effective constitutional provisions enabling the House of Commons to resolve a legislative deadlock and impose its will upon an intransigent upper chamber that lies a further source of the legal powers of the Senate. It is not only that the Senate can reject a measure outright; there is no machinery by which it can be compelled to yield its position or change its stand on a particular piece of legislation. To ensure the superiority of the Lower House, the constitutions of parliamentary systems invariably provide for some kind of swamping techniques, ranging from the ancient prerogative of the British monarch to create enough new peers to outnumber the Government's antagonists in the Upper House to joint votes of the two houses, which secures the preponderance of the Lower House.[75] The delegates of the London Conference, however, both those from the Maritime provinces and the Province of Canada, regarded the power to swamp the Senate as conflicting with the Senate's function effectively to safeguard provincial rights, and emphasized the importance of fixed numbers.[76] Indeed, it was only upon the insistence of the Colonial Secretary, Lord Carnarvon, that a very harmless version of the swamping power was adopted, providing for a maximum of two additional appointments per senatorial section in case of a collision between the two houses.[77] This provision, which would be ineffective in almost any conceivable circumstances, has never been put to use and since long been considered obsolete.[78] Similarly, it was from federal fears that Laurier's tentative attempts in 1897 to get the approval of the provinces

[75]F. A. Kunz, "Second Chambers: A Comparative Study," unpublished MA thesis, McGill University, 1960, pp. 195 ff.

[76]See in particular the remarks of Tupper, Tilley, Howland, and Langevin. J. Pope, ed., *Confederation Documents* (Toronto, 1895), pp. 117 ff.

[77]Section 26 of the BNA Act as amended in 1915. Cf. Sen. Wilmot's remarks, *SD, 1877*, p. 203. Thus, in 1867 it meant a possible total of six additional appointments. It might be mentioned as a historical curiosity that the number 6 was not without precedent. In 1719 the House of Lords passed the Peerage bill, whose main provision was "that the number of English Peers should not be enlarged beyond six above the present number. . . ." The bill was defeated in the House of Commons, due to the opposition of Walpole, thus maintaining the safety-valve which proved so invaluable in 1832 and 1911. Cf. Bromhead, *The House of Lords*, p. 11.

[78]E. A. Forsey, "Appointment of Extra Senators under Section 26 of the

of Quebec, Ontario, New Brunswick, and Nova Scotia for the adoption of joint sittings between the two houses as a device to resolve legislative deadlocks had foundered. We have the evidence of Sen. Dandurand, who accompanied him when he submitted the question to the Quebec cabinet, headed by Mr. Marchand, and who said they "received the unanimous decision of the Cabinet that such a change would not be favoured either by the Cabinet or by the Provincial Legislature."[79]

Thus, the theory of the Senate's contemplated federal function, which greatly determined its veto power and its power in the field of financial legislation, also secured it a co-ordinate position in cases of prolonged disagreements with the House of Commons. Similarly to the other two areas of its powers, however, the Senate has never abused this unique constitutional position, by clinging capriciously to a course which was denounced by the House of Commons. On the contrary, as Table XXIV reveals, the Senate's revisory work has caused, relatively speaking, very little friction between the two chambers during the years from 1925 to 1963. It is a remarkable fact that of the 289 Government measures amended by the Senate in that period (most of them in several particulars) only in thirty-six did certain Senate amendments fail to get prompt concurrence by the House of Commons,[80] and that, further, only eight of the thirty-six produced what might be called a legislative deadlock. In the rest of the twenty-eight cases, the "contentious" Senate amendments were resolved through a simple exchange of messages, each House stating its reasons and trying to adjust its position to the other's: on one occasion the Commons yielded to the Senate's insistence on the amendment it first disagreed to;[81] in thirteen cases,[82] it was the

---

British North America Act, *Canadian Journal of Economics and Political Science*, May, 1946; "Alexander Mackenzie's Memoranda on the Appointment of Extra-Senators, 1873–4," *Canadian Historical Review*, June, 1936; A. Todd, *Parliamentary Government in the British Colonies* (London, 1894), p. 164; A. B. Keith, *Responsible Government in the Dominions* (Oxford, 1928), p. 465. R. M. Dawson, *The Government of Canada* (3rd. ed., Toronto, 1957), pp. 347–8.

[79] *SD, 1925*, p. 510.

[80] What happened in most instances of course, was that the Senate made a great number of amendments to a bill, of which the Commons agreed to some at once and disagreed to others; it is the fate of the disagreed ones that here concerns us.

[81] It was an amendment to the Limitation of Hours of Work bill of 1935. The Commons' decision to give in came after extended informal discussions between Bennett and Meighen. Cf. Bennett's remarks, *HD, 1935*, p. 4307.

[82] Fruit bill of 1925; Root Vegetables bill and Criminal Code bill of 1931; Marketing bill and Fruit bill of 1934; Canadian Farm Loan bill of 1935; Income Tax bill of 1936; Central Mortgage Bank bill of 1939; Debts Due to the Crown bill of 1940; Civil Employment Reinstatement bill and War Risk Insurance bill of 1942; Estate Tax bill of 1958; Income Tax bill of 1959.

TABLE XXIV
The Resolution of Contentious Amendments Made by the Senate in Government Bills, 1925–63

Session	Total no. of bills amended by the Senate	Contentious amendments						
		Total	Resolved through				Lost
			Com-promise	HC yields	Senate yields	Free con-ferences	
1925	11	3	1		1	1	
1926	2	–					
1927	12	1	1				
1928	8	1	1				
1929	4	–					
1930	9	–					
1931	5	2			2		
1932	5	–					
1933	7	1				1	
1934	12	4	1		2	1	
1935	23	5	3	1	1		
1936	19	6	4		1		1
1937	10	1	1				
1938	11	1				1	
1939	13	2	1		1		
1940	16	2			1		1
1941	2	–					
1942	8	2			2		
1943	6	–					
1944	14	–					
1945	7	–					
1946	12	–					
1947	14	–				1	
1948	6	–					
1949	2	–					
1950	1	–					
1951	16	1	1				
1952	3	–					
1953	4	–					
1954	5	–					
1955	5	–					
1956	–	–					
1957	1	–					
1957–8	1	–					
1958	4	1			1		
1959	7	1			1		
1960	1	–					
1961	2	1					1
1962	1	–					
1962–3	–	–					
Total	289	36	14	1	13	5	3

Senate that desisted from the amendment which was objected to by the House of Commons, while in fourteen cases a compromise solution was reached, either through consequential amendments[83] or by each house sacrificing some of its original views for the sake of agreement.[84]

In eight instances, however, simple messages could not iron out the differences between the two chambers—the Senate refused to comply, whereas the Commons continued to insist on their disagreement. To break the legislative impasse, on six occasions the Commons asked for a free conference with the Senate, and in five out of the six cases the Conference was successful in saving the life of the disputed measure. The free conference system, which is based on the same idea as the Conference Committee in Congress, or the highly effective "Vermittlungsausschuss" in the Federal Republic of Germany,[85] differs from the ordinary conferences, used solely for transmitting communication, in that at a free conference the "managers" of the two houses are free "to urge arguments, to offer and combat objections, and, in short, to attempt by personal persuasion and argument to effect an agreement between the two Houses."[86] From this follows that a free conference can only be used in a conflict-situation which has developed over a single text, first passed by the Commons, then amended by the Senate; it cannot be used to resolve *any* kind of conflict. Thus, for example, no matter how desirable it might have been, it was impossible under the rules to arrange a free conference on the constitutional amendment in 1960,[87] not because the issue in question was a constitutional rather than a legislative matter, but because the same resolution was introduced in both houses in identical texts, and, although the Senate's amendment conflicted with the intentions of the Government, it was made in the Senate Address and not in a text that was brought up from the House of Commons.[88]

[83]Customs bill, Customs Tariff bill, Special War Revenue bill of 1936; Canadian Wheat Board bill of 1939; Canadian Forces bill of 1951.

[84]Pension bill of 1925; Excise bill of 1927; Pension bill of 1928; Farmers' Creditors Arrangement bill of 1934; Combines Investigation bill, Weights and Measures bill, Dominion Trade and Industry Commission bill of 1935; National Harbours bill of 1936; CNR Capital Revision bill of 1937.

[85]It was consulted 150 times from 1949 to 1959. See G. Dietze, "The Federal Republic of Germany: An Evaluation After Ten years," *Journal of Politics* (1960) no. 1.

[86]Bourinot, *Parliamentary Procedure*, p. 279; W. F. Dawson, *Procedure in the Canadian House of Commons* (Toronto, 1962), pp. 235–6. Nothing like the free conference system has been developed in Britain. The suggestion of the Bryce Conference for the adoption of a regular conference committee for settling differences between the houses has not been followed up, because, as Bromhead says, "such machinery would scarcely be suitable to the conditions of British politics." Bromhead, *The House of Lords*, p. 133.

[87]Above, p. 326.

[88]*HD, 1960*, pp. 7196, 7203.

The purpose of the conference is best served by small teams, representative of the respective party stands as well as the intellectual resources of the two houses. Indeed, the tendency has been for each house to send three "managers," the Commons' team invariably including the minister concerned, and sometimes more than one minister, while the Senate's team consisting of some of the most illustrious members of the Upper House. Suggestion for the date is usually contained in the Senate's message responding to the Commons' call for a conference. The meetings are held in one of the Senate's committee rooms.

The Senate, it should be emphasized, never came off second best in these encounters with the Commons. Its six "managers" stood fast by the decision of the House in the Home Bank Depositors bill of 1925,[89] in the face of the Commons' team, whose members, including five ministers of the Crown, were given an absolute mandate, unrestricted by the terms of the resolution, to press for the withdrawal of the Senate amendments.[90] However, all they could achieve was a concession from the Senate not to insist on their preamble and accept a consequential amendment to one of their amendments. Their report to the Commons made ex-Minister of Finance Sir Henry Drayton exclaim: "What has he [the P.M.] done . . .? He has commenced a constitutional contest. That contest had for its object the determination of the question as to whether the Senate had any right to interfere with a financial bill or not. How did it end? It ended by . . . accepting the position taken by the Senate. Why, we might as well have had no conference and saved this time and this farce."[91]

[89]Above, p. 342. This was the largest team ever appointed. Its appointment raised the procedural question of who was responsible for naming the managers of the Senate. After selecting four Conservatives, Sen. Lougheed, Opposition Leader in the Senate, asked Dandurand to nominate one from the Liberal ranks. Dandurand declined, on the ground "that the Senate has sufficient confidence in the hon. gentlemen whom [Lougheed] has named to leave the interests of the Senate in their hands . . . those four would fairly represent the opinion of the Senate." Lougheed was adamant; "this Bill," he said, "was . . . the unanimous production of the Senate. Both sides agreed upon it. It is very undesirable that any impression should be created . . . that this side alone is responsible for the Bill." However, according to constitutional usage, as interpreted by Dandurand, the appointment of the conferees was in the hands of those who represented the majority. Dandurand had no objection though to Lougheed's selecting a manager "from among those who are supposed to hold Liberal tenets." (Never say "party"!) Lougheed's choice fell upon Béique and Aylesworth. (*SD*, *1925*, pp. 682–3) In contrast, all the six managers of the Commons were Liberals. This gave the Liberals an 8:6 margin at the conference; however, it had no effect on the outcome. (But cf. n. 100 below.)

[90]*HD*, *1925*, p. 4901.

[91]*Ibid.*, p. 5060.

The three Senate "managers," Meighen, Chapais, and Graham (two Conservatives and one Liberal), who represented the Senate in 1933 over the Criminal Code (Protection of Children) bill, were equally successful in persuading Solicitor General Dupré, Lapointe, and Heaps (Labour) that to pass an act of Parliament virtually compelling a man and his common law wife to abandon their own offspring would be an undue stiffening of the Code. The emerging draft, giving the court full discretion in the matter, was an actual victory of the Senate's stand.[92]

The next time, when the exercise of the Senate's substantive function in connection with appeal procedures under the Excise bill of 1934[93] caused a legislative deadlock between the two houses, it was again two predominantly Conservative teams (Meighen, Côté, and Copp on behalf of the Senate, and Matthews, Minister of National Revenue, Cahan, Secretary of State, and Euler on behalf of the Commons) that were confronted with each other in a free conference. And it was again the representatives of the Commons who finally yielded, by agreeing to the first three, and to a compromise version of the fourth, of the Senate's contentious amendments.[94]

Differences of view between the two chambers over the Farmers' Creditors Arrangement Act occasioned two conferences in the sessions of 1938 and 1940. In 1938 the deadlock was caused by the Senate's amendment putting a time limit upon the operation of the Act in every province except Alberta and Saskatchewan, where the matter of terminating the legislation was to be left to the discretion of the Governor-in-Council. The ensuing conference between Senators Beaubien, Haig, Meighen, and Dandurand (three Conservatives and one Liberal) and the all-Liberal Commons team of Crerar, Euler, Ilsley, and McLean was able to make the way clear for enactment of the measure, by adopting a compromise solution, which postponed the deadline fixed by the Senate from December 31, 1938, to June 30, 1939, but left the principle of a time-limit unaffected.[95] The following session the Government reintroduced the bill, for the sole purpose of placing Manitoba with regard to the progressive termination of the Act by the Governor-in-Council in the same statutory position as Alberta and Saskatchewan. However, the bill was negatived on second reading in the Senate, mainly because of Meighen's strongly felt antagonism to its principle.[96] Then in the session of 1940, in compliance with the unanimous request of the Legislature of Manitoba, the Government again brought forward

[92]*Ibid., 1933*, p. 5580. For further comments, see above, p. 305.
[93]Above, pp. 308–9.
[94]*HD, 1934*, p. 4507; *SD, 1934*, p. 618.
[95]*SD, 1938*, p. 561.
[96]*SD, 1939*, pp. 196–7. See also Roger Graham, *Arthur Meighen*, vol. 3, pp. 70–1.

the measure. This time the bill was allowed second reading in the Senate[97] but was amended on third reading, enabling farmers and creditors alike to appeal to the Appeal Court from a proposal confirmed by the Board.[98] This stand the Senate, its majority in the case being made up of members from both sides of the House,[99] was not willing to abandon, with the result that the conference on July 21 was unable to come to an agreement and the bill was dropped.[100]

The last occasion on which the device of free conference was resorted to came in 1947, when the Commons found two of the Senate's thirty-two amendments to the Criminal Code bill unacceptable, while the Senate insisted on its original position. At the conference[101] the managers of the Senate "had very fine co-operation from members of the House of Commons: they appreciated our point of view, and one of them . . .," Haig recalled, "supported our amendments even more strongly than we did."[102] In the end the controversial clauses (dealing with the grounds for a murder charge) were redrafted by the Minister of Justice, the Deputy Minister of Justice, and the Law Clerk of the Senate in the presence of the managers. The product was in fact a

[97]Meighen's attitude was obviously influenced by a last-minute telegram from Premier Bracken of Manitoba, who urged "that the Bill should at least be sent to committee, and that before final vote is taken members of the Manitoba board of review should be called before the committee to give evidence as to whether ... this is good reason for the Act again being made effective in Manitoba." *Ibid., 1940*, p. 185.

[98]*Ibid.*, p. 265.

[99]Above, p. 130.

[100]*HD, 1940*, p. 2322. Procedurally, there was a slight deviation from the traditional practice. Until now the steps leading up to the conference were as follows; the Commons sent a message to the Senate asking for a free conference; the Senate sent back a message, agreeing to the idea of the conference, indicating a date and naming its managers; upon receipt of this message the Commons named its own managers. This time, in anticipation of the Senate's approval of the idea of a conference, the Commons in the same message in which it proposed the Conference also named its three managers—Ilsley, Crerar, and Tucker. The fact that all three were chosen from among the majority in House of Commons made it imperative in Meighen's eyes "that the three managers to be appointed by the Senate should all be chosen from among the majority in this House." Accordingly, he picked Conservative Senators Beaubien, Calder, and Haig; Dandurand, as fifteen years before, had no objection to leaving to them "the responsibility of presenting to the managers for the House of Commons the point of view of the Senate." *SD, 1940*, p. 401. (It should be noted that when the bill was passed in 1943 it provided for the right of appeal from the decision of the district court judge, who replaced the high court judge in dealing with debt adjustment applications.)

[101]The procedure regarding the naming of the managers was the same as in 1940. All the three from the House of Commons were Liberals. But the Senate team consisted of two Liberals (Robertson and Beauregard) and one Conservative (Haig).

[102]*SD, 1947*, p. 673.

compromise between the original text and its Senate version, the essence of the Senate amendments being left intact.

Thus, the free conferences held between the Senate and the House of Commons during the years from 1925 to 1963 were, with one exception, successful in resolving the legislative deadlocks which threatened the passage of particular measures. However, the Farmers' Creditors Arrangement bill of 1940 was not the only bill which was lost because the amendments made by the Senate were unacceptable to the Government. There were two other instances during our period when bills were dropped for the same reason, and in both their fate can be traced back to the unwillingness of the Government of the day to come to terms with the Senate, and its deliberate refusal to take advantage of the free conference system. One was the Combines Investigation bill of 1936, in which the Senate, in consistency with its action a year before, made certain amendments concerning the production of documents in criminal proceedings.[103] Although the amendments did not nullify the effectiveness of the Combines Act, they enraged Mackenzie King, who contended that the bill was completely useless as returned from the Senate. Both Bennett and Woodsworth, while supporting the stand of the Government, urged that the proper way of facilitating an understanding between the two houses was through a free conference.[104] However, utterly impatient with the Senate, the Prime Minister declined the suggestion, on the rather flimsy ground that "from a reading of the debate in the Senate it would appear that no useful purpose could possibly be served by a Conference." In contrast, Bennett believed that this was "a case for the utilization of such conciliatory powers as we possess, and our constitution has provided for a conference; that is the usual course." He dismissed the suggestion that seeking a conference might imply "that any one House of Parliament goes on its knees to any other House of Parliament. That is entirely beside the question. They have co-ordinate powers of jurisdiction. . . ." A conference, therefore, he pleaded, was "the appropriate method, because in a debate in the House there is not the same opportunity for explanation and contact as there is when a conference is held."[105] These arguments, however, could not change King's mind; no conference was held and the bill failed to pass Parliament.[106] Similarly, the Conservative Government in 1961 was urged, without avail, to take a more conciliatory attitude to the Senate amendments in its Customs Tariff bill.[107] Upon receiving the Commons'

[103]Above, p. 306. [104]*HD, 1936*, p. 3993. [105]*Ibid.*, pp. 4035, 4036–7.

[106]It was passed in 1937, with important judicial safeguards incorporated in the law. See above, p. 307.

[107]Above, pp. 310–11.

disagreeing message to the Senate's amendment, Sen. Macdonald, Liberal Leader of the Senate, suggested on July 11 that a free conference be arranged between the two houses with a view of working out a satisfactory method of appeal under the Act. Although this suggestion was not strictly in accordance with the rules governing conferences, since the proposed meeting was to take place prior to the Senate's decision regarding its reply-message to the Commons, nevertheless at the end of the day's sitting, when it was evident that the Senate's Liberal majority was resolved to reject the Commons' message, Sen. Brunt, Deputy Leader of the Government, stated he had "learned that such a conference might be possible. As long as it is possible, and as long as there is a possibility of saving the bill, let us try to save it."[108] However, the Government had apparently by this time made up its mind; on June 12, its representative, Sen. Aseltine, told the Senate that "no conference is possible at this stage." His motion to pass the bill in its original form was defeated by 38 votes to 17. After the vote there was a final chance of saving the bill, by arranging a last-minute meeting with the House of Commons under the usual procedure. "We on this side," Macdonald said, "are prepared to have a conference. If this bill is not carried, it will not be our responsibility; it is the Government that will be defeating its own bill."[109] But his words went unheeded; Parliament was adjourned the following day, and with it died the whole legislation.[110]

In sum, the Senate has used its varied powers during the period from 1925 to 1963 with a combination of firmness and moderation that does not fail to impress the observer. The exercise of these powers is, of course, fundamentally linked to the operative principles governing partisanship and impartiality in the Senate. Temperateness and detachment in matters of party politics will usually result in reasonableness and self-restraint as regards the use of the Senate's formidable constitutional powers. On the other hand, used wisely and tactfully, these powers can be of great help to the Senate in performing its substantive role as an auxiliary institutional check upon the executive. Not only can these powers be mobilized to achieve the necessary balance of power; their bare presence may compel the Government to think twice before it brings forward any item of policy in Parliament. And this, indeed, sems to be the essence of a second chamber in a modern parliamentary democracy.

[108]*SD, 1961*, p. 1117. [109]*Ibid.*, p. 1126.

[110]When Parliament was reconvened for a short period in September, questions were raised in the House of Commons on September 27 and 28 as to the intentions of the Government with regard to the bill. The replies given indicated no change in the attitude of the Government. *HD, 1960–1*, pp. 9021, 9022, 9091.

CONCLUSION 13

FOR A MORE SYSTEMATIC DISCUSSION of the Senate's work in modern times a theoretical distinction was suggested between the "technical" and the "substantive" functions of second chambers in parliamentary democracies of the cabinet type. While the first derived from the increasing burden on the Commons' timetable, caused by the growing complexity of things Parliament was expected to deal with, the second stemmed from the contemporary constitutional phenomenon of cabinet preponderance, in conjunction with the accompanying trend of the tightening of party discipline in the elected Chamber. Less fettered by the rules of debate and removed from the actual arena of party strife, the Senate has been successful in effecting useful modifications in public legislation under Conservative and Liberal governments alike, for the purpose of introducing technical improvements and of checking executive extravagance; in taking a first look at complex or non-controversial measures and, since 1935, at all private bills; in holding valuable debates on matters of broad national policy and of administration in narrow fields, which, directly or indirectly, have influenced government policies, intentions, and attitudes; in making use, to a greater and greater extent, of its standing and special committee system in the triple field of legislation, scrutiny, and inquiry, with the additional general advantages of bringing affected interests into direct contact with representatives of the administration, and of obliging governments to explain their policies and to reply to serious and constructive criticisms and suggestions; and in representing the territorial and other minorities, by intervening on their behalf and by providing (through the operation of the appointing system) a socially recognized means of acknowledging their relative importance in the federal state. Part of this is work such as the House of Commons also carries out. But the House of Commons, as was noted above, does not have unlimited time and, being the focal point of the political power struggle on the national level, is under the domination of the great rival party machines. As a result, even if some of these functions are performed by both houses, they do not do it in quite the same way, and there are some aspects of the work which are better done the Senate's way than the Commons' way. But all through the years the Senate has exercised its considerable legal powers in a responsible manner, using persuasion rather than obstruction to defend its stand vis-à-vis the House of Commons. In matters of economic and social policy it has wisely taken the lead of the elected House and for the better part of the period under review it has accepted, indeed supported, the policies of successive governments in that regard. The Senate has never, during the last three decades at any rate, posed as an "Upper House" in terms of traditional class values and, unlike some of its Continental counterparts, membership of the House has not been associated with the notions of social superiority. An impartial study of the record of the Senate during the years 1925 to 1963 amply confirms the argument that the Upper House is a useful complement to the Lower.

These considerations do not, however, entitle us to be complacent, or to say that the Senate ought to be left exactly as it is. While appreciating its services in functional terms, we must also admit that it has defects on practical grounds, and although this study is not a treatise on Senate reform, but primarily an essay of the working of the "unreformed Senate," we have to look for the remedies.

Senate reform, strictly speaking, has long ceased to be the subject of serious consideration of political science. It "comes periodically," Henri Bourassa once said, "like other forms of epidemics and current fevers,"[1] and furnishes, as Sen. Roebuck remarked, "those seeking intellectual exercise with an interesting topic of conversation."[2] Not only have innumerable schemes been advocated by conferences and individuals, in the form of books, pamphlets, and articles in the popular press, but parties have included the theme in their manifestos and brought down in motions moved in Parliament. However, these motions and promises have hardly been motivated by the honest desire to grapple with the problem which they urged so badly needed a quick solution; proposals made by governments have not been followed up, while motions moved

[1]*HD, 1926*, p. 648.
[2]*SD, 1951*, p. 94.

by Opposition parties in the House of Commons have mostly been aimed at irritating and embarrassing the Government.[3] Furthermore, no party has been quite consistent in its alternative plans for the present composition of the Senate. Even radical groups, which have habitually considered the Senate an anathema, have occasionally deviated from their hard line of abolition and, in view of political realities, accepted an institution which has no place in their ideals. Thus, spokesmen of the CCF party in the House of Commons had often taken a more "realistic" attitude and held that, abolition being unfeasible under the circumstances, the Senate should be reformed and "democratized."[4]

[3]No constructive purpose has been served by Mackenzie King's crusade against the Senate during the 1925 election campaign (cf. Correspondence of Aylesworth and Murphy, Oct. 1925. Murphy Papers, vol. 1, nos. 337–8); by the promise in the Speech from the Throne the same session for a special federal-provincial conference to consider the constitution of the Senate; by a debate on Senate reform in the House of Commons on Shaw's (Progr., West Calgary) motion, March 9, 1925; by the urgent demands of the Opposition during the successive years that the Government act upon its promise (*HD, 1926*, pp. 208–9, 939, 4030; *ibid., 1928*, pp. 224–5, 616, 659; *ibid., 1929*, pp. 28, 661, 1920–1); by the Dominion-Provincial Conference of 1927, which dealt with Senate reform in a historical perspective (*Canadian Annual Review, 1927–8*, p. 31); by Coldwell's appeals to the Government in 1939, 1940, and 1943 to implement its twenty-year-old campaign plank regarding the Senate (*HD, 1939*, pp. 4917–8; *ibid., 1940*, p. 2322; *ibid., 1943*, p. 56); by the extended debate on the Senate and House of Commons bill of 1947; by Drew's motion in 1950, defeated after debate by 111 votes to 51, for the appointment of a joint parliamentary committee of the two houses to propose constitutional changes affecting the Senate; by a debate on Senate reform in the House of Commons in 1954, arising out of another motion by Drew, that was defeated by 84 votes to 48; by a similar debate in 1955 on Rowe's motion that the Government start "consultation and inquiry respecting reform of the Senate," (*HD, 1955*, p. 5355)—a debate which drew no contribution from the Government side and ended in a hostile vote of 95:62; by a formal Request for Election and Senate Reform by Drew in 1956 following the Pipe Line affair (*HD, 1956*, p. 5332.); by the vague reference to Senate reform in the Speech from the Throne in the session of 1957–8; and by the repeated urging of the Government during the successive sessions to change its words into deeds (*HD, 1957–8*, pp. 1509, 2939; *ibid., 1958*, p. 2206, 3174; *ibid., 1960*, pp. 498, 1708; *ibid., 1961*, p. 4322; *ibid., 1962*, p. 976.).

[4]The official CCF policy for abolition, in harmony with earlier farmer and labour policies and incorporated in the Regina Manifesto of 1933, has of course often been repeated by party members in the House of Commons. However, for more conciliatory statements, see, *inter alia* the remarks of Woodsworth (*HD, 1926*, p. 562; *ibid., 1936*, p. 4038), Lucas (UFA) (*ibid., 1932*, p. 2335); Mitchell (Hamilton East) (*ibid.*, p. 2346; *ibid., 1935*, p. 102); Coldwell (*ibid., 1937*, p. 427; *ibid., 1950*, pp. 2759–60), Thatcher (Moose Jaw-Lake Centre) (*ibid., 1946*, pp. 2431–2; *ibid., 1955*, p. 5339), Irvine (Cariboo) (*ibid., 1947*, p. 5364), Knight (Saskatoon) (*ibid., 1955*, p. 5928), Winch (Vancouver E.) (*ibid.*, p. 6006); the undogmatic stand was perhaps most pronounced in MacInnis' (Vancouver-Kingsway) opinion that if the CCF "formed the Government the first thing we would have to do would be to get somebody in the Senate to represent us there, even at the opening of Parliament, and once having embarked upon that course we probably might consider changing our policy of abolition." *Ibid., 1955*, p. 5345.

Generally speaking, comprehensive proposals for a wholesale reconstruction of the Senate have stemmed from two basic ideas—both founded on a mistaken notion of the Senate's functions and of the nature of the system in which it has to operate. On the one hand, it has been argued, ever since David Mills introduced a motion in 1874, that, the main feature of the Canadian system being its federal structure, the primary and most important function of the Senate is to be a politically active institutional stronghold of the provinces in Parliament, representing provincial or sectional interests in a militant way, if necessary, not only against the federal executive but against the federal legislature as well. To achieve this end, numerous schemes have been put forward, ranging from a total or partial transfer of the right to recommend senatorial appointments from the prime minister to the provincial governments, to a recently advocated scheme, under which the Senate would be turned into a "standing Dominion-Provincial Conference," its members voting under strict instructions from their respective provinces and led in the House by their respective premiers themselves—a true replica of the system obtaining in the Federal Republic of Germany.[5]

The second stream of proposals has centred around the theme that the Senate, an appointed body, is non-representative, non-responsible, and, therefore, undemocratic. To remedy this situation, it has been suggested that the Senate, wholly or in part, should either be directly elected by the people, or, again, appointed by the provincial governments for a fixed duration, or that some sort of term appointment should be adopted under the existing nominative system. The effect of any of these methods, or a combination of them, it has been urged, would not only make the Senate more democratically founded but it would end the lopsidedness of party representation in the Chamber, by making the Senate more representative of the "various minority schools of political thought" in the country.

The misconception behind these reform proposals appears to have been caused by a misreading of the constitutional context in which the Senate, as a parliamentary institution, is placed to function. They have overlooked the plain fact that Canada has a governmental system "similar in principle to that of the United Kingdom." The basis on which the whole machinery of government is organized is that of

[5]Peyton V. Lyon, "A New Idea for Senate Reform," *Canadian Commentator*, July–Aug., 1962. Its author claims that by the adoption of his scheme the problem of "repatriating" the Canadian constitution could also be solved. For an even more controversial proposal, see Trevor Lloyd's article, "A Bi-National Second Chamber," in the *Canadian Forum*, June 1964, and a rebuttal from Eugene Forsey, "A Bi-National Second Chamber?" *ibid.*, Nov. 1964.

responsible cabinet government. A second house of the central legislature acting as an assembly of disciplined provincial delegates would unduly complicate, disturb, and, probably, block the operation of that system. The Senate is not to be expected to do more in the field of provincial representation than what it does; its functions should not be enlarged in the direction of giving provincial politics a formalized and institutionalized expression in the framework of Parliament.

By the same token, it is not the function of the Senate to represent politically polarized current public opinion through direct mandate or otherwise. Leaving aside minor technical objections,[6] the most telling argument against a "representative" Senate is that it would reproduce, without any obvious advantage, party cleavages and foster partisanship in the Senate and would blur the meaning, and confuse the implications, of governmental responsibility. Arguments about a "democratic" or "undemocratic" Senate are not, as a rule, thought through and there is much demagogy in repeating nineteenth century liberal slogans about the virtues of elected offices. What is important is that Canada's political system is democratic; the Senate is part of the system.

Any reform that might with advantage be introduced must, therefore, start from the above-mentioned constitutional premise, and must be aimed at enabling the Senate to perform its technical and substantive functions, as defined throughout this survey, more effectively. There are two defects in the Senate's composition that actually or potentially detract from the effectiveness of the House, and both can be rectified within the framework of the present appointing system. One is the presence of a fairly large number of persons of very advanced age, who may lend dignity to the Senate's work and may render services on a restricted personal basis, but who cannot all regularly take an active

[6]Term appointment, usually accompanied by the notion of re-appointment "would reduce such members to mere puppets of the administration of the day. Their positions would be analogous to that of civil servants with a five-year contract . . . it would utterly destroy the independence of Senators appointed on that basis, and in all probability it would endanger the independence of the Senate as a whole." (Sen. Roebuck's remarks, *SD*, *1951*, p. 96) Even more important, as John N. Turner's (now Liberal member for St. Lawrence–St. George in the House of Commons) figures indicate, the extremes in party representation would have been far greater under term appointments, made either by the federal government or by the provincial governments or by a combination of the two, than they were under the present arrangement. (Cf. J. N. Turner, "The Senate of Canada," unpublished BA thesis, University of British Columbia (1949), pp. 148–65. *passim.*) Indeed, as we have seen (above, p. 70), the natural mortality rate in the Senate takes care of the necessary influx of new blood. As for the method of election, it would, *inter alia,* almost certainly put an end to the practice, so rigorously observed by successive governments, of giving representation to certain minorities, regardless of their numerical strength on a population basis.

part in the Senate's technical business. The result is that, as we have seen, the brunt of work, both in the House and in committees, is borne by a relatively small group of men, who are themselves not very young and whose burden should more equally be distributed among the whole membership. The simplest way of attaining this end seems to be through the adoption of a statutory retirement age, not higher than seventy-five and not lower than seventy. In addition to lowering the average age in the Senate, such a limitation would perhaps also encourage the appointment of younger men—people in their early rather than, as at present, in their late fifties. Opponents of such a scheme usually point to the example of famous octagenarians in the Senate's history, who were apparently not withered by age or decayed by the years. Indeed, it must be admitted that some of those who contributed most to the Senate's work during these thirty-seven years were in this highest age group—Buchanan, Aylesworth, Dandurand, Lynch-Staunton, Graham, Tanner, Ballantyne, King, Robinson, Copp, Black, Jones, Marcotte, Turgeon (Sr.), to name only the most obvious of past figures. However, as Sen. Hugessen convincingly argued in 1951, all these counter-examples were "based very largely upon personal considerations and they have dealt with individual cases of men, who . . . are the exception, and for that reason their names stand out to such a degree. Exceptions are not the general rule." And he subsequently moved a Resolution that "future appointments to the Senate should not be made for life, but should be made subject to retirement at the age of 75 years at the latest."[7] Indeed, one of the positive merits of this reform plan is that it is not controversial; it is practically universally approved throughout the country and it also enjoys general support in the Senate—at least amongst those under 75. Accordingly, after earlier attempts by others during the past decade,[8] the Conservative Government brought down a bill on April 9, 1962, to implement its election pledge for Senate reform, by introducing a compulsory retirement age at seventy-five. The bill was passed on the first reading by 143 votes to 7, only the NDP group opposing it on some rather obscure ground.[9] Although the bill died on the Commons' Order Paper both in 1962 and in the session of 1962–63, due to the dissolution of Parliament, the enactment of a similar measure at some future date can now be taken as a virtual certainty.*

[7]*SD, 1951*, pp. 162–5.

[8]In both 1954 and 1955 Follwell (Lib., Hastings South) introduced a private member's bill to amend the BNA Act to provide for a senatorial retirement age at 75; on neither of these occasions, however, did his bill get beyond the stage of first reading.

[9]See Herridge's statement, Montreal *Gazette*, April 10, 1962.

*A bill to retire senators at the age of seventy-five had passed the Commons and was before the Senate just as this book went to press.

If the purpose of a fixed retirement age is to enhance the competence of the Senate in discharging its "technical" duties, some reform to further neutralize partisan impulses would probably add to the Senate's ability to perform its "substantive" functions. To give the Senate an even more non-partisan character, it has been suggested that either the power of appointment should be taken out of the hands of the prime minister and placed in those of various professional bodies, or that appointments should be made, not on the basis of political allegiance, but on "merit," as "a positive recognition and acknowledgement of community responsibility."[10] These proposals, however, immediately raise serious objections. Whereas the idea of appointment by organized "non-political associations," which comes very close to the principles of corporatism, would scarcely be suitable to the conditions of Canadian government, the scheme of turning the Senate into a body of "notables" would probably deprive the House of membership of men of great legislative experience, which is so indispensable to the effective functioning of the Senate. Having said this, it must nevertheless be admitted that a more equitable representation of the various occupations in the Senate would be a very sound objective to aim at, indeed.

In a sense, then, the main problem is how to reconcile the idea of legislative competence, secured by the presence of many former members of the House of Commons, or other deliberative bodies, with the idea of non-partisanship, which is potentially, at least, always in danger in the presence of so many former MP's. But between these two extremes there are many intermediate grades and the solution to the problem might well lie in developing certain constitutional conventions, which would bind the prime minister in making his appointments to the Senate. That such an idea is not entirely Utopian was amply demonstrated by some of Mr. St. Laurent's appointments during the second half of his administration, when he was faced with the danger of a one-party Senate. To encourage the development of such conventions, it has been proposed that appointments to the Senate should in fact be "seconded" by the leader of the Opposition in the Commons or that the constitution should be amended to provide a statutory maximum and minimum for government supporters and non-government members

[10]Sen. Turgeon, *SD, 1955*, p. 527. For similar views, see in particular the remarks of Woodsworth (*HD, 1926*, p. 562), Lemieux (*SD, 1934*, pp. 153–4), Irvine (CCF, Cariboo) (*HD, 1947*, p. 5364), Hees (PC, Broadview) (*ibid., 1955*, p. 5343), Knight (CCF, Saskatoon) (*ibid.*, p. 5928), Thatcher (CCF, Moose Jaw-Lake Centre) (*ibid.*, p. 5339); Sen. Lambert, "Reform of the Senate," reprinted from the *Winnipeg Free Press*, April 1950; the articles, "A New Senate" and "This Is Why We Need It" in *MacLean's Magazine*, April 15, 1954; the editorial in the *Ottawa Journal*, June 2, 1955; and J. B. McGeachy, "Let's Stir Up the Senate," *Financial Post*, Aug. 2, 1958.

in the Senate at any given point of time.[11] In addition to a compulsory retirement age, some reform along these lines would probably help improve the composition of the Senate, and increase its all-round efficiency.

One of the positive features of the proposals discussed above is that they could be implemented under the BNA Act (No. 2) of 1949, without seeming likely to create any particular constitutional difficulties.[12] Procedurally, of course, their introduction would still require the concurrence of the Senate. But apart from the requirements of the law, it is, indeed, a matter of "constitutional etiquette" that there should be co-operation between the Senate and the Government before any reform is considered. Mackenzie King, who had perhaps more trouble with the Senate than any other prime minister of Canada in modern times, first thought it desirable to have an unwritten pledge exacted from his appointees, ensuring their support for any Senate reform his Government might in future decide to introduce. He later discontinued this practice[13] and, then, towards the end of his career, he gave the following wise

[11]See Sen. Gouin's motion, *SD*, *1951*, p. 407; White's (PC, Middlesex East) proposal, *HD*, *1953–4*, pp. 274–5; also F. O. Baldwin, "Is Senate Reform Necessary?" *Canadian Business*, Nov. 1951. The first idea was embodied in the Trinidad and Tobago (Const.) order-in-council (*SI*, *1962*, no. 1875), according to which the twenty-four members of the Senate are appointed by the governor general, thirteen on the advice of the prime minister, seven on the advice of the prime minister after consultation with those social, economic, and religious bodies and associations from which he considers that such appointments should be made, and four on the advice of the leader of the opposition. The same scheme has been adopted in Jamaica, where a total of thirteen of the twenty-one members of the Upper House are appointed on the advice of the prime minister and eight on the advice of the leader of the opposition.

[12]See Paul Gérin-Lajoie, *Constitutional Amendment in Canada* (Toronto, 1950) in particular pp. xxx and 237–8; E. R. Hopkins, *How Parliament Works* (Ottawa, 1957), p. 22; Dandurand's remarks, *SD*, *1927*, p. 129; and *Canadian Annual Review*, *1926–27*, p. 103.

[13]"The only reference in that connection that I can recall," he said in 1947, "is the matter of Senators being prepared to favour a shortening of years during which service would be given in the Senate. . . . That was not in the nature of making a rubber-stamp out of the Senate; it was if anything to ensure that Liberal members who went to the Senate would be helpful in bringing about that reform. That was a mere understanding, a gentleman's agreement with some of those who went to the Senate at the beginning of my term of office as Prime Minister." "It was an undertaking," he repeated in 1948, "that was given to myself, as the one who was responsible for nominating members to the Senate. How many there were from whom I received that assurance, I cannot say. . . . Nor am I in a position to say just when I ceased to raise that question." But "of late years I have not felt it was necessary to suggest this reform to any Senator; I believe many already favour it." *HD*, *1947*, p. 5366; *ibid.*, *1948*, pp. 853–4. For more on this question of the pledge, for which he was so bitterly criticized by so many, see *inter alia*, *HD*, *1926*, pp. 105, 1099, 3297; *ibid.*, *1927*, p. 355; *SD*, *1927*, p. 51.; *HD*, *1929*, p. 1421; *SD*, *1933*, p. 511; *HD*, *1935*, p. 2381; *ibid.*, *1949*, p. 971; *ibid.*, *1955*, pp. 5331 ff, 6010.

advice during the course of an "intimate and delightful conversation" with Sen. Robertson:

I always had it in mind to do something about the Senate before I cease to be a Prime Minister, but there are so many things to be done from one day to another that it is difficult for me to concentrate on this question. . . . *I think action should be taken at a time when the relations between the two Houses are happy ones, because then the change could be made under very much better circumstances.* . . . My own view, for what it is worth, is that the Senate itself should give consideration to this problem.[14]

Curiously, most of the proposals that have been put forward by various quarters for a wholesale reconstruction of the Senate have been based upon some rational or perfectionist plan, the kind of "Cartesianism" which is so alien to the Anglo-Saxon tradition of bringing about improvements in institutions gradually, through a process of trial and error. Therefore, much more important than these comprehensive reform schemes concerning the Senate's composition have been those piecemeal innovations which the Senate has itself effected in the organization of its work throughout the years. Indeed, the Senate has shown great ingenuity and adaptability in adjusting its work to the demands of developing constitutional practice. Writing in 1925 on the "unreformed Senate of Canada," Professor Mackay listed a few reform proposals which were urged at the time as likely to enhance the effectiveness of the Senate's contribution—such as making the Senate a chamber of first instance with respect to all private bills, changing the rules to allow ministers from the House of Commons to introduce legislation in the Senate, increasing the use of the Senate's committees, and diffusing legislative leadership among a wide circle of Senators. All of these proposals, as we have seen, have been put into effect one by one during the last thirty-seven years. The organic quality of the Senate was exceptionally well illustrated by the story of Rule 18/A, which was adopted after long agitation, and then was quietly dropped when it no longer seemed to serve any useful purpose at all. Similar to these piecemeal improvements, accomplished simply by a change in organization and leadership, are several areas in which the Senate could increase its usefulness. The most obvious ones are connected with a continued

[14]*SD, 1951*, p. 53. Italic added. See also Mr. Pickersgill's remarks, *HD, 1962*, p. 1154. In this spirit it would seem advisable that if and when a statutory retirement age is introduced it should be restricted to future appointments, leaving the tenure of the present incumbents undisturbed. Indeed, the measure to enforce retirement from the Senate at the age of seventy-five, which had passed the Commons and was before the Senate as this book went to press, adopted this principle by making retirement for the present members of the Senate optional.

expansion of the Senate's committee work in the fields of legislation, scrutiny, and inquiry, but particularly in those of scrutiny and inquiry. Greatly helped by the flexibility of its timetable and its ruling spirit of impartiality, the Senate could develop some effective and important means of overseeing certain aspects of financial administration, especially in the sphere of Crown corporations, and checking certain executive practices, especially in the sphere of delegated legislation. The Senate could also increase the number of special inquiries conducted annually, and enlarge their scope and variety. All this requires very little external stimulus and can be achieved through imaginative leadership and, perhaps, a few changes in internal organization. Indeed, the best practical way of "reforming" the Senate seems to lie in further exploiting the potentialities inherent in the structure of the institution itself.

APPENDICES

APPENDIX I

Treatment in the Senate of Bills Passed by the House of Commons

Session	Government bills				Private bills				Public bills introduced by private member				Total				Bills passed by the HC and sent to the Senate
	Amended	Rejected	Passed without amendment	Withdrawn	Amended	Rejected	Passed without amendment	Withdrawn	Amended	Rejected	Passed without amendment	Withdrawn	Amended	Rejected	Passed without amendment	Withdrawn	
1925	11	4	43	—	5	1	10	—	—	1	—	—	16	6	53	—	75
1926	2	3	17	1	3	—	10	—	—	1	1	—	5	2	28	2	37
1926–27	12	2	66	—	1	—	23	—	—	—	—	—	13	2	89	—	104
1928	8	2	46	—	3	2	17	—	—	1	—	—	11	5	63	—	79
1929	4	1	57	—	5	1	24	—	—	3	—	—	9	5	81	—	95
1930[1]	9	—	38	—	5	—	20	—	—	1	3	—	14	1	61	—	76
1930[2]	—	—	3	—	—	—	—	—	—	—	—	—	—	—	3	—	3
1931	5	—	52	—	3	—	9	—	1	—	3	—	9	—	64	—	73
1932	5	—	46	—	1	—	4	—	—	—	1	—	6	—	51	—	57
1932–33	7	1	44	—	3	—	8	—	—	—	—	—	10	1	52	—	63
1934	12	—	44	1	1	1	9	—	—	—	1	—	13	1	54	1	69
1935	23	1	39	—	—	—	—	—	—	1	—	—	23	2	39	—	64
1936	19	—	30	—	—	—	—	—	—	—	1	—	19	—	31	—	50
1937	10	—	33	—	—	—	1	—	—	—	1	—	10	—	35	—	45
1938	11	1	39	1	—	—	—	1	2	2	3	—	13	3	42	2	60
1939	13	1	47	—	—	—	2	—	—	1	—	—	13	2	49	—	64
1940	16	1	32	—	—	—	—	—	—	—	—	—	16	1	32	—	49
1940–1–2	2	—	30	1	—	—	—	—	—	—	—	—	2	—	30	1	33
1942–43	8	—	28	—	—	—	—	—	—	—	—	—	8	—	28	—	36
1943–44	6	—	26	—	—	—	—	—	—	—	—	—	6	—	26	—	32
1944–45	14	—	38	—	—	—	—	—	—	—	—	—	14	—	38	—	52
1945	7	—	28	—	—	—	—	—	—	—	—	—	7	—	28	—	35
1946	12	—	56	—	—	—	—	—	1	—	—	—	13	—	56	—	69
1947	14	—	48	—	—	—	—	—	—	—	1	—	14	—	49	—	63
1948	6	—	48	—	—	—	—	—	—	—	—	—	6	—	48	—	54
1949[1]	—	—	15	—	—	—	—	—	—	—	—	—	—	—	15	—	15
1949[2]	2	—	28	—	1	—	—	—	—	—	1	—	3	—	29	—	32
1950	1	—	33	—	—	—	2	—	—	—	—	—	1	—	35	—	36
1950–51	—	—	10	—	—	—	—	—	—	—	—	—	—	—	10	—	10
1951[1]	11	—	42	—	—	—	—	—	—	—	—	—	11	—	42	—	53
1951[2]	5	—	27	—	—	—	—	—	—	—	—	—	5	—	27	—	32
1952	3	—	41	—	—	—	—	—	—	—	1	—	3	—	42	—	45
1952–53	4	—	34	—	—	—	—	—	—	—	—	—	4	—	34	—	38
1953–54	5	—	51	—	—	—	—	—	—	—	1	—	5	—	52	—	57
1955	5	—	46	—	—	—	—	—	—	—	1	—	5	—	47	—	52
1956	—	—	42	—	—	—	—	—	—	—	—	—	—	—	42	—	42
1957	1	—	28	—	—	—	—	—	—	—	—	—	1	—	28	—	29
1957–58	1	—	27	—	—	—	—	—	—	—	—	—	1	—	27	—	28
1958	4	—	37	—	—	—	—	—	—	—	—	—	4	—	37	—	41
1959	7	—	36	—	—	—	—	—	—	—	1	—	7	—	37	—	44
1960	1	—	36	—	—	—	—	—	—	—	—	—	1	—	36	—	37
1961	2	1	55	—	—	—	—	—	—	—	2	1	2	1	57	1	61
1962	1	—	26	—	—	—	—	—	—	—	2	1	1	—	28	1	30
1962–63	—	—	17	—	—	—	—	—	—	—	—	—	—	—	17	—	17
Total	289	18	1,609	4	31	5	139	1	4	11	24	1	324	32	1,772	8	2,136

APPENDIX II

Treatment in the House of Commons of Bills Passed by the Senate

Session	Government bills				Private bills				Public bills introduced by private member				Divorce bills			Totals				Bills passed by the Senate
	Amended	Rejected	Passed without amendment	Withdrawn	Amended	Rejected	Passed without amendment	Withdrawn	Amended	Rejected	Passed without amendment	Withdrawn	Rejected	Passed without amended	Withdrawn	Amended	Rejected	Passed without amendment	Withdrawn	
1925	—	—	1	—	1	—	6	—	—	—	—	—	—	135	—	1	—	142	—	143
1926	—	—	1	—	2	—	4	—	—	—	—	2	—	137	34*	2	—	142	36	180
1926–7	—	—	1	1	3	1	6	—	—	—	—	2	—	196	—	3	1	203	3	210
1928	—	—	—	—	1	—	8	—	—	1	—	1	—	239	—	1	1	247	1	250
1929	1	—	—	1	—	—	7	—	—	2	—	2	2	238	1	1	4	245	4	254
1930	—	—	—	—	—	—	5	2	—	—	—	—	2	247	—	—	2	252	2	256
1931	—	—	1	—	—	—	7	1	—	1	—	—	—	39	—	—	1	47	1	49†
1932	4	—	—	—	—	—	1	—	—	—	—	—	—	27	—	4	—	28	—	32
1932–3	2	—	2	—	—	—	2	—	—	1	—	—	—	24	—	2	1	28	—	31
1934	2	—	2	—	3	—	—	1	—	1	—	—	1	38	—	5	2	40	1	48
1935	1	—	3	—	1	2	4	—	—	—	—	—	2	30	—	2	4	37	—	43
1936	—	—	1	—	3	3	6	1	—	1	—	—	—	40	—	3	4	47	1	55
1937	—	—	—	—	—	2	8	—	—	1	—	—	—	46	—	—	3	54	—	57
1938	—	—	—	—	1	1	7	—	—	1	—	—	1	85	—	1	3	92	—	96
1939	1	—	1	—	4	—	8	—	—	—	—	—	—	50	—	5	—	59	—	64
1940	—	—	—	—	2	—	5	1	—	—	—	—	—	62	—	2	—	67	1	70
1940-1-2	—	—	—	—	1	—	7	—	—	1	—	—	—	49	—	1	1	56	—	58
1942–43	—	—	—	—	—	—	3	5	—	—	—	—	—	73	3	—	—	76	8	84
1943–44	—	—	—	—	2	—	4	—	—	—	—	—	—	92	2	2	—	96	2	100
1944–45	—	—	—	—	2	—	9	—	—	—	—	—	—	111	—	2	—	120	—	122
1945	1	—	3	—	2	—	13	—	—	—	—	—	—	179	—	3	—	195	—	198
1946	2	—	6	—	—	—	12	—	—	—	—	—	—	290	—	2	—	308	—	310
1947	4	—	11	—	4	1	13	—	—	—	—	—	2	348	1	8	3	372	—	383
1948	6	—	18	—	1	—	12	1	—	—	—	—	2	292	1	7	2	322	2	333
1949[1]	1	—	5	5	1	—	16	1	—	—	—	—	—	184	—	2	—	205	6	213
1949[2]	3	—	8	1	—	—	1	2	—	—	—	—	—	166	—	3	—	175	3	181
1950	7	—	14	—	—	—	10	—	—	—	—	—	—	240	—	7	—	264	—	271
1951[1]	1	—	11	—	11	—	17	1	—	—	—	—	—	294	1	12	—	322	2	336
1951[2]	—	—	1	—	—	—	4	—	—	—	—	—	—	—	—	—	—	5	—	5
1952	1	—	8	—	—	—	15	1	1	—	—	—	—	312	1	2	—	335	2	339
1952–53	5	—	11	—	1	—	14	—	—	—	—	—	—	282	—	6	—	307	—	313
1953–54	3	—	7	—	1	—	13	—	—	—	—	—	3	379	—	4	3	399	—	406
1955	—	—	8	—	7	—	20	—	—	—	—	—	5	402	—	7	5	430	—	442
1956	3	—	5	—	1	—	21	—	—	—	—	—	—	356	—	4	—	382	—	386
1957	—	—	10	2	1	—	15	1	—	—	—	—	1	338	2	1	1	363	5	370
1957–58	—	—	3	—	1	—	10	—	—	—	—	—	—	187	—	1	—	200	—	201
1958	—	—	3	—	1	—	12	—	—	—	—	—	1	318	—	1	1	333	—	335
1959	—	—	11	1	3	—	16	—	—	—	—	—	1	352	—	3	1	379	1	384
1960	1	—	10	—	—	—	22	—	—	—	—	—	6	486	—	1	6	518	—	525
1961	—	—	6	—	4	—	17	—	—	—	—	—	2	354	—	4	2	377	—	383
1962	—	—	1	—	—	—	16	—	—	—	—	—	—	—	327‡	—	—	17	327	344
1962–63	—	—	—	1	—	—	7	9	—	—	—	—	—	—	494‡	—	—	7	503	510
Total	49	—	173	12	65	10	403	27	1	10	—	7	31	7,717	867	115	51	8,293	911	9,370

*Note: Action was not concluded on a number of bills due to dissolution of Parliament.
†Divorce cases fell off due to passing of Divorce Act (Ont.).
‡None of the bills of Divorce sent down to the HC by the Senate were passed by the Commons.

APPENDIX III

Legislation before the Senate*

Session	Government bills introduced in the Senate	Private bills introduced in the Senate	Public bills introduced by private members in the Senate	Divorce bills	Government bills from the House of Commons	Private bills from the House of Commons	Public bills introduced by private members in the House of Commons	Total
1925	1	9	1	135	59	16	2	223
1926	2	5	2	171	22	13	2	217
1926–27	2	11	2	196	80	24	-	315
1928	—	9	3	239	56	22	1	330
1929	2	8	6	241	63	30	2	352
1930	—	8	-	249	45	25	4	331
1930 2nd	—	—	-	—	3	—	-	3
1931	1	9	4	39	58	12	4	127
1932	6	3	1	27	51	5	1	94
1932–33	4	2	1	24	52	11	-	94
1934	4	4	1	39	57	11	1	117
1935	4	9	2	32	63	—	1	111
1936	1	13	2	40	49	—	1	106
1937	1	10	2	46	44	1	1	105
1938	—	11	1	86	52	1	6	157
1939	3	12	1	50	61	2	1	130
1940	—	8	-	62	49	—	-	119
1940–1–2	—	8	2	49	33	—	-	92
1942–43	—	8	1	76	36	—	-	121
1943–44	—	6	1	94	32	—	-	133
1944–45	—	11	-	111	52	—	-	174
1945	4	15	-	179	35	—	-	233
1946	10	12	1	290	68	—	-	381
1947	14	18	1	351	62	—	-	446
1948	25	16	1	295	54	—	-	391
1949[1]	13	18	-	184	15	—	-	230
1949[2]	12	3	-	166	30	1	1	213
1950	21	10	-	240	34	2	-	307
1950–51	—	—	-	—	10	—	-	10
1951[1]	12	30	-	295	53	—	-	390
1951[2]	1	4	-	—	32	—	-	37
1952	12	16	1	313	44	—	1	387
1952–53	18	15	1	282	38	—	-	354
1953–54	10	14	-	382	56	—	1	463
1955	8	28	2	407	51	—	1	497
1956	8	22	1	356	42	—	-	429
1957	14	17	-	341	29	—	-	401
1957–58	4	11	-	187	28	—	-	230
1958	3	13	-	319	41	—	-	376
1959	12	19	-	353	43	—	-	427
1960	11	22	2	492	37	—	-	564
1961	6	21	2	356	58	—	3	446
1962	1	16	1	327	26	—	3	374
1962–63	1	21	1	494	17	—	-	534
Totals	251	525	47	8,615	1,920	176	37	1,1571

*Note: These figures include bills introduced in the Senate but not passed.

INDEX

www.ingramcontent.com/pod-product-compliance
Lightning Source LLC
LaVergne TN
LVHW090801070826
844660LV00022B/1050

* 9 7 8 1 4 8 7 5 9 2 4 7 9 *